Business Ethics and Continental Philosophy

Business ethics has largely been written from the perspective of analytical philosophy with very little attention paid to the work of continental philosophers. Although very few of these philosophers directly discuss business ethics, their ideas have interesting applications in this field. This innovative textbook shows how the work of continental philosophers – Bauman, Deleuze and Guattari, Derrida, Foucault, Heidegger, Jonas, Latour, Levinas, Nancy, Nietzsche, Sartre, Sloterdijk, and Zizek – can provide fresh insights into a number of different issues in business ethics. Topics covered include agency, stakeholder theory, organizational culture, organizational justice, moral decision-making, leadership, whistle-blowing, corporate social responsibility, globalization, and sustainability. The book includes a number of features designed to aid comprehension, including a detailed glossary of key terms, text boxes explaining key concepts, and a wide range of examples from the world of business.

Mollie Painter-Morland is Associate Professor in the Department of Philosophy at DePaul University and Associate Director of DePaul's Institute for Business and Professional Ethics.

René ten Bos is Professor of Philosophy at the Department of Management Sciences, Radboud University.

Business Ethics and Continental Philosophy

Edited by
MOLLIE PAINTER-MORLAND
and
RENÉ TEN BOS

CAMBRIDGE
UNIVERSITY PRESS

CAMBRIDGE
UNIVERSITY PRESS

University Printing House, Cambridge CB2 8BS, United Kingdom

Published in the United States of America by Cambridge University Press, New York

Cambridge University Press is part of the University of Cambridge.

It furthers the University's mission by disseminating knowledge in the pursuit of
education, learning and research at the highest international levels of excellence.

www.cambridge.org
Information on this title: www.cambridge.org/9780521137560

© Mollie Painter-Morland and René ten Bos 2011

First published 2011

A catalogue record for this publication is available from the British Library

Library of Congress Cataloguing in Publication data
Business ethics and continental philosophy / edited by Mollie Painter-Morland and René ten Bos.
p. cm.
Includes index.
ISBN 978-0-521-19904-9 (hardback)
1. Business ethics. 2. Corporate culture. 3. Social responsibility of business.
I. Painter-Morland, Mollie. II. Bos, René ten.
HF5387.B8677 2011
174.4 – dc23 2011023018

ISBN 978-0-521-19904-9 Hardback
ISBN 978-0-521-13756-0 Paperback

Contents

Figures

Boxes

Contributors

David Bevan completed his PhD in Accounting at King's College London. He is currently Professor of Management and Organizational Behaviour at Grenoble Graduate Business School and Academic Director of the Academy of Business in Society (EABIS). David is Senior Wicklander Fellow at the Institute for Professional and Business Ethics, DePaul University, and a member of the editorial board of *Professional and Business Ethics*. He has designed and delivered courses in applied ethics and sustainability in numerous universities and business schools, including King's College London, Royal Holloway and HEC Paris.

Janet Borgerson earned a BA (University of Michigan, Ann Arbor), MA, and PhD (University of Wisconsin, Madison) in Philosophy, and an MA in Islamic Studies (University of Exeter, UK). She completed postdoctoral work at Brown University, and has held faculty positions at Stockholm University Business School and the University of Exeter, as well as teaching in France, Finland, and the US. Her publications include work in *Philosophy Today*, *Journal of Philosophical Research*, *Organization Studies*, *Business Ethics: A European Review*, *Advances in Consumer Research*, *European Journal of Marketing*, and *Consumption, Markets and Culture*.

Stephen Dunne is Director for the Centre for Philosophy and Political Economy and Lecturer in Social Theory and Consumption at the University of Leicester School of Management.

Mollie Painter-Morland is Associate Professor in the Department of Philosophy at DePaul University and Associate Director of DePaul's Institute for Business and Professional Ethics. She serves as Editor-in-chief of *Business and Professional Ethics* and as co-editor of Springer's 'Issues in Business Ethics' series. On a part-time basis, she remains involved with the consulting projects and anti-corruption work of the South African Centre for Business and Professional Ethics at the University of Pretoria, and teaches in its MPhil programme in Workplace Ethics.

Andreas Rasche is Assistant Professor of Business in Society at the Governance and Public Management Group at Warwick Business School. Since 2007 he has acted as a consultant to the United Nations Global Compact Office in New

York. He holds a PhD (Dr. rer. pol.) from the European Business School, Germany and a Habilitation (Dr. habil.) from Helmut-Schmidt-University, Hamburg. He regularly contributes to international journals in his field of study and has lectured widely on corporate social and environmental responsibility at different institutions in Europe. He co-edited *The United Nations Global Compact: Achievements, Trends and Challenges* (Cambridge University Press, 2010).

Carl Rhodes is not a philosopher, but he is very much interested in reading philosophy as a means to gain insight into the goings on in organizations. Most recently this has led him to a questioning of if and how ethics can manifest itself in organizations, and whether or not this manifestation might be a good thing. He is Professor of Organization Studies at Swansea University School of Business and Economics.

Sverre Spoelstra is Associate Professor at the Department of Business Administration, Lund University, Sweden. He received his PhD from Leicester School of Management on the topic of the reception of philosophy in organization theory, published as *What is Organization?* (Lund Business Press, 2007). His current research interests include leadership studies, theology and organization, work/play, rigour/relevance, and the branding of higher education. Sverre is an editor of the journal *ephemera*.

René ten Bos is Professor of Philosophy at the Department of Management Sciences, Radboud University. He has written extensively on a variety of topics ranging from melancholia and masochism to business ethics and our twisted relationship to the animal in and outside us. He is currently interested in such disparate topics as the moral significance of gestures, managerial mediocrity, self-help books, football, cryptobiology, infinity, silence, and water. In his country, he is well known as a public speaker for managerial audiences, but he also teaches at primary schools and in prisons.

Patricia Werhane is the Callista Wicklander Chair in Business Ethics and Managing Director of the Institute for Business and Professional Ethics at DePaul University. She is also Professor Emerita at the University of Virginia. She has published over twenty-five books including *Moral Imagination and Management Decision-making, Adam Smith and his Legacy for Modern Capitalism*, and *Profitable Partnerships for Poverty Alleviation* (together with Laura Hartman, Dennis Moberg, and Scott Kelley). Her forthcoming anthology is titled *Leadership, Gender, and Organization* (together with Mollie Painter-Morland).

Hugh Willmott is Research Professor in Organization Studies at Cardiff Business School. He co-founded the International Labor Process Conference and the Critical Management Studies Conference. He currently serves on the boards of *Academy of Management Review, Organization Studies*, and *Journal of Management Studies*, and is an associate editor of *Organization*. He was a member of the Business and Management Panel for the UK's 2008 Research Assessment Exercise.

Foreword

For too long, business ethics has been the captive of Anglo-American analytic philosophy. Ethical theory to most business ethicists means the traditional trifecta of consequentialism (usually utilitarianism), deontology (usually Kant), and virtue ethics (usually Aristotle). While this has been quite useful in the academic beginnings of the field, it is high time that we begin to connect these now traditional texts and arguments in business ethics with other traditions in the humanities.

Business ethics was born in scandal. It seems to regenerate itself with each succeeding wave of scandal. And, there are two problems here. The first is that our world is so interconnected that we can no longer afford to see business as a separate institution in society, subject to its own moral code. Business must be thoroughly situated in society. This means that we can no longer accept the now rather commonplace narrative about businesspeople being economic profit-maximizers and little else. Business is a deeply human institution set in our societies and interconnected all over the world. The second problem is that business ethics, by being reborn in scandal, never escapes the presumption that business starts off by being morally questionable. It never seems to get any credit for the good it brings into the world, only questions about the bad. In fact, capitalism may well be the greatest system of social cooperation that we have ever invented. But, if it is, then it must stand the critical test of our best thinkers, if for no other reason than to make it better. Simply assuming that capitalism is either unquestionably morally good or unquestionably morally problematic violates both scholarly and practical norms.

Analytical business ethics and its concurrent management theory has produced much that is useful to theorists and managers, from employee rights to stakeholder theory, social contract theory, corporate responsibility and sustainability models, and much more. However, there is almost a non-human quality to some of these ideas, as they take for granted the underlying social scientific reasoning, which is primarily economic in nature. Again, while economics has been an important cornerstone for business theory, there is much more to consider if we are to return the institution of business to its rightful place as a deeply human institution.

There are very few people who could put together this book. Hopefully the old tensions between 'continental' and 'analytic' philosophers have passed. However, I'm afraid they are still alive in business ethics. The late business ethicist, Robert Solomon, when asked whether he was a continental or analytical philosopher, replied 'what are the politics that are at stake by asking that question?'.

What Professors Painter-Morland and ten Bos have done is to make the question moot. They have crafted an outstanding volume that speaks to the issues with which analytical business ethics has been concerned, and then demonstrates how to think about these issues in a very different way. They invoke the theory of Deleuze, Derrida, Foucault, Zizek, and others that may be foreign to many business ethicists and students, yet they show how much these thinkers have to offer us.

They have put together a cutting-edge collection of chapters that has the possibility to transform business ethics as a discipline. They set business in its broadest societal and human context, and ask us to see business as just one more part of the continuum that we humans have woven together. At the end of each chapter I found myself wanting to read more and thinking differently about issues that I had believed to be long settled, even in my own research. There is much here with which to agree and disagree. That means that Painter-Morland and ten Bos have vastly enriched our conversation about business and ethics.

This is an important book for business ethics as a field. It will repay reading, many times over, and we will see the results as a more human, socially conscious, discipline of business ethics.

R. Edward Freeman
Professor, The Darden School, University of Virginia

Acknowledgements

The editors would like to extend a word of thanks to a number of individuals who have assisted us in completing this project. All the faculty and students at DePaul University have been extremely supportive of this project. In particular, we would like to thank William McNeil and Michael Naas, who read drafts of some chapters, and Karolin Mirzakhan, James Murphy, Christopher Turner, and Perry Zurn, who provided invaluable editing assistance. Patricia Werhane and the staff of DePaul's Institute for Business and Professional Ethics have been instrumental in organizing our very first project meetings and have provided support throughout. Mollie Painter-Morland would also like to thank DePaul students enrolled in her PHL/MGT 248 Business Ethics classes during 2009, 2010, and 2011 for their patience and valuable inputs during the piloting of the material. A further word of thanks goes to the anonymous reviewers of the proposal and of the draft chapters, who played a large role in improving the text. We are also indebted to the following friends and colleagues who provided moral support and read parts of the manuscript: Ignaas Devisch, Juliette Helmer, Campbell Jones, Ruud Kaulingfreks, Pieter Leroy, and Arno Morland.

Introduction: critical crossings

MOLLIE PAINTER-MORLAND AND RENÉ TEN BOS

Why read this book?

Authors like to imagine that people read their books out of passion for the subject matter or at least out of a curiosity regarding the new perspectives that the text may yield. Years of teaching have, however, made this team of editors more realistic. This book was more likely assigned by your teacher, and bought with hard-earned money squeezed from an increasingly tight textbook budget. You are most likely opening it now because your teacher assigned the introduction for your first class meeting, or because you are eager, or anxious, or both, to know what will be expected of you in this course within the next few weeks. The other possibility is that you are a teacher yourself, trying to determine what your students should spend their money and time on. It is therefore pointless to convince you that this book is worth the money you or your students have spent and the time that all of you will devote to reading it over the next couple of weeks. We cannot convince you, even if we tried. Reading books is a uniquely personal activity. The journey that reading this book will take you on is shaped by who you are and by what you bring to the table in terms of questions, passions, and expectations. The best we can do is try to explain why we went to the trouble of putting this book together.

At face value, this book may look like a normal textbook. You will encounter facts, figures, tables, text boxes, learning goals, and all other things that one would expect from a decent textbook. Like many other business ethics textbooks, the material is interdisciplinary in nature. It aims to offer some philosophical perspectives on the business environment, and since it deals with the behaviour of systems and institutions, it draws on disciplines such as sociology and psychology as well. The global context in which businesses operate also requires the development of insight into political economy and cultural studies. The authors in this book therefore represent many different disciplines. They are also from different areas in the world. Some are philosophers, others are organizational theorists or business ethicists. They all share an interest in ethical issues about business and society.

A few things set the book apart from many of the other textbooks available within the business ethics field. The most important difference lies in the fact that this book offers some 'critical crossings'. This introduction's title should be read in all of its senses. In the first place, 'critical' means that we consider the themes we address and the way in which we challenge the mainstream literature on these themes as important. We believe that if we can start to reconsider some of our basic understandings of certain business practices, it can make a difference to our world. This can only happen by changing people's orientation and practices. This is why you should understand the idea of 'crossing' not necessarily in the sense of crossing a bridge, or making a link, but rather as a willingness to take a critical stance, to 'cross' positions that may have remained unquestioned thus far, and to formulate a dissenting position if you come to the conclusion that you in fact disagree with a specific standpoint. Engaging in critical crossings by no means entails rejecting the *status quo* out of hand, nor does it mean agreeing with the dissenting position offered by the authors of this book. The important thing is that you formulate your own perspective after having had the opportunity to engage in a critical assessment of a variety of positions.

Another way in which what you are reading here is 'new' or 'unusual' is that it tries to link worlds that typically function miles apart. We are in the business of crossing divides, i.e. the divide which seems to exist between philosophers and business people, and between business ethics and a certain part of the philosophical tradition, i.e. continental thought. These divides are not 'natural facts', but rather something that has emerged over time. The Ancient Greek philosophers like Socrates, Plato, or Aristotle, were all philosophers of the market place (*agora*) where all kinds of activities took place: political, social, and commercial. They practised their philosophy amid the hustle and bustle of the trading and negotiating that was going in ancient Athens and elsewhere. The problem that we face in contemporary society is that this space, where both trade and socio-political and ethical discourses could flourish, was lost in the course of history. With it, the kind of conversations that were so characteristic of ancient philosophy disappeared as well. Nowadays, we do not take for granted anymore that philosophy and business might share the same space. On the contrary, most people would probably claim that business and philosophy belong to completely different realms. This book, however, can be seen as a modest attempt to recreate this space. Of course, it cannot recreate exactly the same kind of space the ancient philosophers occupied. Imagine a bunch of philosophers walking round our contemporary shopping malls asking people tricky questions and debating the socio-political and ethical state of society. They will most likely be removed by the mall security for bothering customers and distracting them from their spending sprees!

It is clear that the context has changed profoundly. We live in a globalized environment and this book is at once a product and symptom of this. New technologies, socio-economic dynamics, and cultural orientations have opened up new possibilities of how we can live, and we have to figure out how we want to do that. It may be difficult to find common ground on how to live given this pluralistic environment. However, we do believe that through a renewed engagement between philosophy and the world of commerce, a space may emerge where dialogue and debate will become just as important as it was in ancient Greece. What we can still learn from the ancient philosophers is that it is important to challenge common wisdom and to critically interrogate the assumptions that we encounter in what we have known so far. In this respect, we need the help of the philosophers, and in this book we will frequently resort to continental philosophers.

The divide between analytic and continental philosophy

This brings us to the second divide that matters to us, namely the one between analytic philosophy and continental philosophy. The distinction is important because business ethics is much more grounded in analytic philosophy than in continental philosophy. This implies that we should tell you a little bit about this notorious distinction.

Nobody knows exactly who is responsible for it. A meeting at a conference in the small Swiss city of Davos in Spring 1929 is often seen as the event that engendered this distinction.[1] At this conference, two very influential German philosophers, Martin Heidegger and Ernst Cassirer, engaged in a discussion about the Enlightenment philosopher Immanuel Kant (1724–1804). One of the attendants at the meeting was a young Austrian philosopher called Rudolf Carnap. This young man, who was already on his way to becoming one of the most famous analytic philosophers of his time, accused Heidegger, who is widely seen as perhaps the single most important continental philosopher of the twentieth century, of talking only 'mumbo-jumbo'. This accusation has led, at least among logicians, positivists, and other scientifically inclined philosophers, to either mirth or downright contempt. But it is not just a meeting between two philosophers that helped to bring about such a distinction. Carnap actually read Heidegger quite closely and remarked, in an article published in 1931, that Heidegger is driven by only one truly 'big question', to wit, 'the question of Being and nothing more'.[2] But what is the meaning of such a big question? Carnap frankly admitted he could not make much sense of such a question and offered some arguments that need not concern us here. The point that is interesting in the present context is that Carnap claims that Heidegger is a 'metaphysical' philosopher. He is adamantly clear about what this means:

> Metaphysical philosophers do not offer us 'propositions', that is to say, statements that describe the world and that are as such either false or true. They rather offer us something entirely different, something that might be an expression of our attitude to life, something that comes closer to poetry than to exact logical thinking.[3]

The allegation that metaphysical philosophy expresses pure artistry rather than logical ingenuity has haunted what came to be known as 'continental' philosophy. In the wake of Carnap, many analytic philosophers have claimed to abhor the 'metaphysics' that seems to underpin continental philosophy. There has been a lot of debate about whether the analytic portrayal of metaphysics is right, but we will not enter into that. However, you should know that there were times that it was taken for granted that metaphysics is the most important kind of philosophy since it allegedly asks the most basic questions that human beings can ask: What is the essence of life? What is the essence of being? Does the human soul exist and is it immortal? Carnap's way of denouncing all these questions as poetry, artistry, or pseudo-science was widely seen as challenging and provocative. The discussion between Carnap and Heidegger became emblematic of the divide between analytic philosophy and continental philosophy. Analytic philosophers think that not just Heidegger, but all continental philosophers are at best metaphysical poets or artists.

How did continental philosophers respond? Most of them simply ignored all these allegations and continued with the kind of work they were doing. But underneath this superficial indifference, it is clear that many continental philosophers think that analytic philosophers lack depth, are not rigorous, and engage in their own kind of metaphysics. Such a different kind of 'metaphysics' implies, for example, a naïve belief in the idea that science has straightforward access to objects in the world and does not experience any difficulties in phrasing unequivocal propositions about these objects. In fact, scientists operate in a world where hard facts have become increasingly exceptional. In this book, for example, we will see that issues such as globalization or sustainability are hardly ever uncontested and do not have the clear factual status some people may long for. Many continental philosophers alert us to the difficulties we may experience in accessing the world.

The following table outlines some of the distinctions between analytic and continental philosophy as seen from the perspective of analytic philosophy.

Analytic philosophy	Continental philosophy (as seen from the perspective of analytic philosophy)
language analysis	poetical analysis, poetry itself
scientific	artistic at best, in fact nonsensical
disciplined	wild, unruly, anarchistic
politically neutral	politically left
methodological	chaotic
believe in the progress of knowledge	situational truths, contingency
really philosophical	rhetorical

Having looked over the distinctions drawn above, you may feel that you would have preferred a business ethics text written from the perspective of analytic philosophy. After all, what is wrong with a disciplined, politically neutral, methodological text that offers 'real' philosophical perspectives on business? As indicated above, this table of distinctions was drafted from the perspective of analytic philosophy, but one could easily redraft it to cast a more positive light on the continental perspective, and be more dismissive about the contributions of analytic philosophy. Many of the commitments of the analytic philosophers, especially their commitment to science, progress, and politically neutral analysis, have been questioned by the continentals. Some of this has its contextual origins in the political events in Europe during the first half of the twentieth century. Especially the events of the second world war were pivotal in shaping the concerns of many continental thinkers. In fact, Auschwitz has been described as 'the collapse of reason'. Therefore, one can detect a distinct disillusionment with reason, science, and technology in the writings of many continental thinkers. The events of the war and the demise of humanity and morality during this time made it eminently clear that science, technology, and the desire for progress are neither politically neutral nor unequivocally 'good'. Continental philosophers made clear that some critical crossings in the realms of science, politics, and philosophy were desperately called for. One cannot continue, as analytic philosophers would propose, to venerate science as a bulwark of reason and objectivity.

However, it is not the purpose of this book to engage in philosophical hair-splitting about the pros and cons of either analytic or continental philosophy. Instead, we'd rather show you how specific continental philosophers do philosophy. Therefore, to give you a foretaste of the kind of philosophical work you can expect to encounter, we thought it may be helpful to introduce you to just some of the basic issues that concern continental philosophers. One example of such an issue is 'truth'. Thinkers like Nietzsche or Heidegger, who are often seen as the precursors of many of the key figures you will encounter in this book, had a problem with the big claims to 'truth' that we find within science or history. Nietzsche proposed that there are always very specific interests of power lurking behind these seemingly 'objective' claims. Heidegger agreed with Nietzsche in the sense that he also thought that language does not straightforwardly correspond to reality. Many continental philosophers would subsequently relate to this issue of truth, for example by arguing that truth is not a state of affairs, but rather an ongoing process. Others argued that instead of looking for all-encompassing explanations of reality, we should rather focus on specificity and particularity. In some cases, this led to a re-evaluation or downright condemnation of what came to be known as 'grand narratives' or 'big stories'. An example of such a big story would be the self-portrayal of science as a heroic quest for truth, or the history of humankind as a march from tyranny to more and more liberty. François Lyotard, a very influential French philosopher, proposed that philosophers and scientists should be more modest and only tell 'small stories'. Historians, for example, should henceforward not focus on the great events in our history (the battles, the revolutions, or the deeds of the big heroes) but on how all of this might have impacted on the lives of smaller communities (particular trades, villages, or families). Small stories, so the argument goes, are taken from real life, whereas big stories lack any connection to it.

The skepticism regarding big and all-encompassing 'truths' led other continental figures such as Jacques Derrida to rethink the very nature of language. His idea of 'deconstruction' opened up the possibility that meaning and sense in language can be very slippery. Indeed, texts and words can obtain a significance that was initially not anticipated. In this book, we will see that many concepts used in business ethics – globalization, responsibility, value, or sustainability – have undergone a constant shift in meaning. Another key figure in this book, Gilles Deleuze, proposed to replace what he understood as 'transcendental' reason with a kind of 'vitalist empiricism' that would take concrete bodily affections and experiences as the point of departure. Like Nietzsche, Deleuze reminded us of the importance of emotion and embodiment, and we will return to this topic in many chapters of this book. For the moment, it suffices to note that many continental philosophers do not think that the pursuit of knowledge is or should be an entirely reasonable and disembodied endeavour. And what counts for knowledge, in this regard at least, also counts for language.

This very brief exposé of some of the issues that continental figures engage with should not, however, be read as a 'position statement' that all continental philosophers would subscribe to. On many issues they do not agree with one another at all. Therefore, they should most certainly not be portrayed as all singing the same tune, as if they were putting forward a homogeneous, coherent position. For instance, the German philosopher, Peter Sloterdijk, responds to the fragmentation that the rejection of big stories might entail by deliberately constructing a new 'big story', which narrates how human beings have always been in the business of constructing and destroying the kind of communities he refers to as 'spheres'. The Slovenian philosopher Slavoj Zizek dismisses Deleuze's vitalism as a philosophy that merely incites people to indulge in their own feelings rather than to be concerned about real problems in the world. Against this conceitedness, he hopes to reinvigorate a revolutionary zeal and clearly argues that big truths are needed for that. Only big stories engage people, not small stories. But this has, in turn, led Sloterdijk to accuse Zizek of flirting with the possibility of violence. If there is one lesson to be drawn from history, Sloterdijk argues, then it is that big stories can be dangerous, especially when they turn out to be political.

This debate between Deleuze, Zizek, and Sloterdijk serves to show that 'continental philosophy' is not a name for a unified tradition. However, what seems important to many of these thinkers – in spite of all their mutual differences – is to engage critically with the tradition that informs their own work, and with each others' work. Contemporary continental philosophers still take their inspiration from earlier philosophers who played an important role in the history of philosophy: Aristotle, Plato, Descartes, Spinoza, Hume, Kant, Hegel, Marx,

and many others. They also reflect on thinkers who can be seen as their immediate predecessors: Nietzsche, Bergson, Blanchot, Batailles, and even someone
like Ludwig Wittgenstein, who is a big name in analytic circles as well. All
these philosophers cast doubt on some central tenets and values not only of
philosophy but also of modern culture as such. However, it is important to note
that continental philosophers never envisaged a radical rift with the history of
philosophy. If, for example, Derrida talks about 'deconstruction', we should
not forget that he never envisaged a wholesale attack on heroes of ancient or
modern philosophy. In fact, it is a distinct characteristic of continental philosophers that they take the history of Western thought very seriously. Subtle and
precise textual analyses of classical philosophical texts are the hallmark of
much continental philosophy, something which has tempted commentators to
label this philosophy as difficult and obscure.

We want to reiterate that the distinction between continental and analytic
philosophy remains opaque and contentious. Also, we should never forget that
the very notion of 'continental philosophy' has been created in the Anglo-
Saxon world. Just a few philosophers in the continent would actually endorse
the distinction even though many of them might deem 'analytic' philosophy to
be boring, superficial, and overly rigid. Be this as it may, business ethics is firmly
rooted in the analytic tradition and has largely ignored continental philosophy
altogether. This is not to say that it does not add meaningful perspectives.
Indeed, business ethics has embraced the analytic agenda and offered clear
normative perspectives on important issues. It has, for example, formulated
codes of conduct for business practitioners, it has developed new and important
insights in the business environment (in terms of stakeholders, politics, and so
on), and it has also raised important issues about worldwide processes such as
capitalism and globalization and what businesses can do about them. Despite
the advances made, however, we do believe that research in this area can be
so much richer when it opens up to a long but neglected continental tradition
of thought.

Continental philosophers suggest that one should always start from where
one is. In terms of this project, it means that we should start with what has been
produced in business ethics, and where that puts us at this specific juncture.
As such the book wants to provide an accessible overview of what is available
in the business ethics field and push us towards a critical reflection on where
that leaves us. What do we mean by 'reflection'? It is clear that the discipline
of business ethics has always been reflective, but in a somewhat different kind
of way than what we will be proposing here. The field of business ethics
reflects issues that are topical in the corporate world; it has indeed an enormous
reputation in doing so. Yet, we maintain that it hardly ever discusses its own
assumptions. Instead, business ethics has always been intent on improving the
status quo, but was, in our opinion, much less inclined to questioning the
status quo. This made it impossible to question commercial motivations such
as yielding more profits, limiting liability, or building reputational value from

a normative perspective. The central question seems to have been how ethics could make business more profitable. The result is that it forecloses critical discussions of the idea of 'profit' and what it might mean for our society. In the process, many business ethicists forgot the most basic ethical question: How should we live? In our opinion, ethics should always remain questioning – if it fails to do this, it ceases to be ethics. Ethics is not primarily about answers, or solutions, but about questions, puzzles, or dilemmas. This does not mean that solutions cannot emerge, but they should always be submitted to the process of critical questioning. We argue that this is an important lesson that can be drawn from continental thought. The importance of this lesson will become more evident as we look into the meaning of concepts such as ethics or morality.

Clarifying some basic concepts

In terms of establishing a common conceptual framework for your reading of the book, we would like to offer a brief description of certain key terms. It is yet another misconception that within continental philosophy 'anything goes' and that argumentation need not conform to rational restrictions. Though it is true that continental philosophy employs a slightly different conception of and stance to 'rational' deliberation, it by no means embraces irrationalism or relativism. Instead, it makes us aware of where our ideas about 'rationality' come from, and gives us an eye for the political, social, and economic context of our judgements. This does not mean that we cannot provide a framework for the concepts and that a certain rigour in argumentation isn't expected in putting forward continental philosophical positions. This makes it important to embark on some reflection regarding the typical terminology that is employed in the field of business ethics.

A few central concepts, such as 'morality', 'ethics', 'norm', 'value', 'principle', 'dilemma', 'relativism', or 'absolutism', are pivotal in the normative discussion and critical evaluation of business practices. The most central term is surely 'ethics'. When one asks any audience or group of students what comes to mind when they hear the word 'ethics', one typically gets the response that it is about right and wrong. But what does it mean to say that something is 'right' or 'wrong'? This question has kept philosophers occupied for centuries, and does not lend itself to simple answers. Suffice to say that 'right' or 'wrong' seems to make reference to what a specific society finds acceptable or unacceptable in terms of judgement, conduct, or institutional arrangements. This has led some theorists to argue that ethics is about morality. Morality can be defined as the whole of the current norms and values, i.e. ideas about 'right' and 'wrong' that exist in society. Certain beliefs about what is acceptable emerge over time and, after a while, some level of consensus seems to develop. The problem is that when ethics is just about what has emerged over time, we get stuck in one of the most basic philosophical fallacies, i.e. the 'is–ought' fallacy. From the observation that something *is* the case, we do not need to infer that it *ought* to be the case. For example, to say that there have always been instances of injustice in our society, does not mean to say that there ought to be injustice. This brings us to an important distinction between ethics and morality. Whereas morality describes the current norms and values in society, ethics is the discipline of questioning whether we still agree with what is commonly accepted as right and wrong in society. It studies the norms and values of society, plots the factors involved in its emergence, and subjects it to critical scrutiny based on a philosophical interrogation of its validity and functioning within specific societies. If ethics loses this critical perspective, we have compromised its essence.

In order to perform its critical function, ethics has to engage particularly with concepts such as 'norms', 'values', and 'principles', since these are the notions that refer to society's beliefs and orientation regarding 'right' and 'wrong'. Values can be defined as enduring beliefs about what constitutes a preferable existence. It indicates what we consider a 'better' way of living. So, after having lived in society for centuries, we may come to realize that it is preferable to treat other people fairly rather than unfairly, either because those who are treated unfairly will revolt and protest against their treatment or because we realize that we ourselves would not like to be treated unfairly and that it would therefore be unconscionable to treat fellow human beings similarly. We therefore come to value certain states of existence.

These beliefs about what is valuable also dictate how we should act. Hence norms, which tell us how we should act from day to day, come into existence. Many modern philosophers have argued that norms provide a more binding perspective on values. But the perspective should not only be more binding, it should simultaneously be more general. The argument for this is that there must be some beliefs about right and wrong that transcend particular contexts. Kant, for example, argued that this transcendence can only be found in our reason. He argued that what set human beings apart was their capacity to come to rational precepts that all other rational creatures will be able to accept as normative. This allows us to formulate principles, which function as moral laws that we adhere to because of their rational appeal. Often terms such as values, principles, ethics, and morality are used as synonyms, and we by no means expected of our contributors to keep them neatly apart. The overall point is that all these terms refer to the same process of delineating 'good' versus 'bad' and 'right' versus 'wrong'. This is not so much a clear-cut conceptual issue as a judgement that is made on the basis of available knowledge, circumstances, and beliefs.

Therefore, some continental philosophers have come to the conclusion that it may be precisely the clear distinction that is drawn between 'right' and 'wrong' that requires ethical interrogation. Often these binary extremes function as political tools to protect those in power from criticism and dissent – in this sense, the 'right' can become pretty 'wrong'. Continental philosophers argue for an awareness of the contextual particularity of norms and values. One aspect of this context is the power interests that lurk behind the use of moral terms such as 'good' or 'bad'. Contextual awareness alerts us to the fact that an appeal to 'what makes rational sense to all human beings' may be an oversimplified way of thinking about normativity. What seems to make perfect sense to one group of people, may not look so 'sensible' to others.

Let us consider an example that we are all familiar with in determining what is 'fair', namely the question whether downloading copyrighted music from the Internet without paying for it is unethical. A discussion of this example may typically reveal what we value. Normally, we are willing to pay people a certain amount because we place a certain value on their contribution, effort, talent, and uniqueness. So, there seems to be no reason why we should not pay for copyrighted music when we download it from the Internet. However, we may find some inconsistencies in these kinds of arguments and here too everything hinges on context: why is it that in normal contexts we would pay for music and why is it that the Internet apparently does not provide a normal context? For instance, we do not necessarily mind paying a few hundred dollars for a concert ticket, even if the famous artist will just make a thirty-minute appearance. But at the same time, we may have no problem justifying downloading that artist's song online without paying for it. If, by paying for the expensive ticket, we have already acknowledged the value of the artist's work, could we justify taking that asset without paying for it in a different context? Surely we don't want to say that we'll only pay the artist what his/her work is worth when we are forced to do so? That will be like admitting that we will steal as long as we do not get caught! But the argument is seldom that simple and we tend to have immense powers of rationalization in arguing what is fair.

Let us consider some more arguments relating to this example. As a relatively 'poor' student, you may argue that popular artists are rich anyway, and therefore do not 'deserve' or 'need' even more money. The question of effort also enters the debate – some students may argue that artists make quite enough money already by doing something that is a lot of fun, comes easily to them, and that they make enough through concerts anyway. They even argue that artists benefit from the marketing that they get when people download their music from the Internet, and therefore require no additional compensation. Another argument that downloaders all over the world would utilize is that it is not the artists who get the money but the record companies. Hence they do not steal any more from artists than others are already stealing from artists, and that the theft of songs online is stealing from the thieves themselves. This assumes a kind of Robin Hood attitude – stealing from thieves does not really amount to stealing. These arguments amount to a combination of the classic 'you too' argument: 'if you do it, why can't I?' Once again, the underlying philosophical fallacy is that *ought* is derived from *is*. The fallacy plays out like this: 'Cheating is a part of life, it happens all the time, and so cheating ought to happen all the time'.

It is worth considering the full implications of such an argument. Are we willing to say that celebrities should not be paid the millions that they earn, because they exert too little effort, because they are already rich, or because they are robbed by others already? Typically, we don't make this kind of argument because we place such high value on having these celebrities around. We like listening to their music, watching their movies, reading about their lives, following their fashion cues. As such, we have given them a certain role in our everyday existence and as long as they play their role we are willing to look beyond the merit arguments. It is clear then that the question of how, how much and when people should be rewarded for their efforts is a complex and controversial one. Does this mean that the pay discrepancies between top executives and other employees or male and female executives can conceivably be justified under certain conditions? We will pursue these kinds of questions in more detail in some of the chapters, but for now, let's consider the conceptual implications of these arguments and debates.

It is often the case that a particular consideration appears to be more pertinent or compelling in one case than in another. In fact, a double standard is being employed – something that seems evidently wrong in one case may be judged perfectly acceptable in another. The application of different moral standards to different ethical problems is called 'relativism'. Most ethicists reject relativism because it assumes that there are no basic goods that need to be protected in society and because it utilizes a logic that is ultimately incapable of offering compelling arguments against abuses. If we were truly relativists, we would have to merely accept it if someone were to take our property, inflict physical harm on us or those we care about, or break their promises. Furthermore, relativism makes it very difficult to resolve disputes, as relativists deny the compelling power of reasonable discourse with others, arguing instead that what is right for others may not be right for them. If there is no reason to believe that some ethical arguments are better than others or that better arguments should prevail and inform our decisions and actions, then there is also no reason why individuals should not simply do as they like. A related problem with relativism is that it allows for ethical subjectivism, i.e. the belief that individuals need not justify their decisions or actions to others.

Does this mean that we will be advocating ethical absolutism instead? Abso-lutism can be defined as the belief that there is one conception of 'right and wrong' that should hold for all people at all times. It can also be related to ethical imperialism, which refers to a position that affords the proponents of one ethical position the right to criticize others and to convince or even coerce these others to adopt their specific point of view. Continental philosophers have always been notoriously skeptical and critical of absolutist claims, especially because of the totalitarian implications of such claims and the power abuse that often accompanies its employment in practice. In fact, it would be incred-ibly difficult to advocate an absolutist perspective if you take the continental philosophers seriously. Continental philosophers are committed to contextual analysis and the specificity it requires. But, we will also see that this is not to say that they succumb to relativism. Especially in the chapter on globalization, you will read more on the problem of relativism. Now, we simply want to point out that another reason why continental philosophy can be so interesting for business ethicists is that it alerts us to context as an important factor in ethics and morality.

Who should read this book, and how?

We wrote this book to offer the opportunity to make critical crossings to a rather broad audience. In the first place, we hope that it will afford students of business administration, economics, and philosophy the opportunity to engage in a sophisticated philosophical analysis of business. It is also written for teachers who want to enrich their teaching with a whole range of novel ideas. This book will also make interesting reading for philosophically minded practitioners, who want to challenge themselves to never stop asking questions about the environment in which they live and function. Whether you are a student, a teacher, or a practitioner, we hope that this book will be only one of the first phases in a lifelong journey with continental philosophy. In ethics and philosophy, our work is never done.

Firstly, this book will require you to practise certain basic philosophical skills. This includes close reading, critical questioning, and independent argumentation. This inevitably means that you can never read something only once. You have to analyse the structure of each chapter, and you then need to formulate a critical response. In doing the latter, you employ quality arguments and avoid philosophical fallacies. In our view, fallacies are signs of sloppy thinking and laziness. For example, resorting to personal attacks or issuing threats to try to convince others of your position is not only unacceptable but ineffective in a philosophical dispute. What you should display instead is a thorough understanding of various positions, a willingness to listen to people who hold different positions, and a readiness to bring in meaningful arguments and perspectives to support your own stance. Part of this involves getting to know yourself. If you can understand the genesis of your own position, the factors that inform it, and its implications, you will be more able to anticipate and understand possible objections against it and to enter into meaningful dialogue with others.

As we have indicated from the outset, this book is not just any kind of philosophical text. It wants to create the space for 'critical crossings'. The way the book is structured reflects our preoccupation with crossing the divide between current business ethics theory and continental philosophy. Each chapter describes a certain topical area: sustainability, reward and compensation, culture, and a number of other priority items that remain on the agenda of business ethicists. The order of the various chapters of the textbook deliberately takes us from a broader consideration of the context that sets the scene for discussions within business ethics, towards more specific thematic issues that require our attention. We therefore start with chapters on more general notions such as corporate agency, stakeholder theory, organizational culture, moral decision-making, and justice. We believe that it is important to have a clear understanding of these notions, and to also consider a possible reframing of them, before proceeding with the rest of the book, which deals with more specific themes, such as whistle-blowing, leadership, reward and compensation, marketing, corporate social responsibility, codes and standards, sustainability, and globalization.

Within each chapter, we asked ourselves what continental thought brings to our understanding of these central themes in business ethics. Every chapter offers a description of the mainstream point of view on the topic and then proceeds to offer some perspectives from within continental philosophy. We therefore start with the wealth of insights that business ethics produced, spending some time in understanding its underlying assumptions. In doing the latter, we open another level of questioning, another space where new possibilities may emerge. If we can identify the assumptions of our current theories, we are in a better position to question them and thereby unsettle beliefs that may have gone unchallenged for too long. Continental philosophers take a different angle on things and as such allow for different perspectives. They allow us to change positions, or to relocate ourselves without physically moving to another continent. Herein lies the excitement of philosophy. This excitement, however, comes at a price. You will find that some chapters contain difficult theory, but we have done our utmost to present this theory in an accessible way, and have selected only those theories that we think may enrich the field of business ethics.

Some chapters may include boxes and lists of important issues that allow the reader to get a better 'background' understanding of what is going on. For ease of reference, some central concepts within the various chapters are explained in the glossary at the end of the text. If you are unsure of what a term means, the glossary is the place to go. This book can be read chapter by chapter, but there is no need to do so: you may also choose your own chapters of interest (it depends very much on what kind of teacher or student you are). Teachers will hopefully use the book so as to make students reflect about issues that are addressed in the chapters. The idea is to allow students to come to a nuanced position on a certain issue. The chapters have been organized in such a way that much of the book can be covered in a typical semester (one chapter a week).

We hope that this book will allow our readers to understand the relevance of continental philosophy for business and organization. This will require of you not only to obtain the particular insights that this kind of philosophy might offer, but also to cultivate the philosophical attitudes and to practise the skills of close reading, critical questioning, and independent argumentation. We hope you will, after having worked through the book, not shy away from the enormous complexity of the world we live in. Texts on business and organization too often encourage a mentality that seeks a simplistic solution for every problem. An over-emphasis on practical solutions is, we believe, one of the problems, not only in standard business texts, but also in business practice. If continental philosophy teaches us one thing, then it is that the problems of the world seldom require quick fixes and that theoretical and practical carefulness and discipline are crucially important in our area. In the end, the kind of philosophers we discuss in this text may help us all to develop a somewhat different attitude towards the world's complexity. Perhaps, this refers to what is perhaps the single most important philosophical skill: the capacity to be transformed. As one of the major figures in this book, Martin Heidegger, once argued, the question should not be about what you can do with philosophy, but about what philosophy can do with you.

NOTES

1 There is vast literature about this meeting of separate minds. The most important text is probably: M. Friedman, *A Parting of the Ways: Carnap, Cassirer, and Heidegger*. Chicago, IL: Open Court (2000). See also: M. Friedman, 'Carnap, Cassirer, and Heidegger: the Davos disputation and twentieth century philosophy', *Journal of Philosophy* 10 (3) (2002), 263–74. Another author is: P. Gordon, 'Continental divide. Ernst Cassirer and Martin Heidegger at Davos, 1929 – an allegory of intellectual history', *Modern Intellectual History* 1 (2) (2004), 219–48.

2 R. Carnap, 'Überwindung der Metaphysik durch logische Analyse der Sprache', *Erkenntnis* 2 (1932), 219–41. A translation of this article was published much later: R. Carnap, 'The elimination of metaphysics through logical analysis of language', in A. Ayer (ed.), *Logical Positivism*. Glencoe, IL: The Free Press (1959), 60–81.

3 Carnap, 'The elimination of metaphysics', 79.

Agency in corporations

MOLLIE PAINTER-MORLAND

Goals of this chapter

After studying this chapter you will be able to:

- understand the discussion of agency theory in business ethics;
- understand how Deleuze and Guattari develop an alternative understanding of agency;
- understand the implications of the move from identity towards multiplicity for discussions of corporate agency.

Introduction

Introducing agency theory

One of the basic questions that business ethics is concerned with is the question of who is responsible for ethical failures in the corporate realm. If we feel disappointed in the quality of products or services we have paid for, or feel that our return on investment in a certain corporation is not satisfactory, or when corporate actions harm the environment, we typically feel that some wrong was done, and we want to hold the wrongdoer accountable. Questions that inevitably arise include: 'How was the decision to harm my interests made?', 'Was this done intentionally?', and 'Who should be held accountable for this?' These questions all assume that someone intentionally decided to act in a way that harmed others, that this is wrong, and that someone must pay the price for such wrongdoing.

The problem is that in the case of ethical failures in corporations, each of these three assumptions that we typically rely on turn out to be more complex than it seems at first glance. In the first place, the question of who made the decision is often difficult to answer. For example, we might think that decisions are typically made by an individual, be it a senior manager or the chief executive officer (CEO), but in the case of corporate misconduct, there are often more people involved in the decision-making process. This brings us to the whole debate around *corporate moral agency*. The first question that confronts us is whether a corporation can make decisions or have intentions in the way that individual human beings do. Ever since the emergence of business ethics as a discipline many decades ago, there has been much debate around this issue. The most prominent theory in this regard was developed towards the end of the 1970s by Peter French, who argued that corporations are moral agents in much the same the way that individual human beings are, because they can intend actions and therefore have to be held accountable for those decisions.[1] They have great powers in society, and so it is in all of our interests that we hold these corporations accountable. He also argued that they have the capacity to make rational decisions through what he termed corporate internal decision-structures (CID-structures), and that they can revise these rational decisions over time. French initially argued that these structures resemble the beliefs and desires of those of human beings, but this position received much criticism. Corporations do not have bodies that can be hurt or desires that need to be fulfilled, so surely one could not argue that corporations are similar to human beings in anything but a metaphorical sense. Some of French's critics argued that he was committing the basic philosophical fallacy of anthropomorphism, i.e. ascribing some human characteristic to non-human entities. French subsequently refined his position by arguing that corporations have intentions not because they are persons but because they have a capacity for moral agency. This means that corporations can have intentions in the sense that they are capable of planning for future events and acting on those plans. They therefore operate as agents even though they are not persons. Denis Arnold, an American business ethicist, takes these ideas one step further to argue that what characterizes corporations is a shared intent that allows the corporations to control their activities and the decisions of their members.[2] The corporate decision-structures actually dictate how people ought to behave, and as such they have a normative function. The fact that there is deliberate planning and the structuring of rules and policies to facilitate the attainment of the planned result, as well as reflection on past intentions and changes to these plans, brings Arnold to argue that a corporation has a kind of moral agency that is more than a mere mental state.

Corporate governance and agency theory

The fact that corporations engage in intended actions raises the question of how decisions are made and who is to be held responsible for those decisions and actions. Here we enter into the realm of *corporate governance*. This important term refers to the processes by which corporations are directed and controlled. Typically, a board of directors is in charge of the governance of a corporation. Some of their tasks include determining the direction of the company and the supervision of management, as well as the acceptance of corporate account-ability and compliance with legal and statutory frameworks within which the corporation operates.[3] In most cases, the board of directors is elected by the shareholders of the corporation to fulfil these tasks. It is important that the board includes independent directors, who are capable of more objective oversight than the corporation's executives, who are intimately involved in the day-to-day management of the corporation. An independent director is someone who 'has no direct or indirect interest, current or previous, professional or personal interest or relationship' in the corporation.[4] Boards also have committees in order to control and supervise important financial decisions, compliance measures, and reporting. A very important part of agency theory in business ethics discusses the fact that board members have a fiduciary duty to act as agents of the shareholders, or the owners of the corporation. They are the people who represent the owners, and should therefore operate according to the desires and needs of those whom they represent. In Milton Friedman's view, this was clearly the owners, or stockholders, and much of this thinking remains prominent within many corporations. However, it is widely acknowledged that other stakeholders have become important in corporate governance processes as well: employees, key suppliers, financial institutions, and certain government agencies all have legitimate claims to participate in the corporations' affairs.[5]

This is even more the case in other countries. Significant differences exist between the Anglo-American, European and Japanese-East Asian governance systems. These differences pertain to how corporations are funded and owned, but also to how other historical, political, social, and economic factors shaped the expectations that societies have of corporations.[6] We will not go into details here. It will suffice to say that in some systems, certain stakeholders have vastly more power in terms of the governance of the corporation than in others. For instance, in Europe, employees have much more influence in the direction that the company takes. This influence is afforded to them by a two-tier board system, which includes a supervisory board or council on which employees have significant representation. This allows employees to put their interests and demands squarely on the agenda when it comes to the governance of the corporation. Because banks are the key financial institutions and are closely involved with ownership of corporations in continental Europe and Japan, they also have a lot of influence on how corporations are governed. This is not necessarily the case in the Anglo-American system, which operates largely on the shareholder wealth maximization model. Anglo-American boards' primary fiduciary duties are towards private individual shareholders, or groups that represent these shareholders. The main interest of these shareholders is the growth of their investment in firms, and hence, ensuring sustained profit-maximization has been a prime governance priority.

The reason why governance is so important for our discussion on *corporate moral agency* is that boards of directors seem to be responsible for many of the important decisions that corporations make as well as for the actions they take. Recent legislative developments have also increased the supervisory duties of the board in order to avoid the kind of unethical behaviour that has led to the demise of many corporations worldwide. The question remains, however, whether these developments will have a positive influence on the decisions and actions of corporations. The belief that seems to underpin most governance structures is that individual human beings are still in charge of corporations, and that these individual agents represent their principals (the owners of the corporation) as moral agents. There is also the belief that individual moral agents are rational in making decisions and taking actions that further the intentions of the principals they are representing.[7] The interaction between individual board members, executives, or other representatives of the corporation, and the corporation as a legal 'person' in and of itself, raises some of the most difficult questions regarding corporate accountability. To address these questions, we will need to take a more critical look at how corporations gained the power and influence that they currently have in our society.

A critical perspective on corporate moral agency

A very critical analysis of the idea of 'corporate personhood' can be found in Bobby Banerjee's discussion of the evolution of corporate entities over the last two centuries.[8] Banerjee makes it clear that the corporation as we know it today does not resemble the role that was originally envisaged in the emergence of these entities in the 1800s. At that time, the state could, and often did, revoke the charter of a corporation if it did not act in the interest of the public good. By the twentieth century, however, these restrictions on corporations disappeared. It was not until the 1960s and 1970s that environmental and consumer activists started campaigning again for a system of federal charters to rein in the power of corporations. Given how the legal persona of the corporation has evolved, this has been easier said than done. Corporations are no longer officially required to serve the public interest, and even though some laws govern their relationships with stakeholders, the law also grants them many rights and freedoms. So much so that some have argued that the rights and freedoms of the corporation as a 'legal person' sometimes trump those of human persons. How did this happen?

Banerjee indicates that it was the landmark court decision of Dartmouth College v. Woodward in 1819 that bestowed property rights on corporations. Legal counsel for Dartmouth College argued that the rights of private corporations should be protected from the changes and fluctuation of political opinions and parties. This led the judge, John Marshall, to conclude that 'a corporation is a legal person' or an 'artificial legal entity' distinct from its owners and officers. This decision had important ramifications. It meant that the corporation was no longer perceived as a creation of the state that should serve the public interest and that it had similar private rights as individuals. For instance, as an artificial legal person the corporation is entitled to protection under the 14th Amendment of the US Constitution.

Since corporations are now for all intents and purposes 'persons' with similar rights, many business ethicists argue for assigning them corresponding responsibilities. The *corporate social responsibility* (CSR) movement is based on the belief that the corporation is interwoven with the rest of society and has at least the following responsibilities: the economic responsibility to be profitable, the legal responsibility to abide by societal laws, the ethical responsibility to do what is right even when not compelled by law, and the philanthropic responsibility to contribute to what is desired in society. This fourth area is not morally or legally mandatory and falls entirely within the discretion of corporations.[9] We will discuss the various developments within the CSR movement in more detail in Chapter 11. For the purposes of this chapter, it will suffice to say that corporations have always played and continue to play a very significant role in the lives of communities and that, as such, there is a legitimate expectation that they should be responsible in doing so – at least in the four ways described above. But is this enough?

What does it really mean to say that corporations should be responsible? In the early years of the CSR movement, corporate social responsibility discourses restricted the forms of corporate participation in community life to charitable contributions and community development. As a result, more active corporate participation in societal governance and the overall impact that it has on society was not adequately acknowledged. More recently, revisions of this understanding of corporate citizenship (CC) have been proposed. The main reason is that the context within which CC operates had changed significantly. The power role that the nation state plays in guaranteeing citizenship rights has been weakened, whereas the power of corporations has increased. Moon *et al.* argue for a more rigorous definition of how corporations should function as 'citizens' in a global context.[10] They claim that corporate citizenship cannot be sustained on the basis of corporations' legal and administrative status. Though they may operate *like* citizens in some respects, they are not citizens in the real sense of the word.

Nevertheless, Moon *et al.* argue that corporations do operate like citizens in three important ways. In the first place, they participate in their communities' processes of societal governance through lobbying, pressure group activity, and even directly in governing in and through everyday economic activities. Secondly, they contend that corporations are involved in developmental democracy to the extent that they safeguard certain civil and social rights of other citizens. This has been particularly important when multinational corporations (MNCs) operate in countries guilty of human rights abuses (China and apartheid South Africa), and in developing countries where the state cannot adequately protect and deliver certain social rights, such as healthcare, education, and infrastructure. Thirdly, corporations also engage in deliberative democracy in and through their involvement in collective problem-solving. The notion of 'stakeholder democracy' is central here – corporations open the possibility for deliberation among societal groups and also respond to stakeholder concerns. Crane *et al.*

argue, therefore, that corporations may not be entitled to certain rights as 'real' citizens would be, but they are powerful public actors who have the responsibility to respect and even protect 'real' citizenship rights in society.[11] In fact, they argue that corporations should be viewed as administrators of certain citizenship rights. The main thrust of this argument is that corporations are taking over what were previously governmental functions. This raises all kinds of questions regarding the participation of those whose rights are defended and administered by corporations in the process of informing, controlling, and accounting for corporate decisions.

Critics of the *corporate citizenship* approach argue that the conflation of the notion of a legal 'person' and a public citizen should not be tolerated. Corporations don't have bodies that can get hurt, age, and die like those of human citizens in society. They don't vote for governments like individual human citizens do. Add to this the fact that many multinational corporations operate all over the world, and one is left with the vague notion of multinational corporations being 'world citizens'. Banerjee points out that even though the law can recognize the metaphoric personhood of a corporation, it is by no means easy to assign corresponding responsibilities to them.[12] What we are left with are 'persons' who have lots of rights, but no real responsibilities.

As we saw above, Crane *et al.* counter this objection by acknowledging that corporations are not citizens in the real sense of the word, but function like citizens, or at least as protectors and administrators of citizenship rights. However, even this position has met with serious criticisms. If we are going to assign to corporations the functions of government, how can we make sure that they will administer these fairly and to the benefit of all in society? Crane *et al.* argue that there are various mechanisms through which stakeholders can participate in the governance of corporations, or exert pressure on them. However, what seems evident is that corporations will be most concerned with protecting the rights of those stakeholders who have a direct impact on their operations, i.e. customers, employees, and suppliers. All these parties are economically empowered in some way – they can influence the corporation by withholding their investment, spending power, or production power. The question that remains is how we can be sure that the corporation will protect the rights of economically disadvantaged groups, like the unemployed, or the poor who don't have spending power. How can we be sure that corporations will be trustworthy custodians of certain common goods, like water, air, and natural resources that belong to all in society? Despite claims by Crane *et al.* that the new corporate citizenship (NCC) model that they propose is descriptive and value-neutral, Jones and Haigh have accused them of betraying a clear neoliberal prejudice and refusing to acknowledge that corporations do not always operate in the best interests of society.[13] Furthermore, even if they wanted to serve societal interests, it is not easily conceivable that corporations will be able to implement participatory decision-making models that take pluralist interests into account. Hence, corporate decisions are not sufficiently safeguarded by democratic processes, as most governments claim to be.

Other objections to the idea that corporations can be citizens draw out the implications that this will have in practice. Why would corporations agree to take on the obligation to act as administrators of citizenship rights? Hans van Oosterhout argues that they would do so because of the concomitant rights that they can claim in the process. He believes that corporations will be interested in attaining some fundamental human rights, like protection against arbitrary interference and expropriation by governments. They would also lay claim to rights that give states and other intra- and international entities privileged status under national and international law. This will have an impact on the status and legal subjectivity of corporations under international law. It would also allow corporations to invoke these rights against real human beings.[14]

Regardless of the objections raised within these theoretical debates, we see that corporations are taking on moral responsibilities in practice. The acceptance of the notion of 'corporate moral agency' and 'corporate citizenship' has brought many corporations to state their moral commitments publicly. The emphasis that is now placed on good governance practices, corporate social responsibility, and corporate citizenship, has led to the development of a plethora of corporate codes and charters that outline the value commitments of corporations. Most corporations, whether they manufacture cigarettes, weapons, or motorcars, make it clear that they intend to do business ethically. This is true even in the case of corporations that failed due to financial misconduct and deceptive business practices, such as Enron Corporation, which sported a glossy code of conduct and won numerous rewards for its excellent corporate social responsibility projects. This has led to significant skepticism regarding the intentions and practical value of corporations' stated value commitments.

However, when it comes to ethical violations, the law has the capacity to hold both the individuals involved in executive decisions and the corporation as a legal entity responsible for any damages caused. The concept of a tort is central in this regard. A tort is a civil wrong that is settled when one party sues another. Business can therefore be liable for intentional or unintentional torts of their agents or employees.[15] This includes strict product liability, and even vicarious liability for unintentional harm done by employees or agents of the corporation. The central assumption seems to be that although it is still individual moral agents who make mistakes, the corporation as a whole is supposed to guide these agents and prevent them from wrongdoing.

There are even attempts to entice corporations to proactively manage their ethics in order to prevent ethical violations. In the US, the most prominent initiative in this regard is the *US Federal Sentencing Guidelines for Corporations*. Within this, seven steps are prescribed that should be taken in the establishment of an ethics and compliance programme. These seven steps include: developing compliance standards, including a code of conduct, assigning a

Box 1.1	The Federal Sentencing Guidelines' seven steps

(1) Formulating compliance standards and procedures such as a code of conduct or ethics;

(2) assigning a senior employee (e.g. a compliance or ethics officer) to oversee proceedings;

(3) taking care when delegating authority;

(4) effective communication of standards and procedures (e.g. training);

(5) auditing/monitoring systems and reporting mechanisms, including whistle-blowing;

(6) enforcement of disciplinary mechanisms; and

(7) appropriate response after detection.

senior employee responsibility for managing the programme, implementing ethics training, making provisions for safe reporting channels, ensuring proper communication of ethical standards and raising ethical awareness, enforcing discipline, monitoring, and auditing, as well as preventing the reoccurrence of misconduct.[16]

If a corporation can indicate that it did everything it could to prevent its agent from engaging in misconduct, it may receive a lesser fine, or escape prosecution altogether. Corporate executives calculated that investing in the development of an ethics programme would probably cost them less than what they stand to lose in the event of a lawsuit. Ethics programmes that were motivated by this kind of logic were therefore no more than relatively cheap insurance policies. As it happened, experience soon showed that a programme in and of itself has little power to curb misconduct.

The spate of corporate scandals that occurred in the early 2000s compelled the Federal Sentencing Commission to take stock of what seemed to be the failure of many corporate ethics programmes. In 2004 they revised the guidelines and significantly elaborated on the criteria that ethics programmes in corporations had to meet. They also assigned significantly more responsibility to the governing authority (i.e. the board of directors) and executive leadership of an organization in overseeing the ethics programme. An important new provision was that an organization has to show that it had promoted 'an organizational culture that encourages ethical conduct and a commitment to compliance with the law'. This has led to renewed interest in the issue of corporate culture in the field of business ethics.[17] The debate is often described as the question of whether ethical failures in corporations are the result of bad apples (unethical individuals) or bad barrels (corrupting organizational structures). It also led to a plethora of articles debating the benefits of a values-driven approach to organizational culture, or a compliance-driven orientation stipulating clear rules and procedures. The emergent consensus in business ethics circles is that the two approaches are not mutually exclusive and that successful ethics management programmes often employ a combination of both values-driven cultural interventions with a strong compliance orientation.

We need to develop more insight into the interaction between corporations and their agents. Despite all of the theoretical discussion of corporate 'personhood' and 'citizenship', the current reality is that moral agency still seems to be located primarily within the individual human agents within corporations. We see this in the way corporate governance systems function, and the way that the law holds corporations responsible for the decisions and actions of their agents. The problem, however, is that once a violation occurs, it is very difficult to assign precise accountability because of the complex nature of decision structures. Many questions remain to be answered: Are individual moral agents within corporations indeed capable of rational decisions and actions directed by clear intentions? Are these agents not influenced by their institutional environments? And if so, who, or what is to blame? And if corporations are to protect citizen rights, who makes the decisions on what to protect and how to go about doing so? These questions cannot be answered if we do not take into account how human beings shape and are shaped by their institutional environments. It is in this regard that the insights of continental philosophers become invaluable.

Continental perspectives on structure and agency

The current debates around corporate agency and individual moral agency within corporations display a number of assumptions that call for philosophical interrogation. In the first place, many theorists seem to assume that corporations, and the individuals that operate within them, have distinct identities that allow them to act as 'agents'. In the case of corporations, their 'identities' are often described in terms of 'organizational cultures'. In terms of individuals, much attention is paid to the fiduciary duties that executives have, and the development of their personal integrity through various kinds of ethics training sessions and awareness raising programmes. But are these 'agents' real and do they have moral identities? How do they come into existence? In this section, we will discuss how Gilles Deleuze and Félix Guattari trace the origins of both corporations and individuals back to the basic flows of desire that make up the world. We will see that they give us reason to be less certain in our claims about corporate and individual identity.

What we have to investigate is how these corporate entities function and whether the focus on 'identity' within these complex organizations is indeed appropriate. Deleuze and Guattari help us understand that the focus on 'identity' often conceals the fluidity and multiplicity inherent in individuals and organizations. In organizational theory, the model of the corporation as a complex adaptive system may also challenge us to acknowledge the more fluid and dynamic nature of both corporations and their agents. A second, related set of assumptions that may merit investigation is the nature of the interaction between corporate structures and the individuals that operate within them. In philosophy, this problem is often referred to as the structure-agency problem. Are individuals determined, or decisively shaped by the institutions within which they function? Or do they maintain their free will, their own sense of agency? Or is this in fact an overly simplistic way of looking at how decisions and actions emerge?

Capitalism and its 'entities'

In *Anti-Oedipus: Capitalism and Schizophrenia*, Deleuze and Guattari offer an analysis of the way in which capitalist practices are related to some of the most basic workings of the human unconscious, which they describe as 'desiring-production'. They position *desire* as central to social production and reproduction, and as such, they posit it as the very infrastructure of daily life.[18] The flow of this desire creates couplings. The reason for coupling in the Deleuzoguattarian scheme of things is related to sensory stimuli linked to the specific details of our embodied reality, like a lock of hair, a smell, a voice. The point of these couplings is that they are not related to identities or over-arching entities. They are not transcendental or hierarchical. For example, Deleuze and Guattari explain that children do not love their parents (the father, the mother), but that they become attached to specific details, like the breast, the eyes, the voice, or a moustache. The attraction is visceral, not an abstract commitment.

For Deleuze and Guattari, desire is a positive and productive force that sustains the material flows that all life requires. Desire is not only permeating the natural or the biological, but also the social – it 'produces' various forms of sociality. It plays, in other words, a role in the creation and sustaining of practices and institutions. Deleuze and Guattari always provide their readership with lots of examples of what they have in mind: bureaucrats may indeed love their files, a judge may be libidinously related to his or her verdicts, exchange business on Wall Street turns people on, fans are enthused in a soccer or football stadium. Here, it is important to understand that 'desire' is *not* what psychoanalysis understood it to be. It is not a sense of lack that permeates our unconscious, it is rather a productive force that constitutes reality, including social reality. We have to understand that for Deleuze and Guattari desire refers to more than just sexual desire. Sexuality is but one flow amid many others that make up desire.

Deleuze and Guattari stress the primacy of historical and political forces in the operation of 'desiring-production'. The notion of *desiring-production* is a neologism for a conception of desire infused with production.[19] This desire is the physical and corporeal production of what we want. Our economic activities therefore have to be understood within the context of this desiring-production. Examples that Deleuze and Guattari offer of desiring machines include a mother's breast and a baby's mouth – the breast produces a stream of milk, the mouth taps it. The mouth is also a productive machine that produces sounds and saliva. Deleuze and Guattari also describe capitalism as a formidable

Box 1.2   **Machines versus mechanisms and organisms**

It is important to distinguish the idea of the machinic from that of the mechanistic or organismic. Living bodies and technological apparatuses are machinic when they are in the process of becoming, they are organismic or mechanical when they are functioning in a state of stable equilibrium. For Deleuze, the machinic is necessary to celebrate and explore the multiplicities that are always present in mechanisms and organisms.

'desiring machine', which is both social and technical.[20] As such, the social and technical structuring, destructuring, and restructuring within capitalism reveal the desiring-production we are all necessarily engaged in. Deleuze and Guattari were very critical of how capitalism came to be the social and economic form that our desiring-production takes. However, they offer a critique of capitalism that nonetheless accepts it as a central part of our existence that has to be analysed and understood.

Deleuze and Guattari's understanding of social, political, and economic activity is premised on the fact that all of life itself is a matter of flows, which must be structured in order for us to subsist. This structuring takes place through societal 'coding' that brings about relatively stable ways of existing. In Deleuze and Guattari's vocabulary, *territorialization* refers to the process by which we as human beings organize our world into spatial patterns such as 'inside' versus 'outside', or 'centre' versus 'periphery'. It relates to the spatial, material, and psychological components that constitute a society, group, or individual. However, rather than being a sedentary place with fixed borders, the territory is itself a malleable site of passage.[21] An *assemblage* has both territorial aspects, to stabilize it, and cutting edges of deterritorialization – therefore, it can be described as a mobile and shifting centre. This notion of assemblage is the translation of the French concept of *agencement*, and as such, offers another way of thinking about agency in corporate contexts. '*Agencement*' refers to the intermingling of bodies in a society, including all the attractions and repulsions, sympathies and antipathies, alterations, amalgamations, penetrations, and expansions that affect bodies of all kinds in their relations to one another. *Agencement* stems from the Latin *agens*, meaning 'directing', 'putting into motion'. *Agencement* allows us to put things into motion, to act, to direct. The fact that the concept of *agencement* is translated as assemblage, is quite significant. As Deleuze and Guattari explain, 'a society is defined by its amalgamations, not by its tools'.[22] One can think here of how a room is appointed, how things are arranged. But the difference is that there is no central agent that arranges, but is rather a kind of emergent patterning that produces something like 'agency', 'identity', etc. The assemblages that allow for this *agencing* (the verb form of agency) capacity are not stagnant. An *assemblage* has both territorial aspects, to stabilize it, and cutting edges of deterritorialization. Therefore it can be described as a mobile and shifting centre.

Territorialization, deterritorialization and reterritorialization presuppose each other. Deterritorialization is the possibility of change and transformation that is part of any territory.[23] For our purposes in this chapter, it is important to understand the constant deterritorialization that is always at work in capitalism. How does this deterritorialization play out in capitalism? To say that capitalism is characterized by 'constant deterritorialization' would mean that capitalism typically disrupts some of the coded societal orders upon which our sense of self and security has been built. Some examples that Deleuze and Guattari mention are: the deterritorialization of wealth through monetary abstraction; the decoding of the flows of production through merchant capital, and the decoding of states through financial capital and public debts. As such, it would seem that capitalism frees up our coded existence and creates new possibilities. However, this is not where the process ends. Capitalism replaces 'codes' with 'axioms'. This axiomatization empties flows of the specific social meaning that codes conveyed, and replaces it with a structure within which everything can be made equivalent based on its monetary value. The example of prohibitions around sex can be used to explain this: within a coded system, the prohibition on sex before marriage is something that signifies the stability of family life and procreation in society. Within a capitalist system, sex becomes a commodity to be sold or to be used to sell other commodities.

How does this happen? Industrial capital leads to the conjunction of all the decoded and deterritorialized flows in taking control of production and driving it towards creating a surplus value. This surplus has to be sold and this can only happen if our desire can be directed at some new kind of 'value'. The problem is that production of surplus value leads to a system in which 'money begets money'.[24] The belief that profit is valuable in and of itself starts to function as an axiomatic universal truth, which structures everyone and everything in its path to perpetuate this truth. In this process, 'value' no longer refers to any actual valuable 'thing', but becomes something with a substance, life, and motion all of its own. 'Value' no longer designates the relations of commodities, but enters into relations with itself. Under these conditions, capitalism functions as a diachronic machine, i.e. a machine operating over time, that organizes all the decoded flows for its own purposes. In the process, some of this coding becomes axiomatic and the functioning of the system mechanistic. The profitability of the firm and its relationship to the market and with commercial and financial capital requires more and more surplus value to fuel its pursuit of value for the sake of value. In this process, both physical labour and 'knowledge capital' (specialized education and information) become part of capitalism's operations.

The implication of all of this for corporations is that it is precisely capitalism's facility for decoding and unleashing flows, and its tendency to pursue value for the sake of value, that put the corporate entity itself at risk. Because the criteria for anything of value is more value, entities that were created for the purposes of value generation, like corporations, have no inherent right to existence. In fact, since these 'entities' have been produced merely as a means to an end, they can easily be replaced. As Ian Buchanan explains, Deleuze and Guattari's analysis of the life of capital allows us to appreciate the precariousness of corporate entities. By seeking out more profitable investment vehicles and lucrative opportunities elsewhere, capital thrives even when giant companies like Microsoft don't.[25] What we have to understand to get a sense of the precariousness of entities in a world characterized by advanced capitalism, is that the kind of connections that are made to facilitate desiring-production can be largely virtual in nature. There is no need for a real product, or even for real people producing something, in order for value to be created. Companies such as Facebook and YouTube trade on their 'cultural value' and do not seem to need mediation through commodity production. There of course comes a time when these start-up companies are bought by larger corporations, making their owners substantial profits, but as such, this merely starts the cycle of seeking surplus value all over again.

Could this view of corporations as dispensable profit-making machines have underpinned the downfall of big corporations like Enron and the broader global financial crisis a number of years later? Their executives did seem to be driven more by the need to uphold the perception of profit-making capacity than with the creation of real commodity value. But even if one did believe that corporations are mere profit-generating machines with no value in and of themselves, they do have implications for real human beings. Within business ethics, there has recently been more acknowledgement of the interdependence between corporations and the individuals that are linked to them. So much so that the new mantra has become 'sustainability' – not just to guarantee the corporation as an ongoing financial concern, but also to ensure environmental and social sustainability. We will return to this topic in Chapter 13. What we will pursue here, however, is the way in which corporations and individuals are part of decision-making processes. If Deleuze and Guattari are right that the human unconscious is subject to the same processes of cyclical turns in production that we witness in capitalist cycles, both individual agency and corporate agency may have to be rethought.

Who are we as individual agents?

In much of ethical theory, the assumption is made that there is an individual, or sometimes a collective entity, which acts as an integrated whole to make decisions about right and wrong. To understand how we come to know ourselves as 'subjects' or 'agents' of decisions and actions, we need to understand our own identity in a radically new way. Deleuze rejects the idea that the self is an integrated whole – instead, he argues that 'the self who acts are little selves which contemplate and render possible both the action and the active subject'. Deleuze explains that what we call 'self' is in fact the result of thousands of little witnesses that contemplate within us.[26]

Our desiring-production is shaping us through what Deleuze calls *passive syntheses*, which create our capacity for imagination, for intuiting the next step or the direction we should follow. By definition, a passive synthesis is something that we do not actively devise. It is something that happens *in* the mind rather than through conscious mindful activity. What we do after the fact is to contemplate how exactly we came to certain conclusions or why we took certain actions, and it is this 'contemplation' that leads us to construct an identity. As Deleuze explains, memory and understanding are superimposed upon and supported by the passive syntheses of the imagination.[27] The 'subject' is something that arises as a side-effect of certain practices and habits that we become part of due to these passive syntheses.

Deleuze and Guattari's view of the subject moves us away from 'identity' towards 'multiplicity'. Within each one of us, there are multiple flows and desires, which connect spontaneously with other human beings and with institutions. Desiring-production is constantly operating, and we interact with other forces such as those operative in capitalism, and this creates multiple effects. Our 'identity' is just one of these effects. It is not something we actively create or choose, but an effect of these multiplicities and the ongoing shifts in the processes of desiring-production that is part of its various cycles.

A further side-effect of these passive syntheses is that we can sometimes be on the receiving end of the negative effects of our own desiring-production. We habitually act in certain ways that then structure our existence in much the same way as a fascist ruler would structure the lives of his subordinates. Fascist desire is the desire for codes to replace the decoding that frees flows under capitalist axiomatics. If the coding is such that it leads to a conjunction (fixing, or stagnation) of desiring flows, such codes create rigid boundaries for thinking and allow human subjects to get stuck in certain patterns of thought.[28] Deleuze and Guattari argue that, paradoxically, fascism is not always the result of external agents such as dictators or state apparatuses. As Foucault succinctly notes in his 'Introduction' to *Anti-Oedipus*, 'the fascist often lies within'. We have internalized certain codes and controls to such an extent that fascist control is a function of our own unconscious. We become part of mechanistic operations that are not necessarily of our own active choosing, and the danger is that we are no longer capable of exploring possibilities of becoming more than we are in certain coded social systems. Why would this happen? What is the interaction between individuals and entities such as corporations?

How do 'agents' come to decisions?

It has to be acknowledged that Deleuze and Guattari have no interest in trying to direct or control ethical decision-making in a corporate setting. In fact, they would argue that 'ethics' obscures the processes of desiring-production that are always at work. Ethical thought projects certain permanent features of human experience and a kind of 'wisdom' about how to conduct interpersonal relations.[29] These are part of the historical and institutional specifics that allow us to operate within certain social settings, but as such, they are merely the 'effects' that hide the actual processes of desiring-production.

The problem may be that in focusing on developing step-by-step processes of ethical deliberation, such as is typically taught in ethics training sessions for individuals, or developing a rule-driven system of rules and procedures, such as we find in best practice governance models, we are misunderstanding the process by which decisions are in fact made. The nature of business organizations and the multidirectional effects that various interactions have on the emergence of agency have to be better understood. Let us start by looking at the nature of organizations. There has been quite a debate regarding whether corporations operate as rule-driven mechanisms, or instead as organisms. This has led some theorists to argue that organizations function like complex adaptive systems. It is important to note that these systems should not be understood as a fixed structure that can succumb to structural analysis by plotting cause-and-effect relationships. Complex adaptive systems are open, changing, and continually responding to new developments. Though order still emerges from within them, they cannot be reduced to the sum of their components. These systems are non-linear and operate far from equilibrium. Importantly, they are not at all structured as orderly, rule-governed grids, nor do they always function as organisms. Any 'structure' comes into effect as an emergent pattern that cannot be directed, or predicted in advance.

Drawing on Deleuze and Guattari, we may come to the conclusion that viewing corporations as mechanisms or as organisms is not our only option. What Deleuze and Guattari would help us understand is that the mechanistic rules that we often witness in corporate structures function as a 'molar order', which hides or covers over what is happening on a molecular level. Similarly, describing organizations as 'organisms' does not get us beyond the molar order either. Just like organizations, organisms remain stuck in the functions and processes that are required to maintain equilibrium. What Deleuze and Guattari are interested in, is exploring the molecular flows of forces that we are typically unaware of.[30]

Molecular flows of belief and desire escape the molar categories that are regulated through codes.[31] Deleuze and Guattari explain that there is a difference between the connection of flows and the conjunction of flows. A connection of flows occurs when decoded or deterritorialized flows join each other spontaneously, boosting and strengthening each other in an autocatalytic, i.e. self-propelling movement. They use mutiny or prison breaks as examples of such flows. Conjunction, in contrast, is the overcoding of flows, which captures them and leads to stoppages, blocking the lines of flight.

It has been argued that contemporary corporations function as open systems and maintain a delicate equilibrium close to the edge of chaos, i.e. close to the point where order disperses completely. From the perspective of this more complex model, then, the conventions and expectations that organize and guide business activity come into being and are developed as people interact with one another. Such order as exists within business life reflects, then, the 'internal logic' of business as a system of functional relationships between various individuals and organizations. The advantage of this understanding of business is that it looks for signs of functional organization within the dynamics of business activity itself, instead of trying to force it to conform to some preconceived operational model.

In order to understand the processes of decision-making, the more fluid relational dynamics that emerge between individuals, groups, and institutions have to be taken into account. The lines of influence between an organization's culture and its employees' moral sensibilities are not one-directional. This engenders a multidirectional flow of verbal, visceral, and mental signals about what is valued and expected by the organization's employees and agents. Employees on all levels contribute to the tacit understanding that emerges among them. Because this understanding emerges in the course of multiple interactions between employees, under various different sorts of circumstances, no one individual can control it. To be sure, certain individuals, like senior executives and charismatic leaders, may play a more prominent role than others, merely because they can also influence some of the structural dynamics that have an impact on patterning. However, it is extremely difficult for a single individual to 'step out' of the web of unarticulated expectations, obligations, and pressures that make an organizational culture what it is, in order to change or challenge it. Even if it were possible for individuals to do so, their agitations would simply be taken up in the multidirectional flow of tacit interpersonal signals within the organization, where they would combine with other, unarticulated expectations to produce any number of unforeseeable effects on the behaviour of employees.

Trying to come up with an 'integrity' strategy that holds individuals and corporations true to their core values may have little effect in dealing with the multiplicities that are part of desiring-production. The process of desiring-production may even lead to passive syntheses that we are not consciously aware of and can therefore not be deliberately operationalized, nor easily changed. This does not mean, however, that change within organizations is impossible. Quite the contrary: if the multiplicity of desiring-production is acknowledged, new forms of agency become more likely. However, to call this agency in the strict sense of the word may be a bit of a misnomer. What it is instead is a form of 'agencing' – i.e. the verb form of agency. This occurs when individuals are no longer perceived as 'functionaries' within the organization as organism, or as 'tools' within the organization as mechanism. Individuals are in and of themselves multiplicities of force, and as such, they are capable of 'agencing' that is unique, surprising, and as such creative. Deleuze and Guattari describe this as the possibility of 'the body without organs'. Within the body without organs, multiplicities are freed to take on new shapes that are not determined by organismic functions. The body without organs is a plane of consistency, or plane of immanence that allows for 'agencing' (*agencement* in French). One can see from the emphasis placed on immanence that all hierarchical structuring is abandoned here. The body without organs is a destratified body of which the organs have been released from the fixed and habituated functions that they assume in its organism form.[32] A singular body without organs is populated by uncoded intensities, and immanent relations of matter and energy flows determine the triggers of production.

Within complexity theory, these lines of flight may be understood as moves within the complex system that triggers bifurcation. A relative line of flight is a move towards a predetermined attractor. Elsewhere, we argue that values can act as strange attractors within an organizational set of dynamics.[33] Values emerge spontaneously from the everyday practices, habits, and interactions between individuals and groups. As such, these values are tacit, unspoken beliefs of which individuals are often not conscious but that can have an influence on their behaviour regardless. Lines of flight are vectors of both deterritorializing and reterritorializing. So seen from the perspective of Deleuze and Guattari, when an individual responds to an unprecedented crisis for which no code, rule, or directive exists in a way that reflects the organization's tacit values, it could be regarded as a relative line of flight. It does not follow a codified strategy, but does retreat to some 'sense' of what is appropriate. An absolute line of flight is when there is an absolute territorialization of the current, and new attractors, bifurcators, and patterns emerge. Bonta and Protevi provide a helpful description of lines of flight as 'vectors of freedom', or at least 'freedom-from'. Sometimes freedom is procured by finding safety in a set of practices, habits, and beliefs that offer immediate security and acceptance, sometimes it entails a more radical departure from any related practice or pattern.

What is important is that we remain open to the multiplicities that lie hidden behind the molar structures, on the molecular level of desiring-production. Individuals who operate in certain fixed roles for a long time and internalize the practices, habits, and beliefs of that role, may find it hard to think beyond those frames of reference. Within organizations, the dangerous phenomenon of group-think often occurs, when individuals become incapable of dissenting from the beliefs and habits of the group as it has become sedimented over time. If this environment's coded reality is one of amoral or even immoral behaviour, the individual will not be able to explore ethical possibilities. But within the notion of absolute lines of flight we may find the possibility of rethinking our own capacities for agency. To be capable of an individual moral response, some of the freedom of flows that is possible within the body without organs will be explored. Individuals who can embrace the idea of a 'body without organs', may be capable of surprising behaviour. It could, in fact, imply that something like 'moral responsiveness' would emerge spontaneously, without any fixed programming. This would make it possible that a sense of moral urgency may overcome all other considerations (as we will explain in the case of some whistleblowers in Chapter 9).

In organizational terms, the body without organs may refer to the various aspects of organizational life that have been moved out of its stable state or comfort zones and now offer a plane of immanence where new, surprising events can occur. Bonta and Protevi make it clear that the body without organs is not the infantile body of our past, but rather the virtual realm of possibilities. We can only reach the body without organs through a practice of disturbing the organism's patterns. Matter, energy, and desire must be able to flow without a centralized or hierarchical control. In a sense, this creates a form of agency that goes beyond our conception of individualized agents. Bonta and Protevi explain that for Deleuze and Guattari, at least in their earlier work, *Anti-Oedipus*, it is the central control that drains off the extra work, the surplus value that is produced. If a body could be structured in a way that allows patterning to remain flexible, to sustain some elements of intensity and of crisis, the body without organs or the virtual possibilities that always exist can more easily be reached.

What happens to the notion of 'identity' in this process? Deleuze and Guattari explain that the body without organs is not 'me', nor is it something that is a product of individual ingenuity. In its indifference towards an 'I' or a 'me', the body without organs is constantly changing form, crossing thresholds, and exploring possibilities. According to Bonta and Protevi, Deleuze and Guattari thematize the subject as 'an emergent functional structure embedded in a series of structures'. Structure may even be too strong a word here – it is more the case that what we come to know as our 'subjectivity' is an emergent patterning that becomes recognizable over time. This would mean that both the individual and the 'corporate' agency of groups are emergent properties of the interactions, priorities, shifts, and challenges that are part of organizational life.

How do we then account for corporate and individual 'decisions'? Deleuze and Guattari describe decision-making as an unspecifiable, unpredictable, rhizomatic activity. The biological term 'rhizome' refers to a form of plant that extends itself through a horizontal, tuber-like root system and can in this way create endless new plants. Examples of rhizomatic systems include ferns, grapevines, the brain, the Internet and terrorist networks. Deleuze and Guattari's description of the rhizome provides an account for the fact that there are strange connections between events, people, and objects. As Scott Lawley explains it, it involves a site of potentiality, a constantly moving set of potential connections, a 'permanent inventiveness'.[34] This does not mean complete flux. The rhizome is a plane of consistency, i.e. what allows for the constant emergence of agency.

It is important to note that hierarchy and rhizomatic canals coexist in the same environment, and continuously unsettle the patterns that are characteristic of each. In the context of corporate governance, they allow us to acknowledge the importance of certain hierarchical structures, and even the foundational principles upon which they rely. However, what the coexistence of rhizomes and hierarchical structures implies is that much escapes from those structures, and that what escapes may be of great interest to those within the field of business ethics.

Exploring the rhizomatic in business ethics requires quite a mind-shift. Where much attention used to be focused on delineated units that operate according to specific foundational principles and checks and balances, we now have to be open to 'dimensions, or rather directions in motion'.[35] Our interest has to be in what we and our institutions are becoming, rather than what they are. This requires a different kind of methodology as well. Where boards are typically concerned with how they can direct their corporations from where they are now, to where they want to end up, the rhizomatic requires starting in the middle, rather than from a beginning or an end. Looking at the rhizomatic map will indicate multiple points of entries and exits, and no, not all roads lead to Rome.

What Deleuze and Guattari seem to offer us is the idea that there is always the possibility that things could be otherwise. But in order to open these possibilities, we have to be aware of the processes of desiring-production, of flow, that allow for the emergence of certain patterns. Deleuze and Guattari offer us no safe position from which we can exert our moral agency. Instead they show that agency as such is an effect, a byproduct, of our desiring-production and the structuring and destructuring that is always part of this process. It is towards exploring the multiplicities of what can be in the process of affirming life, that we should direct our ethical attention. It can, in fact, be a very powerful force for action that is based in the affects that have powerful effects, some of which may come as a surprise to us.

Does this mean that, as such, there is no room for more deliberate ethical judgements? Not quite. Deleuze and Guattari challenge us to continually perform an evaluation of all of the various 'assemblages' that we are involved in. The only criteria they offer us for this evaluation is whether assemblages are life-affirming or life-denying. However, it is important to note that though they are critical of some of the social and economic orderings that have emerged as part of our desiring-production, they are not trying to argue that all territorialization and stratification is necessarily bad, or immoral. In fact, judging something as immoral will merely cover up the important desiring-production processes that lead to the structuring dynamics in which we find ourselves immersed.

This presents us with the possibility of agency without a central agent, which has some important implications for our consideration of corporate agency earlier on in the chapter. Let us briefly explore the critical questions it allows us to pose, and the possibilities that may emerge as a result. We saw that most discussion of corporate agency still puts a lot of stock in the identity of individual agents or corporate entities. Concepts like corporate culture and corporate citizenship are often used as if they depict a fixed entity with specific identity. But, in fact, these notions are molar constructs that cover up the desiring flows on a molecular order. It is these flows that produce these identities as a kind of side-effect of what is going on between people and institutions. This does not mean that we should do away with these notions, or that they are less important. The kind of structuring that they afford us is indeed very important. However, it becomes problematic if these constructs lead to a kind of fixed coding that makes any challenge to them, or exploration of possibilities beyond them, impossible. For instance, we saw some of these concerns raised against the notion of 'corporate citizens', by which corporations start to function as the administrators of other citizenship rights. It may allow us to always think critically about what an emergent molar order like 'corporate citizenship' implies for our embodied interactions with one another and with animate and inanimate entities we interact with. We should understand the inevitable limitations of terms like 'corporate governance', and employ a hermeneutics of suspicion with regard to the kind of safeguards they promise.

This also means that there are multiple other possibilities to explore. The various assemblages of which we are a part create a plane for taking action, and we can embrace this opportunity if we are willing to be affected by our interactions. In a sense, this is a call towards remaining open towards the various ways in which one's body interacts with those of others, and the way one's body takes up its place in the world.

Conclusion

In this chapter, we tracked the emergence of the notion of corporate personhood and corporate citizenship and the implications that these developments have for discussions of moral agency. From the perspective of business ethics, boards of directors govern corporations and these executive or non-executive directors have to exercise their own individual moral agency in determining corporate structures, decisions and actions. The problem is that complex business transactions and structures often make it very difficult to assign moral accountability to specific individuals. Multidirectional influences within organizations as complex adaptive systems also lead to tacit references that go far beyond the hierarchical directives of certain influential individuals. Some business ethicists would refer to corporate cultures as the 'bad barrels' that corrupt the individuals within. Others would lay the blame with immoral individuals, or 'bad apples', who corrupt the system. The interaction between corporations and the individuals within them have puzzled many business ethicists.

Deleuze and Guattari allowed us to see that what escapes this analysis is the broader processes of desiring-production that take on a certain form within the capitalist system. When we understand how desiring-production functions, we see that the 'identity' that we assign to both persons and corporations may, in fact, belie the multiplicity of flows and desires that are at work within our complex interactions in the world. In fact, 'identity' may just be the emergent effect of the structuring, destructuring, and restructuring that takes place as individuals and organizations move through the various cycles and flows that are part of our existence in the world. We need codes and structures, but sometimes these structures cut off the flows that allow us to be open to new possibilities of existence. These structures are not always external, institutional constraints. Often, there are unconscious forces and emergent patterns that operate within us, and afford us our 'agency'.

The challenge that confronts us as we make our way in the world is to seek the life-affirming possibilities that lie within and beyond the various structures within which we operate. This means that we will in some cases have to seek escape routes, or lines of flight, in Deleuze and Guattari's vocabulary. Sometimes we will find our way into other, similar patterns, and at other times we may be confronted with more radical changes. Whatever it is, it is all part of the flow of possibilities that keep us very much alive.

NOTES

1 P. French, *Collective and Corporate Responsibility*. New York: Columbia Press (1984).
2 D. G. Arnold, 'Corporate moral agency', *Midwest Studies in Philosophy* 30 (1) (2006), 279–91.
3 L. Erokovic, 'Corporate governance', in R. W. Kolb (ed.), *Encyclopedia for Business Ethics and Society*. Thousands Oaks, CA: Sage Publications (2008), 471–80.
4 *Ibid.*, 475.
5 E. Freeman, A. Wicks, J. Harrison, B. Parmar, and S. de Colle, *Stakeholder Theory: The State of the Art*. Cambridge: Cambridge University Press (2010).
6 For more detail on these national differences, see *Ibid.*, 473.
7 For further discussion on the issue of the rationality of moral agents and a description of the phenomenon of 'bounded rationality', see Chapter 5.
8 S. B. Banerjee, *Corporate Social Responsibility. The Good, the Bad, the Ugly*. Northampton, MA: Edward Elgar (2007), 45.
9 D. Matten, A. Crane, and W. Chapple, 'Behind the mask: revealing the true face of corporate citizenship', *Journal of Business Ethics* 45 (2003), 110.
10 J. Moon, A. Crane, and D. Matten, 'Can corporations be citizens? Corporate citizenship as a metaphor for business participation in society', *Business Ethics Quarterly* 15 (3) (2005), 429–53.
11 A. Crane, D. Matten, and J. Moon, 'Stakeholders as citizens? Rethinking rights, participation and democracy', *Journal of Business Ethics* 53 (2004), 107–22.
12 Banerjee, *Corporate Social Responsibility*.
13 M. T. Jones and M. Haigh, 'The transnational corporation and new corporate citizenship theory. A critical analysis', *Journal of Corporate Citizenship* 27 (2007), 51–69.
14 H. van Oosterhout, 'Dialogue', *Academy of Management Review* 30 (4) (2005), 677–84.
15 N. Nedzel, 'Business Law', in Kolb, *Encyclopedia for Business Ethics*, 240–9.
16 For a more detailed analysis of the various elements of an ethics management programme, see D.-M. Driscoll and W. M. Hoffman, *Ethics Matters. How to Implement*

Values-driven Management. Bentley, MA: Bentley University Center for Business Ethics (1999).

17 E. Petry, 'Assessing corporate culture part 1', *Ethikos* 18 (5) (March/April 2005).

18 I. Buchanan, *Deleuze and Guattari's Anti-Oedipus. A Reader's Guide*. New York: Continuum (2008), 39.

19 Buchanan, *Deleuze and Guattari*, 43.

20 G. Deleuze and F. Guattari, *Anti-Oedipus. Capitalism and Schizophrenia*. Minneapolis, MN: University of Minnesota Press (1983), 244.

21 K. Message, *The Deleuze Dictionary* A. Parr (ed.). New York: Columbia University Press (2005), 275.

22 G. Deleuze and F. Guattari, *A Thousand Plateaus. Capitalism and Schizophrenia*. Minneapolis, MN: University of Minnesota Press (1987), 90.

23 A. Parr, *The Deleuze Dictionary*. New York: Columbia University Press (2006), 67.

24 Deleuze and Guattari, *Anti-Oedipus*, 227.

25 Buchanan, *Deleuze and Guattari*, 57.

26 G. Deleuze, *Difference and Repetition*. New York: Columbia University Press (1995), 74.

27 *Ibid.*, 71.

28 M. Bonta and J. Protevi, *Deleuze and Geophilosophy: A Guide and Glossary*. Edinburgh, UK: Edinburgh University Press (2004), 86.

29 Buchanan, *Deleuze and Guattari*, 82.

30 Deleuze and Guattari, *Anti-Oedipus*, 283–9; *A Thousand Plateaus*, 256, 395–403, 409–11.

31 Bonta and Protevi, *Deleuze and Geophilosophy*, 87.

32 *Ibid.*, 62.

33 M. Painter-Morland, *Business Ethics as Practice. Ethics as the Everyday Business of Business*. Cambridge: Cambridge University Press (2008).

34 S. Lawley, 'Deleuze's rhizome and the study of organization: conceptual movement and an open future', *TAMARA: Journal of Critical Postmodern Organization Studies* 3 (4) (2005), 36–47.

35 Deleuze and Guattari, *A Thousand Plateaus*, 21.

2 Stakeholder theory

DAVID BEVAN AND PATRICIA WERHANE

Goals of this chapter

After reading this chapter you will be able to:

- understand traditional stakeholder theory;
- discuss its characteristics and indicative shortcomings;
- critically evaluate stakeholder theory by considering Levinas's thinking.

Introduction

> Simply put, a stakeholder is any group or individual who can affect, or is affected by, the achievement of a corporation's purpose. Stakeholders include employees, customers, suppliers, stockholders, banks, environmentalists, government and other groups who can help or hurt the corporation.[1]

With these words R. Edward Freeman is generally regarded as inscribing the stakeholder as a key concept for mainstream business ethics and a theoretical cornerstone for the development of corporate social responsibility (CSR) over the past three decades. It is clear that this was not entirely his original purpose. Indeed, he intended that primarily it would be a new concept for strategic management practice. Nor was it a sudden invention: Freeman had been working on the stakeholder project while at Wharton in 1977 and finished the first full version of this work in 1983. A provisional, retrospective appreciation has recently appeared, in which Freeman and some current collaborators reassess the origins of the stakeholder concept: they analyse the various and multiple iterations and versions that have arisen from the original idea and offer some new possibilities for the stakeholder franchise.[2] In the course of their authoritative recollection of what has happened, over 300 articles (journal articles, books and chapters) which feature the term 'stakeholder' are considered worthy of comment or citation.

Here we do not seek to replicate this scholarly work, nor offer such a variety in detail. Rather, we shall present in this chapter a critical review of a range of positions offered by business ethics regarding stakeholder theory. At the same time we shall introduce a selection of apparent mainstream critics of the stakeholder concept. We then review and discuss the organizing potential, of stakeholder theory as a mental model. The stakeholder concept is central to, and facilitative of, developing a pluralist model of social responsibility across business activities (or CSR), which we interpret as responsibility for others. Finally, and to offset mainstream views from a continental perspective, we shall consider the meaning of stakeholder in terms of this responsibility to others by particular reference to the work of Zygmunt Bauman and Emmanuel Levinas.

Mainstream views of stakeholder theory

Freeman's initial account of the stakeholder concept is not claimed as a personal innovation. It is made quite clear that threads of the concept can be found in Adam Smith as well as Berle and Means.[3] Freeman suggests that its contemporary meaning arises from the work of Igor Ansoff at Stanford in the early 1960s:

> The actual word 'stakeholder' first appeared in the management literature in an internal memorandum at the Stanford Research Institute . . . in 1963. The term was meant to generalize the notion of stockholder as the only group to whom management need be responsive.[4]

The concept suggests a means of identifying persons or groups other than (but not excluding) shareholders without which an organization could not exist or function. These persons or groups 'originally included shareowners, employees, customers, suppliers, lenders and society'.[5] This broad taxonomy of stakeholders is a clear step away from the extreme individualist position of instrumental, managerial economics that suggests only the interests of shareholders are of significance to managers. To exemplify such a position we can recall Milton Friedman who considered that:

> [T]here is only one social responsibility of business – to use its resources and engage in activities designed to increase its profits so long as it stays within the rules of the game.[6]

For Freeman, the stakeholder perspective implies something entirely different:

> [U]nless executives understood the needs and concerns of these stakeholder groups, they could not formulate corporate objectives which would receive the necessary support for the continued survival of the firm.[7]

We do not suggest here that *all possible* readings of Freeman repudiate *all possible* interpretations of Friedman's axiomatic claim. But for Friedman, interviewed in the *Financial Times* in 2003, the concept of stakeholders remained a dangerous, socialist concept embracing a fundamentally subversive doctrine approaching corporate fraud.[8] More specifically:

> Few trends could so thoroughly undermine the very foundation of our free society as the acceptance by corporate officials of a social responsibility other than to make as much money for their stockholders as possible.[9]

The important point here is one of *emphasis*: the stakeholder concept from its conceptualization or development in Freeman marks a significant move in the direction of a socially aware or pluralist apperception of the relationship between business and society. Contemplating Friedman and Freeman – some readers may have seen this juxtaposition framing an essay or exam topic – makes understanding the stakeholder approach a little more emphatic.

From this conceptual starting point, Freeman suggests, we can trace the influences of the stakeholder concept in at least four distinct, mainstream management directions. It is an organizing concept in the corporate planning literature from which it is acknowledged to have emerged. It is also discernible as informing aspects of systems theory, literature on CSR, and organization theory. Further, it is the aggregation of these four fields that will result in Freeman's conceptualization of strategic management. For the interests of this chapter we shall follow mainly the CSR strand of management for its contribution to business ethics. Freeman views CSR literature, rather than in the terms we have just discussed, as applying stakeholder concepts to non-traditional stakeholder groups: 'less emphasis is put on satisfying owners and comparatively more emphasis is put on the public or the community or the employees'.[10]

Freeman argues that isolating economic issues from social issues is intellectually fallacious.[11] In his later work he calls this the 'separation fallacy'.[12] Freeman claims that ethics and economics cannot be separated, just as social issues and economics cannot. It is also significant for us that Freeman believes management theory to be distinctly prescriptive: 'good theories of management are practical'. The stakeholder concept is valuable as the basis of revising and improving existing views of business and management. Further and beyond such evidence of foundational pragmatism, 'the stakeholder model developed here is prescriptive in the sense that it prescribes action for organizational managers in a rational sense.'[13] In a mainstream business ethics setting such claims reinforce the propriety and the essentially emancipating nature of Freeman's theory. Notwithstanding, this perspective will be significant for our discussion in the second part of this chapter.

One of the ways in which Freeman most effectively communicates the stakeholder approach to strategic management is through models of stakeholding. Again these are important to the discussion of mental models later in this section. There are what appear to be spoke and wheel models with the firm

Figure 2.1

A 'traditional' stakeholder map

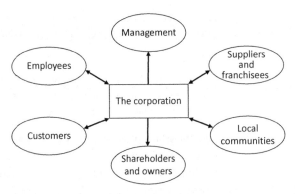

Source: R. E. Freeman, *Strategic Management: a Stakeholder Approach*. Boston, MA: Pitman (1984).

at the centre (hub) and a number of spokes radiating to and from the hub to the outlying stakeholder categories, although Freeman himself argues that this diagram is supposed to demonstrate the interrelated relationships between various stakeholders and the firm (Figure 2.1).[14] There are also taxonomical tables in which each of these categories is then subdivided into a range of possible examples. Other representations include: role set analysis diagrams; two dimensional grids in which stakeholder power and function are explicated; planning process schematics in which activities are displayed; two-by-two matrices in which organizational process and stakeholder transactions are modelled; a stakeholder's dilemma 'game' modelled on the prisoner's dilemma in which voluntary negotiating is one option and 'hardball' (implicating constraint or litigation) is the other.

In the course of these examples Freeman's prescriptivism comes across as strongly in favour of voluntarism for any managers engaging with stakeholders. They 'must go hand in hand' in any successful stakeholder engagement.[15] The importance of Friedman's contribution in the 1980s is perhaps attributable to the prominence it brought to a pluralist conceptualization at a time when this was a radical deviation from the mainstream agency paradigm, which focused on managerial responsibilities to shareholders. While it implicates business ethics in its consideration of CSR, this is not the major focus of his 1984 book. It is a clear explication of the stakeholder concept but written from the narrower, highly pragmatic perspective of management strategy rather than the ethical concerns to which Freeman (and many others) turned subsequently.

Pragmatism features as the implicit focus of a further refinement from Freeman himself, which we consider to make the link to mainstream business ethics from the work of fundamental pragmatists such as Charles Pierce, William James, and John Dewey.[16] Freeman suggests that stakeholder theory is not any single axiomatic theory, but rather that it is a generic *approach* from which 'a reasonable pluralism' may be shown to arise.[17] This generic stakeholder approach allows us 'to blend together the central concepts of business with those of ethics'.[18] As a manifestation of this pluralist tendency we now briefly point to some of the reconsiderations of stakeholder theory as exemplifying the interest from mainstream business ethics, both in general,[19] and in a range of diverse and particular examples: Kant and the ethics of duty;[20] pragmatism;[21] discourse ethics;[22] (integrative) social contracts theory;[23] (social) justice;[24] politics;[25] the common good;[26] critical realism;[27] agency theory;[28] feminism;[29] and many, seemingly endlessly, more. Versions of stakeholder theories are also adopted throughout the business ethics literature and recast variously and experimentally as implicit and explicit;[30] or implicitly contractual and explicitly contractual.[31] Stakeholders can be primary or secondary;[32] legitimate and/or illegitimate.[33] The requisite theories to consider them can be normative or descriptive;[34] these theories can converge and diverge;[35] and be integrated with or decoupled from CSR practice;[36] and – again – so on. This profusion of approaches suggests that unreliable, even maddening,[37] or bewildering,[38] criteria may be whimsically adduced. Numerous others continue to reinforce this view with various perplexing schemas of stakeholder definitions:[39] 'employees, providers of finance, consumers, community and environment, government and other organizations and groups',[40] is typical of such offerings which can include anyone.[41]

Thus stakeholder theory is potentially in problematic disarray,[42] and it sometimes has been regarded as inconclusive, misleading,[43] and confused.[44] The stakeholder model of organization is implicitly open to criticism as a myth,[45] a fad,[46] or a management fashion.[47] Some have criticized stakeholder power for lacunae in theoretical rigour,[48] or for being excessively normative.[49] Others have extensively elaborated the theory with different names and theoretical dimensions.[50]

We will more fully consider two developments based on the stakeholder approach as a means of showing the ways in which other authors in business ethics have adopted the stakeholder concept as the basis of fuller analysis. Both papers divergently employ Freeman's pluralist stakeholder theory to reformulate central concepts of structure in the first instance, and of power relations in the second. The first is Donaldson and Preston, the second is Mitchell, Agle, and Wood.[51]

Donaldson and Preston suggest that stakeholder theory has three typological formulations. Whereas, as we have identified above, Freeman initially volunteers a simple prescriptive intent, for Donaldson and Preston there is a richer potential, which can be understood across the three distinct dimensions of *descriptive*, *instrumental*, and *normative*. A fourth thesis is that stakeholder management 'requires as its key attribute, simultaneous attention to the legitimate interests of all appropriate stakeholders'.[52] The *descriptive* or empirical

Stakeholder theory from the
perspective of Donaldson and
Preston

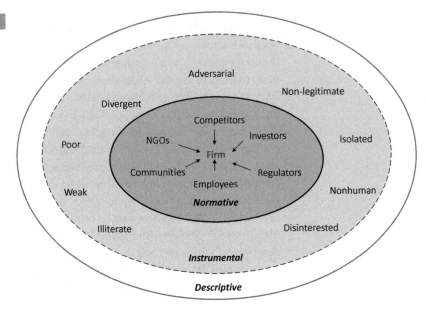

Source: T. Donaldson and L. E. Preston, 'The stakeholder theory of the corporation:
concepts, evidence, and implications', *Academy of Management Review* 24
(1) (1995), 65–9.

dimension arises from the way in which the stakeholder concept sees the firm
as an interaction of intrinsically valuable and potentially collaborative, competitive interests. The *instrumental* dimension suggests that stakeholder theory
permits the exploration of a relationship between CSR and business performance. The *normative* dimension arises in the tendency of stakeholder theory
to permit the consideration of a broad range of interests beyond the share-
holder/owner or contractually engaged parties. All normative theories, seeking
to establish a behavioural norm, propose what someone – here, managers –
should do. Here the stakeholder norm at least apparently contradicts or deviates from Friedman's CSR axiom of the primacy of fiduciary responsibilities
between manager and owner. Donaldson and Preston argue that all stakeholders have intrinsic value, beyond the normative justifications presented in this
book, and rely on 'Western philosophical and moral traditions such as utilitarianism, the social contract, fairness and reciprocity, fundamental human rights,
and respect for human beings'.[53] Friedman's axiom of the value-maximizing
enterprise is in fact 'morally untenable'.[54] This array of three dimensions is
nested in a concentric mental model. The descriptive outer shell of empirical
practice contains and shapes the other two dimensions: the intermediate circle
of instrumental stakeholder theory shows how a correct use of CSR makes
good business; at the centre is the normative core of the pluralistic form of the
firm (Figure 2.2).

Mitchell, Agle, and Wood innovate a notion of stakeholder power in terms of salience. This salience is predicated by the possession, or attribution, of one, some or all of the following qualities:

- the power of the stakeholder to influence the corporation;
- the legitimacy of the stakeholder's relationship with the corporation; and
- the urgency of the stakeholder's claim on the corporation.

These three core constituents of power, legitimacy and urgency have a sense of intangibility.[55] Each of the dimensions lacks any absolute standard – if that is a desirable quality – and so each suffers all the relativist, contextual, epistemological challenges explored above in looking at stakeholders. One possibly unintentional consequence of this theory is that it implicates a potential shareholder primacy in each of the three qualities; a shareholder has each of these qualities through the simple quality of owning a share.

In a 2010 volume, written with Harrison, Wicks, Parmar, and De Colle, Freeman presents a view that stakeholder theory has succeeded in overturning the Friedman delineation of shareholder capitalism, 'the usual understanding of business as a vehicle to maximize returns to the owners of capital'.[56] It suggests that globalization has forced us to reconsider 'the dominant conceptual models we use to understand business'. In such a context, it claims that stakeholder theories are robustly compatible with the intellectual tenets of market idealism, strategic management, agency theory, and transaction cost economics; all of which have been regularly misapplied to undermine it. By this means stakeholder theory is, somewhat ambivalently we suggest, represented as both overturning the normal interpretations of business it seeks to improve or supersede, while also adopting all the characteristics it set out to radically humanize.

Is it that the materiality of the stakeholder concept has been magnified and elaborated so effectively that after twenty-five years it is capable of enfolding and overcoming all objections? One trace of such discourse is the assertion in Chapter 11 of this book that CSR should (i.e. normatively) come to stand for corporate *stakeholder* responsibility. The rationale runs like this: if the stakeholder concept has become so central to a new kind of capitalism – differentiated carefully from Friedman's (1962) market capitalism as the basis of freedom, to Freeman *et al.*'s (2010) capitalism as the basis of freedom and responsibility – then the social, formerly the 'S' in CSR, becomes redundant. It is replaced by the structurally socialized stakeholder concept. So 'by appealing to some principle of responsibility . . . and simply realizing that stakeholders and business people share a common humanity', capitalism can mutate into a system with an ethical core.[57]

Does this sound reasonable? We will venture to agree that on one level it is entirely plausible and rational. Our project, however, will be to add new dimensions to stakeholder theory: its scope, its impact, and its notions of responsibility.

Figure 2.3

A more complex model

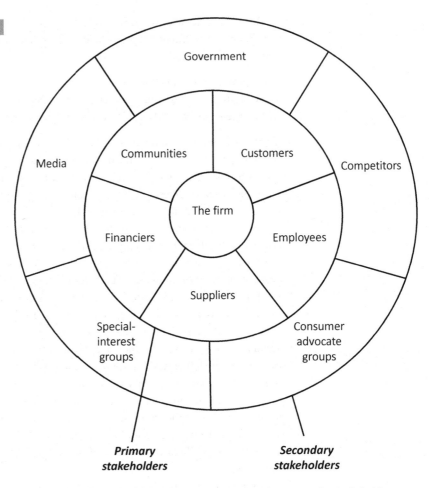

Source: R. E. Freeman, J. S. Harrison, and A. C. Wicks, *Managing for Stakeholders.
Survival, Reputation, and Success.* New Haven, CT: Yale University Press (2007).

Decentring stakeholder models and systems thinking

Most stakeholder models, even those framed by complex graphics that take
into account critical and fringe stakeholders, are depicted with the firm in the
centre. A 'traditional' stakeholder map (Figure 2.1) first proposed by Freeman
some time ago, places the corporation in the centre of the graphic, and that
remains so in Freeman *et al.*'s more complex iteration (Figure 2.3).[58] While
allegedly this is not a wheel-and-spoke model, its focus on the firm as the
centre captures our attention. Our mental model of corporate governance and
corporate responsibility is partly constructed by these graphics. Our focus is
firstly on the company, and only secondarily on its stakeholders, despite the
claim that all critical stakeholders, those who most affect or are affected by the
company, have, or should have, equal claims to importance. This attention to

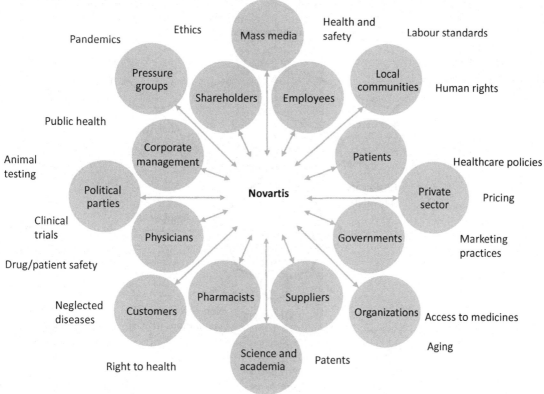

Pandemics Ethics Health and safety Labour standards

Public health

Animal testing

Clinical trials

Drug/patient safety

Neglected diseases

Right to health Patents

Human rights

Healthcare policies

Pricing

Marketing practices

Access to medicines

Aging

Source: ©Novartis, 2008.

Figure 2.4

Companies operate in a challenging environment

the centre, the firm, we suggest, may marginalize other stakeholders even when that is not the deliberate intent.

Global companies have very complicated stakeholder maps, as the Novartis example illustrates (Figure 2.4). But in many (but not all) corporate graphics, the focus of attention is to the centre of the graphic, and often, still, the firm remains in that centre. When one's mental model of corporate governance and corporate responsibilities are framed with the firm in the centre, how one thinks about corporate responsibility is different, say, than when that model is altered. That is, these models are firm-centric so that the company is the agent for these relationships, not an embedded partner. This firm-centric depiction may prevent companies and their managers from viewing the firm from the perspectives of others: their primary and secondary stakeholders who, from the context in which they operate, may be culturally, politically, or economically alien. Thus this sort of thinking may also preclude firms and even their stakeholders from taking into account perspectives that will affect their operations, particularly in diverse cultures.

There are a number of ways to challenge this model, each of which will affect our thinking about corporate responsibility. We shall suggest there are

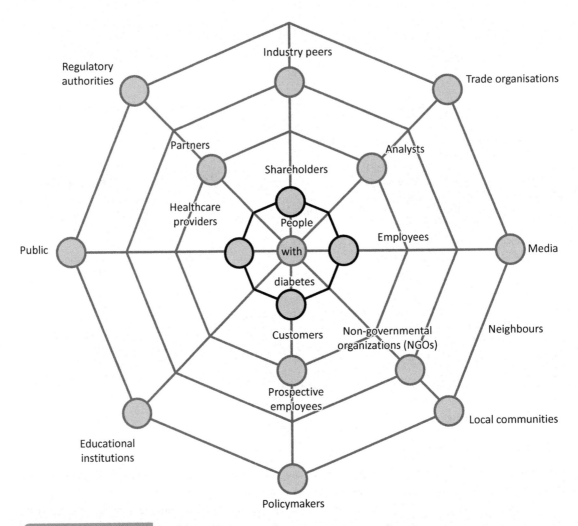

Figure 2.5

Stakeholders at Novo Nordisk

at least four: One can replace the firm in the centre with another stakeholder. In Figure 2.5 from Novo Nordisk, we find patients in the centre, specifically patients with diabetes, thus prioritizing that set of patient-stakeholders for that company. Another way to highlight and refocus attention is to place an actual picture of a stakeholder in the centre. For example, in focusing attention on sweatshop workers employed in factories producing goods for Wal-Mart, one could put an actual picture of a worker in the centre. Figure 2.6 depicts a 14-year-old sweatshop worker, working at a Bangladeshi jeans factory for more hours than she is paid. She is expected to attach a button to a pair of jeans every seven seconds. When her productivity decreases, she will either be transferred to an easier task, or simply be replaced by another, faster, worker.[59] By placing an individual person in the centre of a stakeholder map we achieve two ends: we draw attention to these workers and their plight, and give a 'name and face' to a very large group, probably close to 2 million women in Bangladesh alone

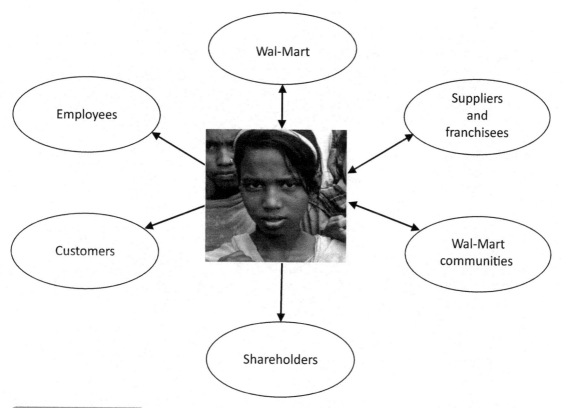

Figure 2.6

'Names and faces'

who work under sweatshop conditions. Freeman himself and John McVea have written on the importance of remembering that stakeholder groups represent a collection of real individual human beings.[60] This point is critical if stakeholder theory is to meet the objections of its continental critics. We shall take up this again in the discussion of Levinas.[61]

A third alteration in our thinking can be elicited by taking a systems approach to stakeholder theory (Figure 2.7). This is particularly useful for global companies. Here, we do not depict systems as closed, deterministic structures, but rather as complex, adaptive systems. 'A truly systemic view . . . considers how a set of individuals, institutions and processes operates in a system involving a complex network of interrelationships, an array of individual and institutional actors with conflicting interests and goals, and a number of feedback loops'.[62] A systems approach presupposes that most of our thinking, experiencing, practices, and institutions are interrelated and interconnected. Almost everything we can experience or think about is in a network of interrelationships such that each element of a particular set of interrelationships affects some other components of that set and the system itself, and almost no phenomenon can be studied in isolation from other relationships with at least some other phenomenon.

Transnational corporations, in particular, are meso-systems embedded in larger political, economic, legal, and cultural systems. Global corporations may

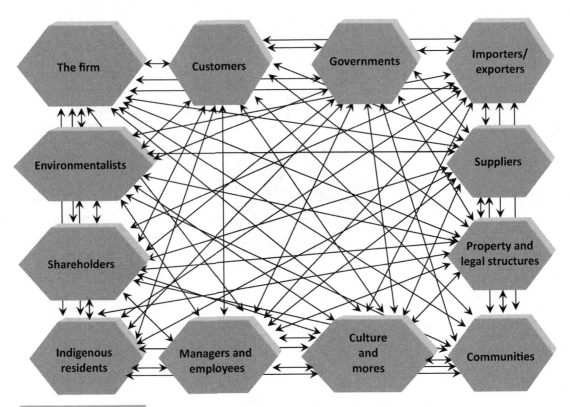

Figure 2.7

Stakeholder system networks

be embedded in many such systems. These are all examples of 'complex adaptive systems', a term used to describe open interactive systems capable of changing themselves and affecting change in their interactions with other systems.[63] What is characteristic of all types of systems is that any phenomenon or set of phenomena that are defined as part of a system has properties or characteristics that are altered, lost, or at best obscured, when the system is broken down into components. For example, in studying corporations, if one focuses simply on its organizational structure, or merely on its mission statement, or only on its employees, shareholders, or customers, one obscures if not distorts the interconnections and interrelationships that characterize and affect that organization in its internal and, more importantly for this argument, its external relationships.

Because a system consists of networks of relationships between individuals, groups, and institutions, how any system is construed and how it operates, affects and is affected by individuals, i.e. names and faces. The character and operations of a particular system or set of systems affects those of us who come in contact with the system, whether we are individuals, the community, professionals, managers, companies, religious communities, or government agencies. An alteration of a particular system or corporate operations within a system (or globally, across systems) will often produce different kinds of outcomes, some of which will have moral consequences. This part of moral

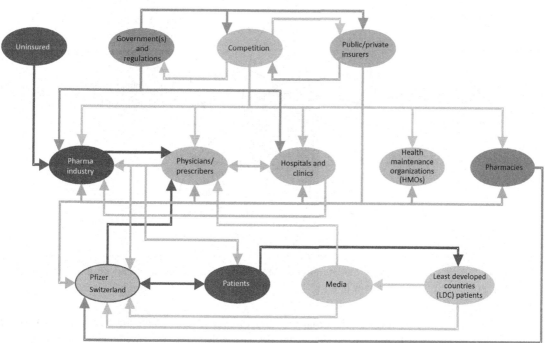

Source: Sybille Sachs, University of Zurich, available at www.pfizer.com/responsibility/cr_report/engagement.jsp.

Figure 2.8

A systems model

responsibility is structured by the nature and characteristics of the system in which a company operates.[64]

On the other hand, what companies and individuals functioning within these systems focus on, their power and influence, and the ways values and stakeholders are prioritized affect their goals, procedures, and outcomes as well as affecting the system in question. On every level, the way individuals and corporations frame the goals, the procedures and what networks they take into account makes a difference in what is discovered or neglected. These framing and reframing mechanisms will turn out to be important normative influences of systems and systems thinking.[65]

Global companies frequently find themselves involved in a complex network of disparate stakeholders where they are not always the centre of attention. Pfizer Switzerland depicts itself in that manner (Figure 2.8). Notice how in this graphic the firm is one of a number of equal players, and this creates a more networked mental model of the global firm. Such a multiple perspectives approach is essential if, for example, a multinational corporation (MNC) thinks of itself as a global company that affects and is affected by its suppliers and their employees *and* the various communities in which it contracts or operates.[66] Still, a multiple perspectives approach does not adequately take into account two important elements of corporate governance and corporate responsibility. Firstly, as we mentioned earlier, the fact that stakeholders are individual human

Figure 2.9

The FHC alliance model

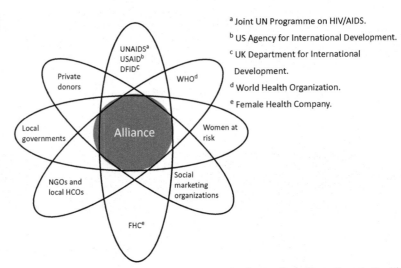

ᵃ Joint UN Programme on HIV/AIDS.

ᵇ US Agency for International Development.

ᶜ UK Department for International Development.

ᵈ World Health Organization.

ᵉ Female Health Company.

Source: Model courtesy of Mary Ann Leeper, chief operating officer, Female Health Company (FHC).

beings implies that they must all be given 'names and faces' rather than be homogenized as 'the others'. Secondly, in the present climate where companies are pressured to take community interests seriously (environmental and social responsibilities as well as creating economic ones) they need to see themselves with a more disinterested perspective of the cultures in which they operate – a less firm-centric perspective. Thus companies appear to have three sets of obligations: a set of corporate agent-centred reciprocal obligations to and with their stakeholders including shareholders, another networked-centred set of obligations to these groups as individuals, and thirdly, from a more disinterested perspective, to see themselves as global players in very complex relationships.[67]

A fourth kind of decentring depiction is useful when global companies form partnerships with non-governmental organizations (NGOs) and local officials in order to break down barriers of entry, cultural differences, or local product distribution. For example, the Female Health Company (FHC), an over-the-counter company, distributes female condoms in the developing world. To be successful (and profitable) it had to form alliances with foundations and aid agencies for financial support, with NGOs and local officials for distribution channels, and with social workers who understand value differences in the countries and villages where this product was to be distributed. FHC then redrew its stakeholder model as an alliance model where the programme for manufacture, education, funding, and distribution, not the product or the company, is at the centre of the alliance (Figure 2.9). And notice that the possible victims of HIV have names and faces as well.[68]

Our argument here is that redrawing stakeholder maps is not merely fun for idle graphic artists. How these maps are drawn affects – or gives structure to – our mental models: the ways companies and managers think about themselves, their products and processes, their responsibility to their stakeholders, and how they are perceived by outsiders in different contexts. The difference, if one uses a systems or an alliance model, is the adaptation of multiple perspectives, trying to get at the mind set of each group of stakeholders from their points of view. A systems perspective or an alliance model brings into focus the responsibilities as well as rights of various stakeholders and communities from their perspectives, not merely from the firm's point of view. It takes seriously a multicultural, global, individualized 'names and faces' approach.

In closing this section on responsibility we suggest that decentring organizational stakeholder narratives and, as we will discuss in the next section, rethinking stakeholder analyses through Zygmunt Bauman's *Postmodern Ethics* and Emmanuel Levinas's notion of 'the Other' helps each of us to understand the extent and limits of organizational involvement in a variety of global contexts where CSR is often defined as 'the responsibility of a company for the *totality* of its impact'.[69,70]

Continental approaches to stakeholder theory

The irreducible responsibility for the Other

In the work of Levinas we encounter some clues regarding distinct, yet overlapping problems within stakeholder theory. Based on Levinas's work, Bauman brings us to question bureaucracy in organizations for its incapacity for moral responsiveness. To introduce the work and our readings of Levinas we begin with the observation that he offers us an ethics based on the theme of unquestioning responsibility.[71] We shall start with the importance of ontology, which can be defined as a branch of philosophy that studies the most general question, i.e. what it means to be. For Levinas, ontology is problematic because it is often assumed that we can understand what 'is' while it is precisely the certainty of this understanding that undermines the ethical relation.[72] Such 'understanding' is seen as a form of domination or violence.

As Levinas and Bauman understand it, there is a tradition in Western philosophy that suggests that understanding what our senses seem to tell us is, very literally, a process of sense-making. Levinas suggests that such sense-making is simply a reduction of these sense data to the terms of each individual's experience – to the self. We thus selfishly reduce everything to our own terms of reference. In Levinas's language, Western philosophy is based on an ontology which reduces others to what is familiar to us (the same).[73]

According to Levinas, the Other is that which is not 'me' (or 'the same' as me). We are all, largely, so enmeshed in the practice of ontology that this simple proposition tends to evade the reduction to comprehension or 'totality'. For Levinas, our understanding is nothing more than a selfish totalization of experience. He contrasts such a totality of knowledge with 'infinity' in the sense of that which is beyond or outside of knowledge, or simply incomprehensible. Thus everything that is not us, is other than us, and Levinas suggests that the otherness of others who are not us can only reasonably – through reason – be reduced to understanding.

The personal or ethical relation that we naturally – in a vulnerable and irrational space – experience in the face of the Other, becomes reduced by reason to a cognitive relation. The problem lies in the reduction or totalization of the Other to 'stakeholders', because the notion of the Other suggests that even questions of knowledge are potentially subjective. Such an ontological perspective presents itself to us contingently. So, 'I' have to resolve knowledge for myself in each moment.

For Levinas, 'the conception of the "I" as self-sufficient is one of the essential marks of the bourgeois spirit and its philosophy'.[74] According to Levinas, such unnatural, self-sufficient egoism is an essential, structural constituent of capitalism; the conception of the 'I' 'nourishes the audacious dreams of a restless and enterprising capitalism . . . presides over capitalism's work ethic, its cult of initiative and discovery, which aims less at reconciling man with himself than at securing for him the unknowns of time and things'. It is as though my identity as 'I' is itself a quality of being: the insecure security which we have from this 'bourgeois' confidence in our being, draws us into a concern 'with business matters and science as a defense against things and all that is unforeseeable in them'. For example, the way that many people invest in their careers or are even obsessed by it, can be seen as an attempt to gain control over insecurity.

Reading Levinas we become aware of the fact that stakeholder theory is concerned primarily with firms, not with individuals. One possible way to think through Levinas's critique is to replace the individual with the firm. It is certainly sometimes true, as we argued in the last section, that stakeholder theory is often 'firm-centric', and that a strictly two-way firm-centric perspective may preclude a global perspective essential to unscrupulous or even value-creating business decisions.

If we take Levinas to the letter, we would inevitably have to come to the conclusion that business folk or managers are unscrupulous: '[Their] lack of scruples is a shameful form of his tranquil conscience'. The need for reasonable security becomes a justification for all business activity. Managers prefer the security of tomorrow to the enjoyment of today. This may be an exaggeration of managerial behaviour in many instances, but it may reflect some cases such as Enron (see Chapter 4), AIG, and other companies where managers became self-interested, ignored their stakeholders as real individuals, and were probably greedy as well.

For Levinas, knowledge or understanding is too often reduced to something that only makes sense to 'me'.[75] But this is, of course, a limited, safe version of knowledge. We are potentially faced in every moment with an infinity of experiences. This infinity is irreducible to any familiar concept. But for Levinas, enlightenment-informed thinking causes us to go through a reductive process in which by negating contradictory propositions to preserve them in a coherent discourse we institute a totality 'in which all Other is included in the Same'.[76] This understanding captures the Other in the terms of the Same. Another way of putting this is that when stakeholder theory treats each of its class of stakeholders as a group rather than acknowledging that group as a collection of individual human beings, we conceive that group as being a collective, as 'the Same', when in fact that is far from the case. The result is that:

> Western philosophy has most often been an ontology: a reduction of the other to the same by the interposition of a middle and a neutral term that ensures the comprehension of being.[77]

We may understand ontology here as 'egology', itself a neologism, meaning 'knowledge in my own terms'. So business ethics, when it is firm-centred, tends to be egological from such a perspective. The responsibility located in stakeholder theory is simply one that is convenient to some within business ethics.[78] Building on the problem of egology for business ethics theorizing is potentially a rational approach: and this act of rationalization reduces responsibility to a collective, not an individual responsibility.

Critical scholars in accounting and organization studies have elaborated on this point in Levinas to challenge orthodox management positions.[79,80] Bevan and Corvellec, for example, argue that for Levinas, ethics itself and any semblance of responsibility unfolds in the relationship with the Other.[81] Our unconditional and unlimited responsibility for the Other is an essential part of our humanity. 'Being ethical – being human – is being open to, (un)prepared for and impassioned by the radical difference of the Other . . . and lurching without compromise into the unknown and unknowable, the infinite and timeless otherness of the Other'.[82] To express ethics or responsibility in such terms stands in counterpoint to some business ethics theories that ignore the face of the Other. Responsibility does not arise from some rationalization of (stakeholder) claims, but in the encounter with the Other and outside of the self. Morality is thus instantiated in the relationship between the human subject and other moral subjects. Levinas brings us to reconsider the thematization or totality of codes of ethics, rules of stakeholder engagement, good corporate citizenship, and ethical principles. Instead he argues that responsibility arises in the emergent complexity of the encounter with the Other.

Levinas unfortunately offers few practical directions about how to operationalize such responsibility. It is in this impracticality that we find a suitable crux for the problems between continental philosophy and business ethics. In fact, what Levinas understands as responsibility for the Other cannot be subsumed under collective stakeholder theory at all, no matter how carefully it is phrased. From his perspective, the rational deliberation of stakeholder thinking is inherently irresponsible. It is not a response; it is a rational cogitation, the contemplation of one category by another, and, possibly only with the intention to control or subjugate it. Stakeholders as a category can, as we have seen above, be used effectively as a means to replicate market capitalism. The understanding of the stakeholder as a collective is an attempted totalization of an irreducible complexity. This would be one way of (mis)understanding the corporate stakeholder responsibility model proposed in Freeman *et al.*[83]

Beyond this multilateral problematization, and inspired again by Levinas, we now turn to the concern of Bauman, which focuses on the ills of bureaucratic organizations. Bauman is disenchanted with the iron-cage of bureaucracy and what he perceives as its determinism.[84] He sees society as constituted in a struggle of structural processes in a state of constant competition facilitated by the bureaucratic arrangements.[85] For Bauman, modern advanced market capitalism is a 'global spread of the modern form of life' which has an 'elemental, unregulated and politically uncontrolled nature'.[86] Bauman adopts Levinas's concept of the Other and the instantiation of responsibility in the encounter with the Other. In this face-to-face encounter, the Other confronts us literally with a moral impulse. Bauman appears to think about responsibility like Levinas, as an immanent, incomplete and unpredictable relation between oneself and the Other. Bauman writes with great attention about the multiple fractures, the effective atomization, of any such rule of responsibility which takes place in an institutional/organizational project. The processes of even small institutional bureaucracies take us away from the face-to-face encounter with the Other. In bureaucratically managed institutions:

> [A]ll social organization consists therefore in neutralizing the disruptive and deregulating impact of moral impulse. This is achieved through a number of complementary arrangements: (1) assuring that there is a distance, not proximity between two poles of action – the 'doing' and the 'suffering' one; by the same token those on the receiving end are held beyond the reach of the actor's moral impulse; (2) exempting some 'others' from the class of potential objects of moral responsibility, of potential 'faces'; (3) dissembling other human objects of action into aggregates of functionally specific traits, and holding such traits separate – so that the occasion for reassembling the 'face' out of disparate 'items' does not arise, and the task set for each action can be exempt from moral evaluation.[87]

These 'complementary arrangements' of bureaucracy – familiar perhaps from Weber's functional and specific division of powers – are an inherent, structural feature in other fields in which the normalization of the unthinkable occurs, such as in the army, a hospital, or a school.[88,89] Here, Bauman offers an explanation of why an individual, perhaps 'names and faces', approach to the Other is more human. For example, we need to know who the 'victims of HIV/AIDS' are individually if we are to respond to their needs ethically. In Levinas's terms, these complementary arrangements atomize all sense of individual moral responsibility for the Other. This does not take away the responsibility, but rather palliates it, diluting the call for subjective responding, concealing the Other with sleights of linguistic obfuscation and indirectness. Responsibility in Levinas and Bauman does not fit neatly into the stakeholder concept, at least not when it totalizes the collection of stakeholders:

> Responsibility means to respond, to respond to the call for responsibility issued wordlessly from the Other and revived pre-voluntarily by the subject.[90]

This structure of bureaucracy is potentially problematic for the concerns central to stakeholder theory. In connection with Bauman's conceptualization of complementary arrangements, stakeholder theory may supply a vocabulary of separation; a means of distancing accountability and responsibility and endlessly interrupting the moral impulse. Thus we may find recourse to the language of stakeholder names and classes employed among those seeking to avoid, rather than to engage with, accountability.[91] Functionally, we could claim there are but two classes of stakeholder in business ethics:

(1) those who own shares; and
(2) those who do not.

Among those who do not, a priority may be established by reference to normal commercial risk criteria as interpreted in Mitchell *et al.*, which by recourse to rational and unemotional, analytic philosophy, again repeats the convenient axioms to which all stakeholder engagement can be used instrumentally to serve the transnational corporations' self-interest in business-as-usual.[92]

But this dissection belies the ontological structure of stakeholder theory, which argues that all stakeholders are on equal footing. What stakeholder theory sometimes fails to do is recognize that each group of stakeholders is a bundle of individuals, each of whom is an irreducible Other to whom each manager and each firm has an irreducible responsibility. More could be made of the names and faces dimensions of stakeholder theory, and an appeal to Levinas helps to do that. Both the Donaldson/Preston and the Mitchell *et al.* analyses fail in this regard. We suspect that Freeman does not, but his contribution can still benefit from the names and faces theory we have discussed in this chapter.[93]

The Levinas/Bauman analyses remind us that all forms of political economy are created by, made up of, and affect, individual irreducible human beings. Any radical confrontation with the Other, whether at the individual or firm level, explicates the myriad almost infinite responsibilities we have to each other, both individually and collectively. We can never escape this accountability; we can only try to understand a bit of it through systems thinking, decentring stakeholder models, and the radicalization of the Other in stakeholder thinking.

Conclusion

To bring this chapter to a conclusion, we see Freeman's contribution of stakeholder theory to business ethics as a great success. Freeman provides an essentially emancipatory makeover for capitalism on the basis of which an ethical industry could emerge. A burgeoning debate has arisen on the relationship between business and academia, where business wants more relevance and less theory, and academia wants more rigour and scholarship. Stakeholder theory has provided an interesting example of how well a theoretical innovation can work in practice, *if* it is continuously engaged. As we have shown in the discussion of mental models, in this case arising from this single idea, it is capable of dynamically affecting the way we engage with the world. We have spoken of the structural tendencies noted by many commentators – and mainly in adverse terms – for regulation and bureaucracy. But are rules and institutions inherently evil to the extent that capitalism is always cruel and bureaucracy inevitably immoral? As individuals (scholars/students/managers) we are all agents in the structural reproduction of the present – it requires our *conscious* engagement.

NOTES

1 R. E. Freeman, *Strategic Management: a Stakeholder Approach*. Boston, MA: Pitman (1984), vi.
2 R. E. Freeman, J. S. Harrison, A. C. Wicks, B. L. Parmar, and S. De Colle, *Stakeholder Theory: the State of the Art*. Oxford: Oxford University Press (2010).
3 A. Smith, *The Wealth of Nations*. R. H. Campbell and A. S. Skinner (eds.). Oxford: Oxford University Press (1776; 1976); A. A. Berle, Jr. and G. Means, *The Modern Corporation and Private Property*. New York: Macmillan (1932).
4 Freeman, *Strategic Management*, 31.
5 *Ibid.*, 32.
6 M. Friedman, *Capitalism and Freedom*. Chicago, IL: University of Chicago Press (1962), 74.
7 Freeman, *Strategic Management*, 32.
8 S. London, 'The long view: interview with Milton man', *Financial Times*, Weekend Magazine, 7 June 2003.
9 Friedman, *Capitalism and Freedom*, 133.
10 Freeman, *Strategic Management*, 38.
11 *Ibid.*, 40.
12 J. D. Harris and R. E. Freeman, 'The impossibility of the separation thesis', *Business Ethics Quarterly* 18 (4) (2008), 541–8; Freeman *et al.*, *Stakeholder Theory*.
13 Freeman, *Strategic Management*, 48.
14 From a private conversation with Ed Freeman, 6 November 2009.
15 Freeman, *Strategic Management*, 80.
16 R. E. Freeman, 'The politics of stakeholder theory', *Business Ethics Quarterly* 4 (1994), 409–21; N. Bowie, 'A Kantian theory of capitalism', *Business Ethics Quarterly* SI (1) (1998), 37–60.

17 Freeman, 'The politics', 414.

18 *Ibid.*, 409.

19 R. E. Freeman and P. Werhane, 'Business ethics: the state of the art', *International Journal of Management Review* 1 (1) (1999), 1–16.

20 W. E. Evan and R. E. Freeman, 'A stakeholder theory of the modern corporation: Kantian capitalism', in T. L. Beauchamp and N. E. Bowie (eds.), *Ethical Theory and Business*. Englewood Cliffs, NJ: Prentice Hall (1988).

21 A. C. Wicks and R. E. Freeman, 'Organization studies and the new pragmatism: positivism, anti-positivism and the search for ethics', *Organization Science* 9 (1998), 123–40.

22 D. Reed, 'Stakeholder management theory: a critical theory perspective', *Business Ethics Quarterly* 9 (3) (1999), 453–83.

23 T. Donaldson and T. Dunfee, *Ties That Bind: a Social Contracts Approach to Business Ethics*. Cambridge, MA: Harvard Business School Press (1999).

24 Freeman, 'The politics'; R. E. Freeman, 'A stakeholder theory of the modern corporation', in T. L. Beauchamp, N. E. Bowie, and D. G. Arnold (eds.), *Ethical Theory and Business Practice,* 6th edn. Upper Saddle River, NJ: Prentice Hall (2001), 56–65; R. Phillips, 'Stakeholder theory and a principle of fairness', *Business Ethics Quarterly* 7 (1) (1997), 51–66; R. Phillips, 'Stakeholder legitimacy', *Business Ethics Quarterly* 13 (1) (2003), 25–41.

25 N. M. Wijnberg, 'Normative stakeholder theory and Aristotle: the link between ethics and politics', *Journal of Business Ethics* 25 (2000), 329–42.

26 A. Argandoña, 'The stakeholder and the common good', *Journal of Business Ethics* 17 (9/10) (1998), 1,093–102.

27 A. L. Man and S. Miles, 'Developing stakeholder theory', *Journal of Management Studies* 39 (1) (2002), 1–21.

28 C. W. L. Hill and T. M. Jones, 'Stakeholder agency theory', *Journal of Management Studies* 29 (1992), 131–54.

29 A. C. Wicks, D. R. Gilbert, and R. E. Freeman, 'A feminist reinterpretation of the stakeholder concept', *Business Ethics Quarterly* 4 (iv) (1994), 475–97.

30 D. Matten and J. Moon, ' "Implicit" and "explicit" CSR: a conceptual framework for a comparative understanding of corporate social responsibility', *Academy of Management Review* 33 (2) (2008), 404–24.

31 A. L. Friedman and S. Miles, *Stakeholders: Theory and Practice*. Oxford: Oxford University Press (2006).

32 M. B. E. Clarkson, 'A stakeholder framework for analyzing and evaluating corporate performance', *Academy of Management Review* 20 (1) (1995), 92–117.

33 R. Phillips, 'Stakeholder legitimacy', *Business Ethics Quarterly* 13 (1) (2003), 25–41.

34 R. K. Mitchell, B. R. Agle, and D. J. Wood, 'Towards a theory of stakeholder identification and salience: defining the principle of who and what really counts', *Academy of Management Review* 22 (4) (1997), 853–86.

35 L. K. Trevino and G. R. Weaver, 'The stakeholder research tradition: converging theorists – not convergent theory', *Academy of Management Review* 24 (2) (1999), 222–7.

36 G. R. Weaver, L. K. Trevino, and P. L. Cochran, 'Integrated and decoupled corporate social performance: management commitments, external pressures, and corporate ethics practices', *Academy of Management Journal* 42 (5) (1999), 539–52.

37 Mitchell *et al.*, 'Towards a theory'.

38 T. Swift, 'Trust, reputation and corporate accountability', *Business Ethics: a European Review*, 10 (1) (2001), 16–26.

39 J. Hasnas, 'The normative theories of business ethics: a guide for the perplexed', *Business Ethics Quarterly* 8 (1) (1998), 127–46.

40 L. J. Mullins, *Management and Organisational Behaviour*. London: FT Prentice Hall (2004), 135.

41 N. Egels, *Sorting out the Mess: a Review of Definitions of Ethical Issues in Business*. Gothenburg: Gothenburg Research Institute (2005).

42 D. A. Gioia, 'Practicability, paradigms, and problems in stakeholder theorizing', *Academy of Management Review* 24 (2) (1999), 229–32.

43 R. Gray, D. Owen, and C. Adams, *Accounting and Accountability*. Harlow: Prentice Hall Europe (1996).

44 C. Stoney and D. Winstanley, 'Stakeholding: confusion or Utopia? Mapping the conceptual terrain', *Journal of Management Studies* 38 (5) (2001), 603–26.

45 A. Geva, 'Myth and ethics in business', *Business Ethics Quarterly* 11 (4) (2001), 575–97.

46 P. P. Carson, P. A. Lanier, K. D. Carson, and B. N. Guidry, 'Clearing a path through the management fashion jungle: some preliminary trailblazing', *Academy of Management Journal* 43 (6) (2000), 1,143–58.

47 C. S. Spell, 'Management fashions: where do they come from, and are they old wine in new bottles?', *Journal of Management Inquiry*, 10 (4) (2001), 358–73.

48 E. Jansson, 'The stakeholder model: the influence of the ownership and governance structures', *Journal of Business Ethics* 56 (1) (2005), 1–13.

49 S. B. Banerjee, 'Whose land is it anyway? National interest, indigenous stakeholders and colonial discourses: the case of the Jabiluka uranium mine', *Organization and Environment* 13 (1) (2001), 3–38.

50 J. Jonker and D. Foster, 'Stakeholder excellence? Framing the evolution and complexity of a stakeholder perspective of the firm', *Corporate Social Responsibility and Environmental Management* 9 (4) (2002), 187–95.

51 T. Donaldson and L. E. Preston, 'The stakeholder theory of the corporation: concepts, evidence, and implications', *Academy of Management Review* 24 (1) (1995), 65–9.

52 *Ibid.*, 67.

53 S. B. Banerjee, *Corporate Social Responsibility: the Good, the Bad and the Ugly*. Cheltenham, UK: Edward Elgar (2008), 26.

54 Donaldson and Preston, 'The stakeholder theory', 88.

55 R. E. Freeman, *Business Ethics: the State of the Art*. Oxford: Oxford University Press (1991); Hasnas, 'Normative theories'.

56 Freeman *et al.*, 'Stakeholder theory', 9.

57 *Ibid.*, 424–5.

58 R. E. Freeman, J. S. Harrison, and A. C. Wicks, *Managing for Stakeholders. Survival, Reputation, and Success*. New Haven, CT: Yale University Press (2007).

59 National Labor Committee, www.nlc.org (2006).

60 J. McVea and R. E. Freeman, 'A names-and-faces approach to stakeholder management', *Journal of Management Inquiry* 14 (2005), 57–69.

61 S. Benhabib, *Situating the Self*. New York: Routledge (1992).

62 S. Wolf, 'Toward a systemic theory of informed consent in managed care', *Houston Law Review* 14 (1999), 1,632.

63 P. Pisek, 'Redesigning of health care with insights from the science of complex systems', in Committee of Quality of Health Care in America, Institute of Medicine Washington, DC (eds.), *Crossing the Quality Chasm. A New Health System for the 21st Century*. Washington, DC: National Academy Press (2001), 309–23.

64 L. Emanuel, 'Ethics and the structure of health care', *Cambridge Quarterly* 9 (2000), 151–68.

65 P. H. Werhane, 'Moral imagination and systems thinking', *Journal of Business Ethics* 38 (2002), 33–42.

66 I. I. Mintroff and H. A. Linstone, *Unbounded Mind: Breaking the Chains of Traditional Business Thinking*. Oxford, UK: Oxford University Press (1993), 98.

67 K. Goodpaster, 'Corporate responsibility and its constituents', in T. Beauchamp and G. Brenkert (eds.), *Oxford Handbook for Business Ethics*. Oxford: Oxford University Press (2009).

68 G. Yemen and E. Powell, *The Female Health Company*. Charlottesville, VA: University of Virginia Darden School Publishing (2003).

69 Z. Bauman, *Postmodern Ethics*. Oxford, UK: Blackwell (1993).

70 G. Chandler, 'Introduction: defining corporate social responsibility', *Ethical Performance: Best Practice* (Fall 2001). See www.rhcatalyst.org/site/DocServer/CSRQ_A.pdf?docID=103, accessed 10 November 2009.

71 A. Zielinski, *Levinas – La Responsabilité est sans Pourquoi?* Paris: University of Paris Press (2004).

72 E. Levinas, 'Is ontology fundamental?', in E. Levinas (ed.), *Entre Nous: Thinking of the Other*. London: Continuum Books (2006), 1–10, 1.

73 E. Levinas, *Totality and Infinity – an Essay on Exteriority*, A. Lingis (trans.). Pittsburgh, PA: Duquesne University Press (1969), 43.

74 E. Levinas, *On Escape*, B. Bergo (trans.). Stanford, CA: Stanford University Press (2003), 50.

75 E. Levinas, *Alterity and Transcendence*, M. B. Smith (trans.). London: Athlone Press (1999), 39.

76 Ibid., 56.

77 Levinas, *Totality and Infinity*, 43.

78 D. Bevan, 'Continental philosophy: a grounded theory approach and the emergence of convenient and inconvenient ethics', in M. Painter-Morland and P. Werhane (eds.), *Cutting-edge Issues in Business Ethics: Continental Challenges to Tradition and Practice*. New York: Springer (2008), 131–52.

79 T. Shearer, 'Ethics and accountability: from the for-itself to the for-the-other', *Accounting, Organizations and Society* 27 (2002), 541–73.

80 J. Roberts, 'The manufacture of corporate social responsibility: constructing corporate sensibility', *Organization* 10 (2) (2003), 249–65.

81 D. Bevan and H. Corvellec, 'The impossibility of corporate ethics: for a Levinasian approach to management ethics', *Business Ethics: a European Review* 16 (3) (2007), 208–19.

82 *Ibid.*, 208.

83 Freeman *et al.*, 'Stakeholder theory'.

84 M. Weber, *The Protestant Ethic and the Spirit of Capitalism*, T. Parsons (trans.). Mineola, NY: Dover (1904; 1930; 2003).

85 Z. Bauman, *Postmodern Ethics*. Oxford, UK: Blackwell (1993), 193.

86 Z. Bauman, *Wasted Lives*. Cambridge: Polity Press (2004), 7.

87 Bauman, *Postmodern Ethics*, 125.

88 M. Weber, *Economy and Society*. London: University of California Press (1922; 1978).

89 H. Arendt, *The Human Condition* (2nd edn.). Chicago, IL: University of Chicago Press (1999); C. Card, *The Atrocity Paradigm: a Theory of Evil*. Oxford, UK: Oxford University Press (2005); G. Deleuze and F. Guattari, *A Thousand Plateaus: Capitalism and Schizophrenia*, B. Massumi (trans.). London: Continuum (2004); R. Jackall, *Moral Mazes: the World of Corporate Managers*. Oxford, UK: Oxford University Press (2000).

90 A. J. Vetlesen, 'Introducing an ethics of proximity', in H. Jodalen and A. J. Vetlesen (eds.), *Closeness: an Ethics*. Oslo: Scandinavian University Press (1997), 1–19.

91 S. Key, L. Bewley, and S. Vault, *Stakeholder Theory around the World: a Twenty-year Retrospective*. Paper presented at the Academy of International Business – South-east (AIB-SE) (2004), Knoxville, TN.

92 Mitchell *et al.*, 'Towards a theory'. See also E. Collins, K. Kearins, and J. Roper, 'The risks in relying on stakeholder engagement for the achievement of sustainability', *Electronic Journal of Radical Organization Theory* 9 (1) (2005), 1–19.

93 McVea and Freeman, 'A names-and-faces approach'.

Organizational culture

HUGH WILLMOTT

Goals of this chapter

After studying this chapter you will be able to:

- understand what is meant by the term 'culture' in the context of business ethics;
- identify the limitations of some approaches to developing an 'ethical organizational culture';
- understand the notion of 'freedom' in Foucault's thought;
- analyse how 'culture' played a role in the Enron case.

Introduction

This chapter explores 'culture' in relation to ethics in business. What might this mean? Box 3.1 presents an extract from a corporate values statement, which distils the core cultural values of Nnore, a major corporation. The statement is typical in emphasizing openness, honesty, and sincerity and in aspiring to excellence in everything that Nnore does. The values statement is affirmed and elaborated in the company's sixty-four-page code of ethics.[1]

Why are such statements and associated codes of ethics drawn up and publicized in internal communications and highlighted in annual reports and on corporate websites? Communicating the core corporate values of a company is intended to build the confidence of stakeholders who include suppliers, customers, and investors as well as employees. Values statements and codes of ethics offer reassurance to these stakeholders that they will receive what is promised – in the form of terms of services provided, payments for supplies, or dividends and capital gains accruing from investments. So widespread have such statements and codes become that their absence might trouble stakeholders if it implies that the organization is unreliable or disreputable.

Establishing and maintaining an 'ethical culture' by communicating core corporate values is intended to minimize the risk of reputational damage, associated erosion of confidence and loss of business. A demonstration of the fragility of business confidence occurred on 13 September 2007 when television

Box 3.1	Nnore* values

Integrity. We work with customers and prospects openly, honestly, and sincerely. When we say we will do something, we will do it; when we say we cannot or will not do something, then we won't do it.

Excellence. We are satisfied with nothing less than the very best in everything that we do. We will continue to raise the bar for everyone. The great fun here will be to discover just how good we can really be.

* Nnore is a pseudonym for a major corporation.

news broadcasts showed lengthy queues of depositors outside branches of Northern Rock, the sixth-largest retail bank in the UK at that time. The queues were a response to a news bulletin in which it was reported that Northern Rock was seeking emergency financial assistance from the Bank of England. When confidence evaporates, stakeholders become reluctant to maintain their 'stake' – in depositing their savings, in committing their labour, in supplying raw materials, in providing capital, in endorsing reputation, and so on.[2] This issue of business confidence is by no means confined, post-2008, to the financial sector or to the UK. In 2009, the annual Trust Barometer produced by Edelman, a public relations firm, reported that 'trust in US business is even lower than it was after Enron and the dot-com bust'.[3]

Building and securing reputation and trust becomes even more critical in an era of consumer capitalism when businesses expand into more domains of society (e.g. culture, sports, or leisure); the branding of companies and services becomes more critical for growth; and the media, including the Internet, become more significant in corporate communications.[4] In this context, the contents of codes and programmes of corporate ethics may underscore the importance of values such as openness and sincerity but also include those of 'social responsibility' and 'citizenship' with regard to the wider society. These developments help to explain why increasing attention is being directed to the strengthening of 'ethical culture', including the promotion of good corporate citizenship.[5,6] In an effort to improve the ethical character and standing of organizations, corporations like Nnore (see Box 3.1), have introduced ethics programmes and even appointed ethics officers to 'communicate important values, standards, and assumptions regarding ethical conduct'.

The objective of this chapter is to present and illustrate the conventional wisdom about instilling ethical conduct by shaping and strengthening corporate culture and then, mobilizing the thinking of Foucault, to interrogate this wisdom. Foucault's ideas provide a way of questioning whether values statements and codes of ethics serve to address or obscure ethical issues, and whether they enhance or undermine employees' capacity to act ethically. It comprises three substantive sections.

The first section reviews the mainstream literature on organizational culture and business ethics by exploring how culture has become a target for making business more ethical. It attends to the limitations of conventional wisdom by highlighting its neglect of cultural diversity, the significance of interpretation, and the operation of power relations in the development and application of norms and values. It also highlights the moral dimension of organizational activity, and considers the possibility of voicing dissent and exiting organizations, as well as being loyal to their espoused value; and it elaborates on the role of 'ethical culture' in winning consent and domesticating resistance. In the final part of the first section, the case of Enron, for which Nnore is a pseudonym, is deployed to illustrate the role of values statements and codes of conduct in strengthening 'ethical culture'.

The second section focuses more directly on ethics in business. It begins by noting how an attentiveness to ethics can open up questions about the morality of business and suggests that the effect of 'business ethics' has been to forestall and domesticate this potential. In this light, values statements and codes of ethics are seen to define and manage ethics in a way that is positive for business. In its more progressive form, this may incorporate diverse sub-cultural values to mitigate the risks associated with 'group think'. The section then explores an alternative understanding of ethics which connects it to the exercise of freedom which is regarded as a defining feature of the human condition. Ethical conduct is related to taking moral responsibility rather than simply mobilizing the capacity of self-direction to ensure conformity with organizationally prescribed norms and values.

This leads, in the third section, to a discussion of an alternative, Foucauldian conception of ethical conduct, which also loosely informs the preceding review of conventional thinking about the relationship of ethics to business. The case of Enron is again used to illustrate an alternative way of interrogating the presence of ethics in business and, in particular, to highlight the role of narcissism in promoting and displacing ethics.

Finally, the conclusion draws together the central themes and concerns of the chapter before underscoring the view that the culture developed at Enron, and more specifically the use of values statements and codes of ethics, only differ in degree from the culture of many other companies.

Organizational culture and the promotion of business ethics

At its simplest, the term 'culture' is used to convey a sense of what is considered to be 'normal', which includes what is morally acceptable. Culture is widely conceived to consist of distinctive and deep-seated values, beliefs, and norms of behaviour that underpin and inform commonsensical ways of doing things and interacting with others. In the context of organizations, the values, beliefs, and norms of culture are understood to enable and coordinate activity in a manner that is ostensibly voluntary and uncoerced. Collectively, these values and norms comprise 'rules of engagement' to which organizational members are conceived to be bound morally (by conscience), and not just instrumentally (by calculation of self-interest).

Culture is, arguably, more complex than the way it is commonly portrayed. That is because within any organization there are often multiple and overlapping sub-cultures. In all but the smallest or cult-like of work organizations there are sub-cultural values and norms based upon, for example, specialist training and activity, social background, occupational affiliation, and so on. To these sources of diversity can be added sub-cultural memberships based upon gender, sexual orientation, leisure interests, religious belief, etc. To illustrate the point, crude and colourful language that one may encounter in a sub-culture of salespeople may be morally unacceptable, and therefore absent, from the sub-culture of a human resources department, where the values of political correctness or 'professionalism' are prized. Within each (sub-)culture, there are valued rituals, symbols, and artefacts that foster and articulate a sense of identity and purpose. That said, because it is likely that employees will be members of several sub-cultures, they may experience and learn to manage divided loyalties and conflicting priorities. Recognition of this multiplicity places in doubt the credibility of attributing a single (unified) culture to organizations.[7]

The complexities associated with sub-cultural diversity are further compounded by differences of hierarchical position. Consider the person who is recruited as a graduate trainee. As a trainee, they may be censured and punished for expressing views that are unacceptably opinionated or politically inept. Yet, when the trainee is promoted to become a manager, very similar behaviour may be tolerated and perhaps openly encouraged and rewarded. What was initially antithetical to certain values – such as taking initiatives or challenging conventional wisdom – may subsequently be applauded. This is not to say that all managers would approve of such behaviour, since within and across the ranks of management there are also sub-cultural differences in norms and values.[8]

By referring to 'culture' as if it were homogeneous and unified, much literature on organizational culture and business ethics conveniently disregards the complexities of sub-cultural differences and hierarchical divisions. When disregarding these differences, it is more readily believed that values and norms can be bestowed upon, our poured into, organizational members as if they were the equivalent of empty vessels waiting to be filled.[9] Lacking here is an appreciation of how values statements, for example, are interpreted and negotiated within particular sub-cultures by employees who engage diverse frames of reference. Consider a mundane decision, such as which team member or member of staff is to be selected as 'employee of the month'. Even if there are clear criteria for making this selection, it will be necessary to interpret the criteria, and to weigh them against each other, even when they are already ranked in an order of importance, before coming to a decision. Considerations come into play that are not reducible to the satisfaction of objective criteria even if, after the fact, a decision is justified by reference to the criteria (see Box 3.5). Similarly, reference to a code of ethics, however detailed, proves to be of limited assistance when making a decision or pursuing a course of action. There is a space of indeterminacy in which a process of interpretation occurs, and for which personal responsibility may be accepted, unacknowledged, or denied. Coming to a decision relies, at least in part, upon understandings that remain tacit and unexplicated, and which are unacknowledged or inadequately covered by the code. Explanations of human behaviour that attribute courses of action to the (determining) presence of cultural norms and values, or which assume that the introduction of codes of conduct will produce desired behaviour, deny or devalue the ethical moment of freedom, and associated responsibility, in all decision-making.

A neglect of the role of freedom and the related uncertainties of interpretation may be compounded by a limited awareness of how power relations mediate processes of communication – as, for example, when employees appear to subscribe to corporate values but then act, in relation to colleagues or customers, in ways that belie any such subscription. Because employees are dependent upon organizations for work-based identity and esteem, and not just for a wage, this dependence may render them amenable to complying with corporate values which, as individuals, they do not hold, and in colluding in practices that are widely judged to be unethical – such as turning a blind eye to, or covering up, bullying, fraud, or sexual abuse. Compliance with corporate norms may seem to be voluntary but it is generally inspired, supported, and incentivized by symbolic considerations (e.g. status and esteem) as well as material dependence (e.g. income from employment) and, not least, by the thinly veiled coercion of peer pressure.

Yet, with some exceptions, employee identification with work and colleagues is incomplete. Other sources of identification – such as family, community, or religion – provide an alternative frame of reference that may lead employees to question, resist, or flaunt corporate values extolled in codes of ethics. In short, the 'doing' of culture is subtle and complex. What is deemed morally acceptable may well differ between departments and work groups as well as between hierarchical levels. Efforts to establish and enforce 'official' norms may be judged, morally, by certain groups of employees as unacceptably intrusive, unreasonable, or unduly harsh. This multifaceted, fragmented, intricate, and opaque quality of the contents of 'organizational culture' helps to account for why it can take some time for newcomers to 'get their bearings' (or they may resist doing so) and also why managing or changing 'culture' is fraught with difficulties and paradoxes.

Why 'ethical culture' matters: instrumental and moral considerations

The Nnore/Enron code of conduct states that employees will fulfil 'moral as well as legal obligations . . . openly, promptly, and in a manner which will reflect pride on the Company's name'. The distinction is an important one. The fulfilment of legal obligations may well be a necessary condition of maintaining a good reputation. But it is rarely sufficient.[10] That is because what is legally permissible may be considered morally dubious or unacceptable. Insisting that no law has been broken may further damage reputation rather than restore it. Failure to appreciate this kind of 'moral hazard' can have calamitous consequences not only for trading, competitiveness, and profitability, but also for employee morale.[11]

Shell's decision in 1995 to 'dump' the Brent Spar oil drilling platform in the North Sea was entirely legal and it even had support from technical experts. But it prompted global moral outrage and led to widespread boycotting of Shell filling stations. Similarly, encouraging employees to place their savings into their employer's pension fund, as Enron did and many other companies do, is not illegal. Nonetheless, it has attracted moral opprobrium as it concentrates, rather than spreads, financial risk for employees whose pensions as well as their jobs are tied to the performance of the company. The difference between what is legally sound and what is morally acceptable helps to explain why values statements and codes of ethics, which in principle commit organizations to conduct their affairs in ways that extend well beyond what is legally required, have sprung up in recent years. Typically, corporate ethical codes prescribe employee commitment to a culture in which staff do not simply operate within the law but work to the 'highest standards'.

Legal rules can be tested in the courts. Moral norms, in contrast, are ambiguous and indeed are 'resistant to legalistic formulation and codification'.[12] Despite this ambiguity, norms and values – such as 'fairness', 'trust', and 'respectfulness' – are vital for accomplishing most forms of organized activity, including business. If, as a prospective employee, you do not expect to be treated 'fairly', why would you apply for a position in an organization, assuming that you have options to work elsewhere? In the absence of physical compulsion or military subjugation, values of 'respect', 'trust', or 'dignity' are pivotal for many, and perhaps all, forms of organized activity – from sporting events to paid employment. These values are not, however, readily manufactured in work organizations, despite the best efforts of human resource specialists.

Of course, acknowledging the importance of norms and values within work organizations does not deny that many people seek employment primarily for the instrumental purpose of securing an income that provides for their subsistence. But work also has a moral dimension that extends beyond the pay packet. That is because it is also of significance for identity, esteem, personal development, and so on. Being treated with a measure of 'dignity' or 'respect' is of importance for most people. That said, and to underscore the point about the ambiguity of moral norms, what counts as 'dignified' treatment is not self-evident. Banter that is playful to one party may be deeply offensive to the other. Work relations are morally charged precisely because some (ambiguous) level of 'dignity', 'fairness', and 'respect' is expected. What this means in practice does not, however, become very clear prior to some behaviour that attracts a moral sanction – in the form, for example, of smouldering resentment, outright hostility, or other kinds of aggressive–defensive reaction. For example, during a conference call with stock analysts and reporters in April 2001, the then Chief Executive Officer (CEO) of Enron, Jeffrey Skilling, responded to a comment complaining about the lack of financial information provided by Enron by saying 'Well, thank you very much, we appreciate that. Asshole'. In this case, the transgression was picked up immediately by other participants in the conference call, leading them to doubt Skilling's suitability as CEO. When questioned about his 'Asshole' remark, Skilling was unrepentant about, and perhaps in denial of, the negative reaction that it had provoked. He made no apology. Instead, he offered the explanation that the comment had been made by 'a short-seller in the market. I don't think it is fair to our shareholders to give someone a platform like that they are using for some personal vested interest related to their stock position'. In other words, Skilling justified his 'Asshole' remark by suggesting that the complaint about lack of financial information was made by a party interested in weakening the Enron stock price.

The key point to be appreciated is that organized activity is endemically normative and moral, regardless of whether the organization is considered to be ethical. Take the example of the Mafia or a terrorist organization. Or take the case of a corporation with a checkered reputation, such as BAE Systems – one of the largest global defence, security, and aerospace companies, which has around 107,000 employees worldwide and reported sales of £22.4 billion (US$36.2 billion) in 2009.[13] Each is widely viewed as corrupt (see Box 3.2). Yet each of these organizations relies upon morally charged norms of behaviour, which its members contravene at their peril. As the saying goes, there is 'honour among thieves'. In such organizations, there is a morally enforced conspiracy of silence that is policed by accusations of 'disloyalty' and is backed by the threat of expulsion or worse. The combination of moral appeals to loyalty and the prospect of exclusion routinely ensures that 'elephants in the room' remain unidentified and 'skeletons in the cupboard' are undisturbed. A survey of BAE Systems' staff published in its annual report for 2008 indicates that only 57 per cent of respondents thought it was 'safe to speak up and challenge the way things are done in BAE Systems'.[14] This was despite the roll-out of its global code of conduct in the same year.[15]

In such organizations, moral conviction and obligation are keenly sensed. After a Mafia boss, Salvatore Lo Piccola, was arrested on 5 November 2007, Ten Commandments of Mafia morality were discovered, which included the following: 'You have the duty always to be ready to render a service to the Cosa Nostra. Even if your wife is just about to give birth'.[16] Fulfilling this duty to fellow Mafiosi would be considered honourable – that is, morally upright – whereas giving priority to one's wife would be shameful. In the BAE Systems code of ethics (which runs to over sixty pages), 'employees are required to comply with the standards set out within the code' and 'failure to comply may result in

Box 3.2	BAE to settle bribery cases for more than $400 million

Britain's BAE Systems plc reached settlements totalling almost $500 million with the US Justice Department and the UK Serious Fraud Office to resolve longstanding corruption allegations that have dogged one of the world's biggest defence contractors.

Under the agreements, London-based BAE will plead guilty to charges in both countries, relating to transactions that took place before 2002. The investigations examined whether BAE had made illegal payments to officials in various countries to secure lucrative contracts.

The settlement allows BAE to continue bidding for government contracts. Investors had feared that a guilty plea might have resulted in BAE's debarment in the US or the European Union. In a sign of investors' relief, BAE shares in London closed up 1.6 per cent on Friday.

The UK's Serious Fraud Office (SFO) in November 2004 launched an investigation regarding BAE's alleged illegal payments in Saudi Arabia, a case that soon expanded to cover the Czech Republic, Romania, South Africa, and Tanzania. BAE's then Chief Executive, Mike Turner, denied the company had acted improperly.

In 2006, the SFO halted the investigation into allegations about BAE's Saudi operations under pressure from then-prime minister, Tony Blair, who had been lobbied by Saudi officials. Mr Blair cited national-security grounds as the reason.

After 2001, prosecutors allege, BAE made payments totalling more than £135 million and an additional $14 million-plus to marketing advisers through one offshore entity, according to the court documents.

The US filing also alleges that BAE paid tens of millions of dollars to a Saudi government official and other associates, as well as to intermediaries, as recently as 2002. The payments were made as part of its management of a long-term agreement begun in the 1980s between the UK and Saudi Arabia to supply military hardware to the Saudis, US prosecutors say.

Derived from the *Wall Street Journal*, 6 February 2010.

disciplinary action'.[17] The key standards are remarkably similar to Nnore/Enron's values statement (see Box 3.1): accountability, honesty, integrity, openness, and respect, the last of these being elaborated as 'we value each individual and treat them with dignity, respect, and thoughtfulness'.[18] Coincidentally, employees in both companies were driven by the moral imperative of deal-making, which was linked to status and esteem, and not just financial reward. In BAE Systems, deals were sealed by the bribing of customers and/or their intermediaries. At Enron, deals were lubricated by huge bonuses and related inducements paid to senior executives and traders. Consider, for a moment, the dilemma for a BAE Systems employee who knows of behaviour that contravenes 'the standards set out in the code'. They do not speak out about it because they fear the loss of employment and its impact upon their family. Is this decision morally defensible in the light of the code of ethics? Are representatives of the company morally justified in taking disciplinary action against this employee? Or consider an employee who challenges the ethicality of behaviour that is not directly proscribed by the code. Is such a challenge morally defective?

The allure of conformity: loyalty, exit voice

It is unity and conformity that is prized by architects of corporate culture and the authors of codes of conduct. Such unity is often claimed, or aspired to, when executives extol the distinctiveness of the culture of their organization. Such claims are presented as credible depictions, or perhaps as realizable aspirations. An alternative perspective interprets such claims as an increasingly central element of a stratagem pursued by corporate executives to reassure stakeholders, especially shareholders rendered nervous by a series of spectacular corporate failures such as Enron, Worldcom, and Lehman Brothers, that the company has a unified and morally upright sense of purpose. Specifically, the provision of values statements and codes of ethics is offered as evidence that the company is committed – by insisting upon consistency in its norms and values – to making employee behaviour morally impeccable. Whether the executives who champion such statements and codes themselves believe in delivering such unity and conformity is difficult to judge; but it is a message that, in their capacity as leaders and guardians of corporate reputation, they appear to be under considerable pressure to endorse and convey.

The unity message is reflected in, and reinforced by, mainstream thinking about business ethics. This thinking identifies ethics – in the form of codes or programmes, for example – as a technique or instrument for addressing the risks occasioned by self-interested behaviour and resulting loss of reputation.[19] The reality of such risks was demonstrated in the demise of Arthur Andersen, one of the 'big five' global accounting firms, in the wake of Enron's collapse. An injection of business ethics is commended as an important means of mitigating risk when the aim of such interventions is to integrate 'responsible corporate processes into organizations' everyday activities'.[20] Advocates of codes and programmes tend to assume their effectiveness in changing behaviour, with the single proviso that their successful implementation depends above all upon the commitment of top management.

Ken Lay, when Chairman and CEO of Enron, was fully committed to the sixty-four-page code of ethics, produced in 2000. He provided its Foreword in which he writes that it is 'absolutely essential' that Enron employees 'comply fully with these policies'. There is little reason to doubt that senior executives at Enron or elsewhere identify any significant conflict between pursuing business-as-usual and satisfying the requirements of ethical codes of conduct, including injunctions which, for example, urge employees to assume 'responsibility for conducting business . . . in a moral and honest manner' (see Chapter 4, especially the Introduction). It is anticipated, or fantasized, that the development of ethical codes and programmes for communicating core ethical values, beliefs, and norms will result in employees accepting and absorbing their content. The benign effects and instrumental importance ascribed to codes and programmes of ethics accounts for why, when asked if they believed that ethics are good for the 'bottom line' of organizations, survey results tend to report that employees:

> did not find business ethics an oxymoron; instead, they perceived that ethics and business can co-exist, values are good for the bottom line, and that it is not necessary to compromise one's values to be competitive.[21]

Many business ethics studies take the values of business for granted as it selectively explores how ethics can be accommodating and supportive of business.[22] Marginalized by this approach is an appreciation of how appeals to deal openly and honestly with others – fellow employees as well as customers and suppliers – may be of *moral concern* to employees, and not just of *instrumental relevance* for doing business. Consider again the Nnore/Enron values statement. If prospective and current employees interpret the Enron values statement literally, the organization may attract well-qualified staff, motivate them to work harder, and secure their *loyalty*, or at least their instrumental compliance may be secured.[23] A conspiracy of silence, supported by a culture of fear, may then emerge or become further entrenched such that raising doubts about the honesty and openness of aspects of 'business-as-usual' provokes anxieties about, or attracts accusations of, disloyalty.

Alternatively, if a corporate values statement is interpreted as phoney or deceptive, prospective or current employees may anticipate that they will be expected to transgress values that they personally esteem and strive to uphold (see Box 3.3).[24] Moral sensibility is again being exercised in interpreting and assessing the meaning and implications of the values statement. When employees feel misled or degraded, a possible outcome is *exit* – whether psychologically (demotivation) or physically (departure). Or, finally, employees may *voice* their dismay in the form of 'resistance' – as Sherron Watkins, an Enron executive, did when she eventually blew the whistle on Enron's claims to honesty and openness by exposing the fraud involved in the Raptor, off-the-books, partnerships. (See also the Enron narrative in Chapter 4 and Chapter 9 on Whistle-blowing).

Box 3.3	The morality of the corporation

[B]ureaucratic work causes people to bracket, while at work, the moralities that they might hold outside of the workplace or that they might adhere to privately and to follow instead the prevailing morality of their particular organizational situation. As a former vice-president of a large firms says: 'What is right in the corporation is not what is right in a man's home ... What is right in the corporation is what the guy above you wants from you. That's what morality is in the corporation ... What matters on a day-to-day basis are the moral rules-in-use fashioned within the personal and structural constraints of one's organization.[25]

Designed to foster compliance and thereby secure loyalty, codes of conduct and similar interventions may stifle voices as well as impede exit, with detrimental effects upon the mental health of employees and potentially disastrous consequences for other stakeholders.

It was noted earlier that the reception of 'ethical culture' is informed by employees' diverse frames of reference, some of which are drawn from identifications extending beyond the workplace (e.g. family, church). It is uncertain which frame of reference, or combined frames, will be mobilized. Will employees take a lead from family values, the values of the sub-culture with which they identify, or with the norms and values attributed to the organization? Managerial efforts to build and manage organizational culture are directed at increasing the likelihood that employee behaviour will be guided, or driven, by the last of these possibilities. Instead of loyalty, however, the preferred response of the employees may be one of 'voice' or even 'exit'. How employees respond is contingent upon a moment of indeterminacy, or freedom, in which, for example, a conviction drawn from family or community membership may result in giving 'voice' rather than showing 'loyalty'. This 'moment' exemplifies a defining feature of the human condition – that is, the absence of instinctual compulsion and an associated responsibility which accompanies the capacity for (collective) self-determination.

Dilemmas associated with the demands placed upon employees by values statements and codes often bring distress and expose the presence of conflicting values – as when, for example, employees come under pressure to suspend 'the moralities that they might hold outside of the workplace.'[26] Nor can such dilemmas be resolved by consulting codes of ethics. Even the lengthiest of such codes cannot provide definitive guidance in addressing issues where there are multiple and conflicting demands and possible resolutions. In this respect, at least, the first principle of the BAE Systems code of practice is credible when it states: 'Accountability: We are all personally answerable for our conduct and actions.' In other words, it is not possible to abrogate responsibility simply by 'following orders', in the form of the prescriptions detailed in the code. Nor is it possible to escape the burden of responsibility for addressing conflicts and dilemmas by 'passing the buck' – that is by placing the burden elsewhere – with 'the organization' or 'the boss'. Yet, perversely, this is exactly what codes of conduct routinely require employees to do. That is to say, their formal requirement is for employees to behave in ways that comply with the code of ethics. Elsewhere in the BAE Systems code, for example, employees are told that they will 'take responsibility for implementing the standards in this Code and will comply with all company policies and processes'. Exercising responsibility by being 'personally answerable for our conduct' is equated with, and confined to, taking personal responsibility for ensuring conformity to company policy.

In this way, the moral significance of personal responsibility is domesticated into something that is placed in the service of the corporation as a means

Box 3.4	Ethical corporate governance: guidelines for an ethical culture

The achievement of a set of ethical values widely shared by all the organization members must inevitably be based on the senior management's commitment to those values. In parallel, this must be accompanied by the existence of a formal corporate ethics programme (although that programme alone cannot consolidate an ethical culture).

Such a programme should incorporate certain elements that could be summarized as follows:

(1) formal drawing up of a *code of ethics* that must articulate the firm's ethical expectations;
(2) creation of *ethics committees*, whose task will consist of developing ethical policies, assessing employees' actions, and investigating violations of ethics;
(3) maintenance of *ethics communications systems* that allow employees to report abuses and receive some action or behaviour guidelines;
(4) appointment of an *ethics officer* as the person in charge of coordinating ethics-related policies;
(5) development of *ethics training* within the firm, helping employees to recognize and respond to ethical issues;
(6) regulation of a disciplinary process that can correct unethical behaviours.[27]

of facilitating compliance with its policies. In addressing tensions between (1) values to which employees are personally committed and (2) values institutionalized in corporate policy and practice, the outcome may be a reluctant bending of personal values to the culture of the organization, a dilution of integrity that may be facilitated by engaging a stratagem that distances the 'real self' from what, for instrumental reasons, employees feel obliged or compelled to do as corporate members. What, arguably, is accomplished by such stratagems is a self-deceptive displacement of the moment of moral responsibility that, arguably, is endemic to the human condition.

Designing (ethical) culture and encountering resistance

So far we have been exploring aspects of organizational culture by emphasizing the role of interpretation and power, highlighting its moral as well as its instrumental facets, and noting how the response to interventions intended to improve 'ethical culture' may be accompanied by 'voice' and 'exit' as well as 'loyalty'. But what exactly is meant or implied by the idea of 'improving the ethical culture' of an organization? It is remarkable how rarely this question is addressed in the business ethics literature. Where 'ethical culture' is examined it is in ways that assume its meaning is self-evident (see Box 3.4). Alternatively, it is discussed in a circular way by, for example, conceiving of it as 'encompassing the experiences, assumptions, and expectations of managers and employees about how the organization prevents them from behaving unethically and encourages them to behave ethically'.[28] There have been some attempts to discern the specific virtues attributed to 'ethical culture' – such as the extent to which ethical expectations are understandable to employees, or the degree to which employees, managers, and supervisors act in accordance with these expectations. But there is no specification of the kinds of expectations that are to be counted as ethical or how they become 'understandable' and are 'acted upon'. This rather begs the question of how such expectations are interpreted and how their exemplification by managers is accomplished and recognized.

What can be said with some confidence is that initiatives introduced to manage ethical conduct assume a degree of malleability of employee values and norms. Such initiatives, as we noted with reference to BAE Systems's code of conduct, are clearly intended to cultivate and harness employees' capacities – for self-discipline and self-actualization – in the pursuit of corporate purposes. The introduction of ethical codes and programmes forms part of a 'modern' approach to management. This approach, which invites greater involvement and identification with the design of work processes and the delivery of services, presents an alternative to an earlier, now seemingly outmoded, conception of employees (as wilful wage-maximizers) that is considered to lack psychological depth and subtlety. In the modern view, employees are regarded as amenable to corporate education and motivated by non-financial forms of motivation, including the moral guidance provided by ethical codes and programmes.

What the prescriptions contained in ethical codes and programmes tend to overlook, however, is the difference between (1) setting out a framework of shared values and (2) institutionalizing those values in employee attitudes and behaviour. Simply to keep their jobs and/or to reduce dissonance with their own values, employees at all levels may comply with the letter, but not necessarily enter into the spirit, of values statements and codes of conduct. Despite a managerial celebration of the 'modern' employee, identification with the contents of these statements and codes may be minimal and their significance may be viewed as predominantly instrumental. *Formal* compliance is, of course, more desirable, managerially, than covert resistance or outright hostility. But mere conformity is not ideal. Management gurus such as Tom Peters and Robert Waterman, and chief executives like BAE Systems's Ian King, aim for nothing less than a full, *substantive* commitment to core corporate values (see Box 3.5). As Ian King writes, in his foreword to the BAE Systems code of conduct, 'I am personally committed to creating an environment where people feel comfortable that they can raise the issues without fear of retaliation. *Every one of us is required to uphold this commitment*'.[29]

Despite the best efforts of culture change gurus and champions, however, full commitment to corporate values is exceptional. Most employees are influenced by allegiances to 'sub-cultural' and extra-corporate memberships that are not necessarily congruent with the prescriptions set out in corporate values statements and codes of ethics. As a consequence, employee behaviour repeatedly

Box 3.5	Modern management thinking

In modern management thinking, it is by establishing, communicating, and reinforcing a set of corporate values that employees are enabled to harness their creative energies to the fulfilment of corporate goals: '[E]very minute, every hour, every day is an opportunity to act in support of [the corporation's] overarching themes'.[30] Such commitment is illustrated, rather painfully, by Peters in the example of the devoted Honda employee who 'on his way home each evening straightens up windshield wiper blades on all the Hondas he passes. He just can't stand to see a flaw in a Honda'.[31]

disappoints those who call for unconditional dedication to corporate values. As a result of other affiliations but also because employees' sense of freedom and individuality may be expressed by transgressing corporate principles and standards, there can be no guarantee of their loyalty. The capacity for 'deviance' extends from different groups of rank-and-file workers to their supervisors, managers, and even, or perhaps especially, to the executives who sign off the values statements and codes of conduct as they alone escape detailed, day-to-day surveillance of their conduct.

For these reasons, efforts to establish or strengthen 'ethical culture' are likely to encounter forms of resistance. Resistance may be fuelled by a defensive attachment to established practices, or it may be provoked when management intrudes into areas – of values, feelings, and identifications – over which it is assessed to lack a legitimate claim.[32] Antagonisms arise when there is a repugnant sense that management is sequestering the right and responsibility of employees to decide on the 'range of practices that constitute, define, organize, and instrumentalize the strategies that individuals in their freedom can use in dealing with each other'.[33] Such antagonism stems from a moral sensibility hostile to the (managerial) goal of channelling employee autonomy into the fulfilment of (managerially defined) corporate objectives, irrespective of their compatibility with employees' ethical concerns and priorities.

Hostility or resentment may be further inflamed when interventions ostensibly introduced to 'promote ethical conduct' are assessed to be motivated by a desire to convey a convincing *impression* of valuing ethical conduct when, in practice, this aspiration is overridden by other priorities. When impression management is the unstated purpose of such interventions, this becomes apparent when little or no evidence can be found of efforts directed to changing the values embedded in the culture or sub-cultures of the organization. The absence of this effort may reflect an assessment by senior executives that the realization of espoused values would require a huge commitment of resources with a minimal prospect of lasting change and the likelihood that, if successful, the organization would not be transformed but destroyed. So establishing or strengthening an 'ethical culture' in any meaningful sense may be a high-sounding aspiration, but it is not something to be acted upon. Projecting a desirable, reassuring image of the company, in contrast, is feasible as it is comparatively undemanding, inexpensive, and free of risk. Publicizing the intention to foster and/or strengthen an 'ethical culture' offers a cost-effective way of enhancing the standing of the company and its executives in the eyes of key stakeholders and gatekeepers (e.g. regulators or politicians).

Enron

What, 'ethics' did 'Enron culture' embody? The company *espoused* a common set of values; and a common set of values was also deeply *engrained* within Enron/Nnore. The espoused values included those that introduce this chapter.[34]

In addition to 'integrity' and 'excellence', Enron's values statement espoused two other key values – 'communication' and 'respect'. Although it is unlikely that many other companies have matched Enron's excesses, the company's values statement and code of ethics is not readily distinguishable from numerous other corporations. Indeed, an 'Enron test' has been devised by Tom Connellan in which the Enron values statement is copied together with equivalent statements from other major companies.[35] All names are then erased from the documents before extending an invitation to identify which is the Enron statement. The exercise underlines how values statements, ethical codes, ethical programmes, and so on, are both widespread and uniform across modern business organizations. As we noted earlier, they have become a standard(ized) means of addressing stakeholders' concerns about the security of their 'stakes'. Before the demise of Enron in 2001, the company's values statement and code of conduct might conceivably have been viewed as indicators of a genuine commitment from business to transform its conduct, and thereby contribute to addressing the declining level of trust in business.[36] More cynically, such statements and codes might have been regarded as window-dressing that places companies in a comparatively favourable light. Post-Enron, it might be asked to what extent such statements, codes, and programmes serve to obscure and displace ethical issues, and therefore form part of a milieu, or web, of institutionalized deceit and corruption.

So much for the aspirational values *espoused* in values statements and codes of conduct. What about the *engrained* and incentivised values? An extract from an Enron press release is reproduced in Box 3.6. It accompanied a gathering of hundreds of Enron executives in January 2001 when the CEO, Ken Lay, unfurled a vision that, he declared, would make Enron 'the world's greatest company'.[37] According to Sims and Brinkmann, in this vision, 'Enron appeared to represent the best a 21st century organization had to offer, economically *and* ethically'.[38] Instructively, however, the press release points primarily to features of Enron culture that are not reflected in its values statement or its code of ethics. Reference is made to the company's 'world-class employees' and the 'fast-paced business environment'. There is no mention of the values of these employees beyond a 'commitment to innovative ideas'. The accolade of being named the most innovative company for the sixth consecutive year

Box 3.6	Enron named most innovative company for sixth year

HOUSTON – Enron Corp. was named today the 'Most innovative company in America' for the sixth consecutive year by *Fortune* magazine.

'Our world-class employees and their commitment to innovative ideas continue to drive our success in today's fast-paced business environment,' said Kenneth L. Lay, Enron Chairman and CEO. 'We are proud to receive this accolade for a sixth year. It reflects our corporate culture which is driven by smart employees who continually come up with new ways to grow our business.'

Enron was placed No. 18 overall on *Fortune*'s list of the nation's 535 'Most admired companies', up from No. 36 last year. Enron also ranked among the top five in 'Quality of management', 'Quality of products/services', and 'Employee talent'.

Corporations are judged primarily from feedback contained in confidential questionnaires submitted by approximately 10,000 executives, directors, and securities analysts who were asked to rate the companies by industry on eight attributes.[39]

is attributed to 'our corporate culture'. But this culture is not characterized in terms of its espoused values of integrity, excellence, respect, and so on. Instead, the reference is to Enron's 'smart employees' who 'continually come up with new ways to grow our business'. Two obvious questions are begged by this description of Enron culture: what enabled the company to attract and retain what Lay calls 'smart employees'? What exactly did these employees do to 'grow the business'?

Central to Enron culture was a dedication to deal-making and the use of performance-related pay to 'come up with new ways to grow the business' – from the use of stock options to the receipt of bonuses related to (often future) revenue generation. As an aside, this became the culture of financial services companies and investment banks in the years following Enron's collapse, and which eventually 'blew up' in 2008. The aim was to pump up short-term stock performance, a goal assisted by financial engineering in which complex accounting dodges served to inflate Enron's assets (see Enron narrative, Chapter 4) and kept liabilities off its books.[40] The construction of Enron culture also relied upon a wider system of business in which bankers, accountants, lawyers, politicians, and charities simultaneously supported, and benefitted from, the company's ostensibly exceptional performance.

Participation of Enron employees in a system that was subsequently shown to be mired in deceit and corruption depended upon an *engrained* culture in which 'employees were afraid to express their opinions or to question unethical and potentially illegal business practices'.[41] At its core was the performance review process, also known as 'rank-and-yank'. This 'up-or-out' evaluation process incentivized key employees, notably traders, to make bigger and better (that is, more lucrative but more risky) deals. 'The best and brightest' talent was hired by Enron from top business schools, where its recruiters competed against investment banks and top law firms offering the biggest remuneration packages and 'perks' (see Chapter 4). The task of these recruits was to meet the expectation that Enron stock would rise by 20 per cent per annum. Pressure mounted as the profits of deals were booked up-front, resulting in intensified urgency to make further, bigger deals. Since the performance review process was arbitrary and subjective in its 'ranking' and 'yanking', it was easy for managers to 'reward blind loyalty and quash brewing dissent'.[42]

What effect did the performance review system have upon the values presented in the Enron values statement? According to Fusaro and Miller, it undermined any prospect of 'work[ing] with customers and prospects openly, honestly, and sincerely'.[43,44] The engrained and incentivized system of values rewarded short-term financial performance. In practice, booking profits from deals was the sole and overriding aim and 'value' of Enron culture. 'No bad news' was an unwritten rule since its reporting was taken to imply a lack of belief in, and commitment to, the organization – with terminal consequences for career.[45] Unwavering loyalty to the organization was expected, and this was demonstrated in one way only – by performing. 'Provided they performed to a high standard, [employees] could count on an unlimited benevolent attitude from Enron's leaders'.[46] Otherwise, they were shown the exit. What about the managers of the traders doing the deals? Why didn't they ensure that the Enron values statement and code of ethics were applied when doing business? According to Sherron Watkins, Enron managers learned to stifle 'voice' as they would be complained about by the Performance Review Committee if 'they did not help commercial dealmakers achieve financial goals by pushing deals through the system'.[47]

Ethics in business

Whenever the term 'ethics' makes an appearance in the domain of business, there is a risk that it will expose the operation and effects of business activity to critical scrutiny – such as environmental degradation, the compromising of personal ethical standards by business pressures, or the use of tax havens to minimize the contribution of corporations to the payment of taxes that ensure the provision of public services. It is difficult to imagine how, for example, at least two of the five 'principles' that introduce BAE Systems's ethical code of conduct can be enacted by its employees without putting the company out of business. These principles are: 'Honesty: there is no substitute for the truth' and 'Openness: when questions are asked we will be frank and straightforward in our answers'.[48] This assessment of the business consequences of enacting the principles may be regarded as unduly cynical. But unless BAE Systems's competitors implement similar principles, the company's apparent preparedness to share its secrets, volunteer sensitive information, and display its dirty washing – all of which are implied by the principles of Honesty and Openness – are likely to place it in a position of commercial disadvantage *vis à vis* its competitors.

Worse yet, associating ethics with business may open up questions about the morality of business *per se*. Competitive pressures to generate shareholder value or become exposed to hostile takeover bids are at the heart of capitalist enterprise and were intensified at Enron. These pressures are resistant to, and corrosive of, even the best-intentioned efforts to make radical, substantive improvements in the ethics of business. Associating ethics with business threatens to pose questions of accountability (e.g. for environmental degradation) that most executives and shareholders would prefer to remain unasked. To the extent that corporations are resistant to, or even subversive of, scrutiny of 'ethics in business', the recurrent challenge for proponents of 'business ethics' is to frame and domesticate the meaning of ethics in ways that render ethics compatible with, and subservient to, business practices. The challenge for advocates of 'business ethics', academics, and executives, is to construct an agenda where fundamental questions about 'ethics in business' – with regard to, for example, fair trade, biodiversity, global warming, and sustainability – are silenced or, better, not voiced. The challenge for 'business ethics' is to domesticate and 'reengineer' thorny questions and issues into amenable assets for bolstering or restoring the legitimacy of business.

Domesticating ethics

The risk of ethics corroding or delegitimizing business is mitigated by circumscribing the meaning of ethical conduct in ways that more readily accommodate business activity. Managing this risk is accomplished by bracketing out, or diluting, wider issues of morality. This is done by underscoring the importance of what is legally permissible, as contrasted with what is morally contestable, with regard to, for example, the use of tax havens by major corporations to minimize contribution, through taxation, to public welfare, the outsourcing of production to sweatshops, or the closure of pension funds. Attention is concentrated upon how ethics can be narrowly defined and applied in ways that are productive for the pursuit of business. The widespread formulation of ethical codes and programmes, the appointment of ethics officers, the introduction of initiatives intended to develop stronger ethical cultures – all of these contribute to legitimizing business objectives by projecting a favourable impression of business paying attention to ethics. Transmitted through culture, ethics becomes a handy, comparatively inexpensive tool for managing corporate image, and perhaps also for improving performance and securing competitive advantage.

Enron has provided an example of how a code of ethics, assembled by doubtless well-intentioned human resources management specialists or consultants, and endorsed by its Chairman and CEO, is deployed as a business tool to

Box 3.7   Codes of ethics and conduct: Enron and BAE

Foreword to the Enron code of ethics

We want to be proud of Enron and to know that it enjoys a reputation for fairness and honesty and that it is respected. Gaining such respect is one aim of our advertising and public relations activities, but no matter how effective they may be, Enron's reputation finally depends on its people, on you and me. Let's keep the reputation high.

Kenneth L. Lay
Chairman and CEO

Foreword to the BAE Systems code of conduct

I am determined that we are recognised both as a high-performing company in terms of our programme and financial performance as well as a leader in standards of business conduct among global companies … business conduct … is essential to sustaining our personal and collective reputations.

Ian King
Chief Executive

reassure stakeholders and attract financial and human resources (see Box 3.7). Another example is Lehman Brothers, which traded for 158 years before its doors were closed in 2008. The company's ethical code stressed the importance of trust, stating that '[t]he lynchpins of that trust are our ethical standards and behaviour.[49] We must always do business in a manner that protects and promotes the interest of our clients'.[50] The authors of the Enron and Lehman Brothers codes of ethics clearly appreciated the importance of securing the confidence and trust of their stakeholders. But it is also clear that, in the end, more potent forces took priority over these ostensibly ethical concerns.

In the short term, codes of ethics as well as the 'advertising and public relations activities' may lubricate business activity by bolstering trust and confidence.[51] Surely, companies like Enron and BAE Systems would not prepare and publish a code of conduct running to sixty-plus pages if they were not serious about ethics? Yet, a focus upon ethics programmes in which codes of ethics play an integral part, may do little more than present an *appearance* of ethicality. This scenario illustrates a wider issue where, as Roberts puts it, 'the problem of ethics is cast merely in terms of the desire to be seen to be ethical'.[52] This desire, Roberts suggests, is *narcissistic*, preoccupied with self-image and a preparedness to do whatever it takes to enhance this image – where the 'self' is that of company executives who, by treating the corporation as a mirror for evaluating their standing, see themselves reflected exclusively in the (dollar) value that is attributed to the company and the bonuses awarded to them.[53] In the case of Enron, the appearance conveyed by the company was evidently beguiling to its 'smart employees', clients, and investors, as well as to its executives. Whatever doubts or reservations they may have harboured, these stakeholders were open and ready to be persuaded that Enron was no less than what it appeared to be, and indeed was reported to be by its auditors, regulators, stock analysts, and media commentators. Reassured that these 'professionals' were sufficiently confident in Enron to take or maintain a stake in the company, the decision to join – as an employee, as a supplier or as a small investor – was a 'no brainer'.

Interrogating soft managerialism

Conventional wisdom suggests that company executives have a duty to nurture elements of culture that improve the ethicality of employee conduct. We have noted how interventions prompted by this executive duty, such as the introduction of value statements and ethics codes, require employees to suspend their personal ethics or the ethics of their sub-culture. In effect, employees are required to give priority to the codes. This implies that personal integrity may, or indeed must, be compromised when it deviates from the morality of the codes. In this respect, the very ethics of initiatives introduced to impress a particular set of values or 'ethical culture' upon employees may themselves be questioned.[54]

Moreover, complying with the code may become a substitute for taking personal responsibility. Once the code has been issued, the values statement read, and the ethics programme attended, employees and managers alike may conclude that little further attention need be paid to the ethics of their conduct. The ethics box has been ticked. It is time to continue with business-as-usual, confident that appropriate steps have been taken to ensure and demonstrate the ethicality of whatever the company does. The resumption of business-as-usual is hardly surprising or unexpected when it is recalled that the prescriptions of ethical programmes and codes compete with other pressures and priorities – such as performance targets and career progression. So, as a consequence, it could well be that the most significant contribution of ethics codes and programmes lies in fashioning an alluring shell for normalized secrecy, rivalry, and fear where what passes for 'loyalty' to the organization and/or pressures to perform and progress make it very difficult to voice more searching questions about business morality.

Addressing such concerns, Sinclair contends that retaining diversity in personal and sub-cultural values can mitigate a tendency for ethics codes and associated programmes to suppress debates about values, and thereby impede continuing reflection on the ethics of business.[55] A challenge for advocates of 'business ethics', she suggests, is to better comprehend, *respect*, and mobilize sub-cultural values 'towards goals which are consistent with, or ideally advance, those of the organization'. Diversity of values, Sinclair contends, is not a problem that requires disciplining by a monolithic 'ethical culture'. Rather, diversity is a potential resource for resisting the uniformity of 'group-think', thereby enriching creativity and contributing to superior performance. Moral diversity within sub-cultures is celebrated for its capacity to challenge the development of a dominant culture which, when 'insulated from those who offer a different definition of ethical actions', is seen to jeopardize the very survival of the organization.

Sinclair's justification for safeguarding the moral diversity of sub-cultures is framed in terms of its *instrumental* benefit for organizational morale, effectiveness, and survival. Her defence of diversity is couched in terms of its contribution to maintaining a hierarchical form of organizing that, at best, *selectively* appropriates sub-cultural elements to serve this form. This is paradoxical as, in the process of appropriation, it is likely that aspects of diversity will be devalued or diluted. Both the unified culture approach, with which Sinclair takes issue, and the alternative of mobilizing the diversity of values within sub-cultures, are harnessed to established priorities. Despite an emphasis upon sub-cultural diversity, there is an unquestioned assumption that organizations have goals that somehow transcend the values or purposes of their members. It is assumed that such goals are both readily identifiable and uncontested, rather than framed and negotiated within relations of power – relations that are reproduced or transformed by those who support or resist established priorities. There is no acknowledgement of how an assumption of a goal that is shared itself reflects and reinforces the distinctive, sub-cultural values or fantasies of an executive sub-culture. Politically, the significance of retaining an assumption of goal consensus is, *inter alia*, its bestowal of a measure of moral legitimacy upon the selective appropriation of sub-cultural values, which otherwise might be regarded as a form of morally indefensible interference.

Debunking social determinism

Fortunately, there is an alternative basis for defending the diversity of sub-cultural values and, more specifically, for protecting and nurturing values capable of challenging the ethics of the *status quo*. Sinclair herself alludes to this when she characterizes the process of being ethical as:

> *taking moral responsibility for a decision* and critically analysing the underlying assumptions of each course of action to better understand value choices, before finally applying decision standards and deciding.[56]

Here Sinclair highlights the significance of 'the process of moral thought and self-scrutiny' which, arguably, forms the basis of any claim to act ethically rather than, say, in conformity with a code of ethics, or simply to maintain appearances. Conceived in this way, the meaning of 'ethical' is reserved for behaviour that involves 'taking personal responsibility'. What, then, are the conditions of possibility for assuming this responsibility?

One possibility is to conceive of 'taking moral responsibility' as a learned response nurtured within particular cultures.[57] The idea of taking personal responsibility can only make sense in a cultural context where responsibility for actions is attributable to human beings, conceived as discrete and autonomous individuals, rather than to a supernatural force, or to a wider collective, such as the 'brotherhood' or the 'company', in which the notion of the autonomous individual lacks plausibility and/or legitimacy. There is, however, another important condition of possibility for taking responsibility, regardless of how it is attributed. To appreciate this condition, it is necessary to dip briefly into the field of philosophical anthropology.

A condition of taking responsibility for one's decisions is the 'relative world-openness' that is 'intrinsic to man's (*sic*) biological make-up.'[58] As *homo sapiens* (co)evolve in relation to the constituent elements of the biosphere, a measure of world-openness or indeterminacy develops. This emergent openness gradually and partially supplants a world of instinctual closure where there is 'a largely fixed relationship to the environment' such that actions are governed by natural forces. Accompanying this openness is ambiguity and uncertainty; and it is this openness that permits the construction of a *social* reality manifest in diverse forms of institution – institutions that include such social objects as 'values statements' and 'codes of conduct'. In this philosophical anthropology, human beings are conceived to be responsible for (re)producing and transforming social realities in which relative world-openness is translated into 'relative world-closedness'. For example, the (ethical) issue of how to exercise the freedom associated with 'relative world-openness' is addressed and resolved, at least in principle, by the introduction of a code of conduct: the code provides instructions for reaching closure. In order to 'take responsibility', however, it is necessary to resist or debunk understandings that locate responsibility elsewhere – for example, in natural forces, predestination, or, indeed, in the agency attributed to work organizations, their values statements and codes which invite employees simply to 'follow orders'.

The idea of 'taking moral responsibility' implies a criticism of forms of social determinism where, for example, society, social background, or organizational membership and associated compliance with ethical programmes and codes are conceived to 'control human conduct by setting up predefined patterns of conduct, which channel it in one direction as against the many other directions that would theoretically be possible'.[59] Of course, debunking social determinism does not deny the role of institutions and institutionalization in processes of self-formation and, relatedly, in the formation of sub-cultural norms and values. It only challenges any suggestion that institutions exert a *determining* influence by appearing to confront and shape human beings as an 'external and coercive fact'.[60] Where this appears to occur, there is a forgetfulness of how each institution is the result of past human activity, and of how the continuing existence of institutions requires ongoing active participation, and associated responsibility, of human beings in their (re)production. Unless this ongoing involvement is recalled and appreciated, social reality, including the sense of self, is 'apprehended as an inevitable fate, for which the individual may disclaim responsibility'.[61] It is precisely an invitation to disclaim responsibility that is extended when employees are required and coerced into complying with the prescriptions of ethics codes. Or, more precisely, they are urged to limit their responsibility to ensure that their behaviour is congruent with such prescriptions – that is, to 'follow the orders' set out in the code.

Ethics and freedom: Michel Foucault

The absence of determinism in social life or, more positively, the presence of freedom is, as Foucault argues, a crucially important condition of ethics.[62] That is because freedom – or release from determination – is a condition of the possibility of taking personal responsibility for whatever (social) kinds of closure are established and maintained. Forms of closure are conceived by Foucault as the enactment of 'governmental technologies' that regulate social life and 'often' facilitate 'states of domination'.[63] In the absence of an 'openness' that defies and disrupts determinism, ethics makes little sense. When the primacy of 'openness' and associated freedom is posited, then forms and processes of control, including the ethics codes and programmes, are seen to exemplify practices of 'governmentality' through which 'free individuals' mobilize diverse instruments to govern others.[64]

Even the most mundane of actions is understood to be underdetermined by instinctual and institutional forces, and therefore to involve ongoing moments of decision-making – even when these moments may appear to be habitual, unconscious, or contextually determined. At the heart of Foucault's concept of governmentality, then, is freedom: 'the concept of governmentality makes it possible to bring out the freedom of the subject [e.g. the CEO or the employee] and its relationship to others – which constitutes the very stuff of ethics'.[65] When understood in this way, the human condition is defined by its inherently and profoundly ethical quality. It is a quality that supports the reflexivity and self-scrutiny to which Sinclair points when she describes the process of being ethical as 'taking moral responsibility for a decision', and which is also at the centre of what Foucault calls the 'conduct of conduct'.[66] In human institutions, forms of self-scrutiny are integrated into, or become resistant to, techniques of control and forms of domination.

This capacity for self-scrutiny is referenced by Ken Lay in his foreword to the Enron code of ethics where he urges employees to 'reflect upon your past actions to make sure that you have complied with the policies'.[67] However, as this quote indicates, the capacity is reserved for, or restricted to, the 'responsibilization' of employees who are asked to mobilize this capacity to ensure their compliance with Enron policies. For Foucault, this is more a limitation of freedom than an expression of it. In his thinking, ethics is 'a conscious practice of freedom' in which the 'ethical subject' is disclosed 'in relation to (or even against) those social and organizational rules and norms which seek to determine or dictate what a person should or should not be'.[68] Such 'disclosure' occurs when the possibility of non-compliance is contemplated, and not when the capacity for self-scrutiny is engaged to ensure conforming to 'social and organizational rules'.

Ethical conduct is, according to Foucault, 'the considered form that freedom takes when it is informed by reflection'.[69] A distinguishing feature of such conduct, Bauman has suggested, is that it is never assured of its ethicality.[70] It retains the suspicion that the action taken is morally deficient.[71] Actions are ethical only when full personal responsibility is taken for them; and this would include a decision to act in a way that conforms to the requirements of an ethical code. From this it follows that an 'ethical culture' is not one in which employees comply with the letter of an ethical code. Rather, from a Foucauldian perspective, an 'ethical culture' is one in which members are enabled to take responsibility for 'self-scrutiny, weighing up individual obligations and responsibilities, then weighing up professional and organizational responsibilities . . . before finally applying decision standards and deciding'.[72] A culture or sub-culture in which 'values and norms become so entrenched that self-inspection is unnecessary' is not, in this sense, ethical.[73] It is not ethical because, in such a culture, the sense of self has become so encrusted and self-assured that only the reproduction of cultural norms, or conformity with the code of ethics, counts as ethical. In such cases, employees have become so identified with the dominant norms or values statement that they effectively deny, or refuse, the freedom that, as argued above, is a defining feature of the human condition. To personalize this point, your conduct is ethical when you are no longer narcissistically preoccupied with reproducing or defending your 'self-certainty as an enclosed and isolated subject'.[74] You abrogate ethical responsibility when you attribute this responsibility to others (or to a code of ethics or a 'boss') who, in effect, do the 'ethical work' for you. And, paradoxically perhaps, in doing so, you become more vulnerable as you become dependent upon transient values and norms to affirm an inherently precarious sense of 'self-certainty' (Box 3.8).

This may strike you as implausible. After all, aren't most people inclined to associate (our) goodness with conformity to the values privileged by authorities and other dominant regimes of truth, such as those encountered in work organizations, and not with how we exercise our freedom to accept or to transgress those values? Foucault, by contrast, invites us to engage in 'ethical work' in which the 'ethical subject' is disclosed through processes of self-scrutiny. This process necessitates engaging with, and interrogating, our (power-invested) accounts of the self, including those that have become integrated into, and colonized by, our involvements in practices of domination. As Faubion notes, Foucault 'never takes the ethical for granted. [He] acknowledges the considered

Box 3.8	Skilling's faltering self-certainty

The possibility of what is meaningful to us becoming dislocated and even evaporating is ever-present; and this possibility is terrifying as it threatens to annihilate the reality of the 'encrusted' self. It seems likely that the possibility materialized for Jeffrey Skilling, ex-CEO of Enron, who suffered a nervous breakdown two months after being arrested and charged with fraud, insider trading and other misdemeanours, and for which he subsequently received a twenty-four-year jail sentence.

Seemingly overtaken by paranoia, Skilling reportedly harassed several persons and accused them of being undercover FBI agents before police were called. Skilling's resignation (reportedly in tears) as CEO of Enron for 'personal reasons' had occurred three years prior to this arrest. His resignation coincided with a slide in the Enron stock price from a fifty-two-week high of $90.56 on 23 August 2000, to $42.93 on 14 August 2001, the day before he resigned.[75] The month following his resignation, Skilling sold 500,000 Enron shares and, in total, is reported to have made $70 million from the sale of Enron stock. By the time of his trial, it seems that Skilling had regained his composure by rebuilding his encrusted self. Indeed, in an interview given to the *Wall Street Journal* (17 June 2006), a month after receiving his sentence, Skilling says that he sought psychiatric help and emerged from a lengthy 'malaise' (he became a recluse, staying in bed and obsessively following media coverage of the scandal) only after his 2004 indictment: 'The indictment, in a lot of ways, that was the turning point', Skilling told the newspaper. 'That's when I started climbing back.' At his trial, Skilling continued to protest his innocence, saying that 'the company's collapse was the work of a small number of rogue staff – not including Lay or himself – and that its implosion was hastened by the feeding frenzy following the earnings restatement in October' (BBC News, 2006).

practice of freedom as a human possibility. Ethical work requires a refusal to conflate moral acts with those that conform to rules, laws, values or codes'.[76]

The dis-closure of the ethical subject is perhaps best conceived as a process of struggle, in which diverse available narratives of self are assessed to enable or inhibit self-scrutiny. Inhibiting narratives include those of business ethics where, as we have seen, self-scrutiny is restricted to monitoring and ensuring conformity with value statements and codes. Conventional wisdom denies, or at best marginalizes, the significance of the practice of freedom as a condition of ethical conduct.

Rethinking Enron and beyond

In returning to the example of Enron, it is possible to appreciate how attentiveness to corporate means of developing 'ethical cultures' can displace and obscure more probing ethical questions and weaken the capacity to act ethically.

Instead of appreciating and nurturing human freedom, it is effectively suppressed or channelled to fulfil corporate objectives. Employees are conceived not as free, but as self-interested agents who must be induced – rewarded or punished – in order to ensure that self-interest is funnelled in desired directions. In academic circles, this thinking is distilled in agency theory.[77] From an agency theory perspective, issues of governance and ethics are couched within, and preoccupied with, the question of how to incentivize self-interested, opportunistic managers and employees so that their behaviour becomes more closely aligned with those of shareholders. The pursuit of this alignment extends to compliance with the principles and standards contained in codes of ethics that all employees are 'expected to follow'.[78]

A corporate culture dominated by agency thinking, Kulik argues, is one in which 'employees tend to explain their behaviour as controlled by governance mechanisms' in a way that effectively denies personal responsibility for their behaviour.[79] In Foucauldian terms, agency thinking assumes a sovereign view of power in which one party, in the form of shareholders, strives to ensure that it is in the self-interest of employees to respect their ownership and increase the value of their holdings. The challenge of governance, from this perspective, is to induce managers and other employees – for example, by using share options and bonuses or threatening disciplinary action – to be compliant. Roberts notes how the assumptions of agency theory 'have been read onto corporate governance, and informed its reform in recent decades; they have resulted in what are now an almost universal set of techniques and practices designed to control the conduct of executives both within the corporation and externally'.[80] Roberts concludes that the remedies favoured by proponents of agency theory to resolve corporate misdemeanour are 'better seen not as the solution but as the source of the governance problem'. Policy guided by agency theory has, if anything, contributed to an elaboration of self-interested opportunism, not to its reversal let alone its demise.[81]

The Foucauldian critique of conventional wisdom, as distilled in agency theory, is based upon the understanding that human nature is not inherently 'good' (altruistic) or 'bad' (self-interested) but instead is indeterminate or open. As we have seen, Foucault retains an emphasis upon the importance of freedom informed by reflection as a basis for distinguishing conduct that is informed by 'ethical work' from conduct that simply conforms to a culturally or organizationally favoured set of norms or values. Importantly, the Foucauldian concept of governmentality places the exercise of freedom articulated in ethical work within relations of power that take the form of 'political rule and economic exploitation'. In other words, 'governmentality' points to, and insists upon, the irrevocable and irreversible freedom of the human condition while also acknowledging its framing and articulation in social relations.

At Enron, an individualized model of human nature became the basis for staff recruitment and reward and also provided the criteria for monitoring and evaluating executives and other employees. It is a model that promotes, preys upon, and reinforces 'a narcissistic preoccupation with how the self is seen and judged'.[82,83] Individual visibility and personal judgement were geared directly to pumping up the stock price. Techniques of corporate governance, including the establishment of an ethical culture, were primarily responsive to this priority. These applications of agency theory institutionalized a self-interested model of human nature as they spawned a particular, individualized, type of 'governable person'.[84] The 'rank-and-yank' system of performance review, in particular, served to assuage any lingering doubts about the sovereignty of the selves to whom it was applied and to dispel any enduring suspicions of the fabricated nature of their apparent solidity. To put it in personal terms once more: your sense of self is confirmed by striving to meet performance standards that, at the same time, you conceive to be imposed upon yourself and for which, therefore, you bear no responsibility. Still, your complicity is not invulnerable to disruption. Your sense of sovereignty as a successful individual may be challenged as well as affirmed by your 'performance'.

At Enron, traders were as successful as their last deal. Water-walking 'A's could become shipwrecked 'C's, as painfully illustrated by Jeffrey Skilling's fall from grace as the celebrated CEO became Prisoner 29296-179 with a release date of 21 February 2028. It is at moments of disappointment, or failure of expectations, that the precariousness and vulnerability of sovereignty can be glimpsed, and also when a moment of openness to, and responsibility for, one's actions may be fleetingly experienced.[85] When 'top performers' discover that they are subject to intense pressures and closer scrutiny, a narcissistic response is to insist that 'being the best deserves better', where 'better' means the pursuit of unfettered self-absorption. Self-absorption requires the opportunity to exercise power invested in an elevated and privileged position that seems to make real the fantasy of being a sovereign individual. Convinced that the mirror of performance measurement objectively demonstrates human superiority, the successful holders of these positions become 'scornful of the abilities of others and punishing of any expression of difference or dissent'.[86] An illustration is the response of Ken Lay, then CEO and Chairman of Enron, to some accounting issues that puzzled Sherron Watkins (who subsequently blew the whistle on fraudulent activity at Enron). Outraged by her impudence in voicing her concerns, Lay demanded to know how she might be fired.[87] Sensitive to such (ab)uses of position, many subordinates will be fearful, and become sycophantic, thereby reinforcing the imperious, self-interested behaviour exemplified by Lay and emulated by his fellow executives Skilling and Fastow. Where there is domination, manifest in the absence of downward accountability, not only is narcissistic behaviour indulged but there is also no effective channel for employees to challenge executives. Speaking (their sense of) truth to power is silenced irrespective of what may be written about 'speaking up' in the corporate code of ethics.

Conclusion

Conventional wisdom presumes that moral qualities, such as honesty or sincerity, can be established or instilled by clearly presenting key elements of a normative order which stakeholders in this order, notably employees, are urged to enact. These elements are condensed in values statements and elaborated in codes of ethics. Critics who question their effectiveness argue that reliance upon codes overlooks, or at least marginalizes, the significance of human beings' capacity to interpret communications in the light of their own, diverse frames of reference, which may include the understanding that, in the pursuit of more pressing priorities, minimal attention is to be paid to their prescriptions.

To its author or advocate, a values statement may sound reasonable, even impressive, and entirely justifiable. The assumption is that employees share a common culture and will readily comply with it. Yet, a values statement or code of conduct may be interpreted by some stakeholders as an irrelevant or unwelcome imposition or as mere window-dressing. The process of interpretation is critical, and it is framed within relations of power that condition which interpretations are available and compelling. So, for example, if values statements or codes are interpreted in ways that doubt their relevance or discredit their authority, then their impact is likely to be marginal, and their introduction may well contribute to cynicism and demoralization.

A related and even more penetrating challenge to the claims of ethical codes and programmes comes from critics who argue that they can undermine the capacity to act ethically. The suggestion is that compliance may become a substitute for deliberation over the ethical contribution of such codes and/or the merit of complying 'automatically' with their prescriptions. This challenge arises from the understanding that acting ethically is ultimately a matter of recognizing and nurturing *a capacity and preparedness to take responsibility*, and that ethical action is not equivalent to complying with, or deferring to, the authority of values statements or codes.

To elucidate this insight, we engaged Michel Foucault's reflections upon human beings as 'ethical subjects'. The capacity to become responsible, personally and collectively, for particular forms of social closure or normative order, which includes the closure commended by codes of ethics, is ascribed to an openness and freedom that is a distinctive feature of the human condition. From this perspective, values statements and ethics codes, with which employees are expected to comply, are seen to do little to develop and strengthen the (moral) capacity to take personal responsibility for one's conduct. Instead, these statements and codes are seen to invite employees to believe that they have fulfilled their responsibilities by complying with the codes' requirements. When personal responsibility is accepted, then the claim that one was simply 'following orders' by complying with the statement or the code is not credible, and so loses legitimacy as a defence.[88] Such defences are seen to lend a spurious justification to a disinclination to reflect upon the ethics of conduct. They also demonstrate how the corporate requirement to adhere to ethical codes and programmes gives little encouragement to (1) take personal responsibility for the decision to comply with, or transgress the code; or (2) reflect critically upon the belief that compliance is equivalent to fulfilling such responsibility. Instead of nurturing human freedom and responsibility, the introduction of codes is seen to risk displacing it.

Conventional wisdom is challenged by doubting its presumption that ethical conduct is enacted and strengthened when the norms and values of corporate culture are prescribed and absorbed. Conventional wisdom takes no account of whether pressures for compliance weaken or heighten moral sensibility and the capacity for making ethical judgements. Its concerns are limited to the question of whether members of staff adhere to, or manage the impression of complying with, the codes of ethics, and not whether their capacity to make judgements or take personal responsibility is enhanced or impeded. From a Foucauldian standpoint, by contrast, there is a concern that efforts to strengthen ethical culture run the risk of increasing the ethical deficit and/or sense of moral decay that such codes ostensibly are intended to remedy. If members of an organization are resistant to unethical pressures, then the introduction of codes and programmes is largely irrelevant but, over time, the codes may have a corrosive influence if compliance with them becomes a substitute for such resistance. If, on the other hand, this resistance is weak or absent, then the most significant effect of such codes and programmes, whether intended or not, will be to mask the institutionalized deficit in ethical conduct and/or to further fuel skepticism and incredulity about 'business ethics'. To be clear, this assessment does not imply that interventions to improve ethical conduct are *necessarily* pointless or counterproductive.[89] Rather, the intent is to raise the issue of how such interventions are received. Does the promotion of 'ethical culture' through values statements and codes of ethics encourage moral sensibility and enhance the capacity to take personal responsibility? Or does it disregard and weaken this capacity?

In this chapter, we have cast some doubt upon the claims, potency, and effects of values statements, codes, and ethics programmes that are intended to strengthen ethical conduct. Among the more significant and perverse effects of such interventions may be the masking of a corrosion of moral propriety, a degradation of moral imagination, and a dimming awareness of morally dubious forms of conduct that, in the era of neoliberalism, have become commonplace and normalized. Instead of conceiving of 'ethical culture' as an instrument for facilitating 'business ethics', a shift of focus to 'ethics in business' attends to processes of self-formation within social relations, including those of business, as a basis for developing conduct that is more actively and reflexively ethical.

It is when other priorities and pressures – to meet targets, earn bonuses, or gain promotion – compete with the values and principles set out in codes of ethics (e.g. openness, honesty, sincerity) that 'business ethics' can, in practice, be more relevant for conveying an impression of probity than for developing an 'ethical culture'. The example of Enron was given to illustrate this argument. Enron presented the appearance of a highly reputable company whose commitment to probity was broadcast by its values statement and detailed in its sixty-four-page code of ethics. This appearance was carefully managed even though Enron's business model and methods – particularly its financial engineering – were exceptional outside of the financial sector whose trading culture Enron sought to emulate. More typical is the culture of secrecy, rivalry, fear, and worse that pervades the contemporary corporate landscape and which is by no means restricted to companies, like Enron, whose excesses proved to be undisguisable. As Trevino and Nelson note, managers as well as non-managerial employees:

> have repeatedly reported their own cynicism – the pressure they feel to compromise their personal ethical standards on the job – and they're even more cynical about their peers' ethics than their own. They blame business's preoccupation with gain, the lack of reinforcement of ethical behaviour, competition, the existence of generally unaccepted ethical practices in certain industries, a sense that only results are important to superiors, and the ineffective enforcement of ethical codes.[90]

To this list of articles of blame may be added values statements, codes of ethics and associated efforts to develop 'ethical culture'. In Enron's case, the compromising of ethical judgements in the service of 'business's preoccupation with gain [and] a sense that only results are important to superiors' was intensified by the source of its recruits (business schools), its selection procedures (to identify candidates with an appetite for aggressive risk-taking) and its methods of performance evaluation and reward.[91] Enron was, arguably, a modern corporation with a 'normal' corporate culture in which a narcissistic reluctance to take personal responsibility, concealed by its values statement and codes of ethics, was writ large and reached its logical conclusion.

NOTES

1 The Enron code of ethics can be found at: www.thesmokinggun.com/documents/crime/enrons-code-ethics, accessed 21 March 2011.

2 Reputation is endorsed by association. For example, legal and accountancy firms put their own reputations, such as they are, on the line when agreeing to act as advisers or audits. The point is illustrated by the example of Enron (see Chapter 4).

3 G. Colvin, 'A powerful asset', *Fortune* (2 March 2009). See http://money.cnn.com/2009/02/27/news/companies/colvin_intro.fortune/index.htm, accessed 13 December 2009.

4 M. Schultz, M. J. Hatch, and M. H. Larsen, *The Expressive Organization: Linking Identity, Reputation, and the Corporate Brand*. Oxford: Oxford University Press (2001).

5 See S. Key, 'Organizational ethical climate: real or imagined?', *Journal of Business Ethics* 20 (1999), 217–25; L. K. Trevino, K. D. Butterfield, and D. L. McCabe, 'The ethical context in organizations: influences on employee attitudes and behaviours', *Research in Ethical Issues in Organizations* 3 (2001), 301–33.

6 P. Edward and H. C. Willmott, 'Structures, identities and politics: bringing corporate citizenship into the corporation', in A. Scherer and G. Palazzo (eds.), *Handbook of Research on Global Corporate Citizenship*. London: Edward Elgar (2008), 405–29.

7 M. W. Grojean, C. J. Resick, M. W. Dickson, and D. B. Smith, 'Leaders, values, and organizational climate: examining leadership strategies for establishing an organizational climate regarding ethics', *Journal of Business Ethics* 55 (2004), 231.

8 A. Gouldner, *Patterns of Industrial Bureaucracy*. New York: Free Press (1954).

9 H. Drummond, 'Living in a fool's paradise: the collapse of Barings Bank', *Management Decision* 40 (2002), 232–8.

10 M. S. Schwartz, 'A code of ethics for corporate code of ethics', *Journal of Business Ethics* 41 (2002), 273–843.

11 The idea of 'moral hazard' is more commonly used to describe a situation where, as a consequence of being insulated from risk, a party behaves more recklessly than they would if more exposed to the consequences of risk-taking.

12 M. Painter-Morland, 'Refining accountability as relational responsiveness', *Journal of Business Ethics* 66 (2006), 97.

13 S. Lilley, *BAE Systems' Dirty Dealings*. See www.corpwatch.org/article.php?id= 9008, accessed 6 April 2010.

14 Of BAE's 100,000 employees, 10 per cent were sampled and there was a 41 per cent response rate.

15 K. West, *Worried BAE Staff Turning to 'Whistleblower' Helpline*. 2 April 2010, see   www.dailymail.co.uk/money/article-1263174/Worried-BAE-staff-turning-whistleblower-helpline.html, accessed 6 April 2010.

16 Y. Mounk, *Mafia Morals – Not so Tarantino After All . . .* (9 November 2007). See http://aeuropeanview.blogspot.com/2007/11/mafia-morals-not-so-tarantino-after-all.html, accessed 6 April 2010.

17 BAE Systems, *Being a Responsible Company: Code of Conduct* (2008). See www.baesystems.com/BAEProd/groups/public/documents/bae_publication/bae_pdf_759of003_001.pdf, accessed 22 April 2010.

18 See www.baesystems.com.

19 J. Stansbury and B. Barry, 'Ethics programs and the ethics of control', *Business Ethics Quarterly* 17 (2) (2007), 239–61. See http://papers.ssrn.com/sol3/papers.cfm?abstract_id=962499, accessed 22 December 2009.

20 G. R. Weaver, L. K. Trevino, and P. L. Cochran, 'Corporate ethics practices in the mid-1990s: an empirical study of the Fortune 1000', *Journal of Business Ethics* 18 (1999), 550.

21 A. Jose and M. S. Thibodeaux, 'Institutionalization of ethics: the perspective of managers', *Journal of Business Ethics* 22 (1999), 133–43, 139.

22 E. Wray-Bliss, 'Ethics at work', in D. Knights and H. C. Willmott (eds.), *Introducing Organizational Behaviour and Management*. London: Thompson Business Press (2007); C. Jones, M. Parker, and R. ten Bos, *For Business Ethics*. London: Routledge (2005).

23 A. O. Hirschman, *Exit, Voice and Loyalty: Responses to Decline in Firms, Organizations, and States*. Cambridge, MA: Harvard University Press (1970).

24 R. Jackall, *Moral Mazes: the World of Corporate Managers*. Oxford: Oxford University Press (1988).

25 *Ibid.*, 4.

26 *Ibid.*; see also Box 3.3.

27 Extract from J. Lopis, M. R. Gonzales, and J. L. Gasco, 'Corporate governance and organizational culture. The role of the ethics officers', *International Journal of Disclosure and Governance* 4 (2) (2007), 96–106, 100 (emphases added).

28 M. Kaptein, 'Ethical programs and ethical culture: a next step in unraveling their multi-faceted relationship', *Journal of Business Ethics* 89 (2009), 262–81, 262.

29 BAE Systems, *Being a Responsible Company*, emphasis added.

30 T. J. Peters and R. H. Waterman, *In Search of Excellence. Lessons from America's Best-run Companies.* New York: Harper and Row (1982), 324.

31 *Ibid.*, 37.

32 R. ten Bos and C. Rhodes, 'The game of exemplarity: subjectivity, work and the impossible politics of purity', *Scandinavian Journal of Management* 19 (4) (2003), 403–23.

33 M. Foucault, 'The ethics of concern for self as a practice of freedom', in P. Rabinow (ed.), *Ethics, Subjectivity and Truth.* New York: The New Press (1997), 300.

34 See Box 3.1.

35 T. Connellan, *Can You Pass the Enron Test?* See www.prwebdirect.com/releases/2006/2/prweb342169.htm, accessed 26 May 2010.

36 Edleman, *Edleman Trust Barometer* (2009). See www.edelman.com/trust/2009, accessed 23 April 2010.

37 K. Eichenwald and D. B. Henriques, 'Enron's many strands: the company unravels; Enron buffed image to a shine even as it rotted from within', *New York Times* (10 February 2002). See www.nytimes.com/2002/02/10/business/enron-s-many-strands-company-unravels-enron-buffed-image-shine-even-it-rotted.html?pagewanted=1, accessed 22 December 2009.

38 R. R. Sims and J. Brinkmann, 'Enron ethics (or: culture matters more than codes)', *Journal of Business Ethics* 45 (2003), 243–56.

39 Enron press release, 6 February 2001. See www.propagandacritic.com/articles/examples.enron.html, accessed 13 December 2009.

40 Financial engineering was key to Enron's ostensible profitability – a form of engineering that was emulated and upscaled in the reckless development and trading of derivatives (CDOs and CDSs) that precipitated the financial crisis of 2008.

41 D. Tourish and N. Vatcha, 'Charismatic leadership and corporate cultism at Enron: the elimination of dissent, the promotion of conformity and organizational collapse', *Leadership* 1 (4) (2005), 455–80, 470.

42 *Ibid.*

43 P. Fusaro and R. Miller, *What Went Wrong at Enron? Everyone's Guide to the Largest Bankruptcy in US History.* New York: John Wiley and Sons (2003), 52. Cited in Tourish and Vatcha, 'Charismatic leadership', 470.

44 See Box 3.1.

45 B. Cruver, *Anatomy of Greed: the Unshredded Truth from an Enron Insider.* New York: Carroll and Graff (2002), 176.

46 Tourish and Vatcha, 'Charismatic leadership', 467.

47 H. Hala, 'If capitalists were angels – Sherron Watkins – the fall of Enron – interview', *Internal Auditor* (April 2003). See http://findarticles.com/p/articles/mi_m4153/is_2_60/ai_1000075073; see also Jackall, *Moral Mazes.*

48 See the BAE Systems code of ethics: www.baesystems.com/aboutus/ourglobalCodeofConduct/index.htm, accessed 21 March 2011.

49 B. Stevens, 'Corporate ethical codes as strategic documents: an analysis of success and failure', *Electronic Journal of Business Ethics and Organization Studies* 14 (2) (2009), 14–20, 17.

50 Codes of ethics can be revealing in what is excluded. In the Lehman Brothers code, for example, there is nothing about protecting the natural environment or any commitment to community.

51 To which Ken Lay revealingly associates such codes in his foreword to the Enron code of ethics (see Box 3.7).

52 J. Roberts, 'Agency theory, ethics and corporate governance', paper presented for the *Corporate Governance and Ethics Conference*, Macquarie Graduate School of Management, Sydney, Australia, 28–30 June 2004, 11.

53 J. Roberts, 'Corporate governance and the ethics of Narcissus', *Business Ethics Quarterly* 11 (1) (2001), 109–27; and Roberts, 'Agency theory'.

54 H. C. Willmott, 'Strength is ignorance; slavery is freedom: managing culture in modern organizations', *Journal of Management Studies* 30 (4) (1993), 515–52.

55 A. Sinclair, 'Approaches to organizational culture and ethics', *Journal of Business Ethics* 12 (1) (1993), 63–73.

56 *Ibid.*, 65 (emphasis added).

57 In such cultures, the institution of 'the individual', or some equivalent, has become established to which the capacity of autonomy is attributed.

58 P. L. Berger and T. Luckmann, *The Social Construction of Reality: a Treatise on the Sociology of Knowledge*. Harmondsworth: Penguin (1967), 69.

59 *Ibid.*, 72.

60 *Ibid.*, 76.

61 *Ibid.*, 108.

62 M. Foucault, *Ethics: Essential Works of Michel Foucault, 1954–1984*, Vol. 1, P. Rabinow (ed.). Harmondsworth: Allen Lane/Penguin (1997), 284.

63 M. Foucault, 'The ethic of care for the self as a practice of freedom,' in J. Bernauer and D. Rasmussen (eds.), *The Final Foucault*. Cambridge, MA: MIT Press (1988), 19.

64 Foucault, *Ethics: Essential Works*, 500.

65 *Ibid.*; T. Lemke, *Foucault, governmentality and critique*. See www.andosciasociology.net/resources/Foucault$2C+Governmentality$2C+and+Critique+IV-2.pdf, accessed 21 March 2010. Also published in Rethinking Marxism 14 (3) (2002), 49–63.

66 Sinclair, 'Approaches to organizational culture and ethics', 68.

67 Enron code of ethics.

68 E. Ibarra-Colado, S. R. Clegg, C. Rhodes, and M. Kornberger, 'The ethics of managerial subjectivity', *Journal of Business Ethics* 64 (2006), 45–55, 46.

69 Foucault, *Ethics: Essential Works*, 284.

70 Z. Bauman, *Postmodern Ethics*. Oxford: Blackwell (1993); BBC News, 'Profile: Jeffrey Skilling', (23 October 2006). See http://news.bbc.co.uk/1/hi/business/6077062.stm, accessed 26 May 2010.

71 Willmott 'Strength is ignorance', 94ff.

72 Sinclair 'Approaches to organizational culture and ethics', 69.

73 *Ibid.*, 71.

74 C. Jones, 'As if business ethics were possible, "within such limits" . . . ', *Organization* 10 (2) (2003), 223–48, 227.

75 See www.enronblog.com/bloggers/jeff-kosty (30 July 2005), accessed 21 March 2011.

76 J. D. Faubion, 'Towards an anthropology of ethics: Foucault and the pedagogies of autopoiesis', *Representations* Spring (2001), 83–104, 88.

77 M. C. Jensen and W. H. Meckling, 'A theory of the firm: managerial behavior, agency costs and ownership structure', *Journal of Financial Economics* 3 (1976), 305–60.

78 BAE Systems code of ethics.

79 B. W. Kulik, 'Agency theory, reasoning and culture at Enron: in search of a solution', *Journal of Business Ethics* 59 (2005), 347–60, 358.

80 J. Roberts, 'The manufacturing of corporate social responsibility: constructing corporate sensibility', *Organization* 10 (2) (2003), 249–65. Roberts points to the relation between agency thinking and how corporate governance is conceived primarily in terms of forms of regulation and the role of directors, regulators, politicians, accountants, lawyers, and academics (including the architects of agency theory). Codes and programmes of ethics are among the techniques and practices designed to control the conduct of employees, including executives. Largely absent from the worldview of agency theory is any appreciation of, or room for, personal responsibility. The collapse of Enron and other cases of corporate corruption (e.g. Worldcom), as well as the more recent meltdown of the financial sector, has presented an opportunity to reflect upon personal responsibility. But this opportunity has not, so far, been taken up as remedies favoured by agency theory are being reapplied. Little consideration is being given to how personal responsibility might be emphasized, encouraged, and supported. Instead, emphasis is placed upon the need for improved external regulation that will accommodate the same (irresponsible) speculative activity and bonus culture. Shareholders, which now include governments, are, it seems, content to accommodate the excesses of the financial sector so long as super-profits are generated, some taxes are collected, most loans are repaid, and the public deficits are eventually cleared. It may be, as Roberts has suggested, that the remedies favoured by proponents of agency theory are 'better seen not as the solution but as the source of the governance problem' (*ibid.*, 3). Policy guided by agency theory has contributed to an elaboration of self-interested opportunism, not to its reversal, let alone its demise.

81 *Ibid.*, 6.

82 A preoccupation with how judgements about corporate image and performance reflects upon the self betrays a form of self-absorption that has become deeply institutionalized in contemporary systems of schooling, sports, and even in the arts. This preoccupation promises reassurance of the existence of the self as an autonomous entity, the level of attainment of which is a source of pride. This (narcissistic) narrative of self is, arguably, not essential to human nature but, rather, is a product of the disciplinary power of particular techniques – of contemporary parenting as well as corporate control – that are untempered by self-scrutiny so that receipt of high grades, for example, is equated with enhanced self-worth.

83 P. Miller and T. O'Leary, 'Accounting and the construction of the governable person', *Accounting, Organizations and Society* 12 (3) (1987), 235–65.

84 Jeffrey Skilling's breakdown in 2004 (see Box 3.8) is an example of this vulnerability. Anxieties about the charges of fraud and insider dealing he was facing led him, paranoically, to suspect that the friendliness of acquaintances he and his wife met in a New York bar were actually FBI agents laying a trap for him to voice some self-incriminating indiscretions. In business, part of being 'socially skilled' is to repress or smooth over such anxieties and associated awkward moments by mobilizing resources that reaffirm a sense of sovereignty in a manner that abrogates all personal responsibility for business processes and disregards how the other affects us despite ourselves.

85 Roberts, 'The manufacturing of corporate social responsibility', 6.

86 S. Watkins, 'Ethical conflicts at Enron: moral responsibility in corporate capitalism', *California Management Review* 45 (2003), 6–19; S. Watkins, 'Former Enron vice-president Sherron Watkins on the Enron collapse', *Academy of Management*

Executive 17 (2003), 119–27, cited in Tourish and Vatcha, 'Charismatic leadership', 472.

87 This defence has been unsuccessful in many legal cases, including its use by Nazi leaders at the Nuremberg tribunals following the second world war. The defence failed because the actions that it seeks to justify are themselves deemed to be illegal. After the Vietnam war, the defence was invoked by a soldier who was court-martialled for killing an elderly Vietnamese citizen after being ordered to do so by an officer. His defence failed because the order to shoot was declared to be 'of such a nature that a man of ordinary sense and understanding would know it to be illegal'. In other words, the soldier was assumed and expected to be capable of exercising a degree of judgement and of accepting a level of responsibility when assessing the legality of the order. It is instructive, in terms of the operation of power relations and the defence of authority, that the corporal who issued the order to kill was found to be insane – that is, incapable of exercising such judgement and taking personal responsibility – and acquitted.

88 R. ten Bos, '*Essai*: business ethics and Bauman ethics', *Organization Studies* 18 (6) (1997), 997–1,014.

89 L. K. Trevino and K. Nelson, *Managing Business Ethics: Straight Talk about How to Do it Right* (4th edn). New York: John Wiley (2006), 4. See http://media.wiley.com/ product_data/excerpt/45/04712305/0471230545.pdf, accessed 13 November 2009.

90 *Ibid.*, 4.

91 E. Levinas, *Otherwise than Being or Beyond Essence*. Dortrecht: Kluwer Academic Publishers (1991).

4   Enron narrative

HUGH WILLMOTT

> We're taking on the entrenched monopolies. In every business we've been in, we're the good guys... We're bringing the benefits of choice and free markets to the world.[1]

> I don't think Enron is that unusual. After all, we have a chief executive class which act like dictators of small Latin American countries.[2]

Introduction

No business scandal has precipitated greater interest in the ethics of business than the spectacular rise and precipitous fall of Enron. Enron was widely acclaimed as a highly reputable, model company. It enjoyed the confidence of the banks and credit rating agencies as well as top-flight law and accounting firms. Celebrated by consultants and business school academics, Enron was praised for blazing a trail that other, less innovative and progressive firms were urged to follow. Companies aspiring to receive equivalent plaudits were entreated to emulate and outshine Enron, including its reputation for philanthropy. Following its collapse in 2001, many Enron executives were convicted of tax and securities fraud, insider dealing, money laundering, and other offences. Nonetheless, Enron continues to have its admirers and defenders.[3]

Confidence in Enron was most clearly signalled by its appeal to seasoned investors. At its peak, Enron stock reached $90 with a market capitalization of $60 billion, and the company was estimated to be the seventh largest in the US based on revenue. Enron was a flagship of modern business practice – in its aggressive pursuit of shareholder value, in the performance-driven design of its remuneration systems and packages, and in its asset-lite strategic use of financial engineering.[4] Not surprisingly, then, it is the Enron story, rather than other scandal-mired failures, such as Worldcom, Tyco, and Global Crossing, that has been retold as a film/documentary (*The Smartest Guys in the Room*) and a play/musical (*Enron*).[5] The central themes of the story continue to resonate a decade later as Enron's business methods and excesses parallel those that contributed to the global financial meltdown of 2008 and its aftermath. The flashlight of Enron illuminates the workings of contemporary, financialized business practices including the antipathy of business to, and its subversion of, regulatory agencies, its use of 'creative' and deceptive accounting and financial engineering to hide debt, its manipulation of prices, and its extensive tax avoidance and/or evasion.

A potted history

Some key actors

Based in Houston, Texas, Enron was formed in 1985 from a merger of a natural gas company and a pipeline company. The merger left the company massively in debt. To address this problem, Enron's Chief Executive Officer (CEO), Ken Lay, who held an economics PhD, hired top-tier consultants McKinsey & Co to advise on how the company might innovate to improve its profitability and cash flow. McKinsey sent Jeffrey Skilling, who had received an MBA from Harvard Business School, worked in banking and risk management, and had become one of McKinsey's youngest ever partners.

Skilling proposed that Enron could take advantage of deregulation by diversifying from its established business of providing physical plant (e.g. pipelines) to become a leading trader in energy. Skilling's vision involved creating a 'gas bank' where, acting as an intermediary, Enron would guarantee a price for suppliers and consumers while charging them fees and, in effect, making money by gambling on price differences and changes which, as a dominant player, it would also be in a position to influence. Impressed by Skilling's vision, Lay hired him in 1990 to head up a new division (Enron Finance Corporation) and in 1991 Skilling became Chairman of Enron Gas Services. This arm of Enron's operations came to dominate natural gas contracts, and the company used its market power to generate super-profits. Evangelists of market deregulation (to build monopoly power in markets) and the pursuit of shareholder value (to make personal fortunes), Skilling and Lay persuaded the wider financial community of banks, analysts, and rating agencies that the trading model developed by Enron could be applied to other markets – notably, electricity. This required the deregulation of the electricity industry for which he and Lay lobbied very hard and successfully. Skilling rose to become CEO of Enron in February 2001 when Lay became its Chairman.

Key to Enron's success as an energy trader was its lobbying of the Securities and Exchange Commission (SEC) to permit its use of mark-to-market accounting, something that had not previously been allowed outside of the financial sector. This accounting method enabled Enron to book future earnings arising from long-term contracts based upon its assessment of expected revenues and costs, and then to report annually gains or losses on contracts against expectations as these occurred.[6] The use of this accounting method presented an opportunity to inflate expected revenues by underestimating the future purchase price of energy in a way that made current earnings look very positive; and it also made possible the offsetting of future unrealized earnings associated with such underestimations by making even bigger deals with higher expected revenues. In 1997, Skilling became Chief Operating Officer, and number two to Lay.

As Enron developed its trading activities, in 1990 Skilling recruited Andrew Fastow, another MBA holder with a banking and risk management background. Fastow had been working at Continental bank on complex, asset-backed securities deals.[7] He was the conduit, if not the architect, of many of Enron's most 'innovative' (or dubious and/or illegal) financing methods (e.g. the creation of numerous special purpose entities [SPEs] and the associated use of 'pre-pays', discussed below).[8] At the heart of Enron's business strategy, masterminded by Skilling and facilitated by Fastow, was an 'asset-lite' philosophy based upon securitization. In 1998, Fastow became Enron's Chief Financial Officer.

Enron's asset-lite business strategy

Securitizing assets by using SPEs, which lies at the heart of the financialization of business, enables companies to remove assets and associated risk from their balance sheets and create an income stream against which further loans for business expansion can be issued. Such 'structured' financial instruments, famously described by Warren Buffet as 'financial weapons of mass destruction', were at the heart of Enron's turbo-driven expansion and meteoric share-price movement as well as at the centre of the financial meltdown of 2008.[9,10] In effect, securitization transforms the risks of retaining assets, the value of which is volatile and ties up capital, by converting them into securities. This enables the future revenues deriving from assets to be made available immediately, thereby releasing funds for further investment and repeated securitization.

The principal appeal of securitization to executives and investors is its turbo-charging of growth and boosting of the stock price. However, it also increases vulnerability to a downturn as it reduces the scope for retrenchment by selling assets or by restructuring debt. When pursuing an asset-lite strategy, day-to-day operations are financed either through earnings and/or by securitizing further assets, including any income streams arising from earlier securitization. This strategy is sustainable so long as the assets (e.g. contracts) that back the securities maintain their value and, relatedly, as long as the company retains its investment grade status either by minimizing its debts or, in Enron's case, by hiding these debts by using SPEs and other dodges, such as pre-pays (discussed later). Operating difficulties arise if trading conditions deteriorate and/or there is a restatement of the value of the company's assets, which reduces the stock price and/or downgrades its credit rating. Such a downgrade places downward pressure on the stock price which can trigger demands for debt repayment. If repayments cannot be met from earnings, from further securitization, or by obtaining loans, the company enters a vortex of decline ending in illiquidity and insolvency.

Rise and fall

In 1997, Enron was identified by *Fortune* magazine in its Most Admired Companies survey and the company had previously been the subject of glowing Harvard Business School case studies.[11] The same year, Lay was named one of the top twenty-five managers of the year by *Business Week*. In 2000, Harvard business guru Gary Hamel published *Leading the Revolution* in which Enron is unequivocally praised for its innovations. Enron had all its 'best practice' boxes – corporate social responsibility, business ethics tools, and philanthropy – carefully ticked. In 2000, *Chief Executive* magazine included Enron among its five top corporate boards. Only a few months prior to the company's collapse, *Fortune* magazine named Enron the most innovative company for the sixth consecutive year.

External observers of Enron (e.g. academics, investment analysts) admired the company for the quality of its management, its products and services, its pool of employee talent, and its capacity to be continuously innovative. Enron's board of directors was populated by experienced and well-regarded members. As with so many aspects of Enron's activities and associations, including its appointment of Arthur Andersen as its auditors, their credentials were above reproach. Enron was also popular from a societal point of view. Ken Lay enjoyed a local and national reputation as philanthropist who 'contributed generously to a number of charities and politicians' campaigns with personal and Enron funds . . . [and] one could conclude that Enron had built up a considerable amount of reputational capital – with politicians, minorities, local business people, charities, academia, investors, and the local business press'.[12] The public face of Enron was flawless.

By 1997, Enron had become the largest US wholesale buyer and seller of natural gas and electricity. From this point, Skilling promoted the vision of Enron as company with a 'core competence' in trading. Central to Skilling's vision was the claim that expertise developed in trading gas and electricity could be applied to contracts in other areas – such as coal, paper, steel, water, broadband, and even weather. In the next three years, revenues increased very rapidly as Enron continued its asset-lite strategy by using SPEs to move assets off its balance sheet. Between 1996 and 2000, the reported increase in revenues was from $13.3 billion to $100.8 billion, a rise of 750 per cent. Unprecedented in any industry, this performance made Enron the darling of Wall Street. Enron's stellar results raised expectations about future earnings, which its senior executives, who held substantial stock options, did nothing to dampen. Past results, combined with a bullish assessment of future prospects, produced a speculative fever. This was fuelled by dotcom mania that in August 2000 raised Enron's stock to $90 – a figure that had been calculated to imply that Enron could earn a return on equity of 25 per cent indefinitely.[13] Even during the weeks immediately preceding its demise, 'almost every brokerage on Wall Street rated Enron a "strong buy"'.[14] Financial journalists even continued to tip Enron stock when it fell steadily during the third quarter of 2001 and after the *Wall Street Journal* in late October observed that 'rarely have so many *analysts liked a stock they concede they know so little about*'.[15]

The opaqueness of Enron's accounts was a condition and consequence of its 'innovative' business methods that were geared to pumping up the stock price, thereby enhancing its investors' reputation for astuteness as well as their (paper) wealth. An unplanned consequence of Enron's exceptional performance was the fuelling of expectations about future earnings. Investor expectations increased pressure to contrive creative ways of hiding liabilities and overstating revenues. Among these was mark-to-market accounting and off-balance-sheet financing using SPEs. It is relevant to note that these methods required the full participation of the banks and Enron's advisors and also received board approvals. A combination of creative accounting and financial engineering delivered huge gains for shareholders, including Enron employees, as the specifics of their design and operation was 'cleverly' hidden from investors and analysts in the impenetrable detail of the small print of its financial statements, or was overlooked by them so long as Enron's stock price remained buoyant.

So gullible were investors and creditors – reputationally and financially – and so trusting of, or dependent upon, the preservation of Enron's success and reputation, that the opacity of its accounts was widely interpreted as confirmation of the company's innovative strategy, novel business model, and path-breaking trading methods, and not as a tell-tale sign of systematic deception, manipulation, and evasion. And, of course, if any doubts were harboured, reassurance was at hand: Andersen, one of the biggest and most reputable of auditing firms, had approved Enron's accounts.

Viewed in this light, the fall of Enron is, arguably, attributable not to a few rotten apples among its most senior executives but, rather, to a wider business system that engendered and endorsed Enron's business methods and its staffing policies. Its business methods included lobbying politicians and regulators, inflating earnings by using financial engineering and creative accounting, silencing advisors and board members, and hiding its debts. Enron staffing policies and decisions pivoted around a single, overriding consideration: would they have an immediate, positive financial impact, irrespective of any longer-term consequences or sustainability?

Business methods

Lobbying

Enron's fortunes in the 1990s were founded upon the successful lobbying of the SEC in 1992 to become the first non-financial company permitted to use mark-to-market accounting practices. Then, in 1993, its lobbying gained Enron an exemption from regulation by the Commodity Futures Trading Commission (CFTC). The Chairman of the CFTC, Wendy Gramm, agreed to the concession five weeks before the end of her tenure, when she then joined the Enron board.[16] In combination, these regulatory changes enabled the rapid expansion of Enron's trading activities that, so long as investor confidence held, produced exceptionally good returns, although it eventually resulted in derivatives liabilities of $18.7 billion, which compares with Lehman Brothers' reported derivatives liabilities of $24.1 billion in May 2008 prior to its collapse.[17]

It was during the 1980s that the CEO, Lay, developed close ties with the Bush family and became a major fundraiser for George Bush Sr. When George W. Bush became Texas governor in 1994, Lay became head of the Governor's Business Council. Lay recruited onto the Enron board members who were closely involved with organizations to which the company had made major charitable donations or which benefitted from Enron largesse.[18] For example, in 1993, the Enron Foundation pledged $1.5 million to the M. D. Anderson Cancer Center in Texas and Lay personally donated $600,000 to the Center. Two of Enron's board members, Dr LeMaistre and Dr Mendelsohn, had served as President of the Centre.[19]

From 1992 to 2001, US government agencies – the Overseas Private Investment Corporation (OPIC), Export-Import Bank, Maritime Administration, and Trade and Development Agency – cleared Enron's path with $3.68 billion worth of support for twenty-five projects in numerous countries, notably India, where privatization and deregulation, advocated by Enron, opened up highly lucrative markets. During this period, the World Bank provided $761 million in support for Enron-related overseas projects as well as giving the company an *entrée* to developing countries to expand their energy and power sector.[20] In the George W. Bush presidency, the US Trade Representative, Robert Zoellick, was an Enron employee. A former Secretary of the Army, Tom White, was the head of Enron Energy Services. A former Secretary of State, James A. Baker III, was also an Enron lobbyist, as was the head of the Republican National Committee (RNC), Ed Gillespie, and his predecessor at the RNC, Mark Racicot. Another top Enron lobbyist was Ralph Reed, a former head of the Christian Coalition. Bush's political guru, Karl Rove, advised Enron to hire Reed, and so Reed got a job that paid him several hundred thousand dollars. Lay was able to attend White House lunches and private meetings with the Vice-President, Dick Cheney, during the formation of the national energy policy.

Creative accounting and financial engineering

Successful lobbying for deregulation laid the foundations for Enron's exponential growth but the fuel for its expansion was creative accounting and financial engineering.

The use of mark-to-market accounting enabled Enron to make very optimistic forecasts of income based upon the present value of net future cash flows. Income from these projects could be recorded in advance of their operation, thereby increasing earnings. An early example was Enron's creative financing of a power plant in Teesside (UK) which it part-owned. This project was approved by a British member of parliament (MP), John Wakeham, who subsequently joined the Enron board (in 1994) and served as a member of its Audit Committee. Five years earlier, Wakeham was the UK Secretary of State for Energy. By acting as its own general contractor, Enron booked as much as $100 million in revenue while the Teesside plant was still being built. Enron also paid its managers a bonus of 3 per cent of the value of deals when they were struck, a policy that did little to discourage the deal makers' inflation of their projected returns.[21] A related method of boosting earnings was 'pre-pays', where Enron received a large sum in advance to deliver energy products over a number of years.[22]

SPEs, of which Enron eventually had over 3,000, were initially designed to fund the purchase of forward contracts with gas producers to supply gas to utilities. Energy contracts were pooled and securitized through bonds sold to investors. From the mid-1990s, SPEs were increasingly used to overstate equity and earnings by concealing debt. In February 1999, members of the Audit Committee (a sub-committee of the board) were explicitly told that Enron was using accounting practices which 'push limits' and were 'at the edge' of acceptable practice; and on three occasions in 1999 and 2000 the board approved the setting-up by Fastow, the CFO, of SPEs, but also of a pseudo company called LJM, 'to do business with Enron for the sole purpose of improving Enron's financial statements'.[23] By October 2000, Enron had $60 billion in assets. Of these, almost half were lodged in SPEs owned by unconsolidated affiliates.[24]

The most notorious of the SPEs were Whitewing, JEDI, Chewco, LJM (1 and 2), and the Raptors. (As an aside, it later emerged that Andersen was paid $5.2 million for advice in setting up the Chewco and LJM SPEs.)[25] The JEDI and Chewco SPEs alone served to inflate Enron's profits in 1997 by 75 per cent.[26] But, to repeat, these SPEs were not hidden from the board members and some reference to them was generally made in the small print of the annual financial statements signed off by Andersen. According to the assessment of the Senate Committee of investigation, the board 'knew of them and took no action to prevent Enron using them. The board was briefed on the purpose and nature of the Whitewing, LJM, and Raptor transactions, explicitly approved them, and received updates on their operations.[27] Enron's extensive off-the-books activity was not only well-known to the board, but was made possible by board resolutions authorizing new unconsolidated entities, Enron preferred shares, and Enron stock collateral that was featured in many of the off-the-books deals'.[28] Instead of scrutinizing and challenging the SPEs, the board 'routinely relied upon Enron management and Andersen representations with little or no effort to verify the information provided, that readily approved new business ventures and complex transactions, and that exercised weak oversight of company operations'.[29]

In general, the SPEs devised by Fastow's team, who were solicited and advised by bankers, lawyers, and accountants, served to circumvent accounting conventions and, in certain cases (e.g. the Raptors), relied upon the illegal use of Enron stock and guarantees to hedge against the downside risk of its investments. Fastow's LJM deals were supported by CEO Lay and seconded by the Chairman of the Audit Committee at a meeting of the board and later disclosed in the small print of the 2000 annual report.[30] Their effect was to boost the flow of funds which, in the case of LJM, was recorded as $2 billion with $200 million in earnings.[31] Not only did the board approve a code of conduct waiver for Fastow, knowing that the LJM partnerships were with Enron and were designed to improve the company's financial statements, but it also failed to 'ensure the LJM transactions and Mr Fastow's compensation were fair to Enron . . . [and] to monitor Mr Fastow's LJM-related compensation.[32] The result was that the LJM partnerships realized hundreds of millions of dollars at Enron's expense'.[33] Again, these figures were reported to the board but were accepted without challenge.

The shady and even illegal design of the SPEs from 1999 onwards might have been exposed by Enron's internal audit department, had Fastow not outsourced this function to Enron's external auditors, Andersen.[34] In 2000, Andersen earned $27 million in consulting fees from Enron, including its provision of the internal audit function, in addition to $25 million in audit fees.[35] As Sherron Watkins later observed, 'junior auditors at Andersen were not going to challenge deals that senior Andersen auditors and senior Andersen executives had approved'.[36] Staff at the Houston office of Andersen had every reason to ignore or suppress any concerns about Enron's business methods and financial engineering. And, indeed, the Houston office 'was permitted to overrule critical reviews of Enron's accounting decisions by Andersen's practice partner in Chicago.[37]

Enron's lawyers, as well as its bankers (e.g. Citigroup, JP Morgan Chase, Merrill Lynch) and auditors, enabled and approved Enron's business methods, including the construction of SPEs.[38] The complicity of the banks in the use of financial instruments was critical in stoking and satisfying market expectations, as was the role of credit rating agencies in awarding Enron a top investment grade status. The complicit role played by the banks is highlighted by the testimony of Robert Roach, the Chief Investigator in the Senate's inquiry into the role of financial institutions in Enron's collapse:

> The evidence indicates that Enron would not have been able to engage in the extent of the accounting deceptions that it did, involving billions of dollars, were it not for the active participation of major financial institutions willing to go along with and even expand upon Enron's activities. The evidence also

indicates that some of these financial institutions knowingly allowed investors to rely on Enron financial statements that they knew or should have known were misleading.[39]

Some of the more notorious SPEs involved Enron employees, notably Fastow. These SPEs were effectively loans provided by financial institutions that enabled Enron to hedge against falls in its investments and/or to trade and service its debt. LJM 1 and 2, for example, were funded by equity of around $400 million from JP Morgan Chase, Citigroup, Credit Suisse, First Boston, and Wachovia banks, and also by Merrill Lynch who marketed the offering. The SPE arrangements were financially highly rewarding to Fastow who received upwards of $30 million.[40] This aspect of the LJM (1 and 2) deals was not disclosed to the board but, equally, its members asked no questions about Fastow's financial interest in the SPEs.[41] Meanwhile, the new ventures trailed in Skilling's grandiose vision – into broadband, for example – were slow to materialize, were aborted, or rapidly lost significant sums of money.[42] By the late 1990s, other companies (e.g. Dynegy, Duke Energy, El Paso, and Williams), eyeing the super-profits made by Enron in energy trading, were entering Enron's markets and squeezing its margins. Simply to maintain its earnings expectations, Enron increased its leverage and the riskiness of its transactions.

The chief limitation of some key SPEs – such as LJM (1 and 2) and Raptors, was that Enron would begin to default on its obligations to them if the stock price weakened substantially. This happened from mid-2000 to mid-2001 when Enron's stock fell by over 30 per cent, as increasingly desperate efforts were made to reverse this fall, which had dire consequences for the many Enron employees who had bought company shares or who had pensions that depended upon their performance. Deals, especially in the finance division, were being made at a rapid pace with the primary, or perhaps sole, aim of booking income immediately. An employee described the period as: 'Good deal vs. bad deal? Didn't matter. If it had a positive net present value (NPV) it could get done. Sometimes positive NPV didn't even matter in the name of strategic significance'.[43] However, the economic slowdown that followed the bursting of the dotcom bubble had depressed energy prices, which reduced opportunities to make large trading gains associated with volatility that had existed during the electricity crisis in California in the last quarter of 2000.[44] All that mattered to Enron's traders, however, was doing deals that could be shown to increase the NPV of the company. And, indeed, they were highly successful at this as trading operations were up by $2.9 billion during the first eight months of 2001.[45] Evidence of Enron's profitable trading is provided by the bonuses paid to its traders in the days between the company's downgrading to 'junk' status and its bankruptcy. It paid a total of $55 million in 'retention bonuses' to a handful of energy traders. John Lavorota received $5 million and John Arnold received $8 million 'in exchange for agreeing to stay at the firm just three months longer (and for agreeing to keep quiet about what they knew)'.[46]

In August 2001, Skilling resigned unexpectedly, prompting negative specula-
tion about the reliability of Enron's financial statements and further depressing
the stock price. The following day, Sherron Watkins, an internal whistleblower, wrote anonymously to Lay, expressing concern that a worsening trading
environment and associated falls in the stock price would be the consequence
of exposing the extent and nature of Enron's off-balance-sheet financing, and
trigger repayments occasioned by these falls. When her concerns, subsequently
expressed personally, received no satisfactory response, Watkins communicated
them to a partner at Andersen where she had worked prior to joining Enron.
Watkins's actions resulted in Andersen producing a restatement of Enron's
earnings and liabilities over several years.

On 16 October 2001 Enron announced a third-quarter loss of $618 million
and a correction of $979 million for the period 1997–2000.[47] Over the follow-
ing days and weeks, further bad news and financial restatements were posted.
There was a reduction of $1.2 billion in shareholder equity relating to LJM 2
and Fastow's compensation for managing the LJM partnership was disclosed –
with predictable consequences. Enron's stock price continued to dive, falling
heavily on the day that Fastow's involvement was revealed and again during
the days prior to the announcement of an SEC 'informal enquiry' into the
company. In response to the weakened stock price, the credit rating agencies
recalibrated Enron's status, eventually reducing it to below investment level
so that the repayment of large amounts of debts was automatically triggered
that the company could not finance. The company's earnings were insufficient
to cover the repayments, and its credit rating made it impossible to undertake
further securitization or to obtain bank loans. Enron's asset-lite strategy, which
had come to rely increasingly upon shadowy and illegal forms of financial
engineering, could not be sustained. On 29 October, Enron sought $1–2 billion
in additional financing from banks, which they refused, prompting the rating
agencies eventually to lower Enron's credit rating to marginally better than
'junk'. During October and November, Lay attempted to call in favours from
his earlier philanthropy and political bank-rolling. Lay 'called Treasury Secretary Paul O'Neill, Commerce Secretary Don Evans, Federal Reserve Chairman
Alan Greenspan, and Robert McTeer, president of the Dallas Federal Reserve.
Enron President Greg Whalley made several calls to Peter Fisher, the under-
secretary of Domestic Finance . . . But none of these men would agree to help
Enron'.[48]

Over the following weeks, as Enron desperately sought a buyer, confidence
completely evaporated, liquidity dried up and the company was unable to continue trading and filed for bankruptcy on 2 December 2001. The paradox was
that until the very eve of its declaration of bankruptcy, Enron was trading highly
profitably, making $1 billion trading natural gas derivatives alone in 2001.[49]
What sunk the company was the web of deception that had concealed $25 bil-
lion in debt, of which at least $8 billion was in pre-pays (JP Morgan Chase $3.7
billion and Citigroup $4.8 billion) – a deception that secured the company's

investment grade rating – a rating that was radically downgraded when it was no longer possible to conceal the debt.[50]

Enron's growth was propelled by incentivizing profitable innovation with minimal regard to risk, an approach facilitated by operations that were highly segmented: 'very few understood the big picture . . . That segmentation allowed us to get work done very quickly, but it isolated that institutional knowledge into the hands of very few people'.[51] This segmentation extended to the relationship between board members and senior executives, in which management entirely escaped challenge and scrutiny by the board of directors and its Audit Committee.[52] For example, the two annual reviews of the key LJM transactions, considered below, conducted in February 2000 and February 2001, 'were superficial and relied entirely on management representations, with no supporting documentation or independent inquiry into facts'.[53]

Yet, the Audit Committee comprised highly qualified and experienced persons including Dr Robert Jaedicke, a retired professor of accounting and former dean of Stanford Business School; Paulo Pereira, a former president and CEO of the State Bank of Rio de Janeiro; John Mendelsohn, a president of the University of Texas's M D Anderson Cancer Center; Wendy Gramm, a former Chairman of CFTC; and John Wakeham, who had formal accounting training and professional experience and had also been Secretary of State for Energy in the UK.[54] Despite their impressive credentials, the members of the Audit Committee took no close interest in the design of Enron's SPEs and the risks to which the company was exposed by their use.

Meetings of the Audit Committee were brief and covered huge amounts of ground.[55] The Senate Report into the Enron collapse found that the board of directors 'chose to ignore' numerous 'indicators of practices which included high-risk accounting, inappropriate conflict of interest transactions, extensive off-the-books activities, and excessive executive compensation'.[56] Their minimal scrutiny of reports prepared by the auditors and the representations made by management was probably not simply a function of the volume of business placed before them. Their preparedness to deal with complex items of business in a perfunctory manner may also have been lubricated by substantial payments and gifts made by Enron to board members for consultancy services or donated to their institutions (e.g. a hospital and a university).[57] According to the Senate Report on the role of the board in the Enron collapse, the compensation of $350,000 received for acting as board members was 'significantly above the norm and much of the compensation was in the form of stock options which enable board members to benefit from stock rises without risking any investment loss'.[58] For example, John Wakeham received an annual salary of £80,000 as a non-executive board member.[59] In 2000, Enron paid John Urquart, another Enron board member, $494,000 for consultancy services. The Chairman of the Audit Committee, Robert Jaedicke, 'made nearly $1 million from Enron stock'.[60]

Staffing

Enron recruited the 'brightest and the best' who would otherwise have been hired by banks, law firms, or consultancies. To become a trader at Enron, applicants had to survive a gruelling recruitment procedure, in which those who reached the second round were interviewed for fifty minutes by eight different interviewers, with only a single ten-minute break. In Fusaro and Miller's account of the recruitment process, candidates 'had to demonstrate that they could maintain high levels of work intensity over an extended period of time'.[61] They also note how the Enron work environment shared many of the characteristics of a top law firm, 'typically filled with brilliant young associates willing to do whatever it takes to make partner'.[62]

The prizes for Enron recruits were considerable – $20,000 golden hellos, $80,000 starting salaries, and initial annual bonuses of up to 100 per cent, which subsequently became limitless.[63] There were additional perks for high performers, which included visits to strip clubs 'where they charged their $575 bottles of champagne and their prostitution expenses to Enron credit cards'.[64] Ken Rice, while head of Enron Broadband Services, bought two high-end motorcycles, Confederate Hellcats, each costing more than $25,000, to decorate his office.

To keep key staff on their toes, Enron operated a performance review process that, in principle, was based on the company's values of respect, integrity, communication, and excellence. In practice, 'excellence' was prioritized and measured exclusively in terms of contribution to earnings. There was no limit to 'merit'-based bonuses. Employees were ranked twice per year on a scale of one to five using ten criteria and then divided into three groups. 'As', described as 'water walkers', were given large rewards but were then tasked with even more challenging assignments and targets.[65] The 'Bs' were encouraged to do better. And the 'Cs', known as 'losers', 'damaged goods', or 'shipwrecks', were given six months to become 'Bs', or be fired.[66]

Enron employees referred to this system as 'rank-and-yank'. In practice, the short period between reviews meant that substantial improvement was unlikely. 'Bs' feared that they would become 'Cs' as a consequence of the arrival of smart replacements for the 'Cs'; and the 'As', who were responsible for the most challenging work, could not be confident of retaining their position. As Thomas describes the situation, 'fierce internal competition prevailed and immediate gratification was prized above long-term potential. Paranoia flourished . . . Secrecy became the order of the day for many of the company's trading contracts, as well as its disclosures'.[67,68]

Incentives and promotions were linked to a single dominant value: demonstrated commitment to maximizing shareholder value, including of course the value received by executives who held stock options. Most staff would not know or might not care if what they were doing was illegal, rather than simply loyal, expedient, and/or entrepreneurial. There was every incentive not to raise questions that might be damaging for stock price performance. Enron pressured some of the largest banks to invest in its businesses by making huge (and lucrative) loans disguised as commodity transactions (pre-pays), or risk the loss of these and other substantial revenue streams by becoming ex-clients and ex-advisors. Enron executives reportedly arranged for investment analysts to be fired if they dared give the company negative ratings. In the film *Enron: The Smartest Guys in the Room*, there is an interview with an analyst who was fired from Merrill Lynch for refusing to bow to pressure from Enron executives to place a 'strong buy' rating on its stock. Once the analyst was removed, Merrill Lynch was rewarded with $50 million in investment banking business.

Only later was it discovered that Enron's top executives had been cashing in their lucrative stock options while simultaneously reassuring investors and employees that the future of the company had never been brighter. It emerged that a number of clandestine payments had also been made to senior executives, notably to Fastow. In the three years prior to Enron's bankruptcy, Lay's stock sales totalled more than $184 million and Skilling's $70 million.[69] That was, of course, in addition to their salaries and bonuses. Enron executives fused deception with corruption – and their dishonesty subsequently extended to the shredding of incriminating documents.[70]

Caught out by and/or locked into their stock ownership (on 17 October the Enron 401(k) retirement plan was frozen), many investors – institutional as well as individual – were badly burned.[71] More generally, investors feared that there would be other Enrons – which there were, in the shape of World-Com and Tyco International, for example. Compounded by the impact of the 9/11 terrorist attacks that occurred in the midst of Enron's fall from grace, the total collapse of an apparently solid and reputable company shook public and investor confidence in business. More specifically, it placed in question the probity of institutions and players (e.g. banks, regulators, rating agencies, law and accounting firms, etc) that had been complicit in perpetuating, or had been duped by, Enron's deception.[72] Enron's 20,000 employees lost their pensions provision and medical insurance and at least 4,000 lost their jobs.[73] For employees, the average severance pay was $4,500 and $1.2 billion was lost in retirement funds, while retirees lost $2 billion in pension funds. The reputation of Andersen, which employed 28,000 employees in the US and 85,000 worldwide, was destroyed by the Enron debacle and the firm was subsequently convicted of the crime of obstruction of justice.[74] Elements of the Andersen business were acquired by other accounting firms and its payroll was reduced to around 200 staff who handled the lawsuits and the orderly dissolution of the company. Enron's collapse also damaged the reputation of leading business school faculty and their alumni as many of Enron's smartest, high-flying executives had passed through those schools.[75] Among their faculty, the Enron debacle prompted extensive hand-wringing over the presence or, rather, the absence of ethics in management education.

The exceptional normality of Enron

The scale and scope of ruses and abuses at Enron may be exceptional. Yet, there is widespread evidence, dramatically demonstrated by exposure of the conduct of financial institutions in 2008, that the values and techniques prized within Enron's corporate culture, and exemplified in the use of SPEs, are symptomatic of contemporary, financialized capitalism, as are the (in)effectiveness of regulation and the collusion of politicians, regulators, accountants, lawyers, and bankers in facilitating its design and legitimation.[76,77]

Accounts of Enron have tended to dramatize the role of a few personalities – the key executives (Lay, Skilling, and Fastow) and also the whistleblower (Watkins). In focusing on their 'greed' or heroic interventions, sight of the bigger picture tends to become lost or blurred. A wider-angled examination of the conditions of Enron's rise and the circumstances of its fall reveals the involvement of banks, regulators, and professional accountants in facilitating, orchestrating, and covering up a culture in which the (mis)use of corporate authority for purposes of personal gain, both symbolic and material, are normalized.

Enron has been portrayed as the 'unacceptable face of capitalism' but it is more credibly represented as an extreme manifestation of neoliberal corporate normality. In other companies, executives may act less recklessly than at Enron as they recognize how growth and profitability, which rely upon excessive risk-taking, financial engineering, and/or abuse of staff, are difficult to sustain. In other companies, responsiveness to pressures to deliver shareholder value – by engaging in forms of creative accounting and financial engineering – may be tempered by limited opportunities to become asset-lite.[78] Elsewhere, responses to pressures of financialization have taken the form of outsourcing, offshoring, and pumping value from intangibles, such as brand names – sometimes with unanticipated and disastrous consequences, as in the case of companies' reliance upon contractors to undertake their drilling operations. In other corporations, the normalized oppression associated with institutionalized secrecy, rivalry, and fear is grudgingly accommodated where it is not positively relished. Enron's spectacular collapse has presented a window into this world but, as the financial crisis of 2008 makes clear, the lessons of Enron and Long Term Capital Management (LTCM) before it, were not learned.

Perhaps if Enron employees had been less fearful of bringing evidence of the dubious and wilfully misleading accounting practices to the attention of the board or its Audit Committee, remedial actions would have been taken in time to avoid the most damaging and illegal of Enron's multiple financial manipulations and accounting dodges. But, as Deakin and Konzelmann comment, the design of the appraisal and remuneration systems at Enron made it highly unlikely that the board 'would receive the information it needed about the company's accounting practices'.[79] In any event, in the light of the evidence produced by the Senate report on the role of the board at Enron, it is probable that the board, or its Audit Committee, would have done no more than refer such concerns to its auditors and/or lawyers, leading to the issuance of reports that provide soothing reassurances. Prior to the emergence of an Enron employee (Watkins) prepared to blow the whistle within the company, and then to communicate directly with Andersen, board members had every reason to ignore or deny any problems. Indeed, in response to the concerns expressed by Watkins, Lay invited a Houston-based law firm, Vinson and Elkins, to investigate the issue, despite the fact that Watkins, anticipating this course of action, had drawn the conflict of interest to Lay's attention. Vinson and Elkins duly delivered a report in October which stated that Arthur Andersen approved of Enron's accounting procedures, and that Enron had done nothing wrong. In an interview given in 2003, Watkins was asked if she ever went to the internal auditors within Enron to voice her concerns about the 'creative accounting' that she had discovered, to which she replied: 'Who knew who they were? There was no place for me to voice my concerns, either to the internal audit function or the Audit Committee. Remember, I was not in the accounting department. But even if I were, I think I would have known it would have been fruitless, because I would have had access to junior auditors who were simply not in the position to raise the flags that would have hurt their senior auditors and account executives'.[80]

As the tide went out, Enron's collapse revealed a corrupt group of executives, aided by an inattentive, complicit board of directors, who presided over a mode of corporate governance that took the pursuit of shareholder value to its logical and perverse conclusion. Yet, in the end, it was not the booking of income from increasingly risky deals that was of greatest significance for the future of the company. The deeper vulnerability lay elsewhere – in the asset-lite strategy, the relentless pursuit of shareholder value and the widespread application of creative accounting and financial engineering. Less obviously, Enron's fall exposed, for those inclined to see it, the systemic rot and/or incompetence of a (financialized) business system – comprising bankers, regulators, politicians, accountants, lawyers, and capital market intermediaries – that nurtured Enron's expansion by facilitating and validating the company's business methods. Indeed, it has been suggested that 'it was parties outside of Enron that were most to blame: the credit rating agencies that had propped up Enron's credit rating and then pulled out the carpet at the end; the investors who had not scrutinized Enron's public filings, and the legislators and regulators who had not only passed the rules Enron used to rationalize its dealings, but then stood by for years while those rules distorted the dominant corporate and financial culture so much that Enron's dealings, which should have been reprehensible, became permissible'.[81]

Notwithstanding the Sarbanes-Oxley Act passed in response to Enron, the parallels between the circumstances leading to Enron's collapse and the meltdown of financial markets eight years later are remarkable. The Enron business model, which assumed that future earnings would conceal and eventually cancel mounting debts; and the financial institutions which invested in or insured AAA–rated collateralized debt obligations (CDOs) assumed an era of uninterrupted growth in which the cycle of boom and bust had been managed out of existence by sophisticated risk management models and financial instruments.

Enron, like the banks and insurance companies bailed out by governments in 2008, is illustrative of an institutional phenomenon. Its collapse is by no means attributable to the presence of a few 'rotten apples', whether of a Lay or Madoff variety. Enron, as Roberts has so cogently put it 'speaks not of the failure but rather the success of corporate governance that had been progressively reformed – that is, weakened – through the decade that preceded Enron's demise'.[82] And, in the financial sector, this weakening continued as a blind eye was turned to the parallels between 'Enronomics' and the use of leveraged debt to engage in the creation and trading of exotic financial products.[83] 'Apples', whether good or bad, do not grow spontaneously. Their germination and ripening are products of the circumstances in which they are cultivated, nourished, and enabled to thrive. These circumstances are constructed by lobbying for (deregulated) conditions in which, for example, forms of creative accounting and financial engineering become conceivable and permissible. Enron's collapse was an early warning signal of how the business system that fostered the company's growth and validated its reports was, and remains, rotten to its core.

The beliefs, values, and norms ascribed to Enron culture played their part in building trust and confidence in the company, fuelling its rapid growth, and delivering its profitability. But the creation and operation of Enron's business model depended, above all, upon the regulators, bankers, credit rating agencies, accountants, lawyers, politicians, academics, and others who collectively enabled, legitimized, masked, and contrived to ignore its business methods, including the financing of its activities. It is by no means clear that the conditions that produced Enron, including the funding of political parties, the lobbying of regulators, and the constitution and operation of company boards, have changed significantly in their composition or *modus operandi* during the intervening years. To the contrary, these years have witnessed a series of corporate scandals culminating in an Enron-writ-large, global financial crisis. As in the case of Enron, which produced much fear and loathing but prompted little radical scrutiny of the business system, the collapse of the banks and the socialization of their losses has not been accompanied by a radical restructuring and public redirection of financial institutions. As the debts of corporations have been socialized into sovereign debt with the associated risks of a flight of capital from government bonds and speculative gambling against currencies, the temporarily interrupted but unchecked financialization of the world economy leaves the global community, including the corporations that have come to dominate its development, exposed to mounting hazards and financial risks.

NOTES

1 Jeffrey Skilling, CEO Elect, quoted in W. Zellner, C. Palmeri, P. Coy, and L. Cohn, 'Enron's power play', *Business Week* (12 February 2001). See www.businessweek.com/2001/01_07/b3719001.htm, accessed 3 June 2010.

2 Sherron Watkins, Enron whistleblower, quoted in L. Curwen, 'The corporate conscience: Sherron Watkins, Enron whistleblower', *The Guardian* (21 June 2003). See www.guardian.co.uk/business/2003/jun/21/corporatefraud.enron, accessed 24 April 2010.

3 See, for example, Cara Ellison's blog at http://caraellison.wordpress.com.

4 M. Ezzamel, H. C. Willmott, and F. Worthington, 'Manufacturing shareholder value: the role of accounting in organizational transformation', *Accounting, Organizations and Society* 33 (2–3) (2009), 107–40.

5 The failure of WorldCom in 2002 was actually bigger than that of Enron as it had $107 billion, compared with Enron's $63 billion, of assets.

6 For example, in July 2000 Enron signed a twenty-year agreement with Blockbuster Video to provide entertainment on demand in a number of US cities using its broadband network. It then booked $110 million in estimated profits from the Blockbuster deal before the technology was tried and tested and before it had received any substantial revenues from the venture.

7 A few years after Fastow's appointment to Enron, Continental became the largest bank failure in American history.

8 It has been questioned whether Fastow was a 'financial genius' or simply someone who, working in Skilling's shadow, was eager to please his boss. In any event, he welcomed a way of addressing Enron's precarious financial status when bankers (Citigroup, JP Morgan Chase, and others) made available financial products (e.g. 'pre-pays') that had been devised to assist clients looking for similar earnings inflating 'solutions'.

9 BBC, *Buffett Warns on Investment 'Time Bomb'*. London: BBC (4 March 2003). See http://news.bbc.co.uk/1/hi/2817995.stm, accessed 3 June 2010.

10 M. Lewis, *The Big Short: Inside the Doomsday Machine*. Harmondsworth, UK: Allen Lane (2010).

11 V. K. Rangan, K. G. Palepu, S. Srinivasan, A. Bhasin, and M. Desai, *Enron Development Corp.: the Dahbol Power Project in Maharashtra, India*. Boston, MA: Harvard Business School Press (1996); P. Tufano and S. Bhatnagar, *Enron Gas Services*. Boston, MA: Harvard Business School Press (1994).

12 B. W. Kulik, 'Agency theory, reasoning and culture at Enron: in search of a solution', *Journal of Business Ethics* 59 (2005), 347–60: 349.

13 P. M. Healy and K. G. Palepu, 'The fall of Enron', *Journal of Economic Perspectives* 17 (2) (2003), 3–26: 17.

14 J. Chaffin and S. Fidler, 'Enron's alchemy turns to lead for bankers', *Financial Times Special Report* (28 February 2002), 4. See http://specials.ft.com/enron/FT3E9GX09YC.html, accessed 3 June 2010.

15 *Ibid.*, emphasis added.

16 M. Stein, 'Oedipus Rex at Enron: leadership, Oedipal struggles, and organizational collapse', *Human Relations* 60 (9) (2007), 1,387–410. For further details

of Wendy Gramm's involvement and that of her husband, Senator Gramm, who was one of the five co-sponsors of the Commodity Futures Act of 2000, which was beneficial to Enron, see Public Citizen, *Blind Faith: How Deregulation and Enron's Influence over Government Looted Billions from Americans* (2001). See www.citizen.org/documents/Blind_Faith.PDF, accessed 21 March 2011; and *Sen. Gramm, White House must be Investigated for Role in Enron's Fraud of Consumers and Shareholders* (2001). See www.apfn.org/ENRON/Blind_Faith.pdf, accessed 29 May 2010. Wendy Gramm was not alone in having conflicting interests. Another member of the board, John Mendelsohn, was the director of a clinic that had received donations of over half a million dollars from Enron or Ken Lay. The Enron code of ethics prohibited board members from being involved in another business entity that does business with the company. Yet, another board member, John Wakeman, received $72,000 for providing consultancy services to Enron in 2000, and Robert Belfer involved his oil and gas company in various ventures with Enron.

17 R. Schultes, L. Jeffs, and L. Vaughan, *Lehman Sets Derivatives Test Case* (2008). See www.efinancialnews.com/story/2008–09-22/lehman-sets-derivatives-test-case, accessed 3 June 2010.

18 Congressional Investigative Report, quoted in J. D. Knottnerus, J. S. Ulsperger, S. Cummins, and E. Osteen, 'Exposing Enron: media representations of ritualized deviance in corporate culture', *Crime Media Culture* 2 (2) (2006), 177–95, 183.

19 Senate Report, *Senate Permanent Subcommittee on Investigations of the Committee on Government Affairs: the Role of the Board of Directors in Enron's Collapse* (2002), 55. See http://fl1.findlaw.com/news.findlaw.com/hdocs/docs/enron/senpsi70802rpt.pdf, accessed 29 May 2010.

20 Sustainable Energy and Economic Network/Institute of Policy Studies, *Enron's Pawns: How Public Institutions Bankrolled Enron's Globalization Game* (2002), 3. See www.apfn.org/enron/pawns.pdf, accessed 3 June 2010.

21 T. Fowler, 'The Pride and the Fall of Enron', *Houston Chronicle* (20 October 2002). See www.chron.com/CDA/archives/archive.mpl/2002_3592430/the-fall-of-enron-a-year-ago-enron-s-crumbling-fou.html, accessed 29 May 2010.

22 Senate Report, *The Role of the Board of Directors*, 7; see Chapter 3, Box 1.

23 *Ibid.*, 12; see Chapter 3, Box 2. Interestingly, LJM was named after Fastow's wife and children: Lea, Jeffrey, and Michael.

24 See Chapter 3, Box 2.

25 L. J. Brooks, *Business and Professional Ethics for Directors, Executives and Accountants* (4th edn). Cincinnati, OH: Thomson South-Western College Publishing (2007), 59. Further details of the make-up and significance of these SPEs can be found in 66ff. and 96ff.

26 A. Sloan, 'Enron's failed power play', *Newsweek* (21 January 2002), 34–9.

27 See Chapter 3, Box 3.

28 Senate Report, *The Role of the Board of Directors*, 13; see Chapter 3, Box 3.

29 *Ibid.*, 14.

30 *Ibid.*, 33.

31 *Ibid.*, 24.

32 N. Hala, 'If capitalists were angels – Sherron Watkins – the fall of Enron – interview', *Internal Auditor* (April 2003). See http://findarticles.com/p/articles/mi_m4153/is_2_60/ai_100075073, accessed 29 May 2010.

33 Senate Report, *The Role of the Board of Directors*.

34 S. Watkins, 'Presentation for the Institute of Internal Auditors, UAE chapter', The 8th Annual Gulf Regional Audit Conference, 11 March 2007. See www.iiadubai.org/pdf/day1/Sherron%20Watkins%20-%20%20Anatomy%20of%20corporate%20bankrupt.pdf, accessed 13 December 2009; Hala, 'If capitalists were angels'.

35 Healy and Palepu, 'The fall of Enron', 15.

36 P. Lattman, 'The Vinson and Elkins–Enron connection: the plot thick-ens', *Wall Street Journal* (2006). See http://blogs.wsj.com/law/2006/06/01/the-vinson-elkins-enron-connection-the-plot-thickens, accessed 13 December 2009; D. L. Rhode and P. D. Paton, *Lawyers, Ethics and Enron*. See www.thecorporatescandalreader.com/forms/04c%20rhode.pdf, accessed 13 December 2009. [An earlier version of this article appeared in the *Stanford Journal of Business and Finance*.]

37 R. Roach, *Testimony of Robert Roach, Chief Investigator to the Permanent Sub-committee of Investigations into the Role of the Financial Institutions in Enron's Collapse* (2002), 1. See http://hsgac.senate.gov/072302roach.pdf, accessed 3 June 2010.

38 Enron, *The Code of Ethics* (2000). See http://bobsutton.typepad.com/files/enron-ethics.pdf, accessed 13 December 2009.

39 J. S. Lublin, 'Enron audit panel is scrutinized for its cozy ties with the firm', *Wall Street Journal* (1 February 2002). See http://bodurtha.georgetown.edu/enron/Enron%20Audit%20Panel%20Is%20Scrutinized%20For%20Its%20Cozy%20Ties%20With%20the%20Firm.htm, accessed 29 May 2010.

40 In 2001, the value of Azurix, a water business aquired in 1998, was written down by $287 million, the broadband investment by $180 million, and other investments by a further $544 million (Healy and Palepu, 'The fall of Enron', 3–26).

41 C. W. Thomas, 'The rise and fall of Enron: when a company looks too good to be true, it usually is', *Journal of Accountancy* (April 2002), 41–52. See www.journalofaccountancy.com/Issues/2002/Apr/TheRiseAndFallOfEnron.htm, accessed 13 December 2009.

42 Brooks, *Business and Professional Ethics*, 59.

43 Fowler, cited in N. B. Rapoport, 'Enron, Titanic and the perfect storm', *Fordham Law Review* 71 (2002), 1,375–97, 1,386 and N42 and N57.

44 Although Enron is widely blamed for escalating, or even engineering, this crisis by manipulating markets, it made more money elsewhere. See F. Partnoy, *Infectious Greed: How Deceit and Risk Corrupted the Financial Markets*. London: Profile (2010), 326–7.

45 Partnoy, *Infectious Greed*, 327.

46 *Ibid.*, 341.

47 See Chapter 3, Box 4.

48 Partnoy, *Infectious Greed*, 333.

49 *Ibid.*, 327.

50 See Brooks, *Business and Professional Ethics*, 76ff. This helps to explain why the banks that had participated in the pre-pays were eager to place maximum pressure on the rating agencies to maintain Enron's investment grade status. Specifically, Robert Rubin, co-Chairman of Citygroup, called Peter Fischer at the US Treasury Department to request that he ask the credit rating agencies to find some alternative to downgrading Enron. See Partnoy, *Infectious Greed*, 335.

51 See also note 5.

52 Healy and Palepu, 'The fall of Enron'.

53 Senate Report, *The Role of the Board of Directors*, 3.

54 Healy and Palepu, 'The fall of Enron', 14.

55 A. Grice, 'Enron and the shadow over Lord Wakeham: is this a fix too far for the ultimate fixer?', *The Independent* (31 January 2002). See www.independent.co.uk/news/uk/politics/enron-and-the-shadow-over-lord-wakeham-is-this-a-fix-too-far-for-the-ultimate-fixer-671909.html, accessed 29 May 2010.

56 Senate Report, *The Role of the Board of Directors*, 56.

57 P. C. Fusaro and R. Miller, *What Went Wrong with Enron?* New York: John Wiley and Sons (2002), 49.

58 *Ibid.*, cited in D. Tourish and N. Vatcha, 'Charismatic leadership and corporate cultism at Enron: the elimination of dissent, the promotion of conformity and orga-nizational collapse', *Leadership* 1 (4) (2005), 455–80, 466; see also Knottnerus *et al.*, 'Exposing Enron', 185–6.

59 D. M. Boje, G. A. Rosalie, R. A. Durant, and J. T. Luhman, 'Enron spectacles: a critical dramaturgical analysis', *Organization Studies* 25 (5) (2004), 751–74, 760.

60 Partnoy, *Infectious Greed*, 341.

61 Fusaro and Miller, *What Went Wrong with Enron?*; M. Swartz and S. Watkins, *Power Failure: the Inside Story of the Collapse of Enron*. New York: Broadway Business (2004).

62 K. Peraino, A. Murr, and A. B. Gesalman, 'ENRON's dirty laundry', *Newsweek* (11 March 2002), 22–30, 26.

63 Thomas, 'The rise and fall of Enron', 2.

64 See Chapter 3, Box 5.

65 A. Jacobius and V. Anand, 'Enron: 401(k) and cash balance plans battered as com-pany crashes', *Pensions and Investments* 29 (25) (2001), 1–34; R. Jenkins, 'Crisis in confidence in corporate America', *Mid-American Journal of Business* 18 (2003), 5–7.

66 B. E. Ashforth and V. Anand, 'The normalization of corruption in organizations', in R. M. Kramer and B. M. Staw (eds.), *Research in Organizational Behavior*. Stamford, CT: JAI Press (2003), 1–52, 2; K. Eichenwald and D. B. Henriques, 'Enron's many strands: the company unravels; Enron buffed image to a shine even as it rotted from within', *New York Times* (10 February 2002). See www.nytimes.com/2002/02/10/business/enron-s-many-strands-company-unravels-enron-buffed-image-shine-even-it-rotted.html?pagewanted=1, accessed 22 December 2009.

67 Thomas, 'The rise and fall of Enron'.

68 Jenkins, 'Crisis in confidence'; see Chapter 3, Box 5.

69 Knottnerus *et al.*, 'Exposing Enron'.

70 The conviction was subsequently overturned on a technicality by the US Supreme Court.

71 L. R. Dean, 'A challenge to change business education', *Mid-American Journal of Business* 18 (1) (2003), 5–6.

72 See Chapter 3, Box 2.

73 G. F. Davis, 'The rise and fall of finance and the end of the society of organiza-tions', *Academy of Management Perspectives* 23 (3) (2009), 27–44; H. C. Willmott, 'Creating "value" beyond the point of production: branding, financialization and market capitalization', *Organization* 19 (5) (2010), 517–42.

74 S. Deakin and S. Konzelmann, 'Learning from Enron', ESRC Centre for Business Research, University of Cambridge, Working Paper No. 274 (2003), 12.

75 Hala, 'If capitalists were angels'.

76 S. Watkins, 'Former Enron vice-president Sherron Watkins on the Enron collapse', *Academy of Management Executive* 17 (2003), 119–27. It was this vulnerability that Watkins identified in her anonymous letter to Lay and later shared with an ex-colleague at Andersen.

77 See Chapter 3, Box 6.

78 J. Roberts, 'Agency theory, ethics and corporate governance', paper prepared for the Corporate Governance and Ethics Conference, Maquarie Graduate School of

Management, Sydney, Australia (28–30 June 2004), 5. See www.le.ac.uk/ulsm/research/cppe/levinas/pdf/roberts2.pdf, accessed 3 June 2010.

79 S. Deakin and S. Konzelmann, 'Learning from Enron', ESRC Centre for Business Research, University of Cambridge, Working Paper No. 274 (2003), 12.

80 Hala, 'If capitalists were angels'.

81 Partnoy, *Infectious Greed*, 345.

82 Roberts, 'Agency theory'.

83 R. Klimecki and H. C. Willmott, 'From demutualization to meltdown: a tale of two wannabe banks', *Critical Perspectives on International Business* 5 (1–2) (2009), 120–40.

5

Moral decision-making

MOLLIE PAINTER-MORLAND

Goals of this chapter

After studying this chapter you will be able to:

- understand the most prominent rationalist approaches to moral reasoning typically employed in business ethics;
- understand the theories of moral development and its limitations;
- develop insight into rational choice theory and its limitations;
- understand the criticisms of and alternatives to rationalist approaches to decision-making;
- understand Derrida's notion of undecidability;
- identify some *aporias* in everyday business life.

Introduction

Those in business have many reasons to be concerned about the way moral decisions are made. The success of business organizations depends on their ability to generate fair profit from their goods or services. For this to happen, employees must show up for work and labour diligently in the firm's interest, suppliers must keep contracts, customers must continue to believe in the value of the goods or services they receive from the corporation and pay for them on time, and shareholders must continue to trust in the corporation to invest their money in its pursuits. If in any one of these respects individuals or groups stop making decisions that are fair, honest, and trustworthy, the whole enterprise will fail. In what we have argued thus far, we have employed a form of reasoning that is probably the most influential in business ethics, namely consequentialist reasoning. Consequentialists argue that it makes sense to do the right thing because good consequences result from such decisions and behaviours. A very important presupposition that underpins consequentialist thinking is that people will always choose those decisions and actions that will best serve their interests. This way of thinking about human beings is called 'rational choice theory', and is used by practitioners in economics, management, philosophy, and psychology. Rational choice theory argues that given a choice, decision-makers will select optimal options in the pursuit of happiness, i.e. decisions are made based on *utility*.

Introducing popular approaches to moral decision-making in business ethics

Consequentialism: utilitarianism

The main type of consequentialist thinking that we encounter in moral theory and that is employed in business ethics is called utilitarianism. One can see from the name of this approach that its adherents believe the right course of action is to be determined by whatever maximizes utility, i.e. useful consequences. The philosopher who is most closely associated with this approach and did much to develop and refine it is John Stuart Mill (1806–73). Mill refined the utilitarian theories of his teacher, Jeremy Bentham (1748–1832), who developed what was called the 'hedonistic calculus'. Bentham basically argued that making moral decisions amounts to a cost–benefit calculation that aims at maximizing the pleasure of the decision-maker. He had a special interest in finding a clear, rational process for making good decisions. In the eighteenth century, religious values caused a lot of conflict, and Bentham wanted to establish clear objective grounds for resolving these disputes. In his mind, a utilitarian approach to moral reasoning would settle disputes by means of a set of clear-cut, rational procedures. One can, however, imagine the objections against this theory from a moral point of view (especially among puritans) – surely one cannot condone an approach that says that whatever is pleasurable is right?

This is where Mill stepped up to clarify what is meant by the utilitarian approach.[1] In the first place, he explained that utilitarian decisions are not just about individualistic, hedonistic pleasure, but rather about maximizing pleasurable outcomes for the greatest number of people in society. His definition of the basic principle of utilitarianism, called the 'greatest happiness principle', made it clear that utilitarians consider the good of others, too, and that there are specific standards for thinking about what is considered pleasurable, and hence good. Mill writes:

> According to the 'greatest happiness principle'. . . the ultimate, with reference to and for the sake of which all other things are desirable, whether we are considering our own good or that of other people, is an existence exempt as far as possible from pain, and as rich as possible in endowments, both in point of quantity and quality: the test of quality, and the rule for measuring it against quantity, being the preference felt by those who in their opportunities of experience, to which must be added their habits of self-consciousness and self-observation, are best furnished with the means of comparison.

We see that Mill distinguishes between quantity pleasures and quality pleasures, and in his writings he makes it clear that he considers certain pleasures to be higher pleasures, and others lower pleasures. Mill argues that, while animals might be happy with the fulfilment of only their immediate needs, human beings are not satisfied with food, drink, and sex; they require the satisfaction of higher pleasures, such as education and culture. How one comes up with a list of higher and lower pleasures can clearly be a great cause of dispute, and this is why Mill argues that the determinations should be made by certain 'competent judges', i.e. those whose experience and habits of self-reflection have best equipped them to make these determinations. Mill, however, can't get himself completely out of trouble here. Do we have to accept that the standard for what should be worthwhile pleasures to pursue should be left in the hands of a few? What will happen if these few happen to be opera lovers who despise any other kind of music, or if they insist on everyone wearing suits all year round for all occasions, and argue that only those with advanced degrees in mathematics should be considered 'educated'? Would we feel comfortable with this determination of 'pleasure'?

Overall, the cost–benefit analysis that utilitarians employ in making decisions has led to serious debate. Not only is the value of what is pleasurable to be disputed, but, in doing a cost–benefit analysis, we have to assume that all pains and pleasures are measurable on a single scale. Here enters the problem of the incommensurability of goods. Can we really argue that it is an acceptable practice to employ children in sweatshop conditions, because, overall, it makes money for the firm and its stakeholders, gives the children some livelihood, and produces cheap products for the customers? Is it right to consider this an acceptable balance of pleasures over pains? We have to keep in mind that utilitarians do not believe that absolutely everyone should be made happy immediately, and this is why utilitarianism can so easily be utilized as a legitimization of certain capitalist practices, such as sweatshops, retrenchments, and other tough decisions that certainly sacrifice some for the benefit of others. Imagine yourself in a situation where you have to make a decision in the interest of the survival of your own small business, which inevitably will entail negative consequences for others. Say for instance, you own a small beauty salon, which because of a financial downturn experiences very serious financial difficulties. You employ five employees, all of whom are friends or family members. In order to help your small business survive and guarantee your own livelihood and that of three of the employees, you have to fire at least two employees. In this case, a utilitarian analysis may suggest that the desired balance of pleasures over pain would dictate that you have to let two employees go. Unfortunately, things aren't so simple in all cases. Would you for instance, compromise people's lives or safety to keep your business afloat? Take for instance the decision made by some businesses to cut their costs by outsourcing their production to sweatshops or suppliers with environmentally unfriendly production methods.

However, most utilitarians would argue that the way some business people use utilitarianism in their decision-making does not adequately reflect the intricacy of the moral reasoning process prescribed by utilitarianism's prime proponents, such as Mill. Often, business managers who employ a cost–benefit analysis do not take into account the happiness of *all* stakeholders, nor do they consider long-term consequences. Furthermore, a real utilitarian would consider the pleasure of protecting lives, and especially the quality of the lives of all involved, much more important than the quantity of money one could make.

Non-consequentialism: deontology

It is important to consider an alternative approach to moral reasoning and it is easy to guess what the main alternative to consequentialism might be – it is what is referred to as non-consequentialism. The most important non-consequentialist approach is called deontology, from the Greek word *deontos*, or duty or law. This approach is radically opposed to judging moral issues based on consequences, precisely because this form of instrumental reasoning sacrifices important duties, rights, or moral principles. The main proponent of deontology is Immanuel Kant (1724–1804), who argued that what makes human beings unique is their capacity for giving themselves rational, moral commands completely autonomously.[2] Rationality and autonomy are both extremely important to Kant. But, of course, he realized that autonomous moral decision-making should not amount to subjectivism, i.e. everyone just doing what he or she likes. Hence there must be certain standards for what will count as a moral law. In the formulation of his basic moral principle, called the 'categorical imperative', Kant makes clear what these standards might be. The first formulation of the categorical imperative states that human beings should never be subjected to any form of instrumental thinking. Kant argued that one should never treat anyone as a means to an end, but always as ends in themselves. The second formulation of the categorical imperative gives us guidelines on how to go about formulating moral laws for ourselves. He argued that we should only act on those maxims that could be made a universal law for all people at all times. Why this guideline? Well, Kant believes that for something to count as a moral law, it must be categorical, i.e. it must hold for all people at all times, and hence it must pass the 'universalization test'. This is a kind of logical test for the rationality of whatever one is thinking of making a moral law. Kant believed that if one were to universalize something immoral, it would simply fail to make logical sense. Say for instance, if one is considering breaking a promise to a friend, one should employ the universalization test by asking: can a broken promise be universalized? Clearly, it will be rationally impossible to will this as a moral law. If all promises are broken, the notion of a promise will cease to exist. The idea that 'all promises must be broken' is logically inconsistent and therefore it cannot be made a moral law.

But proponents of deontology run into a problem here: what should one do when one is confronted with two equally rational moral duties – say, for instance, the duty to protect life and the duty to always keep a promise? Imagine for instance, a very close friend, Joe, wants to share something with you that is troubling him a lot. He asks you to promise that you will keep whatever he tells you a secret, and you swear that you will tell no-one. He then goes on to share with you the fact that he has just heard that he is HIV positive and does not want to tell his girlfriend, Sandy, about this because he fears that he will lose her if he does so. Sandy is also a close friend of yours and often shares her dreams and thoughts about the future with you. You also know that the two of them are not practising safe sex and that, in fact, Sandy is eager to get married and start a family. As it happens, you and Sandy went for an HIV test together just last week and were relieved to receive the news that you are both negative. The dilemma now is, should you break your promise to Joe and tell Sandy to start practising safe sex with Joe since he is HIV positive?

What we confront here is the case of competing duties, and we can see that here Kant is not of much help. He would not allow you to universalize broken promises, nor can one universalize compromising a friend's health, and hence both actions would be considered immoral. Many have criticized Kant for his unwavering universalistic approach. However, Kant would acknowledge that there are situations where morality simply cannot apply at all, because they are not situations of freedom. Kant believed that freedom and autonomy are essential for moral decision-making. One also has to understand that this is Kant's attempt to remain true to the ideals of rationality, which he realized are never completely within our reach, yet must be pursued relentlessly. Business ethicists tend to focus on Kant's *Groundwork for the Metaphysics of Morals*, but his three critiques attest to an awareness of the difficulties of moral thinking. In these works, we encounter a much less self-assured Kant, who is fascinated by the moral law within us and acknowledges its puzzling characteristics.

Moral development theories and its critics

Lawrence Kohlberg

One cannot deny, however, that Kant's deontological approach has been extremely influential in modern moral theory, and that it has led to a belief that the rational capacity to identify universal principles is the epitome of moral thinking. This belief is clearly displayed in the most influential theories of cognitive moral development. Lawrence Kohlberg drew on Jean Piaget's distinction between two basic types of morality, i.e. a morality of constraint and a morality of cooperation. Kohlberg expanded Piaget's two basic moral orientations, and postulated a six-stage linear path towards moral maturity. On the first level, named the preconventional level, individuals respond to the fear of punishment (stage 1), or to the expectation of reward or the need for satisfaction (stage 2). Over time, however, individuals come to recognize that there are certain expectations regarding their societal role and that good behaviour pleases others; hence, in stage 3, individuals seek to please others to earn their trust. In stage 4, individuals come to accept the standards of law and order in society and conform to its codes and procedures. The third level of moral development is reached when individuals can define moral values and principles without it being dictated by society, and hence in stage 5, individuals can negotiate social contracts and seek what they consider best for themselves. In stage 6, individuals develop the capacity for universal reasoning, much like the identification of moral laws that Kant thought all rational people should be able to identify. It is, therefore, clear that for Kohlberg the epitome of moral reasoning is the ability to engage in impartial, rational decision-making and the capacity to abstract in order to identify universal principles.[3]

Critics of development towards rational moral decision-making

Carol Gilligan suggested that there is a gender bias inherent in Kohlberg's theories. She argued that because most of the subjects who participated in Kohlberg's experiments were male, his theories are skewed to consider what is characteristic of certain male stereotypes as normal and ideal. Gilligan believed that women tend to privilege enduring personal relationships in their moral decision-making, which would mean that in terms of Kohlberg's model, they have not yet reached moral maturity. In fact, women may never reach 'moral maturity' in Kohlberg's terms, because they value emotional connections and their personal responsibilities towards others. For instance, the role that women occupy as mothers and the love and care that characterize their relationship with their children may influence how they view their moral responsibilities.

This skepticism towards the influence of emotion has long characterized many approaches to moral decision-making. Emotion was cast as the opposite of rationality, and hence it was argued that decision-making that takes emotions into consideration is irrational. For instance, Kant did not trust the influence of emotion on moral decision-making. In Kant's opinion, emotions undermine the individual's capacity for autonomous reasoning and for universalization. Many philosophers have since argued that this is not at all the case. For instance, Martha Nussbaum indicated that emotions are reliable indicators of what we value, and, hence, are extremely important in making rational decisions. Her analysis of the role of emotion in decision-making allows us to revisit one of the most important debates in Western philosophy, i.e. that between the two Ancient Greeks, Plato and Aristotle. According to Nussbaum, Aristotle wanted to restore emotions to the central place in morality from which Plato had banished them. In Aristotle's conception, emotions function as modes of vision and forms of recognition. He believed that a person's emotional response, rather than detached thinking, guides appropriate decisions and behaviour.[4] Nussbaum argues that emotions have a rich cognitive structure and reflect particular beliefs.[5] As agents, we ascribe value to things that we do not necessarily control. Consequently, we desire things and experience strong emotions as we seek and pursue the things we value. Our interactions with other people shape our sensibilities. They provide us with a strong sense of what is socially appropriate and appreciated in our behaviour. In this way, socialization continually conditions us to respond in an emotionally appropriate way. If we ignore the role that emotion plays, it will become impossible for us to understand our own motivations, decisions, and actions.[6] To explore this idea in more depth, we now turn to Aristotle's perspectives on moral reasoning.

Alternative approaches to moral decision-making

Virtue-based ethics

It is very important to understand that virtue-based ethics has its roots in Ancient Greek society and that, as such, it operates within a unique worldview that reflects some ontological and epistemological assumptions vastly different from our own. This simply means that the Ancient Greeks had another perspective on how things are (ontology), and on how we come to know them (epistemology). For Aristotle (BC384–322), whose *Nicomachean Ethics* is central to understanding virtue-ethics, knowing one's position and role in society is very important in developing a sense of what the right thing to do would be.[7] The Aristotelian city-state (*polis*) was an extremely hierarchical society, and it was virtually impossible to change your social and professional position. The best thing to do, according to Aristotle, is to contribute to the happiness (*eudaimonia*) of your society by fulfilling your specific purpose. In order to do so, you had to cultivate those virtues that are essential in fulfilling your particular role in society. Just like the oak tree grows from the acorn seed, each individual has an inherent purpose (*telos*) that must be realized. Since all of us have different roles in society, we all require different virtues. If you were a soldier, you needed to be brave. If you were a worker, it was important to be diligent. If we practise the virtues that are required to fulfil our purpose consistently, doing the right thing will become a habit and feel like second nature. This can be compared to the best of golf-swings. Lots of time and effort goes into practising it, but when it is perfectly executed, one is not thinking about it. By practising virtues, we accomplish the cultivation of certain habits, or predispositions, which allow us to reach our purpose. This is why Aristotle's ethics are described as *teleological*, i.e. they allow you to reach your purpose (*telos*) and contribute to the happiness of your society.

Another important notion in Aristotle's ethics is that of *ethos*, the Greek word for dwelling place. One may describe the virtuous character that we come to inhabit as a certain *ethos*, which is essential to living a good life. In developing these habits, Aristotle argues that it is extremely important to steer clear of extremes, i.e. of any excess, or deficiency. He therefore suggests that we respond to what could be extreme emotions by seeking the 'golden mean'. Moral virtues are cultivated in and through participation in practices. For instance, the virtue of bravery can be described as finding the mean between foolhardiness and fear, while generosity is the mean between stinginess and wastefulness in very practical circumstances. In addition to the moral virtues, we need to develop intellectual virtues, the most important of which is *phronesis*. This refers to a kind of practical wisdom that helps us to know what the right thing to do is.

In all of this, Aristotle acknowledged the importance of not denying or excluding one's emotions, but instead cultivating the appropriate way to live with them. He believes that theatre, poetry, and physical exercise are all conducive to having a fully embodied sense of agency, which he thinks is essential to developing a strong character, especially when it comes to moral and intellectual virtue. We see that Aristotle did not subscribe to Plato's rational universe of forms and ideals, and argued instead for developing a sense of what is right and wrong in and through everyday practices. Aristotle did not believe we could reach a universal notion of right and wrong conduct, especially since we encounter certain 'blockages' or 'puzzles' that make it difficult to identify the exact mean between the extremes that confront us. We shall discuss these difficulties in more detail when we explore Derrida's discussion of *aporias*. An *aporia* is a dilemma that seems impassable – something that seems irresolvable via our typical strategies of reasonability. Though Aristotle already had a sense of the difficulties that we face when confronted with such impasses, his theories are often applied in simplistic ways, as if finding the 'golden mean' is just seeking a comfortable middle ground or finding an amenable compromise.

This is one of the reasons why some business ethicists who have drawn on Aristotle's work have been criticized. They often underestimate the difficulties that are always part and parcel of practical wisdom. One of the business ethicists who has been credited for doing much to acknowledge the value that both Aristotle's emphasis on practical wisdom and his appreciation of the emotions have for business ethics, is Robert Solomon.[8] He argues for viewing business organizations as similar to Aristotelian communities, and that the development of certain virtues is central to business excellence. Solomon deals with the issue of 'moral mazes' by positing the solution of developing the virtue of moral courage. Solomon's Aristotelian approach to business ethics has been criticized by some authors in critical management studies because it draws overly simplistic parallels between corporations and Aristotle's city-state. Corporations can hardly be described as communities in the strict sense of the word.[9] It soon becomes clear that it is by no means easy to describe the process of moral decision-making in simple terms.

Bounded rationality

There are a number of other approaches to ethics that display attempts to develop more nuanced alternatives to 'rational choice theory' and to explore the limits of 'rationality' as such. For instance, Herbert A. Simon, who won the Nobel prize for Economic Science in 1978, developed the theory of bounded rationality. He believed that most decision-makers are only partly rational, and otherwise irrational. The reason for this is the fact that decision-makers may have limited resources at their disposal. Proponents of neoclassical economic theory make certain flawed assumptions, namely that individuals have precise information, that they are fully aware of all possible alternatives, with their costs and potential benefits, and that there is enough time for decision-makers to weigh these options.[10] So we see that there are both cognitive constraints, as well as time limitations, that have an impact on the 'rationality' of decisions. Some scholars even argue for something like 'rational ignorance', which occurs when the opportunity cost of weighing all the options is perceived to be higher than the possible benefits of careful consideration.[11] One also has to take into account that human perception is limited because it is typically subjective and selective. For all these reasons, people do not always make the most 'rational' decisions. We just try to make satisfactory decisions under the constraints that we operate within, and hence we can be described as what Simon calls *satisficers*. So, if I am playing chess and have to decide which move I am going to make, I generally stop looking for better alternatives if the move I have found pleases me and is *satisficing*. Simon argues that we do have intuition, which functions as a kind of coping mechanism to deal with situations of bounded rationality. It is characterized by pattern recognition, which, because it is synchronous, comes to us all of a sudden, in a moment, and does not require time for rational deliberation. For example, in the movie *Backdraft*, we see something of the capacity that a fireman has for sensing danger, even though there are not always rational reasons for making certain decisions.

Moral imagination

Developing a more deliberately imaginative approach to moral decision-making is something that business ethicists have grappled with for some time now. Patricia Werhane's theory of 'moral imagination' is the most prominent contribution in this regard. Drawing on the work of Adam Smith, Immanuel Kant, and Mark Johnson, she has developed an account of how imagination may be employed in making sense of moral dilemmas. It involves three consecutive phases:

> (1) [b]ecoming aware of social, economic, organizational, and personal factors that affect perception of a business problem and understanding how these might conflict; (2) [r]eframing the problem from various perspectives to understand the potential impact of different solutions; and (3) [d]eveloping alternatives to solve the problem that can be morally justified by others outside the firm.[12]

The deliberate unpacking of all relevant considerations and the conscious envisioning of alternatives that Werhane associates with the employment of imagination in moral decision-making shows some correspondence with Michael Polanyi's observations.[13] In a sense, both describe the employment of imagination as a process that involves a direct, intentional effort to draw on the tacit knowledge resources that are available to the individual. However, there is also a significant difference in how they see this process unfolding. For Polanyi, imagination and intuition are codependent. Intuition, as he sees it, is a process of understanding that is spontaneously initiated as the individual engages with the concrete contingencies of a problem. As such, it is not something that can deliberately be operated from a position of disengagement. It is on this point that he and Werhane differ. Werhane acknowledges that 'conceptual schemes' influence the way individuals think about moral dilemmas. She also recognizes the role that social dynamics and metaphoric language plays in the way that individuals conceptualize moral dilemmas. Despite this, Werhane insists that: 'moral imagination entails the ability to disengage'.[14] In this way, Werhane's theory is still committed to the rational process of thinking through a problem step-by-step and identifying imaginative solutions. We see that this step-by-step approach is popular in business ethics, and various scholars have tried to incorporate a variety of philosophical approaches into a single model that they believe can help us resolve moral dilemmas.

Process-driven decision-making: a combination of approaches

Figuring out how decision-making works, and developing step-by-step guidance on the process, has been the focus of many business ethics scholars and consultants. Multiple decision-making toolkits and decision-trees advise decision-makers on the required steps of the process and the 'right' (i.e. normative) questions to ask at each step. A quick look at how these decision-trees function reveals their assumptions (see examples at the end of this chapter). In the first place, decision-makers are instructed to gather the 'facts' of the case, to describe the dilemma that confronts them, to come up with a set of options for consideration, to weigh these options with the help of certain normative guidelines, and finally to defend their position by referring to the ethical reasons for subscribing to this specific course of action. Kenneth Goodpaster's case analysis template scan (CAT scan) identifies 'describe', 'discern', 'display', 'decide', and 'defend' as distinct steps that have to be followed in making moral decisions.[15] In each of the steps, normative tests are employed to determine how the case is described, how dilemmas are discerned, and finally which options are decided upon and how they are defended. Goodpaster's model includes justice-based reasoning, duty-based reasoning, outcomes-based reasoning, and virtue-based reasoning. Since this decision-making model seems to combine many normative perspectives in an easy-to-understand methodology, many corporate audiences find it very helpful.

Many corporate decision-trees work in a very similar way. At most of the decision-points, decision-makers are instructed to answer simple 'yes' or 'no' questions: 'Is this legal? Yes or no?', or 'Is this employee under 14 years of age? Yes or no?'. 'If yes, proceed to step 2'. Sometimes there is the option of choosing 'Don't know', to which the decision-tree's advice is 'Try to find out'. The assumptions here are those of rational choice theory, i.e. decision-trees assume that decision-makers can gather the necessary information, are capable of weighing options, and have the time to do so. But even the proponents of bounded rationality, or those arguing for the importance of emotions in the decision-making process, still assume that options can be defined in opposition to one another, and that a proper process and a set of rules by which ethical decisions are made will yield an ethical result.

The problem with these assumptions is that it makes ethics a mere device that is 'instrumental' in management decision-making. It seeks to make ethics an easy set of rules, instead of confronting the decision-maker with some real ethical problems. Furthermore, it pretends that the right recipe will always lead to the perfect result. Continental philosophers would raise serious objections to this blind faith in the process and in the instrumental use of moral reasoning, to which we now turn.

Continental responses

The way that business ethics approaches moral decision-making can be challenged on various fronts. The idea with this challenge is not to argue that moral decision-making should not take place, or that thinking about how it takes place is unimportant, but rather that one should understand the limits of such approaches. These limits often have everything to do with the assumptions that these approaches are based on. Some of the main challenges to what is available in business ethics concerning decision-making can be described as: (1) the abdication of individual responsibility that often characterizes rule-driven approaches to ethics; (2) the loss of specificity that enters by means of universal formulations and overgeneralizations; and (3) a risk that is inherent in both (1) and (2), instrumental reasoning makes ethics 'handy' in business while refusing to ask real ethical questions.

The problems of rule-driven moral decision-making

Within organizational theory and critical management studies, the instrumental use of philosophy to help firms devise clear-cut decision-making structures has met with some serious criticism.[16] In most cases, these critics draw on continental philosophers in formulating their objections. The most prominent figures they draw on are Emmanuel Levinas (1906–95) and Jacques Derrida (1930–2004), as well as the sociologist Zygmunt Bauman (1925–), who does much to draw out the ethical implications of Levinas's and Derrida's work.

Zygmunt Bauman's resistance to moral rules and codes lies in the fact that he believes that these instruments of moral guidance undermine and even efface the possibility of moral responsibility. For Bauman, rules are dangerous because they undermine the moral impulse. When one sees a child in danger, one would immediately sense the obligation to help, without deliberation entering into the equation. He draws on Levinas to argue that the problem with codes and rules lies in their appeal to universality, which undermines the possibility of a singular response. Levinas made it clear that ethical responsibility is not something that someone else can do for you. It is a matter of responding to the person in front of you, or, as Levinas would put it, to the face of the 'Other', in a uniquely singular way. Bauman places the blame for irresponsible actions on the depersonalization that takes place when we dissolve the unique individual response into the 'all-embracing we'.[17] He argues that the 'we' can never simply be the plural form of 'I' when it comes to ethical responsibility. This is why some scholars have been notoriously critical of drawing on Levinas to describe corporate responsibility – it threatens to make the same mistake of talking about collective responsibility in the same terms as a uniquely individual ethical response.[18] Why is this a problem? In the first place, the 'we' glosses over the specific relationship between 'me' and the 'other' individual whose face confronts me with the need for a very specific response. The second and related problem is that others are lumped together as 'them', or described in terms of categories, such as 'migrant labourers' or 'child labourers', which makes it impossible to recognize and respond to the specific needs of individuals within these groups.

Scholars in critical management studies point out further dangers of approaching ethics by means of routinized rules. The first charge that these authors make is that the decision-making process that business ethicists often employ allows people to hide behind the rules in their consideration of moral issues, and hence never to take responsibility for the outcomes. As Clegg *et al.* indicate, the infamous defence of Adolf Eichmann, the very efficient Nazi administrator responsible for dispatching Jews from the city centres to the gas chambers, is a case in point. Eichmann's defence was commented on at length by Hannah Arendt in her book *Eichmann in Jerusalem: the Banality of Evil*. Arendt argued that Eichmann confronts us with the very real question of how it was possible that someone that seemed so ordinary, so hard-working, so much like us, was responsible for the death of thousands of Jews. In his defence during the trials in Jerusalem, Eichmann argued that he was just following orders, and actually being quite diligent and precise in the process. The fact that he played a role in killing real human beings simply never occurred to him. These considerations weren't included in the list of things he had to do as part of his job. Now, we can argue that this is not what decision-trees do – of course they require us to ask some ethical questions as part of our work in organizations. But what continental philosophers would help us understand is that the way that these questions, as well as the information guiding their answers, are set up may be part of the problem.

Derrida's thinking about moral decisions

Undecidability

The philosopher Jacques Derrida made us aware of the fact that for a decision to exist in the first place, it cannot be something that is fully determined by the rules or procedures by which it is reached. If this were to be true, it would cease to be a decision.[19] If decisions were in fact foregone conclusions that could be identified via a set of steps or rules, we could programme computers to make those decisions for us.[20] In fact, they would not be decisions any longer – just formulas that contain within themselves predetermined answers. For Derrida, the idea of a decision relies on the possibility of undecidability, i.e. on the existence of a real choice that cannot be calculated in advance. It is important not to confuse undecidability with indecision or an unwillingness to make decisions. John Caputo explains that undecidability is not the opposite of decision, but the condition of its possibility that underscores how difficult the decision is.

A further problem lies in the fact that decisions are guided by options, which are phrased either as oppositional alternatives, or at least as mutually exclusive sets of alternatives. Undecidability not only causes us to waver between the two 'either–or' options, but it also makes us realize there is no clear break (*de-cidere*) between them. Caputo points out that life is a messy affair and that binary terms are often 'contaminated by each other, each inwardly disturbed' by the other.[21] And, in fact, the oppositions and alternatives that confront us often presuppose each other.

Aporias

Business ethicists tend to talk about the choice between two equally important duties as a moral dilemma. It is in the nature of a moral dilemma that you are stuck between a rock and a hard place, or as some say, you are damned if you do and damned if you don't. No matter what you choose, there may be someone who may raise a moral objection against what you decided. This would be close to, yet not completely synonymous with, what Derrida describes as an *aporia*. We may describe moral dilemmas as *aporias* that have forgotten their own *aporetic* character, and are now defined in terms of a certain oppositional logic uncritical of the co-contamination of those very oppositions. As such, it is a kind of metaphysical blind-spot.[22] This would explain why many business ethicists seem to prefer dealing with moral dilemmas rather than *aporias* – they want to offer decision-making tools to help us out of the discomfort of a dilemma, or at least offer us some immutable set of reasons for choosing one option over the other. Derrida wants to maintain the discomfort.[23] When Derrida writes about a moral decision, he describes it in terms of a struggle or an 'ordeal'. In fact, Derrida describes the instant of decision as madness. He talks about how any decision is haunted by the ghost of undecidability. This 'ghost' resides in our decision, and unsettles any kind of self-assurance that we may have regarding the fairness, honesty, or beneficence of that decision.[24] If that were to disappear, the decision would cease to be a decision and the 'fairness' or 'honesty' that we may have striven for in making the decision would be lost as well. This is the conundrum – that something like justice always eludes our grasp, and if it would cease to do so, it would no longer be justice.[25]

It is not that business ethics has taken no account of the fact that resolving a moral dilemma has its costs. Business ethicists would argue that this is just the necessary price of the decision, and whether you are a utilitarian or a deontologist, you can make good arguments for why you chose (a) over (b). What business ethicists can't fully account for, however, is that the 'ghost' that haunts the decision is not just the external ramifications of the decision, i.e. who gets hurt, how much it costs in terms of both money and reputation, etc., but rather that what is haunting lies *in* the option that was decided upon itself.

One of the ways in which Derrida tries to explain the functioning of *aporias* is to talk about specific concepts like 'the gift', 'forgiveness', or 'hospitality'. For example, Derrida points out the difficulties in giving a real 'gift'. He goes so far as to suggest that 'the gift' is ultimately impossible.[26] For something to be a gift in the real sense of the word, it must be given without the expectation of any form of reciprocity. If one gives a gift and receives something in return, the gift ceases to be a gift and instead becomes one element of a transaction. Even a simple 'Thank-you' note can serve to build in a kind of reciprocity that would destroy the 'pure' notion of the gift. Still, gifts stubbornly remain part of our everyday interactions.[27]

Is it possible for us to acknowledge the cold economic rationality inherent in all of our social interactions? This may seem like a radical position, but there are many that doubt the possibility that human beings are capable of selfless behaviour. In fact, adherents of the theory of psychological egoism argue that all decisions are self-interested, and that even the most self-sacrificing individuals or philanthropists do what they do for their own sake. They would argue that even Mother Teresa lived the way she did because of the rewards that she expected to receive in the afterlife, or for the satisfaction of being seen as a good person. Even those philanthropists who never disclose their good deeds derive internal pleasure from them.

If one thinks of the types of objections against corporate social responsibility, it becomes possible to understand the problem. The problem with corporate social responsibility donations or gifts is that they operate within a calculative framework of what the corporation stands to gain in return; hence, they are not gifts at all. Anonymity and no benefit would make them true gifts, but what corporation would give gifts if those were the terms? Also, the rationale for an ethics programme that maintains that the corporation has financial benefits through reputational value, undermines the possibility of ethics. If we want to leave a place for ethics, gift-giving, forgiveness, and hospitality, we must acknowledge that these notions in and of themselves contain impossibilities. Yet the impossibilities should not prevent us from pursuing these things. They only come into being in the messy realities of life, and hence they are never the full embodiment of 'ethics', 'forgiveness', or 'giving' – they never render these notions completely present.

Why does Derrida want to maintain the discomfort of the decision? Why remind us of that which haunts our decisions? Remember, he does not want us to avoid making the decision; he just wants to make us less comfortable with it. Now this may seem like a pretty bad deal he is making us here. So what could the benefit be? Derrida's thought may make us more skeptical about the way we construct various options to choose between, as well as of the 'rational reasons' we offer in defence of our decisions. What happens in the construction of alternatives? As was pointed out earlier, decision-trees assume that individuals using them have the capacity for rationality and access to all the information and time required to make the decision. What they do not take account of is that these individuals receive information regarding the relevant facts of the case, as well as the options that they have to choose among or between, from sources with specific power interests.

Instrumentality as preoccupation with goals or purposes

What we see here is that pursuing ethics as something that has mere instrumental value will undermine ethics as an immediate moral response. Instrumental reasoning is directed at some kind of purpose, or end (*telos*), and hence is calculative and deliberate. Yet a teleological structure underpins so much of our society, and especially of our business lives, that it is very difficult to think about anything in other terms. This happens as part of the simplest business decisions and the most complicated moral dilemmas. There is always a process by which options are identified, weighed, and chosen, even if that happens intuitively, as some philosophers contend. If undecidability is circumvented through rules and procedures, we are not forced to confront the hidden *telos*, or goal, that has already slipped into our thoughts, affects, or intuitions.[28] No framing of a dilemma, or gathering of the 'facts', is ever value-neutral, nor is any construction of the alternatives that we choose between. In each case, it would be possible to identify a certain *end* that is always already present in each aspect of our decision-making. In his essay, 'The ends of man', Derrida plays with the double meaning of the word *end*, namely end as goal, and end as final termination, which in the case of human beings is death.[29] Our relation to our own death or limits informs the values and power interests inherent in facts, acts, and decisions. He wants to make us aware that all of our theories speak of certain goals, which by their very nature tend to function as unquestioned and unquestionable truths, i.e. they operate in a metaphysical way. In organizations, the options in decision-making and the way facts are gathered and weighed always already speak of very specific power interests and purposes, and if they cannot be identified and questioned, they bear a metaphysical character as well.

Now you may ask: why is this goal-directedness a problem? Surely all of us have goals that we are pursuing as individuals or groups – especially since we are all rushing towards our own death and have only so much time to do all the things we want to do? Without goals, surely society would come to a standstill? These are all valid objections. However, the point here is not so much to get rid of the teleological structures, but to understand how they function and to guard against falling into certain patterns of instrumentality without giving it a second thought. These teleological structures could take the shape of a powerful corporate mantra, a suffocating organizational culture, or a decision-making model that gets 'agents' to the foregone conclusion that serves the purposes of the corporation. (Recall here the discussion of corporate and individual agency in Chapter 1.) The problem is that if we are unaware of these teleological structures and the way that they may impact our own values, thoughts, and motivations, we can never challenge or revise them. Furthermore, we tend to view our positions, which are always already informed by the teleological structures that we favour, as natural, and hence desirable for everyone all over the world. This is where cultural imperialism starts. It is also where ethical responsiveness/responsibility ends.

Intentionality

This relates to another important implication of Derrida's thoughts on undecidability, i.e. its ability to confront us with the issue of intentionality. As such, it offers some insights into the limits of rationality and subjectivity that we confronted earlier on in the chapter. This is an issue that he explores in both his early and later work.[30] In Derrida's earlier work, he reflects on the ability of speakers to communicate what they intend. In order for communication to succeed, signs (i.e. words, marks, sounds, gestures) have to be able to be repeated, and with each repetition, what is being communicated is different. This is what Derrida refers to as the iterability of any sign, or word. Things only make sense in relation to other things, and hence any conceptual description of things can only function as such if it is repeated. Though each repetition of the same concept draws on the similarities across various iterations, each iteration is also different. Repetitions are never 'pure'; they always lead to alterations.[31] Derrida never argued that an individual who speaks, writes, or makes decisions has no intentions, but he did warn us against thinking about intentionality in simple terms. Derrida's work helps us understand that the 'intentions' of an author, speaker, or decision-maker have to be understood as open to many contextual influences, and also to many possible interpretations. This also has implications for how our subjectivity operates, or who we are as agents.

In terms of the concepts that we employ in business ethics, it is important to take account of this iterability as well. If someone says, 'Do not bribe!', they are drawing on some notion of 'bribery' that is operative in any such statement, but the ethical intent – which is never fully present in that statement in any self-identical way – can never be said. Hence, one can intend to say something about bribery, but can never be sure that the injunction against bribery is understood in exactly the same way as it was intended. We should note that Derrida is not saying that there is 'pure' intent, and misinterpretation of that intent, but rather that *all* language defies the possibility of the existence of such clear-cut content. In his concept of *différance*, Derrida points out that the meaning of any concept is always deferred (postponed), and always different.[32]

What are the implications of this for moral decision-makers, i.e. the subjects, or agents, who believe that they consider certain options and make a conscious choice? Though not denying the existence and role of consciousness, Derrida points out that the consciousness of the speaker or agent does not fully determine meaning; instead, it is how the act of speaking, deciding, or acting is performed that determines meaning in ways that we can hardly fathom. In fact, the way that we perform a certain speech act, like 'Do not bribe!', may in itself contain, or be haunted by, exactly that which that specific imperative opposes.

Implications for decision-making in business ethics

At this point, it may be helpful to consider a few practical business examples, which may allow us to think through the various implications of what Derrida argues. Let us return, for instance, to the issue of child labour, which has been an important topic for business ethics scholars and civil society activists alike. Many theoretical criticisms of child labour employ both consequentialist and non-consequentialist reasoning to describe child labour as an immoral practice. Yet, in reaching this conclusion too quickly, these well-meaning scholars and activists bracket certain important moral questions in order to place the equally important moral question of avoiding harm to children at the forefront. It is clear that from both deontological and utilitarian perspectives, children should not be harmed. What studies into child labour indicate, however, is that, in trying to avoid harm to children, other bad consequences arise and other principles are sacrificed.

For instance, in a study of how child labour was eradicated in the production of soccer balls in Sialkot, Pakistan, the complex nature of giving a moral response to a moral dilemma became clear.[33] In a bid to eradicate child labour, all home-based soccer ball manufacturing operations were closed down, and all workers had to work in closely monitored factories. This had all kinds of pernicious effects. For instance, many women lost their livelihood. Women could not afford to be away from home all day, nor did they want to work in a factory environment that has a social stigma and perpetrated unfriendly, discriminatory working conditions. The researchers also found that all the focus on 'the protection of children' allowed the manufacturers to hide the fact that they were not paying other workers a living wage. Add to this the fact that children, when asked, indicated that abolishing all child labour did them no favours, and one sees how difficult the dilemmas we confront are. What has to be taken into account is that in developing countries, children who lose their jobs do not go back to a childhood of school, sport, and slumber parties – they often have no option but to turn to prostitution, crime, or begging. Another case of this problem is AIDS-ridden communities in sub-Saharan Africa, where children as young as 13 are often the head of households after the death of their parents. What we see in the case of child labour is that the differences in the meanings of concepts such as the 'good life' or 'childhood', in different contexts and at different times, are not at all acknowledged. Also, by focusing on one injustice, such as child labour, the injustice of unfair wages and gender discrimination is hidden from view. What seems to happen is that the ever-troubling nature of a moral *aporia* and the difficulty of finding an appropriate moral response are avoided. These are actually made impossible to recognize by the self-congratulatory claim that a moral good, i.e. the elimination of child labour in Pakistan's soccer ball manufacturing industry, has been procured. Real individuals, i.e. the women and children that require a response from us, are often effaced, i.e. they have no voice or real presence in our deliberations because of our simplistic commitment to principled rules.

Another issue, which presents an interesting perspective on the implications of Derrida's theories, is that of corporate gift-giving. The specific type of gift-giving we will focus on here is the ever-pressing challenge that corporate managers have in explaining to their employees the difference between a gift and a bribe. We saw above that Derrida considers the gift as one example of an *aporia*, i.e. it is the very impossibility of the gift that makes gift-giving possible.[34] This may sound paradoxical, but it allows us to take a critical look at some of the rules that corporations suggest their employees follow in accepting gifts. In the first place, it should bring us to consider whether any corporate gift can in fact be a gift in the real sense of the word. Even when the gift is a 'Thank-you' for something the corporation received from another stakeholder, or something it offers to build good relationships with stakeholders, it would be an act that attests to reciprocity and hence undermines the concept of the gift itself. But the fact that most of the gifts we give or receive fail to pass the test of non-reciprocity does not mean that we should stop giving or receiving them. What it does suggest is that we can become more aware of the teleological structures that underpin the way we think about an everyday practice like gift-giving. Gifts are given for a purpose that may make an ethical statement long before we start employing normative tests to determine whether it is appropriate or not. There is clearly instrumentality at work here, and, though we may not be able to avoid it, we should at least seek to see it for what it is and not let certain practices become so routine that they take on a life of their own. Furthermore, it challenges us to ask a number of other questions

Box 5.1	BP's self-approval test for the acceptance or giving of corporate gifts

In addition to applying the principles above, ask the following questions to determine whether a gift or entertainment is appropriate.

(1) Intent – is the intent only to build a business relationship or offer normal courtesy, or is it to influence the recipient's objectivity in making a business decision?

(2) Materiality and frequency – is the gift or entertainment modest and infrequent or could it place you (or the other party) under an obligation?

(3) Legality – are you sure that the gift or entertainment is legal both in your country and in the country of the third party?

(4) Compliance with the other person's rules – is the receipt of the gift or entertainment allowed by the recipient's organization? Special care must be taken when dealing with government officials, since many countries do not allow officials to accept gifts or entertainment.

(5) Transparency – would you be embarrassed if your manager, colleagues or anyone outside BP became aware of the situation? If so, there is probably something wrong.

(6) Hypocrisy – are you adopting double standards? We should only offer what we would be comfortable accepting (and vice versa).

regarding the typical ways that corporations suggest we think about normative tests.

When one looks at corporate guidelines on gift-giving, it becomes clear that corporations seek to guide employees' discretion in moral decision-making by suggesting a certain number of normative tests, which includes (1) intention, (2) materiality, (3) legality, (4) compliance with rules, (5) transparency, and (6) hypocrisy. (See BP's guidelines on gifts in Box 5.1.) Now, already at (1) we see that we will have much to consider from Derrida's point of view. How does one determine the intent of the person or company offering the gift? If it is true that the actual act of giving (the performance of the act) itself is important in establishing the meaning of the giver employing a certain sign, and that there is no 'intent' that can be made fully present, how can we follow the corporation's rule here? If a corporate gift arrives with a note saying 'With compliments from M R Corporation', how is the giver's intent to be established? It is already extremely difficult, if not impossible, to do this in the case of an individual. In the case of the corporation, the problem is exacerbated by the distance between the giver and the receiver, which marks the impersonality of much of corporate gift-giving (like computer-printed cards with electronic signatures).

The second problem with the first corporate guideline is that it states that if the intention of the person offering the gift was to influence a business decision, it would be an unacceptable intent, but if it were merely for relationship-building, that would be acceptable. In creating these two options, one would assume that they create an 'either/or' question with clear answers. The way in which BP's alternatives are framed makes it very clear what the problem is. How can one be sure that the establishment of a business relationship does not also imply that objectivity will be lost? Building a relationship can surely be as much of an 'investment', i.e. something done with the expectation of yielding some benefit in future, as a bribe? In fact, do all relationships not endanger the 'objectivity' of decision-making in business?

Moving on to the second corporate guideline, i.e. that of materiality, we are confronted with the tricky problem of the meaning of terms like 'modest' which, like all language, is iterable and value-laden. The self-test asks us to consider whether this is a modest gift, given infrequently. If so, it will be acceptable to receive it. But the question is how a term like 'modest' is to be defined in any clear sense. If we take the idea of *différance* into consideration, a modest gift may be perceived and received differently. The one factor is time, the other the difference that creeps in at every repetition of a sign. The meaning of 'modest' is postponed, and can be quite different in different cases. One can never capture it completely. If a sales representative is having a very bad day, a simple bunch of flowers from a supplier may still be modest, but modest here has a very different meaning on the next day, when she barely notices the flower delivery while happily working on an exciting project. As Derrida would explain, the given object and the act of giving both alter the meaning of the act every time it occurs.[35]

Legality seems to be one of the most clear-cut guidelines that a corporation can impose. If something is illegal, one would tend to accept that it is clearly wrong. However, this discounts not only the fact that some laws can be immoral, but also makes it less likely that the individual will be morally responsible beyond what is required by the law. If you were working in Apartheid South Africa and you knew that your company's big donation to fund the Apartheid government's latest township project close to mines was completely legal, would it then become unimportant to ask moral questions about supporting segregation in this way?[36]

The fourth step of the self-test requires of us to be responsive to the context within which we are operating when thinking about gifts. The way BP phrases this is 'in compliance with the other person's rules'. Is it an acceptable practice in that specific country, or the specific company? Again, the problem is the way in which the existence of a rule blunts the individual's own moral responsiveness to the problem. In this specific case, there is also the danger that 'when in Rome, you do as the Romans do', i.e. conforming to another person's sense of what is appropriate rather than asking difficult questions about whether it is in fact the right thing to do in the specific circumstance. Routine conformance to rules is a danger that we have come across many times in this chapter. It creates patterns of behaviour that influence 'intention' in ways that are often hard to identify, yet cannot be denied.

The test of transparency is often employed to guide corporate employees' decision-making. It is also referred to as the 'sunshine test' – if something cannot be brought to light without shame, it should not be done. The obvious objection to this test is that it assumes a certain cultural homogeneity in terms of agreement on what is considered shameful. What is also important to consider, however, is whether the word 'transparency' itself does not have certain *aporetic* implications. The opposition that seems to be assumed is that between making known and keeping hidden; but again, the two alternatives codetermine and contaminate each other.[37] Transparency sheds a certain light on a specific issue, but can only do so by glossing over something else. For example, in a holding structure, the mother company may want to render the economic and social performance of the daughter company transparent by focusing on numbers. Lots of facts and figures are generated in the pursuit of this 'transparency'. But this transparency hides as much as it discloses. The inefficiency of social audits is a case in point here. Sweatshop conditions often persist regardless of all the data generated and the expensive audits done.

The last guideline that we encounter in BP's gift-giving policies is the requirement that one should not be a hypocrite, i.e. offer something that your company would not have allowed you to receive, nor take something that you know your company would never have offered. The standard here is one of consistency, which is highly prized in many decision-making models. The question here is whether the test of consistency always allows for individual moral responsiveness. Consistency can very easily function as yet another routinized standard or rule that nobody thinks twice about. For instance, just because my company routinely takes customers out to very expensive sporting events, am I allowed to take the same gratuity from a supplier? For a small company supplier, it may be a huge investment, and with it comes great expectations, which will not even occur to me if I am just comparing what seem to be apples with apples.

We therefore see that in these guidelines, the same concerns keep cropping up. The loss of individual responsiveness, specificity in decision-making, and glossing over the implications of seemingly mutually exclusive options, all undermine ethics as such. In business ethics, we should always guard against rules or guidelines that make ethics seem easy, because, by definition, it is not.

So what may be the alternative? Well, if we were to come up with a new set of tests, procedures, or normative questions, we would be stepping in exactly the same trap as many business ethicists have done before us. The best we can do is to suggest, with Clegg *et al.*, that organizations seek to create more opportunity for undecidability to be an acceptable aspect of any decision. This is not to say that decisions should not be made. Of course not! A case could, however, be made for organizations creating more room for dissent and discussion of how options are phrased and what they imply. What is important here is the acceptance that the decision is never completed, or done with, when a certain course of action has been chosen. A decision is always something that has to be pondered over time. It challenges us to an ongoing process of questioning, wondering whether we could not have done better. Also, every decision is haunted by what it excluded and hence it is always in a sense incomplete. It also becomes part of our history and our future. We are made who we are as a result of our decisions – developing the capacity for moral responsiveness demands an ongoing process of consideration and reconsideration. Organizations should not allow individuals to hide behind the rules. In fact, challenging the rules should be encouraged, because it may get people to think about why the rules are there in the first place.

Conclusion

In this chapter, we have explored the most prominent philosophical approaches to moral decision-making in business ethics. Both utilitarianism and deontology rely on the existence of rational moral decision-makers, but we soon discovered that 'rationality' might not exist in the way that many philosophers, economists, and other scientists assumed. We explored alternatives that include the roles that emotion, intuition, and a variety of other influences play in decision-making, and studied the process-driven approaches to moral decision-making that seek to help us through the decision step by step.

The problem with all these models, however, soon became clear. Standardized decision-making models have become 'tools' to make decision-making easier, and may have undermined ethics as such. Zygmunt Bauman's rejection of rule-driven ethics was helpful in understanding that individual moral responsibility and ethical obligation is lost if one relies on rules to make decisions. Jacques Derrida's made us aware of the fact that for something to be a decision in the first place, it cannot be made through clear-cut procedures and calculations. If that were possible, it would no longer be a decision. Derrida's description of *aporias* also casts doubt on the clear-cut way in which alternatives are framed as a choice between two or more alternatives that exist in opposition to one another. Derrida's objections to the positioning of alternatives in binaries or even trinaries could bring us towards an awareness of what we are in fact doing when we develop certain 'options'. Undecidability is not hesitation in the face of opposing options, but it is an unsettling of the oppositions themselves.

The way in which critical management scholars like Hugh Willmott, Stewart Clegg, Martin Kornberger, Carl Rhodes, and Campbell Jones reflect on the implications of Derrida's thought for organizations makes us aware of three possible dangers, i.e. the loss of specificity that comes about as part of gener-alizing universals, the abdication of individual responsibility in rule-following, and the instrumentalization of ethics in order to attain particular goals.

In the last part of the chapter, we explored what the implications may be of Derrida's positions for the employment of corporate guidelines on gift-giving. We also explored the kind of practices and predispositions that could offer alternatives to the way in which many corporations approach decision-making. It is, however, important not to reinscribe the same old problem in our new suggestions, hence we must allow ourselves to remain aware of the ends, the all too human purposes, inherent in even our most caring proposals.

NOTES

1 J. S. Mill, *Utilitarianism*. Whitefish, MT: Kessinger Publishing (2004).
2 I. Kant, *Groundwork of the Metaphysics of Morals*. Mary Gregor (trans.). Cambridge: Cambridge University Press (1998).
3 J. Webber and R. Derry, 'Cognitive moral development', in Robert W. Kolb (ed.), *Encyclopedia of Business Ethics and Society*. Thousands Oaks, CA: Sage Publications (2008), 333.
4 M. Nussbaum, *Love's Knowledge, Essays of Philosophy and Literature*. Oxford: Oxford University Press (1990), 79.
5 M. Nussbaum, *Therapy of Desire*. Princeton, NJ: Princeton University Press (1994), 88.
6 R. ten Bos and H. Willmott, 'Towards a postdualistic business ethics: interweaving reason and emotion in working life', *Journal of Management Studies* 38 (6) (2001), 769–93.
7 Aristotle, *The Nicomachean Ethics of Aristotle*. D. P. Chase (trans.). New York: E. P. Dutton (1911).
8 R. Solomon, *Ethics and Excellence. Cooperation and Integrity in Business*. Cambridge: Cambridge University Press (1993).
9 C. Jones, M. Parker, and R. ten Bos, *For Business Ethics*. London: Routledge (2005).
10 G. P. Lantos, 'Bounded rationality', in Kolb, *Encyclopedia of Business Ethics*, 187.
11 Opportunity cost is defined as what you must give up to get what you want.
12 P. Werhane, *Moral Imagination and Management Decision-making*. New York: Oxford University Press (1999).
13 A. F. Sanders, *Michael Polanyi's Post-Critical Epistemology. A Reconstruction of some Aspects of Tacit Knowledge*. Amsterdam: Rodopi (1988), 10.
14 *Ibid.*, 104.
15 K. Goodpaster, 'Teaching and learning ethics by the case method', in N. E. Bowie (ed.), *The Blackwell Guide to Business Ethics*. Malden, MA: Blackwell (2002), 117–41; see also K. Goodpaster, *Conscience and Corporate Culture*. Malden, MA: Blackwell (2007), 227.
16 C. Jones, 'As if business ethics were possible, "within such limits"', *Organization* 10 (2) (2003), 223–48 and 'Theory after the postmodern condition', *Organization* 10 (3) (2003), 503–25; S. Clegg, M. Kornberger, and C. Rhodes, 'Organizational ethics, decision making, undecidability', *Sociological Review*, 55 (2) (2007), 393–409; R. ten Bos, 'Essai: business ethics and Bauman ethics', *Organization Studies* 18 (6) (1997), 997–1,014; H. Willmott, 'Towards a new ethics? The contributions of poststructuralism and posthumanism', in M. Parker (ed.), *Ethics and Organizations*. London: Sage (1998).
17 Z. Bauman, *Postmodern Ethics*. London: Blackwell (1993), 47.
18 See in this regard the special edition on 'Levinas and business ethics', *Business Ethics: a European Review* 16 (3) (2007).
19 J. Derrida, *The Gift of Death*. Chicago, IL: University of Chicago Press (1996), 24.
20 J. Derrida, *Limited Inc. Afterword*. Chicago, IL: Northwestern University Press (1990), 116.

21 J. Caputo, *Against Ethics. Contributions to a Poetics of Obligation with Constant Reference to Deconstruction*. Bloomington, IN: Indiana University Press (1993), 63.

22 N. Lucy, *A Derrida Dictionary*. Malden, MA: Blackwell Publishing (2004), 1.

23 J. Derrida, 'Force of law: the "mystical foundation of authority"', in D. Cornell, M. Rosenfield, and D. Grey Carlson (eds.), *Deconstruction and the Possibility of Justice*. London: Routledge (1992), 24.

24 *Ibid.*, 24.

25 J. Derrida, *Specters of Marx*. New York: Routledge (1994), 30.

26 J. Derrida, *Given Time: 1. Counterfeit Money*. Chicago, IL: University of Chicago Press (1992), 29.

27 *Ibid.*, 42.

28 *Telos* is the Greek word for goal, and hence teleological means that which is directed to certain goals.

29 J. Derrida, 'The ends of man', *Philosophy and Phenomenological Research* 30 (1) (1969), 31–57.

30 Initially, in works like *On Grammatology* (1974); *Margins of Philosophy* (1982), and *Limited Inc.* (1988), Derrida explores the nature of language and subjectivity, and later on, in texts like *Specters of Marx* (1994), *The Gift of Death* (1995), *On Forgiveness*, and the *Politics of Friendship* (1997), he draws out the ethico-political implications of his theory more clearly.

31 J. Derrida, *Limited Inc. Afterword*, 145.

32 J. Derrida, '*Difference*', in *Margins of Philosophy*. Chicago, IL: University of Chicago Press (1982), 3–27.

33 F. R. Khan, Kamal A. Munir, and H. Willmott, 'A dark side of institutional entrepreneurship: soccer balls, child labour and postcolonial impoverishment', *Organization Studies* 28 (2007), 1,055–77.

34 Derrida, *Given Time*, 37.

35 *Ibid.*, 49.

36 Derrida actually has much more to say about the relationship between law and justice, and we may get back to this in another chapter.

37 One could also bring in Derrida's discussion of the relationship between responsibility and secrecy. Responsibility involves the kind of resistance and dissidence that keeps itself apart from what is publicly declared. See Derrida, *Gift of Death*, 26.

6

Organizational justice

CARL RHODES

Goals of this chapter

After studying this chapter you will be able to:

- articulate the ways in which management and business ethics researchers have approached and developed the idea of organizational justice;
- distinguish between the three most commonly defined dimensions of organizational justice: distributive justice, procedural justice, and interactional justice;
- explain how management and business ethics researchers have understood the relationship between justice and ethics;
- explain how the concept of justice is understood in the philosophy of Emmanuel Levinas and contrast this with the concept of justice used in the literature on organizational justice;
- consider the radical implications of Levinas's understanding of justice for organizational justice;
- understand the meaning of the term *pleonexia* and its relationship with justice in organizations.

Introduction

The idea of justice is philosophically sophisticated, culturally embedded, and practically enacted. Justice has had massive uptake in Western society and culture over some thousands of years. With this longevity 'justice' is part of our normal lexicon and is an idea that forms the basis of some of the main national and international institutions that serve to govern our everyday lives. The breadth of juridico-political structures that regulates interactions between people in both national and global settings rests in one way or the other on the idea of justice. Business organizations are also sites where the idea of justice is meaningful, and it has therefore not escaped the attention of those who study, theorize, and practice management and ethics – especially in terms of the just treatment of employees.

This chapter concerns itself with the idea of 'organizational justice' that has been developed and researched in relation to business ethics as well as in organization and management theory more generally. In this tradition justice is understood as the extent to which people at work perceive that they are treated fairly by their organizations, their managers, and their colleagues. Following an introduction to this understanding of organizational justice, the chapter turns to continental philosophy. We contrast the 'justice' in 'organizational justice' with Emmanuel Levinas's (1906–95) theorization of the relationship between ethics and justice. This reveals a very different perspective: one that does not so much attend to whether people perceive they are being treated justly, but focuses on how one might be able to be just to others.

For 'organizational justice', the principle subject is one who seeks not to be treated unfairly by others. For Levinas the principle subject is one who desires to treat others justly. This Levinasian inversion suggests that justice is not so much (as the organizational justice literature would have it) about how one feels, but more about who one is in relation to others. To assist with this discussion the ancient notion of *pleonexia* – a greed that desires one to have more than one's fair share – is deployed as a conceptual motif that draws the various discussions of ethics and justice together.

Justice: then and now

In his *Nicomachean Ethics*, Aristotle praises justice not just as one virtue among others, but as a 'complete virtue'.[1] Justice is complete because it is a virtue that is focussed not on the self, but on the self's relation to others. Aristotle writes:

> The worst person is the one who exercises his wickedness in relation to himself and in relation to his friends, and the best is not he who exercises his virtue in relation to himself but the one who exercises it in relation to others, since this is the difficult thing to do.

This exercise, for Aristotle, occurs in two possible ways. Firstly, justice is concerned with lawfulness and the obedience to the rules and norms governing the community or society in which one lives. So, to break the law is to commit an injustice, just as today if you break the law then you must account for your actions in court, as well as take any punishment or retribution seen as befitting the injustice committed. Similarly, if you transgress the rules and regulations set out by the organization that employs you, for example by stealing from that employer or engaging in fraudulent activity, you can expect to be held to account as to whether your acts are just as judged by those rules. By this account the just person is a 'good citizen' – one who lives by the rules set out for the community.

Secondly, Aristotle associates justice with fairness and equality – virtues he sees as being distinct from lawfulness. This form of justice is concerned with the distribution of those resources, for example goods and money, that are to be shared among a community. Again, we can see Aristotle's definition of justice at play in contemporary society and organizations. For example if you find out that your colleague at work is earning more money that you for doing the same work you might claim that this is unfair on the basis that you expect remuneration to be distributed in a manner commensurate with tasks, duties, and responsibilities. This has, of course, been the subject of much debate, for example, in relation to the persistence of pay inequalities between men and women (see Chapter 7 for further discussion).

What the two types of justice distinguished by Aristotle share is the idea that injustice occurs when a person furthers their personal advantage at the expense of someone else or at the expense of the community. Injustice is connected to greed, covetousness, and selfishness in place of living reasonably with others – a condition that Aristotle identifies as *pleonexia*. Often translated into English as 'greed', pleonexia literally translates as 'having more', and takes in the nuanced meaning of 'getting more than one's share'.[2] *Pleonexia* is a desire for excessive gain for oneself that is beyond the fair share that might be reasonably expected. This is an unjust desire because realizing it can only be at the expense of those others who would receive less than their fair share or would have what belongs to them taken away.[3]

Fast-forwarding somewhat rapidly from Ancient Greece to modern America, it is John Rawls's 1971 book *A Theory of Justice* that is commonly regarded the most influential contemporary theoretical reflection on the topic.[4] Rawls recognizes Aristotle's argument that achieving justice includes refraining from *pleonexia*, articulated by Rawls as:

> gaining some advantage for oneself by seizing what belongs to another, his property, his reward, his office, and the like, or by denying a person that which is due to him, the fulfilment of a promise, the repayment of a debt, the showing of proper respect, and so on.[5]

It is against this that we can consider Rawls's famous dictum of 'justice as fairness'. Moreover, given that justice is concerned with the relations between people and that these relations are organized institutionally, 'justice is the first virtue of social institutions'.[6] For Rawls, justice is not so much an individual virtue, but rather a social ideal to which actual societies might aspire in terms of cooperation between their citizens. Rawls is interested in how justice relates to principles that are required for the just structuring of society. His definition of justice as institutional fairness makes sense for organizations as well, provided we consider an organization as a form of micro-society or community. Businesses and states may be different, but those differences do not necessitate political theories of justice from being irrelevant to them.[7] Notwithstanding the heat of the debates over the meaning and practice of justice, both ancient and modern, we can consider organizational justice in relation to how organizations set up a quasi-social contract that distributes rights, duties, and benefits to its employees in a manner that is fair and equal.

What is organizational justice?

Despite the long-standing philosophical concern with justice as an individual virtue and an ideal form against which to structure society, in terms of the study of ethics in business and management, the meaning of justice has taken a somewhat different direction. The term 'organizational justice' has been institutionalized as meaning the extent to which people perceive their organizations to be fair – the key focus being the personal perception of justice of the self (rather than for anyone else). Research on the topic has therefore concentrated on the nature and effects of these self-related perceptions.[8] Cropanzano and Stein summarize: 'organizational justice research generally understands fairness [justice] as a subjective perception by a person or persons . . . a workplace event is "fair" or "unfair" because an individual or individuals believes it to be so'.[9] Key issues, for example, include fairness as it relates to remuneration and benefits, recruitment, promotion, and work allocation. The concern that has become privileged in the conceptualization of such a justice is not so much whether a person acts in accordance with the virtue of justice, or whether organizations themselves are just, but whether people feel that others are treating them unjustly. *Pleonexia*, if we can import the term into this field, is considered as a feature of other people who might seek to unfairly attain a disproportionate share of the fruits borne on the organizational tree. The self here is not involved in a reflection of their own just treatment of others, but only with how they are treated by others. In a sense, and not without irony, justice is regarded as a matter of self-interest.

Research into justice and fairness perceptions in organizations has gathered steam since the 1960s and 1970s up to a point where it is now an established mainstay of business ethics and management theory. This development is one built, in part, by distancing itself from philosophical approaches such as the two introduced above. Those who research organizational justice make a sharp distinction between what they see as the central interests and goals of philosophical theories of justice and their own organizational/social scientific interests. Outlining the history of research into organizational justice, Colquitt *et al.*, like most other theorists in this area, make this distinction with an élan for extreme generalization.[10] They argue that the array of philosophical approaches can be collapsed into one commonality – that they 'share a common prescriptive orientation, conceiving of justice as a normative ideal'. Conversely, they sum up the social scientific study of justice as being supplemental to the philosophical by employing a 'descriptive approach' that focuses on 'justice not as it should be, but as it is perceived by individuals . . . of what people perceive as fair'.[11] For the organizational theorist qua social scientist an 'act is just because someone perceives it to be just'.[12] Moreover, despite the anti-normative proclamations, normativity lies not far beneath the surface in the sense that this research commonly assumes justice to be a 'good' thing that should be advocated by organizations; the overtly descriptive intent renders this normativity unexamined and untheorized.

The notion of the perception of fairness has dominated organizational justice research to the extent that justice appears less as an Aristotelian virtue or a Rawlsian social ideal, and more as a valid construct that can be identified as a variable related to other (non-justice related) organizational outcomes. With this 'scientization', organizational justice comes to be understood not as something to be pursued for its own good or for the good of others, but because, for example, it discourages disruptive behaviour in organizations, promotes the acceptance of organizational change, reinforces the sense of trustworthiness in people in positions of authority, reduces people's fear of being exploited, provides an incentive for worker cooperation, and satisfies individual needs for control, esteem, and belonging.[13] Fortin sums this up:

> Organization justice is concerned with people's fairness perceptions in their employment relationships . . . Justice perceptions have been shown to have effects on people's motivation, well being, performance, attitudes, behaviours and other outcomes relevant for organizations and organizational members.[14]

What we have is not so much a concern with justice as an individual or communal ideal associated with the relations between people in society, but rather as a matter of perception – if it feels good, it can't be injustice! The focus is invariably on whether people perceive that others are being unjust to them. By definition we have a type of upside-down *pleonexia* at play – justice relates to me ensuring that I do feel that I am not being taken advantage of by others, rather than relating to any social or ethical feeling, thought, or action on my part towards others. In other words, the social scientific approach to justice is one of 'me first' and based on my 'perceptions'. As such, it runs the danger of inadvertently supporting a solipsistic and relativist idea of justice – one robbed of the social and political by its obsession with individualized perceptions and their numerical aggregation.

Dimensions of organizational justice

The most common way that organizational justice is understood is in terms of its separation into three distinct 'dimensions' – those of distributive justice, procedural justice, and interactional justice. The identification and study of each of these dimensions has developed progressively since the early interest in organizational justice in the 1950s. Until the 1970s the research efforts were almost exclusively dedicated to distributive justice and the ways in which resources were or were not perceived to be distributed fairly in organizations. From the 1970s through to the 1990s this was augmented by a concern for procedural justice and the extent to which employees felt that the processes used for the distribution of resources were administered fairly. Building from the 1980s was interest in a third dimension, that of interactional justice, which concerned how fairly people felt they were treated in interpersonal interactions in organizations.

Distributive justice

One of the earliest approaches to organizational justice focussed on whether people in organizations believe that the various resources and rewards available through work are distributed fairly among employees. A central concern has been the distribution of pay and other benefits, especially in terms of whether these distributions are based on a principle of merit. Although people do not hold it unjust for some to be paid more than others, what does come under scrutiny is whether this unequal distribution is fair. That is, are those people who deserve more financial reward (for example on account of greater responsibility, higher qualifications, or greater productivity) being rewarded fairly? Such issues are very much at play in the public sphere as well, as can be seen in debates over the fairness of excessive executive compensation (see Chapter 7).[15]

Studies in distributive justice usually cite the equity theory of Adams from the 1960s as being the main source of theoretical inspiration.[16] Adams's theory suggested that in assessing their own work, people calculate an input/output ratio that involves an assessment of the rewards they receive as related to the contributions that they have made. This ratio is then compared to how one imagines the same ratio would be for others. It is posited that those who believe they have a higher input/output ratio than others would feel angry and cheated; those who have a lower ratio would feel guilty; and those who have a relatively equal ratio would feel satisfied and fairly treated. Justice, in this sense, can be understood as the absence of *pleonexia* being manifested either by myself or by others.

Equity theory also suggests that people will seek to adjust their own input/output ratios so as to achieve a sense of fairness, for example reducing their work output if they feel that their ratio is too high. So, for example, if I feel that I am doing a lot more work than one of my colleagues but being remunerated equally, then I can be expected to perceive that an injustice is being perpetrated. To remedy this situation I might seek to get a pay rise, but if that is unsuccessful I would wilfully withhold parts of my labour so as to equalize the input/output ratio in accordance with the norm. Studies by organizational justice researchers suggest that in work situations, equity theory holds strong sway as a predictor of people's behaviour.[17]

Procedural justice

From the 1970s researchers focussed attention not just on the perceived fairness of outcomes themselves (distributive justice) but also on their perception of the fairness of the processes and procedures by which those outcomes were arrived at (procedural justice). This attention to procedural justice followed on from research by Thibaut and Walker who showed that unfavourable distributions were more likely to be accepted by people if they perceived that the process by which those distributions were made was fair.[18] Thibaut and Walker's research was in relation to decisions made in courts of law. This was applied and generalized elsewhere, especially in relation to conflict resolution at work. The uptake of this is that if one is in a conflict with a colleague at work and that a process perceived as fair is used to resolve that conflict, then one might accept an unfavourable outcome for oneself.

In another influential study, Leventhal *et al.* identified six attributes of fair processes: consistency, freedom from bias, accuracy, representativeness of stakeholders, correct ability, and consistency with ethical standards.[19] In relation to the study of management, this has led to a focus on procedural justice as it is, or is not, present in a variety of procedures including performance appraisals, pay allocation, recruitment and selection systems, employee retrenchments, and work allocation processes. So, for example, if three people apply for one position and the best candidate gets the job, it might still be perceived as unfair if the recruitment process involved a powerful manager bullying the others involved to make the decision that the manager wanted in the first place, instead of following due process.

Interactional justice

The third dimension of interest to organizational justice researchers is 'interactional justice' – the extent to which people feel that they are treated fairly in their interactions with people in organizations and the nature of the communication involved in those interactions. Building on the seminal work of Bies and Moag, particular attention has been on how people are treated in their interactions with managers and others in positions of authority.[20] On this basis, interactional justice is defined as 'the fairness of the interpersonal treatment that one receives at the hand of authority figures'.[21] A central implication of this research is that even though a person might feel that they get their fair share of an organization's rewards, and that they are treated equally in terms of process, they might still believe that they are subject to an injustice if managers treat them with disdain or disrespect. Injustice may also be perceived by those people who feel that information is being withheld from them, or that decisions about them are made without their involvement or consultation.

With interactional justice, justice becomes aligned with being treated with dignity and respect, as well as the extent to which people are furnished with information and explanations about decisions which affect them.[22] Together this sums up the four main concerns of interactional justice:

- truthfulness – the extent to which one perceives that those in authority communicate with honesty;
- justification – the extent to which one perceives that decisions are adequately explained;
- respect – the extent to which one perceives that one is being interacted with in a manner that is polite and respectful; and
- propriety – the extent to which one's interactions with those in positions of authority is free from prejudicial statements and inappropriate questions.[23]

Ethics and organizational justice

Surprisingly, research and writing in organizational justice has not traditionally made explicit connections between justice on the one hand and ethics and morality on the other. This omission, however, has not been total and there has been some recent attention paid to this matter. Fortin has observed that when organizational justice researchers do turn their attention to ethics, most commonly it is done so at an individual level, for example in relation to what is taken to be an individual's moral principles and their level of moral development.[24] The 'behavioural ethics' perspective generally adopted by organizational justice researchers sees ethics as being all about 'individual behaviour that is subject to or judged according to generally accepted moral norms of behaviour'.[25] The key distinction is between justice, regarded as perception of fairness, and morality, regarded as those normative standards against which the relative goodness of those acts is judged. In this vein ethics is reduced to a set of 'moral principles' used to judge right from wrong. A commitment to justice is regarded as one such principle.[26]

The implication of behavioural ethics for organizational justice is that rather than seeing justice simply as a matter of people securing their own material self-interest, it might also be possible that people feel they are treated unjustly at work on account of their moral principles having been transgressed. This would mean that in some situations 'justice is sought for its own sake' rather than for the sake of instrumental control or social relationships.[27] Such an approach does not seek to identify or problematize the source or nature of moral principles, but it does go to suggest that justice may be valued for reasons other than a desire to ensure that a person gets their own fair share of whatever resources are being divided up. In Aristotelian terms this would mean that *pleonexia* is a 'vice' on its own terms such that it is to be policed and eradicated on purely moral terms. The relationship that is posited is one where justice and ethics are related to each other in the sense that 'moral thinking impacts fairness perceptions and associated behaviours'.[28] So, for example, one might oppose gender discrimination at work not just because of its personal effects, but because one believes it is wrong. Moreover, such a moral belief could lead a man to support decisions, such as positive discrimination, that could well mean the potential of fewer opportunities for him personally.

Continental philosophy and organizational justice

So far, we have reviewed the dominant meaning of the term organizational justice as well as its relationship to behavioural ethics. This is a justice understood in terms of a person's perception of fairness at work, whether that justice be distributive, procedural, or interactional. Despite the considerable attention that researchers have paid to these issues, when those who study organizational justice consider the meaning of justice, ethics, and morality, they do so with scant reference to philosophy, let alone to continental philosophy. As explained earlier, philosophical inquiry into justice is seen as a largely different exercise to what the social scientists do. Philosophers, organizational justice researchers maintain, are normative and prescriptive about justice. Social scientists, on the other hand, are descriptive and explanatory. This distinction might be a convenient counterpoint on which to mount a loose justificatory rhetoric for one's own scholarly endeavours, but it does not hold up to scrutiny. It may be true that much philosophical thought on justice seeks to develop ways to think through justice in terms of individual conduct, personal virtues, and social arrangements. But it is also true that philosophy has attended to exploring the very meaning of justice without normative intent. Moreover, whereas organizational justice researchers see 'justice' and 'morality' as somewhat separate, with moral convictions having been largely deemphasized or ignored in organizational justice research, in philosophy ethics and justice are often theorized as being intrinsically related.[29]

A turn to continental philosophy can deeply question, if not usurp, the assumptions of organizational justice research, especially if that turn is in the direction of Emmanuel Levinas. Levinas most avowedly does not perform the sort of philosophy that can be classified under the headings of normative or prescriptive. As Critchley describes, against the tradition of legislative approaches to moral philosophy, Levinas is best understood as a 'moral perfectionist' who expressly theorizes the relationship between ethics and justice. Levinas argues that 'ethics has to be based on some form of basic existential commitment or demand that goes beyond the theoretical strictures of any account of justice or any socially instituted ethical code'.[30] Further, Levinas argues that justice itself must be justified on the basis of a more primary understanding of ethics. As we will now go on to explore, this has significant implications for how we might understand justice in organizations.[31]

Ethics and other people

To begin to understand a Levinasian notion of justice, we must first consider what Levinas means by ethics. Levinas does not use the term ethics to refer to some system of procedures, practices, or dispositions that can ensure a sense of 'goodness' or righteousness on the part of one who adheres to them. Neither is he developing a set of prescriptions intended to guide or inform how people might live or respond to situations in which they find themselves. Levinas's project is to delve into the very meaning of ethics. He himself described his work by saying that his task 'does not consist in constructing ethics' but rather in trying 'to find its meaning'.[32] This meaning, for Levinas, does not start with the self as it would for a person who asks first whether she has been treated unjustly by other people in their penchant for *pleonexia*. Levinas's ethics begins with 'the Other' – the actual other person who is thought of not as another of me but as radically different and unknowable.

Levinas contrasts knowledge (which involves categorizing the other person in one's own terms and thus reducing them to being a part of one's own systems of thought) and ethics (which involves accepting that the other person is beyond those systems). By this account ethics 'cannot be reduced to an act of knowing in which truths are constituted'.[33] Hence, the other is 'irreducible to objective knowledge'.[34] Instead of being a subject of categorization and comparison, each other person is approached in terms of their extreme particularity and incomparability – their infinite distance from the self, even when that other person is in physical or social proximity. Managers might, for example, categorize and identify employees in terms of their occupation, job function, gender, and age. They might even subject people to personality and aptitude tests so as to assess their suitability for various jobs. All of this knowledge, however, serves to make employees comparable and manageable. For Levinas, this type of management knowledge would not be about ethics because it is always about putting people into preestablished categories. An ethical approach to another person would resist such categories, being instead open to the other person as being so unique that they can never be adequately 'captured' by them. That is not to say that identifying people through categories is 'unethical'. Instead what flies in the face of ethics is the assumption that one can use such common categories to get to the heart of who another person really is.

Levinas refers to the other person in terms of 'face' and his ethics is expressed in the face-to-face relation – a relation where the other person can never be totalized as a known entity identified by categories of knowledge. I am face-to-face with the Other but that Other is at the same time always infinitely different to me and not able to be known by me. For Levinas, it is the awe inspired by this infinity that gives rise to ethics, and to a relation with the other person not based on reciprocity, self-advantage or exploitation, but on generosity, respect, and humility. The ethical relation is akin to a relation of love, never reverting to the pursuit of one's own advantage, the furthering of one's own needs, or even the expectation of reciprocity. The ethical self is not only void of *pleonexia*, but also does not judge the Other on those terms.

Levinas's ethics rest on the idea of a self who is never self-sufficient, but is always, in his terms, held hostage by the Other to whom that self holds itself responsible. In his major work, *Totality and Infinity*, Levinas explores this relationship in terms of what he refers to as *enjoyment*.[35] Enjoyment, understood as the self pursuing their own needs without concern for anything or anybody that exists outside of that self, is, for Levinas, an egoism. Enjoyment is, however, essential. With it, the self achieves a separation that enables it to regard itself as a self – as an individual who is separated from other individuals and who has a sense of identity.

Levinas explains that 'the separated being affirms an independence that owes nothing, dialectically nor logically, to the other who remains transcendent to it'.[36] The separated self holds no concern for other people, pursuing instead their own enjoyment: 'in enjoyment I am absolutely for myself... entirely deaf to the Other'.[37] This 'pursuit of happiness', however, is ruptured by the presence of the other person, and the invocation of a desire for something outside of ourselves that goes beyond selfishness – a recognition that 'I am not alone'.[38] For Levinas, ethics is a 'calling into question of my spontaneity by the presence of the Other' – a calling into question of my own selfish enjoyment.[39] Ethics contrasts with enjoyment because ethics is a generosity, a welcoming of the Other and a hospitality – that is not to say that it is necessarily unpleasant, but rather that it is not motivated by the pursuit of selfish pleasures without thinking about the effects of that pursuit on others. Ethics does not lead one to seek the unfair share of *pleonexia*, nor even to seek justice for oneself. Ethics puts the other person first. With it, the other person is not just a thing that can be exploited for the purposes of one's own enjoyment or happiness, but is an Other who disrupts such a quest for exploitation. Ethics is not about self in enjoyment, but about the relationship between people in interaction with each other and where the self becomes vulnerable to the Other and desiring of the Other. This ethics begins when the self, in its enjoyment and freedom, is called into question. '[G]oodness consists in taking up a position in being such that the Other counts more than myself'.[40] In ethics, *pleonexia* is reversed – my share is that which I have to give freely and generously.

Ethics at work

Levinas's philosophy is not just an abstract theorization of ethics in relation to otherness, it also speaks directly to the purpose and functioning of work and organizations. In *Totality and Infinity*, Levinas suggests some important distinctions between work, labour, and commerce. In one sense the very enter-prise of organized work immediately affronts ethics. This affront is realized in the forms of exchange that characterize work – forms of exchange that render people already substitutable and stripped of their difference and uniqueness. In work we have 'a humanity of interchangeable men, of reciprocal relations [where] [t]he substitution of men for one another, the primal disrespect, makes possible exploitation itself'.[41] With commerce and the language of money all difference can be reduced to a form of symbolic and economic exchange which renders everything comparable – a trading of selves through peaceful systems of exchange and agreed reciprocity. With work and commerce the face of the other dissolves in an 'imperialism of the same'.[42]

This imperialism is one where, at work, the right of each person to unique-ness is nowhere to be found. This is so when '[a]t worst employees are viewed as numbers and not as people, let alone "faces" in the Levinasian sense'.[43] Moreover management practice is replete with attempts to judge and monitor employees through a mode of reasoning that 'starts with a category and ends with a judgment relative to that category . . . [and] through this move the "Oth-erness" of the Other, the exceptional, is neatly bracketed and "covered over"'.[44] In organized work the other person is reduced to comparative categories par excellence. Even well-meaning managerial interventions such as diversity man-agement can be understood as 'an attempt to capture the elementary experience of self and other in the sphere of managerial control' by locating people into comparable groups of difference rather than regarding each other person as mysterious and unique.[45]

There are other things at play here as well. Even though work and commerce might affront ethics through anonymization, it would be premature and simplis-tic to say that relations of work are unequivocally unethical. For Levinas, 'we live from our labour which ensures our subsistence; but we also live from our labour because it fills (delights or saddens) life'.[46] Labour and the possession that it affords serve to stave off the uncertainty of the future – one has to live from one's labour in order to be at home with oneself – in order to have a self which can receive the other in the first place. In other words:

> relations of work are necessary for ethics . . . not as an accidental feature of certain socio-economic arrangements, nor a curse that might signify a fallenness from a truer state, labour is 'access to the world' that enables the goals of need to be met such that the elements of the world can be brought back to the 'dwelling' of home and human welcome.[47]

Although work might recast the ethical approach of the other person in terms of reciprocity and exchange, the labour that goes into work also creates the very conditions through which the other person can be welcomed; the condition for ethics. Hospitality requires a home from which one can be hospitable. The disjuncture, then, is that economic life is the basis for relations with the other person, the basis on which the self can be maintained such that it is able to relate to that other in the first place. In Levinas's words 'no face can be approached with empty hands and closed home'.[48] Cast in this way, it is not so much that ethics is absent at work, but rather that there is an ethical tension between the anonymizing force of commerce and exchange and the hospitality that they can make possible. Again, if we turn our attention to diversity management we see an organizational focus on accounting for and managing various forms of difference among employees, most notably gender and racial difference. At the same time, however, the ethical impetus of respecting difference that might have informed a drive to diversity management, when practised, involves categorizing people into groups, and hence rendering the people in those groups as being 'the same' rather than different.[49] The practice of diversity management thus exists between a desire to respect the difference between people, and the practicality of managing that difference by placing people in stereotypical categories.

With Levinas we see that ethics is not just a matter of the mind, but relates directly to embodied material experience in a world with others. It is through work, and the rewards of work, that people sustain themselves – quite literally 'earning a living'. And this living that is earned is a precondition for being able to be for the other person; a precondition that provides one with those things that can be given. And not just material things; one cannot give of oneself unless the being of that self is sustained and empowered. It is here that organizations garner an ethical purpose; that purpose being:

> that of gathering and organizing the exercise of power so that needs – of 'others' – can in some way be provided for. Maximising this power – without waste, special pleading, and in the interests of the production of genuine goods – is a necessary implication of recognizing, in the one for the Other, the other Others who are also 'the stranger', 'the neighbour'. They, too, all of them, must be recognized and attended to. This drive – the drive to find structures, which express this imperative – is the drive for justice.[50]

Impossible justice

Levinas's ethics are conceived in the context of the self and the other person being situated in the relationship of the face-to-face. In organizations, as in other social settings, things get much more complex than this original scene of ethics. Organizations are always contexts in which people encounter a multitude of others such that any ethics or generosity to the one Other is always undermined by the presence of the other Others. In Levinas's terms, the critical point is the one where the third person enters the scene previously characterized as the face-to-face between the self and Other:

> It is the third party that interrupts the face to face of a welcome of the other man, interrupts the proximity or approach of the neighbour, it is the third man with which justice begins.[51]

It is here that we begin to understand the meaning of justice as it extends from Levinas's ethics. Justice is where ethics becomes both practical and impossible. In attending to the one Other, the self, in ethics, retains an infinite responsibility to that singular Other. The entry of the third party shifts attention from the face of the one Other to the face of the other Other as well as to the relationship between the two Others. The infinite responsibility can thus no longer be considered as a possible direction because in the face of all of the Others responsibility will always be both divided and obscured. This need for sharing – to give to more than one Other, and thus to divide what is given between them – is where justice rears its head. In sociality, and thus in organizations, justice becomes necessary to enact ethics. Simultaneously, justice can never live up to those demands for ethics. Justice always ushers in the requirement for ethics to be compromised:

> Justice is necessary, that is comparison, coexistence, contemporaneousness, assembling order, thematization, the visibility of faces, and this intentionality and the intellect, the intelligibility of a system, and thence also a copresence on an equal footing as before a court of justice.[52]

This is a justice that is still concerned with fairness – concerned with the idea that all of the people might be treated equally in comparison with one another. If, as for Levinas, ethics resides on the absolute Otherness, and hence uniqueness, of each and every other person, then this comparison immediately confronts ethicality. What this suggests is that while ethics gives rise to justice, it is also in tension with it. While organizational justice researchers might posit a clear difference between justice as perceived fairness, and ethics as internally held moral principles, with Levinas both the meaning and relationship between ethics and justice has changed as well as complexified. For Levinas ethics always comes first and is the only basis on which justice can be justified. Fairness then must have an ethical basis in generosity as well as realizing that that basis is always already compromised.

Justice demands 'a comparison of what is in principle incomparable'.[53] The ethical questions that this poses are:

> How is the unbounded and infinite obligation that I have to the (one) Other to be rendered compatible with the equally incalculable being and claim of the other Other, the third person? How are the rights of all the others to be respected within the infinite relation of the face-to-face?[54]

Levinas presents justice, in our case organizational justice, with an ethical conundrum – ethics demands justice to be applied in social situations, but justice, by its very nature can never live up to the ethical demands that invoked it. It is certainly not enough to revert to the assumptions made by organizational justice researchers that the main concern should be with whether or not people perceive that they themselves are being treated justly, and where ethics merely refers to those normative standards against which such a perception is rendered. To do so individualizes justice to such an extent that the attention is always on the self and its egoistic pursuit of enjoyment and avoidance of *pleonexia* in others. By this account organizational justice is that which does not prevent me from pursuing my enjoyment as judged by personal moral standards that require no justification outside of myself. Organizational justice is egoism and not really a justice at all – it is a justice 'all about me'.

To revert to the terms of the organizational justice literature, justice understood as fair distribution among the many requires procedures – it requires a sort of law, norm, or policy through which justice is to be achieved. As discussed earlier, justice is concerned with ensuring that everyone is treated in the same way, so, for example, that different people doing the same job all get paid the same wage, that workloads are allocated equally among people, and so forth. The dilemma that Levinas's ethics brings into such procedures, however, is that in treating everyone the same, the ethical relationship with the other person (regarded as absolutely singular rather than a member of a group) is inevitably compromised. It is in this sense that Jacques Derrida, in the same vein as Levinas, has elucidated so clearly that justice can only be experienced as an ethical *aporia* – an impasse or dilemma that defies resolution while demanding attention:

> How are we to reconcile the act of justice that must always concern singularity, individuals, irreplaceable groups and lives, the other or myself as other, in a unique situation, with rule, norm, value or the imperative for justice which necessarily have a general form, even if this generality prescribes a singular application in each case? If I were content to apply a just rule, without a spirit of justice and without in some way inventing the rule and the example for each case, I might be protected by law (*droit*), my action corresponding to objective law, but I would not be just.[55]

What this means is that by applying the same just rule to all, one is not really making an ethical decision about how to treat each other person, but risks dealing with people in a formulaic fashion. Think, for example, of a manager who has been instructed to retrench two of their ten staff as part of a downsizing exercise. If all of these people are doing the same job, then the 'rule' presented to the manager might be that they have to select the two poorest performers for retrenchment. But what if that same manager realizes that one of those classified as a 'poor performer' relies on their salary to singularly support a large family? What if the manager also knows that several of the so-called better performers are all single and would easily find alternative employment if they lost their jobs? The dilemma that such a manager might face would be whether to consider the individual needs and circumstances of the people involved – to treat them as 'individuals' – or just to apply the rule and retrench the 'poor performers' irrespective of those circumstances.

What Derrida calls for is not the law of justice but the 'spirit of justice' – the ethical spirit by which each other person is treated with absolute particularity and not in comparison with any other Others. Justice demands that one decides how to act but can never prescribe the action to be taken – this includes not just the following of rules, but the personal decision of whether to follow the rules. To be just, then, is not just about abiding and enforcing the rules, but involves a relationship with those rules. The dilemma that this creates in practice is:

> the experience of that which, though heterogeneous, foreign to the order of the calculable and the rule, is still obliged – if it is of obligation that we must speak – to give itself up to the impossible decision, while taking account of laws and rules.[56]

When justice is at stake a decision cannot exactly be predetermined by any procedures, rules, or laws that preexist it – otherwise to make a decision would mean that no ethics were at play in that decision being made. Just like the manager in the hypothetical example of downsizing, the rules and expectations of the organization are not adequate to the actual situation that is encountered. The manager must decide herself what to do, even if that decision ends up being to apply the rule strictly. Moreover, if ethics requires the others to be approached in full acknowledgement of their ethical uniqueness they cannot just be treated as substitutable beings against which the same standards can be blindly applied. At least to some extent the moment of justice is a moment where the case at hand does not apply to any given rule even though those rules are there to inform the decision.

Institutionalizing justice in person

What does this mean, then, for organizational justice? The starting point for a response to this question is the requirement to manage the inevitable but necessary tensions between ethics and justice as well as to recognise that it is the presence of those tensions that are the sign of ethical self-questioning in organizations.[57] Justice is not about assessing perceptions so as to judge whether this or that action or decision is classifiable as 'just'. Only in the anxious space between ethics and justice can an ethically grounded justice be approached and pursued. Moreover, in this space, justice and procedural or administrative arrangements that seek to pursue it can never justify themselves on their own terms. Justice is no measure for the justness of justice. Justice is only meaningful when it is justified from the outside – justified by the externality of the other person in whose name it is exercised. For managers, justice is not limited to treating everyone equally and without favouritism, it must also be done in the name of caring for other people.

With Levinas, ethics is not to be considered as a separate domain from justice, it is not an independent 'construct' – instead, ethics is the very basis on which justice is justified. Without ethics there can be no justice. This is exemplified through the management practice of generating codes of conduct to ensure just and ethical business dealings. Such codes may be a mere window dressing to obscure other practices, and they may also be a response to legal requirements experienced as little more than a burden of doing business, but this need not be the case:

> Some [codes] do arise from a prior determination on the part of the orga-
> nization to decide and adhere to practices that are genuinely grounded in
> ethics – such as transparency in decision making, or arm's-length commercial
> arrangements. Insofar as these principles express a commitment to fairness
> in the exercise of the organization's power, codes can have an origin in ethics.
> However, when this informing basis is forgotten and the principles outlined
> in the code function as mere formal requirements on or limitations to the
> action of individuals, they cease to establish and secure the organization as
> ethically sensitive.[58]

This focus on codes of ethics and codes of conduct has indeed been a vexed issue for business ethicists. On the one hand, organizations commonly use such codes as an exclusive means through which to assert their own ethical status. On the other, they might easily be dismissed as being bureaucratic practices that have little to do with any 'real' sense of ethics, especially if they do not manifest in responsibility.[59]

Beyond the obvious case of ethical codes, the quality of justice does not just lie in the extent to which individuals perceive that they personally are treated justly, but more in the nature and use of the principles by which an organization governs its (often considerable) exercise of power. And these principles, whether explicit or implicit, cover all aspects of organizing, especially those that do not go by the name of ethics. Think of strategy development, human resource management, industrial relations, downsizing, and outsourcing, as but a few examples. All of these practices involve decisions that affect others in material ways, and are therefore open to scrutiny in the name of ethics and justice. There is more to organizational justice than codes and laws – this is so even in cases where those codes may be an unreflective organizational response to calls for justice, where those codes may be designed to serve purposes other than justice, and where those codes might even relate directly to ethical relationships with others.[60]

It is all exercises of power by organizations that are open to scrutiny by justice, and it is the principles that govern that exercise – as manifest in the very act of management – that constitute a system of justice. For justice itself to come alive one must concern oneself with the enactment of these principles in concrete situations – that is in being face-to-face with the Other in an act of what Introna calls 'singular justice'.[61] It is not 'moral principles' that inform judgements about justice, but the extent to which those principles are applied to the unique encounter with other people. Again the question is not about whether I perceive the Other as being unjust towards me, but about how I exercise my responsibility to be just to the Others:

while justice requires rules and principles, they must always be rendered, by me, before the Other in proximity, face to face, in a relation of honour. Justice should not here serve as an excuse for distancing or blinding me from the Other, nor one of ethically absolving me from the exercise of power . . . I must render the rule in person, to the Other, and to all the Others. I must do this in order to constitute the original ground of authority from which all justice springs and without which it is a parody of justice.[62]

This original ground is ethics – the ethical unknowability and non-comparability of the Other; the Other to whom one is wholly responsible in generosity and charity. Justice will always violate this ethics, but it must never forget ethics if it is to retain its own justification. For an organization to be able to continually put itself and its practices into question – to review and rearticulate its commitment to justice through conversation and consideration – is the harbinger of a justice that will always be 'to-come'. The task is not to achieve justice once and for all, so, for example, that it can be ticked off a managerial checklist, reported on in an annual report, or submitted for an award for corporate responsibility. Rather, justice comes alive in organizations when people are open to questioning the justness of their own practices on an ongoing basis, and open to engaging with the difficult ethical dilemmas that those practices portend. Justice demands more than good intentions, and although sourced in a recognition, respect, and generosity to the Other, it 'cannot be realized without objective institutions [that] permit people to liberate themselves from all participation in unjust structures or customs'.[63] The question for organizations is not only about whether employees perceive them to be just, but whether members of the organization are willing and able to be included within and participate in forms of organizational self-critique and ethical deliberation that are institutionalized as part of everyday practice.

Conclusion

We started this chapter with a consideration of the ancient notion of *pleonexia* – a desire to have more than one's fair share. What we have seen is that the driving concern in the organizational justice literature is for people to not feel that their share of the organizational pie is being eroded by others and their *pleonexia*. From this perspective an organization is just only when people stop complaining about the injustices done to them. While proclaiming itself as anti-normative, organizational justice's practical prescriptions to organizations are never far beneath the surface – make sure people don't feel they are being treated unfairly, or else their commitment and contribution to the organization will wane.

As we have seen, Levinas is less concerned with the negative and self-serving justice implicit in 'organizational justice', and more concerned with a positive and Other-focussed justice. Levinas does not use the term himself, but we might say that Levinas worries little about the *pleonexia* of other people. Instead, he is keenly focussed on how the self might approach ethics and justice with a kind of selflessness and generosity void of *pleonexia*, indeed a form of generosity that reverses *pleonexia* through the giving of one's 'share' to others. The ethical subject for Levinas is not groping for justice to be done to it, but rather grapples with the conflict between the ethical impossibility, yet necessity of justice to the Other and the other Others. This is a subject not secure in the pursuit of its own egoistic enjoyment, but one interrupted and fractured by the presence of the other person, and by the demand to do justice to that other.

Pursuing justice, for organizations and the people who manage them, has serious implications. As we have explored, these implications involve scrutiny over every instance where an organization's often considerable power is exercized. For an organization (especially a business organization) to be driven by the generosity that this entails, while almost inconceivable, is ethically necessary. The ethical challenge for organizations is in making justice in organizations conceivable as a horizon of possibility. It is with Levinas that this horizon can be glimpsed. At the risk of being glib, the Levinasian call is 'ask not what justice can do for you, but what you can do for justice'. What an organization can do for justice is a demand that does not quit.

NOTES

1 Aristotle, *Nicomachean Ethics*. Cambridge: Cambridge University Press (1987), 83.
2 The Greek word *pleonektein*, meaning to be greedy, is derived from *pleion* (more) and *ekhein* (have).
3 C. M. Young, 'Aristotle's justice', in R. Kraut (ed.), *The Blackwell Guide to Aristotle's Nicomachean Ethics*. Oxford: Blackwell (2006), 179–97.
4 My concern here is not to provide an overview of the vast philosophical endeavour that has gone into debating the idea of justice, but just to draw attention to some of its central tenets and continuities by highlighting its main contributions from the ancient to the modern. For a comprehensive selection see M. J. Sandel (ed.), *Justice: a Reader*. Oxford: Oxford University Press (2007).
5 J. Rawls, *A Theory of Justice*. Cambridge, MA: Harvard University Press (2005).
6 Rawls, *A Theory of Justice*, 3.
7 For a discussion of the debates surrounding the relevance of political theory to management and business ethics, with specific reference to Rawls, see J. Moriarty, 'On the relevance of political theory to business ethics', *Business Ethics Quarterly* 15 (3) (2005), 455–73. Moriarty is largely in favour of the use of political and moral theory to inform ethical behaviour in business. For an alternative view, see R. A. Phillips and J. D. Margolis, 'Towards an ethics of organization', *Business Ethics Quarterly* 9 (4) (1999), 619–38. For the purpose of this chapter I will not dwell on those debates, focussing instead on the idea of 'organizational justice' in relation to contemporary continental philosophy – the latter not coming under the purview of Moriarty, Phillips, or Margolis.

8 For a detailed review of the nature of this tradition and what goes on within it, see J. Greenberg and J. A. Colquitt (eds.), *The Handbook of Organizational Justice*. Mahwah, NJ: Lawrence Erlbaum (2005). This notion of organizational justice is concerned with justice for employees. Critically important issues of social justice and social responsibility in relation to business behaviour have also been discussed in relation to business ethics; however that is not the focus of this chapter.

9 R. Cropanzano and J. H. Stein, 'Organizational justice and behavioral ethics: promises and prospects', *Business Ethics Quarterly* 19 (2) (2009), 193–233, 195.

10 J. A. Colquitt, J. Greenberg, and C. P. Zapata-Phelan, 'What is organizational justice? A historical overview', in J. Greenberg and J. A. Colquitt (eds.), *The Handbook of Organizational Justice*. Mahwah, NJ: Lawrence Erlbaum (2007), 1–53.

11 *Ibid.*, 3.

12 M. Fortin, 'Perspectives on organizational justice: concept clarification, social context integration, time and links with morality', *International Journal of Management Reviews* 10 (2) (2008), 93–126, 94.

13 Colquitt *et al.*, 'What is organizational justice?', 5–6.

14 Fortin, 'Perspectives on organizational justice', 93.

15 J. D. Harris, 'What's wrong with executive compensation', *Journal of Business Ethics* 85 (1) (2009), 147–58.

16 J. S. Adams, 'Toward an understanding of inequity', *Journal of Abnormal and Social Psychology* 67 (1963), 422–36.

17 J. Greenberg, 'Organizational justice: yesterday, today and tomorrow', *Journal of Management* 16 (1990), 399–432.

18 J. Thibaut and L. Walker, *Procedural Justice. A Psychological Analysis*. Hillsdale, NJ: Lawrence Erlbaum (1975).

19 G. S. Leventhal, J. Karuza, and W. R. Fry, 'Beyond fairness: a theory of allocation preferences', in G. Mukula (ed.), *Justice and Social Interaction*. New York: Springer (1980), 167–218.

20 R. J. Bies and J. Moag, 'Interactional justice: communication criteria for fairness', in R. Lewicki, B. Sheppard, and M. Bazerman (eds.), *Research on Negotiation in Organizations*, 2 vols. Greenwich: JAI Press (1986), vol. 1, 43–55.

21 Z. C. Byrne and R. Cropanzano, 'The history of organizational justice: the founders speak', in R. Cropanzano (ed.), *Justice in the Workplace: from Theory to Practice*. Mahwah, NJ: Lawrence Erlbaum (2001), 3–26, 17.

22 Cropanzano and Stein, 'Organizational justice and behavioral ethics'.

23 Fortin, 'Perspectives on organizational justice'.

24 *Ibid.*

25 L. K. Trevino, G. R. Weaver, and S. J. Reynolds, 'Behavioral ethics in organizations: a review', *Journal of Management* 32 (6) (2006), 951–90.

26 R. Folger, R. Cropanzano, and B. Goldman, 'What is the relationship between justice and morality?', Greenberg and Colquitt (eds.), *The Handbook of Organizational Justice*.

27 Cropanzano and Stein, 'Organizational justice and behavioral ethics', 204.

28 *Ibid.*, 212.

29 *Ibid.*

30 S. Critchley, 'Introduction', in S. Critchley and R. Bernasconi (eds.), *The Cambridge Companion to Levinas*. Cambridge: Cambridge University Press (2002), 1–32, 28.

31 Although not specifically related to the research tradition in 'organizational justice' outlined above, the implications of Levinas's ethics for justice in organizations is something explored in some depth in my work with Damian Byers. The ideas presented in this chapter extend and borrow heavily from that work. See: D. Byers

and C. Rhodes, 'Ethics, alterity, and organizational justice', *Business Ethics: a European Review* 16 (3) (2007), 239–50.

32 E. Levinas, *Ethics and Infinity*. Pittsburgh, PA: Duquesne University Press (1985), 90.

33 E. Levinas, *Outside the Subject*. London: Continuum (1993), xxi.

34 E. Levinas, *Totality and Infinity*. Pittsburgh, PA: Duquesne University Press (1969), 68.

35 *Ibid.*

36 *Ibid.*, 60.

37 *Ibid.*, 134.

38 *Ibid.*, 101.

39 *Ibid.*, 43.

40 *Ibid.*, 247.

41 *Ibid.*, 298.

42 *Ibid.*, 69.

43 R. ten Bos and H. Willmott, 'Towards a post-dualistic business ethics: interweaving reason and emotion in working life', *Journal of Management Studies* 38 (6) (2001), 769–93, 781.

44 L. D. Introna, 'Workplace surveillance "is" unethical and unfair', *Surveillance and Society* 1 (2) (2003), 210–16, 212.

45 B. Costea and L. D. Introna, 'On the mystery of the other and diversity management', in L. D. Introna, F. Ilharco, and E. Fay (eds.), *Phenomenology, Organisation and Technology*. Lissabon: Universidade Catolica Editora (2008), 187–207, 187.

46 Levinas, *Totality and Infinity*, 172.

47 Byers and Rhodes, 'Ethics, alterity, and organizational justice', 244–5.

48 Levinas, *Totality and Infinity*, 172.

49 See S. L. Muhr, 'Othering diversity – a Levinasian analysis of diversity management', *International Journal of Management Concepts and Philosophy* 3 (2) (2008), 176–89.

50 Byers and Rhodes, 'Ethics, alterity, and organizational justice', 239–40.

51 E. Levinas, *Otherwise Than Being or Beyond Essence*. Pittsburgh, PA: Duquesne University Press (1998), 150.

52 Levinas, *Otherwise Than Being*, 157.

53 E. Levinas, *Entre Nous*. London: Continuum (2006).

54 Byers and Rhodes, 'Ethics, alterity, and organizational justice', 245.

55 J. Derrida, 'Force of law: the "mystical foundation of authority"', in D. Cornell, M. Rosenfeld, and D. G. Carlson (eds.), *Deconstruction and the Possibility of Justice*. New York: Routledge (1992), 3–67, 17.

56 Derrida, 'Force of law', 24.

57 Byers and Rhodes, 'Ethics, alterity, and organzational justice', 241.

58 *Ibid.*, 248.

59 S. L. Muhr, 'Reflections on responsibility and justice: coaching human rights in South Africa', *Management Decision* 46 (8) (2008), 1,175–86.

60 C. Jones, 'As if business ethics were possible within such limits', *Organization* 10 (2) (2003), 223–48.

61 L. Introna, 'Singular justice and software privacy', *Business Ethics: a European Review* 16 (3) (2007), 264–7.

62 Byers and Rhodes, 'Ethics, alterity, and organizational justice', 249.

63 A. T. Peperzak, *Beyond: the Philosophy of Emmanuel Levinas*. Evanston, IL: Northwestern University Press (1997).

7

Reward, incentive, and compensation

MOLLIE PAINTER-MORLAND

Goals of this chapter

After studying this chapter you will be able to:

- identify the ethical issues that arise in and through reward, incentives, and compensation practices in organizations;
- understand the limitations of justice-based arguments in dealing with these issues;
- explore the importance of revaluation in rethinking reward, incentive, and compensation in organizations;
- recognize the corporate ethos created through reward structures;
- question the reward and compensation practices employed in corporations.

Introduction

Debating rewards, incentives, and compensation after the financial crisis

With the onset of the financial crisis that hit the world in 2008–9, the question of what constitutes a fair reward for contributions to the success or failure of corporations once again became a matter of fierce debate. In fact, the large bonuses received by executives of some failed companies became the source of moral outrage among politicians and citizens alike. One of the reasons for this outrage is the fact that the compensation paid to some executives seemed to ignore the mistakes they made in running their companies. Nor did it account for the irresponsible, and perhaps even immoral, risks that some took, or of the pernicious effect that it ultimately had on the lives of millions of people around the world. The decisions and behaviour of these highly compensated executives substantially contributed to the 'housing bubble', which ultimately precipitated a domino effect of failures in multiple financial institutions. Many people lost their life savings as a result, yet corporate executives seemed to be largely shielded from the effects of their bad decisions through carefully constructed bonus structures and severance packages, or 'golden parachutes'. It is little wonder, then, that many people began to question whether such payouts were fair or ethical. The compensation that executives receive is, however, only one instance of the way in which reward systems in organizations can have significant ethical ramifications. Besides the issue of executive compensation, the problem of fair reward and compensation in organizations is manifested in controversies about equal pay for equal work, employee stock ownership options, and bonuses and other incentive schemes, as well as in debates around fair performance management and retrenchment processes for all employees.

In this chapter, we will start our discussion by focusing on executive compensation, and the move towards the broader implications of other reward systems within organizations. The reason for this focus is that so-called golden parachutes and other forms of executive compensation like bonuses and stock options have come to represent some of the main points of ethical contention in recent debates. A golden parachute can be defined as a severance package that includes substantial compensation for the possibility of lost earnings in the event of a change in company ownership or changes in, or the severance of, the employment contract. Severance packages also often allow executives to retain their health benefits, travel allowances, retirement funds, and personal benefits such as secretarial staff, after they have left the company. One of the problems with such executive employment contracts is that they are typically agreed upon before an executive joins a company, i.e. before the value of his of her contribution to a company can be gauged.

Some of the recent 'golden parachutes' that have elicited fierce debate, and even legal disputes, include the more than $100 million severance payment that Michael Orwitz received from Disney, the $114 million exit package that Philip Purcell received after being ousted as chief executive officer (CEO) of Morgan Stanley, and the $165 million that compensated Jim Kilts, CEO of Gillette, after his company was acquired by Procter and Gamble.[1] The compensation packages of Goldman Sachs, the company that had to be saved from certain collapse by the US government in 2008, amounted to $3.44 billion. Though the perception is that the compensation of US executives is most outrageous, these kinds of compensation packages are paid out all over the world. For instance, the SABMiller CEO Graham Mackay's package amounted to £6.2 million. In 2009, Porsche's CEO was sacked and got a €50 million bonus. This seems excessive for an executive who has been accused of indebting his company and failing to protect shareholder interests.

The rationale behind such enormous payouts seems to be that they seek to remove considerations of self-interest so that executives are more likely to make decisions that benefit the companies that employ them. Goldman Sachs CEO, Lloyd Blankfein, defended these compensation packages by arguing that the company had trouble retaining its talented staff, and needed these incentives to motivate them to continue to work in the interest of the shareholders rather than pursue outside alternatives. If an executive knows that his own financial future is secure, so the argument goes, he will be more likely to objectively make decisions that are in the best interests of the corporation and its shareholders. It may be argued, however, that if protecting the best interests of the corporation is part and parcel of the job description of any executive then surely objectivity and good judgement should not have to be bought at such a high price. What causes further outrage is the increasing earnings gap between the executive suite and 'average' corporate workers. In the last ten years, CEO pay increased from 100 times the pay of the average worker to somewhere between 350 and 570 times that of a typical worker.[2] Executive compensation packages often include cash salaries of between \$1–3 million per annum, with bonuses of up to fifteen times that amount. The question that inevitably arises is: how can these discrepancies be morally justifiable?

Some explain the large compensation packages by making reference to the fact that, in the US, the principle of 'employment at will' (EAW) guides the relationship between employers and employees. EAW means that, in absence of any other agreement to the contrary, the employment relationship is considered 'at will' and that either party can terminate and/or alter the relationship at any time, for all but illegal reasons. There are some basic legal requirements regarding working conditions, but, beyond that, employers can use their discretion in determining the terms of the employment relationship. For instance, in the case of private companies, employees' contracts can be terminated without an employer having to provide a rationale for the decision, or having to provide the employee with an opportunity to respond to concerns. In public companies, due process is more often than not recognized as an employee right. The reality is that senior executives' livelihoods and privileges are routinely safeguarded through employment agreements, while those of other employees lower down in the pecking order are usually not.

Another assumption that explains why executive compensation has been viewed as an essential part of the employment contract is the reliance on agency theory, which holds that agents will respond optimally to rewards and seek the best possible outcomes for themselves and those on whose behalf they act. Even from the perspective of bounded rationality, rewards clearly motivate agents.[3] Add to this the fact that there is some evidence that certain forms of executive compensation may actually increase the risk of financial misrepresentation, and we have reason to be even more concerned. Jared Harris and Philip Bromily found that a stock option is a form of compensation that display a strong relationship to financial misrepresentation among executives. Whereas bonuses tend not to have an effect on executives' decisions to misrepresent the financial situation of their companies, stock options do have such an effect. This can be demonstrated by the fact that the average options grant (\$5,699,512) is valued at approximately twenty times the average bonus (\$350,000). Stock options influence misrepresentation largely for firms with the highest percentage of compensation options, namely the top third of Harris and Bromily's sample (the average option grant for this group being \$15,100,100). Their research indicated that this effect persists even when sound corporate governance mechanisms are in place to deter such practices. It seems that when big money is at stake, ethics goes out of the window.

The question, from an ethical point of view, is whether the excessive remuneration practices of companies can be morally justified at all. Harris claims that arguments that CEO pay is unreasonable because of the sheer gross magnitude of it, or arguments that view it as unreasonable because of its comparative magnitude, do not go very far in helping us think about executive compensation.[4] The reason why Harris judges these arguments to be unhelpful is because they are based on personal sentiments regarding what is excessive, and hence turn out to be self-referential. What seems excessive to some may not be excessive to others and no single yardstick can easily be found to judge excess. Harris also argues that comparing executive pay to that of typical workers is like comparing apples with oranges. We do not typically compare the salaries of physicians to those of flight attendants, or software programmers to those of taxi drivers. The reason we do not do that, according to Harris, has to do with the fact that the market economy can only function if different jobs, with different educational requirements and differing levels of skills, can be compensated differentially. Instead of provocative arguments around comparative excess and greed, Harris argues for the employment of justice-based reasoning, to which we now turn.

Justice as fairness

For many business ethicists the issue of just reward and compensation revolves around the notion of fairness. This is due in part to the continuing influence of ideas proposed by the American philosopher John Rawls (1921–2002). Rawls argued that, ideally, we need a social and political order that would be fair in the sense that it would give everyone in a particular society a fair chance at a good life. But the question is: how do we know what is fair to all? Rawls devised a way to try and guarantee impartiality and objectivity in determining what is fair. This path consists of a thought experiment called the 'veil of ignorance'. Rawls argued that if we were to be ignorant of the position we would occupy within the social order that we were constructing, we would design a society that would be fair to all. If one would apply this same notion to judging the fairness of corporate reward and compensation practices, one would be required to imagine oneself in a position to design them without knowing in advance whether you will be at the top or at the bottom of the corporate hierarchy, whether you will be male or female, disabled or healthy, formally educated or not, and talented or not. Rawls believed that under these imagined constraints all reasonable people would agree that social institutions and practices have to conform to at least the following principles:

(1) each person is to have an equal right to the most extensive basic liberty compatible with similar liberty for others;

(2) social and economic inequalities should be arranged so that they are both
(a) reasonably expected to be to everyone's advantage and (b) attached to
positions and offices open to all.[5]

It soon becomes clear that, based on a particular reading of these Rawlsian principles, there are some arguments to be made in favour of large executive compensation packages. It could conceivably be argued, for instance, that companies are free to pay executives whatever they like, as long as they do not thereby interfere with the freedom of others to do as they choose. It could also be argued that executive remuneration may be disproportionate to that of other employees, as long as the relevant executives guarantee adequate profit for stockholders, and provided that companies pay fair taxes on their profits. When these basic provisions are met, society on the whole arguably benefits, while nobody is negatively affected. Arguments of this nature are based in part on the belief that free markets are efficient in distributing wealth and resources among all members of society, so that the profit-making activities of some ultimately benefit all members of society. A rising tide, it is claimed, lifts all boats. If this argument holds, then those who are perceived to be central to the success, not only of individual companies, but also of the economy and therefore of society as a whole, could justifiably claim a greater share of the spoils.

While variations of these arguments remain convincing to many, there are both factual and normative objections to be raised against them. The claim, for instance, that the profit-making activities of some always benefit the whole of society is open to dispute. It could be argued that the dynamics of liberal free market capitalism have tended to exacerbate the differences in income between the wealthiest and poorest members of societies worldwide. Such a pronounced widening of the wealth gap often precipitates the disgruntlement of the poor and thereby serves to destabilize society as a whole. Another objection is that the compensation of talented individuals does not always correspond to their success. During the financial crisis of 2008–9, even executives who had demonstrably contributed to the failure of their companies received huge bonuses and other severance benefits. On a normative level, questions can also be asked about the fairness of the distribution that does take place. Is it fair for executives to be shielded from the effects of the financial crisis, while workers inevitably lose their jobs, and investors lose their life savings?

It could conceivably be claimed that the Rawlsian principle, stating that freedom should be guaranteed only insofar as this does not interfere with other people's freedom, has been violated by executive compensation practices. The failure of some distressed companies to adjust their executive compensation practices in lieu of their leaders' role in precipitating the financial crises of 2008–9, as well as the public financing that they received, fails the Rawlsian test of fairness. Irresponsible management practices have clearly curtailed the freedoms of many other people – millions of people worldwide lost life savings, jobs, homes, etc. The effects of a global financial crisis were also much more severe for those at the bottom of corporate hierarchies or in the low-income sector of society. It could therefore be argued, on the basis of the Rawlsian principle, that a society may allow inequalities as long as the most disadvantaged group in society is not negatively affected, i.e. that it is unfair to allow top executives to be paid large bonuses while other employees are retrenched and the taxpayer has to bail out embattled companies. However, the question that has to be asked is whether Rawls would in fact believe that losing one's job is a case of one's freedom being limited. He seems to believe that inequalities resulting from the application of his principles can be solved via other means. For instance, this is reflected in his opinion on whether there should be a minimum wage. Rawls argued that once a suitable minimum is provided by transfers, it may be perfectly fair that the rest of total income be settled by the price system (i.e. the market).

Part (b) of the second Rawlsian principle of justice, which is also described as the 'open position' or 'fair equality of opportunity principle', might hold the strongest injunction against executive compensation, since it is quite clear that not everyone can reach the position of CEO. Yet even this principle has been invoked in defence of executive compensation. The idea that a society should guarantee equal opportunity for all its members is at the basis of what is often referred to as the 'American dream'. Inasmuch as the US is seen as a society that conforms to this Rawlsian fairness principle, the US holds out the promise of social advancement solely on the basis of merit. Those who have faith in this promise therefore insist that anyone can pull themselves up by their own bootstraps, irrespective of who they are, their social background, and their personal circumstances. Failure to do so is, therefore, usually attributed to a lack of application and/or a lack of talent on the part of the individual. Barack Obama's rise from humble beginnings to the US presidency is often cited in support of this view. What is important to note, however, is that this kind of optimistic position was particularly prominent in financial boom times when everyone's faith in the market was intact and people wanted to ride the wave for as long as possible. It has since become clear that though it may be possible for some individuals in exceptional cases to climb the ranks of corporate hierarchies from the most disadvantageous of circumstances, this rise remains effectively impossible for most. In other words, the exceptions do not prove the rule, however compelling and inspirational those exceptions may be.

The phenomenon of the so-called 'glass ceiling' is particularly pertinent in this regard. The glass ceiling refers to invisible barriers, such as unacknowledged chauvinist and patriarchic prejudices, which prevent many women from advancing to positions of power and authority within organizations. Though most corporations claim to be committed to equal employment practices, the dismally small percentage of women in CEO or other executive positions and on corporate boards suggests that there is still a significant difference between what is professed and what is practised within organizations in this regard.

Even if women manage to work their way into positions commensurate with their skills, qualifications, and experience, they are unlikely to earn what their male counterparts do. Researchers continue to find significant pay discrepancies between male and female employees. Even female executives continue to be underpaid compared to their male counterparts.[6] This suggests that the full realization of Rawls's principle of equal opportunity for everyone may yet remain an elusive ideal in most societies and organizations. As such, the invocation of this principle in defence of disproportionate executive compensation is likely to remain controversial.

Though Rawls's justice as fairness principles were aimed at procuring more equality in society, the reality seems to be that the current inequalities in society do not seem to benefit everyone. Rawls would have been the first to point out that most societies fail to conform to his principles. He might also have explained the persistence of these inequalities by pointing out that certain institutions have failed to provide adequate support for these principles to be translated into political and social realities. In fact, as we shall see later on in the chapter, some institutions may have had a decidedly corrupting effect.

Since 2009, debates around the acceptability of executive compensation in the US have led to legislative reform, including tax reform, which restrict corporations' ability to deduct excessive payments of bonuses or golden parachutes. New emphasis on performance pay structures that require risk-prudent decision-making has also emerged.[7] The question, however, remains whether justice-as-fairness principles present our best resources in thinking about executive compensation.

Arguing for or against executive compensation on the basis of Rawls's fairness principles does not seem to lead to conclusive judgements in all cases. One reason for this might have to do with Rawls's assumption that it is possible to judge the fairness of a practice such as disproportionate executive compensation in an unbiased or 'objective' manner. Rawls seemed to believe that once these principles were formulated behind a veil of ignorance, they would be self-evident. But is this truly the case? Consider, for instance, the fact that the justification of disproportionate executive compensation on the basis of Rawls's fairness principles was much less controversial prior to the financial crisis of 2008–9. After the onset of the crisis, however, those very same principles could be invoked to argue that disproportionate executive compensation was unfair and unjust. What this seems to show is that our perspective on the fairness of disproportionate executive compensation may in fact be influenced by our participation in either a favourable or unfavourable economic environment. This suggests that the historic and material context, within which a judgement is made, tends to be significant. However, its significance is usually not recognized until later. Time and change are often required to reveal the limitations and prejudices that pertain to a particular historical perspective. The most well-formulated general principles may not guarantee the equitable interpretation of these principles in all cases. This is why Rawls's fairness principles can be invoked both to support and to criticize disproportionate executive compensation. The specific implications of Rawls's fairness principles remain irrevocably open to interpretation and people inevitably and unwittingly interpret them from the perspective of the specific historical context in which they participate. Friedrich Nietzsche described it thus: 'Lack of historical sense is the original error of all philosophers.'[8]

Role responsibility

We therefore need to start realizing what we always attribute value within a specific historical context. Only then can we determine how what is valued should be negotiated and protected. But who decides what is valued and protected? If valuation were to be merely individual or based on societal context, we would be left with the problem of ethical subjectivism, i.e. the belief that individuals need not justify their decisions or actions to others. This would cause all kinds of problems.

If your teacher were to follow the logic of ethical subjectivism, they could wake up one morning and decide to assign a failing grade to every student paper they read without feeling compelled to provide any justification for doing so. Or they might rise in a somewhat less punitive mood and decide to give 'A's to all the blue-eyed students in the class. No doubt this kind of behaviour would spark an instant classroom revolt. Students would be quick to complain that it is terribly *unfair* for a teacher to choose an arbitrary thing, such as the colour of students' eyes, as the criteria for assigning a grade.

What are essentially at stake here are the grades that students *deserve* for their academic efforts. In your defence, you and your fellow students could argue that the estimation of fair reward should not merely be a matter of subjective judgement. After all, your teacher has assumed a professional role within a formal academic institution. A teacher's professional role demands that they use their skills, training, and good judgement to safeguard a basic good in society, something we all value. In this case, it would be the value of a good education procured through hard work and dedication. You and your fellow students can therefore justifiably expect that your teacher allows only the formal standards of their profession to inform their judgements with regard to your grades.

Arguments of this nature draw on a view of ethics first proposed in Ancient Greece by Aristotle. However, they also have a modern reiteration in what is called 'communitarian' ethics. One of the main proponents of communitarianism, Alasdair MacIntyre, argues that what has gone wrong with ethical arguments grounded in 'justice' and 'rights' is that they have lost touch with the societal framework within which these arguments make sense. He points out that notions of 'justice' always develop within particular social or professional contexts. People's understanding of justice is therefore shaped and informed by the contingencies and dynamics that pertain to the specific social contexts within which they function. Without this context, moral notions are mere words that have lost their meaning.

An important part of communitarianism is the notion of practices, which involve the cultivation of certain norms and virtues within certain societal contexts. *Practices* in and of themselves contain the normative guidelines that have to be followed. MacIntyre's example of such a practice is chess.[9] The chess game is still a contest, it allows for inequalities in skill, and for cunning, but there are certain normative guidelines, for instance those against cheating, without which the game of chess would not make sense. The 'normative' aspects of a practice are considered an 'internal good', i.e. their protection belongs to the game itself. MacIntyre famously claims that something like business can never be a practice, because it seeks 'external goods' like money and status. Despite MacIntyre's insistence that a business organization can never be a practice, one could argue that the professional role of the executive in some respects requires characteristics similar to those a good chess player displays, such as cunning, competitiveness, and concern for the rules of the game (legal boundaries).[10]

Could this idea of internal goods and role responsibilities within a certain practice offer a better guide for dealing with the ethical issues around compensation? The contemporary application of role-specific virtues and duties has become very important in establishing expectations around professional ethics. As a society, we expect professionals to fulfil their role properly by displaying certain virtues and responding to specific moral obligations.[11] We trust professionals to be custodians of specific public goods; legal professionals serve justice and therefore have to be fair; medical professionals protect and nurture our physical well-being and thus have to display the virtue of care; and accountants vouch for the veracity of financial statements and hence have to be honest. If professionals fail to protect these basic goods or neglect these virtues, society can no longer allow them to fulfil this specific role. Arthur Andersen, the auditor in the Enron scandal, serves as an example of how a lack of honesty and failure to protect the public can result in the loss of an auditing practice. The role responsibility of executives is typically defined as 'fiduciary duties', i.e. they are *trusted* to act in the best interests of the companies they serve (*fide* being the Latin word for trust).

From this perspective, one can develop a critical position on the argument, made earlier, that executive compensation must be structured in a certain way in order to ensure that the self-interest of executives is aligned with their company. From a role-responsibility perspective, owners and other stakeholders' ability to trust an executive is an essential part of their role. Jeffrey Moriarty has even argued that the fiduciary duty of the executive can be employed to contend that executives themselves should resist accepting excessive compensation.[12] He argued that executives should only accept what he called the minimum effective compensation (MEC) that is required to procure their services, because it is their fiduciary duty to do so. The MEC is a CEO's 'reservation wage' for the job, i.e. the amount necessary for them to accept and retain it. Essentially, this is determined by comparing what the executive could reasonably expect to be paid elsewhere. This 'market-driven' duty argument, however, does not get away from the sticky questions regarding what is minimal or excessive. Surely the fact that everyone is paying CEOs too much does not mean we should continue doing so. In fact, arguing that we 'ought' to continue a practice merely because it 'is' currently the prevalent one, would be considered a philosophical fallacy.

Though there certainly is some advantage to arguing that one's role could frame quite clearly what the criteria for merit may be, there are also other problems with this approach. The danger that lurks here is that there may be a significant difference between the roles played by the same individuals in different contexts. Role morality is sometimes contrasted with personal moral-ity. The virtues and duties required in a specific role may conflict with one's personal sense of what is morally appropriate. It was Max Weber's contention that individual morality is subjugated to the functionally specific rules and roles of the bureaucratic organization. The danger that this subjugation presents is that of the compartmentalization of an individual's life. Alasdair MacIntyre points out that individuals lose a sense of overriding concern for what it means to be human, and they stop asking moral questions outside of those required by specific roles.[13] For example, executives may have two radically different opinions when asked about the need for environmental protection in two dif-ferent capacities. When confronted with this issue in their capacity as parents, executives will typically support environmental protection, but in terms of their fiduciary duties within the corporation, they will often not feel responsible for implementing environmentally friendly business practices.

The phenomena of amoralization, i.e. the inability or unwillingness to rec-ognize something as a moral issue, has also been linked to the limitations that role morality imposes on one's sense of moral imagination. This problem is exacerbated by the fact that society tends to assign legal responsibility for the avoidance of harm only to those within a specific role, and not to human beings in general. For instance, within most jurisdictions, failure to assist a drowning person is not technically illegal, but allowing one's child to die of neglect is. In the business environment, this seeming 'double standard' is manifested in the fact that legal concepts like the 'business judgement rule' assign executives certain rights and liberties to take risks in order to maximize shareholder value. How can we be sure that executive efforts to benefit their companies do not compromise other ethical imperatives?

Continental perspectives on reward and compensation

Though continental philosophers do not typically write about specific topics in business ethics, some of them do offer interesting perspectives on why role responsibilities often don't solve problems relating to merit and fair compensation. Roles tend to encourage a routine practice of certain tasks. As such, they do not afford us the opportunity to reconsider what it means to be a human being, and hence do not allow us to understand our own value. Furthermore, they do not allow us to recognize the valuation that is already at work in our arguments about justice and merit. One should not think that there is one, coherent 'continental' perspective on rewards in organizations. Instead, various continental philosophers offer different perspectives that present unique, yet related, angles on the topic of this chapter. In what follows, we will focus on Friedrich Nietzsche and Michel Foucault.

Nietzsche's perspective

This cursory exploration of the debates around disproportionate executive compensation serves, among other things, to illustrate how complex and contentious an apparently straightforward principle such as 'fairness' can be. The observations of the nineteenth century German philosopher, Friedrich Nietzsche (1844–1900), may offer a compelling explanation for why this is so often the case. It is not that Nietzsche would have made a negative (or positive) moral judgement on executive compensation. In fact, in Nietzschean terms, calling the material success of some exceptional individuals unfair would be a typical case of *ressentiment* (resentment). He argued that less talented individuals adopt moralistic positions because they have given up much of what makes life worthwhile, and now need to make those who still possess exceptional qualities suspect. In fact, Nietzsche blamed moral ideals for the *bad conscience* that brings human beings to deny their bodies and sacrifice their own life-affirming forces.[14] Nietzsche's insights can therefore hardly be used to support one or the other moral judgement. Instead, he describes our interactions in terms that are in fact 'beyond good and evil' or 'extra-moral'. We are merely making sense of the world by schematizing it in terms of metaphors, which eventually lead to concepts. Based on these concepts, we enter into agreements with each other to protect ourselves from harm and to procure what we need to flourish.[15] Nietzsche would therefore argue that the clever rational principles that we devise to shape our societies and guide our moral judgements are in fact very contingent ways in which to deal with our own vulnerability.

By offering this description of the world, Nietzsche allows us to tap into what motivates us as individuals and hence helps us develop some perspective on issues of reward. Nietzsche recognized that we are all constantly subject to the dynamic influence of various combinations of fears and desires, as well as social expectations and material contingencies. He describes our interactions with one another and with the world that surround us as 'a play of forces'.[16] We develop conscious and unconscious strategies to deal with these forces. Morality is but one iteration of the various strategies, conventions, and habits that we develop. Therefore, in Nietzsche's understanding, 'truth' is essentially an estimation of value linked to very practical concerns.[17] Our 'truth' can, therefore, never be fixed, because to do so would be to deny life as such.[18] Nietzsche insists on the importance of recognizing moral truths for what they are, namely attempts to come to terms with contingent and immediate concerns. Though 'truth' can be a useful construction, it paradoxically becomes a lie when people begin to see it as something permanent and unchangeable.

Nietzsche notes the recurring tendency to try and elevate contingent values to the status of immutable truths. His criticism of priests and other religious people is directed at the fact that these societal authority figures make claims to a transcendental authorization of their views, and hence mislead others into believing that their religious and moral views are the ultimate truth. It is not that Nietzsche is against absolutely all ascetic practices; in fact, he is all for disciplining ourselves or exploring and challenging our own limits. But he wants us to realize just what we are doing and not find some kind of ultimate or final legitimization of these practices.[19] We should also realize that, in most cases, morality is not of our own making but is determined by those in power. Less powerful parties are forced to accept whatever settlement the powerful make.[20] Nietzsche essentially sees universal truth claims as a form of social manipulation. His insights draw our attention to people's almost limitless capacity for self-deception and false consciousness.[21] This leads us to what Nietzsche depicted as the *herd instinct*.[22] This refers to the tendency that human beings have to uncritically follow whatever direction their group takes.

It is when convenient strategies are accepted as unquestionable 'truths' that we lose our capacity to think for ourselves. Many people seem to have little difficulty, for instance, in deceiving themselves into believing that a company's success in generating profit during a favourable economic cycle is directly and primarily attributable to the exceptional leadership of its top executives. Conversely, others have no problem convincing themselves that a company's failure to generate profit in an unfavourable economic climate is primarily attributable to the effect of prevailing market conditions. Over time, the belief that investments must be protected, and that growth most be guaranteed at all costs, becomes a 'truth' that is no longer questioned. Many deliberate rationalizations, as well as subconscious fears and expectations, conspire to make us believe that profit is the most important thing of value, which must be pursued vigorously, as long as it has no negative effects on others. What happens when we start believing that our own convenient strategies are in fact truths, is that these truths are uncoupled from the relations that allowed them to emerge. In financial terms, the supposed relationship between executive compensation and society's well-being is lost from sight. As a result, companies and their executives may even continue to believe that compensation is due even when society did not benefit from their actions at all! As such, 'truths' become useless dogmas that make it impossible to navigate the practical challenges that confront us. For Nietzsche, 'truths' are only sustained by conventionalized lying, i.e. lies that cover up the particular powerful interests that they serve.[23]

The question that then crops up is: was the executive compensation the result of corporations and CEOs deceiving themselves, deceiving others, or both? Have we simply been conditioned by social convention to uncritically accept convenient 'truths'? Nietzsche argues that social convention leads to certain language conventions that make us forget the pragmatic nature of truth construction. The 'truths' that we construct as part of social conventions are based on nerve stimuli, which we then try to approximate by using metaphoric language. Metaphors lead to concepts, which generalize from one specific instance or entity to all the other entities that resemble it. Nietzsche argues that language tends to hide, or fog up, our perception of reality instead of helping us own up to the fact that we can never create perfect, final depictions of reality. One example is the metaphor of the 'invisible hand' which is supposed to distribute the benefits of capitalism, procured through brilliant executive leadership, to everyone in society. This metaphor allows us to maintain our belief in justice, even when that belief cannot be seen in real terms. The metaphor also gets translated into concepts like the 'freedom of the market', which should be protected from interference at all costs. These kinds of concepts make asking critical questions about how well the system actually works very difficult.

How do we get out of this kind of conventionalized thinking? In Nietzschean terms, we need to develop the capacity for recoil and self-overcoming. This means that we must become self-conscious about our constructions of truth and develop practices that allow us to overcome the comforts of social convention. Nietzsche urges us to embark on a re-evaluation of all values. He wants us to question our own constructions of truth on an ongoing basis. We have to use language to do this. So again, we are in the realm of metaphor. We are again merely going to simulate a response based on our own previous experiences and constructions. How do we question our own constructions of truth, which are formulated in metaphoric language, by using the very same language? Nietzsche helps us to reconsider the possibility of critical recoil. We need to be pushing against social convention by questioning the very ethics that are employed to prop it up.

In terms of executive compensation, we could start by acknowledging the metaphorical roots of the word 'fairness'. Etymologically, the notion of fairness can be traced back to the idea of 'harmony', 'order', and even 'beauty'. As such, the concept fairness, in its current use as a moral concept, could be taken as a reference to that which is necessary to live a beautiful or pleasing life. The point is that any description of a value such as fairness has to contend with the differences in people's experiences and circumstances. Nietzsche would argue that the word fairness is a generalized concept that can by no means do justice to the specificities of various situations, or of individuals in particular jobs. What may be a pleasing, beautiful reality in one set of circumstances may not be in the next. The reason for this is the fact that we come to value things differently at different times. In thinking about issues of fairness we must, therefore, always take into consideration the processes of valuation that are necessarily in play when making determinations about what people 'deserve'.

Foucault's perspective

Continental thinkers want to inspire us to remain aware of the forces that shape us in order to reclaim our humanity and to protect the possibilities that lie therein. What are, then, the alternatives to thinking about rewards and compensation in instrumental terms? We are confronted with the question of how individual autonomy is maintained within a network of relationships and power interests. In this regard, the work of Michel Foucault provides some important insights. Foucault's earlier works help us unpack the histories of the power dynamics and discourses that shape our sense of self. Foucault's analysis makes it clear that our self-understanding is ultimately bound up with the way power is distributed in society and the specific interests that need to be served in and through these power relationships. As a result of power dynamics, knowledge structures emerge that shape the way people conceive of themselves and others. Foucault's later work suggests an active engagement with these forces through disciplined participation in practices that cultivate the capacity individuals have for freedom.

Foucault describes the ethics that he develops in his later work as a 'care of the self and the practice of freedom'. Foucault makes it clear that there can be no ethics without freedom. In fact, he describes freedom as the ontological condition of ethics, and ethics as the considered form that this freedom takes.[24] This means that freedom has to exist in order for ethics to emerge in and through our consideration of the interests, forces, and power dynamics that we have to navigate in our daily lives. On closer analysis, it becomes clear that Foucault has a very peculiar definition of freedom. It is not a freedom that allows one to rise above one's context and attain a vantage point from which it is possible to judge autonomously. It also does not refer to a 'veil of ignorance' that erases self-knowledge in order to procure objectivity. Instead, our ability to choose comes from our closeness to events. It is from this position of intimate involvement that we are able to establish the right kind of relationship to the present.[25] Ethics entails navigating, negotiating, and manipulating power relationships and knowledge components within oneself and within one's environment. The self is always located at the nexus of a wide array of power relationships and is constituted by various discourses. According to Foucault, one cannot be free if one does not understand the various ways in which these discourses construct the self. Neither can one be free from power relationships or from the desire to influence events and other people. Freedom has to do with how one understands and conducts the self as one navigates the contingent realities of life.

Like Heidegger, who is discussed in the chapter on corporate social responsibility, Foucault draws on the Greek conception of *ethos* to offer an alternative view of how normative structures come to operate in society. According to Foucault, the Ancient Greeks saw *ethos* as a way of being and a form of behaviour that is firmly rooted in relationships.[26] These relationships between people, and within practices, shape the individual. Foucault is not trying to say that some practices are bad and others are good, he merely wants to make us aware of how they shape our lives. No matter how well-intentioned these practices are, or how rooted they are in moral principles, they change the way we develop and function, and hence they are *dangerous* if they are not frequently questioned. They structure our lives by making divisions between people (smart versus average, mad versus sane, sick versus healthy) and developing rationales for differential treatment. We cannot change this about our human societies, but that does not mean that we should just uncritically accept the *status quo*. However, we have to understand that here again the issue is not the establishment of an ethic of liberation (often replacing one bad situation with another), but rather an appeal for an ethics of continual questioning. So, on the issue of reward, Foucault's insights would challenge us to unpack our ideas about why we accept exorbitant remuneration for executives, how we came to accept the pay discrepancies between men and women, and why we seem to be willing to guarantee job security for some but not others. The question here is not so much one of fairness but one of how we view ourselves and others, and how this view emerged over time and through practices. If that view changes, societal structures are bound to change as well. In turn, societal institutions are constantly shaping or influencing our views. Foucault allows us to develop a keen sense of the intricacy of these interactions.

How do we go about creating the right conditions for an ethic of questioning to flourish? Foucault reimagines Ancient Greek practices of note-taking, memorization, and confessions to describe what he calls 'care of the self'. Through his analysis of these Greek practices, Foucault helps us to understand how certain activities influence our view of ourselves. In some cases, discipline and certain stylized routines could disrupt our everyday humdrum and allow for reflection. Other practices, such as confessions, could mislead us in terms of our own identity. It must be made clear that Foucault does not want to present certain practices as a new normative standard, or a kind of 'recipe for the good life'. Instead he analyzes these practices to show us how they develop or hamper our abilities to question the truths and institutions that form part of our daily lives. Foucault encourages us to understand the power dynamics that are in play, which will allow us to ask more questions. The questions we ask are influenced by power relationships too, and the questions we ask often determine the answer. Foucault can therefore not help us to come up with the 'right answers' and would advise us to analyze the 'right' answers that we do come up with. This analysis could also bring us to experiment with new practices. Foucault wants us not only to critique but to experiment with ourselves and thereby multiply new ways of thinking and being.

Implications of rewards for a corporate ethos

Foucault refers to this as the capacity for recoil, a notion that is, as we have seen, also very important in Nietzsche's thought.[27] It means that whatever we come up with in terms of 'truths', they always in and of themselves create more questions that may undermine their original form. Even those practices that may seem to be a good idea, like giving workers a voice through union activity, or creating employee stock ownership plans (ESOPs), or providing more shareholder oversight in the determination of executive compensation, need to be scrutinized in order to understand and take account of the power dynamics at play. For instance, employee stock ownership plans may seem like a good idea because it at least allows workers to share in the wealth created by the corporation, but this fact also has other implications. For instance, if all employees know that the largest part of their pension fund is tied up with the company's stock, they may be willing to cut significant corners and manipulate the rules to ensure that the stock price keeps rising. Other experts also point out other negative effects pertaining to taxation implications and other administrative difficulties. What is, however, even more important than these practical outcomes or consequences is the kind of assumptions that we buy into when we argue for something like ESOP. When we make employees 'owners', we make the greatest measure of value 'stock'. Employing these alternative remuneration practices may mean that other categories of people are disowned in the process, and that other important values may be ignored.

Power is everywhere, and all institutional arrangements are strategies that seek to deal with this fact. Institutions have histories, and they display the workings of specific power interests in society over time. We deal with each other freely, and in and through these freedoms we also have an impact on the freedoms of others. This led Foucault to develop the notion of *governmentality*, which describes power relations as strategic games between liberties. In Foucault's words:

> Governmentality implies the relation of the self to itself and the range of practices that constitute, define, organize and instrumentalize the strategies which individuals in their freedom can use to deal with each other.[28]

We all try to control the conduct of others and the states of dominion that people ordinarily call 'power'. But Foucault's definition of power goes far beyond the typical definition of power as an oppressive force. Foucault also views power as a productive force, as something that individuals wield in order to give shape and form to their lives. This includes how we relate to others and how we participate in certain practices.

Foucault uses the concept of subjectivation to discuss the capacity of individuals for self-stylization or form-giving in their own lives. He wants us to think about the way we, as individuals, establish our relation to the rules we are confronted with and to think about how we become obligated to put them into practice. Understanding our relationship to power, which includes the power of others over us, but also our own power to participate in and interact with other forces, helps us understand why we obey societal rules and why we adopt the values of society and function according to the goals of certain institutions. This is very important in thinking about what we consider an acceptable reward, both for others and for ourselves.

Everything we do, every decision we make, every interaction with others, is part of the process by which we shape our lives. These actions, decisions, and interactions change us and impact others. In terms of organizational life, this will entail asking questions about why we work and how we relate our work to those things we value in life. Do we work to live, or do we live to work? Is work something we do for a reward that lies outside of work, like a nice car, house, clothes, and gadgets? Foucault would not argue that an affirmative answer here is right or wrong. Reading Foucault may just bring us to think about it, and may even cause us to change our minds now and then. What is the alternative? Foucault would not have a specific kind of life in mind, but he would want to make sure you know how to ask serious questions about any kind of life.

Conclusion

In this chapter, we considered the way in which justice-as-fairness principles help us to think through issues of executive compensation and fair reward. We saw that though there may be Rawlsian arguments to put forward in defence of inequalities in compensation, these arguments tend to make sense only in a specific context. The standards of objectivity, or the removal of bias in what is considered fair, seem very difficult, if not impossible, to maintain in practice. We can try to locate the criteria for certain 'fair' judgements in certain professional roles that some individuals fulfil, but those criteria are also specific to the institutions that shape them.

A very important insight of this chapter is that our ability to judge what is fair, or what is morally acceptable in various situations, is influenced by the tacit expectations with which we are gradually inculcated in and through our participation in society. Nietzsche made us aware of the processes of valuation that are always implicit in societal interactions. Foucault helped us understand why this happens, and how these tacit expectations shape all our embodied, visceral responses to the world, including our moral judgements.

This does not mean, however, that we are mere puppets on a string, fully determined by our circumstances and institutions. Both Foucault and Nietzsche envisage the cultivation of questioning and recoil as central aspects of our human lives. They emphasize the importance of carefully cultivating a lifestyle that allows for reflection, for revaluation, and for criticism of everyday practices that often go unquestioned.

Taking these philosophical perspectives seriously may lead to a life that has its own rewards. These rewards may be very different, or may even bring the whole idea of 'reward' as a direct outcome of an activity into question. At the very least, philosophy may serve to put into perspective all the other rewards that are bound to come our way.

NOTES

1 R. Kolb, 'Golden parachutes', in R. W. Kolb (ed.), *Encyclopedia for Business Ethics and Society*. Thousands Oaks, CA: Sage Publications (2008), 1,022.
2 J. Harris and P. Bromily, 'Incentives to cheat: the influence of executive compensation and firm performance on financial misrepresentation', *Organization Science* 18 (3) (2007), 352.
3 Harris and Bromily, 'Incentives to cheat', 352.
4 J. D. Harris, 'What's wrong with executive compensation?', *Journal of Business Ethics* 85 (2008), 147–56.
5 J. Rawls, *A Theory of Justice*. Harvard, MA: The Belknap Press (1971/1999).
6 N. Mohan and J. Ruggiero, 'Influence of firm performance and gender on CEO compensation', *Applied Economics* 39 (9) (2007), 1,107–13; S. Williams, 'Inequities persist in CEO compensation', *Association Management* 55 (11) (2003), 22.
7 C. Poster and R. A. Furniss, 'Pay for risk-prudent performance is the new pay for performance', *Corporate Governance Advisor* 17 (4) (2009), 12–16.
8 F. Nietzsche, 'Human, all too human', in W. Kaufmann (ed.), *The Portable Nietzsche*. New York: Penguin Books (1982), 51.
9 A. MacIntyre, *After Virtue*. London: Duckworth (1981), 114.
10 M. Painter-Morland, *Business Ethics as Practice. Ethics and the Everyday Business of Business*. Cambridge: Cambridge University Press (2008).
11 This paragraph on professional responsibility is based on M. Painter-Morland's own entry on 'Role responsibility', in Kolb (ed.), *Encyclopedia of Business Ethics and Society*.
12 J. Moriarty, 'How much compensation can CEO's permissibly accept?', *Business Ethics Quarterly* 19 (2) (2009), 235–50.
13 A. MacIntyre, 'Social structures and their threats to moral agency', *Philosophy* 74 (1999), 311–29.
14 F. Nietzsche, *On the Genealogy of Morality: a Polemic*, M. Clark and A. J. Swenses (trans.). Cambridge, MA: Hackett Publishing Company (1998), 19.
15 F. Nietzsche, 'On truth and lie in the extramoral sense', in W. Kaufmann, *The Portable Nietzsche*, 42–7.
16 F. Nietzsche, *The Will to Power*, W. Kaufman and R. J. Hollingdale (trans./eds.). New York: Vintage Press (1968), 1,067.
17 M. Heidegger, *Nietzsche Volumes III and IV: the Will to Power as Knowledge and as Metaphysics and Nihilism*, D. F. Krell (ed.). San Francisco, CA: HarperCollins (1987), 57.
18 *Ibid.*, 66.
19 Nietzsche, *On the Genealogy of Morality*, 70–1.
20 *Ibid.*, 46.
21 Nietzsche, 'On truth and lie', 45.
22 Nietzsche, *On the Genealogy of Morality*, 11.
23 *Ibid.*, 47.
24 M. Foucault, *Ethics: the Essential Works*. London: The Penguin Press (1994), 284.

25 See P. Rabinow's introduction to Foucault, *ibid.*, xviii.
26 Foucault, *Ethics*, 287.
27 C. Scott, *The Question of Ethics: Nietzsche, Foucault, Heidegger.* Bloomington, IN: Indiana Press (1990), 58.
28 M. Foucault, 'The subject and power', in J. D. Faubion (ed.), *Power (Essential Works of Foucault).* New York: The New Press (1994), 326–48.

8

Leadership

SVERRE SPOELSTRA AND RENÉ TEN BOS

Goals of this chapter

After studying this chapter you will be able to:

- understand how business ethics portrays leadership as necessarily ethical;
- understand the problem with 'the Hitler problem' in discussions around ethical leadership;
- understand how the Slovenian philosopher Slavoj Zizek sees leadership;
- understand how leadership is not only related to ethics but also to aesthetics.

Introduction

Leadership has fascinated us throughout the ages. Ever since the ancient philosopher Plato (*c.* BC 427–347), discussions around leadership have been intimately linked to discussions about morality. For Plato, only people with the right moral character are capable of leading. This basic idea is still very much present in ideas (and fantasies) about leadership. Even today, some follow Plato when they take for granted that leadership is all about having a good character. The mere suggestion that there is bad leadership is likely to be dismissed by arguing that bad leadership is not leadership at all.

So, we often hear calls for 'strong' or 'visionary' leadership, as if these are the kinds of leadership that miraculously can solve the moral or economic problems in which businesses and organizations regularly find themselves. A lack of good leadership is deemed to have caused whatever crisis there is. Somehow leadership is assumed to show us the way out of trouble. It is hardly ever seen as that which created the trouble and yet it is this possibility that we would like to alert you to.

One of the problems that we encounter in this chapter is the relationship between business ethics and leadership studies. Many business ethicists have an interest in leadership since leaders are obviously involved in moral decision-making in organizations. Business ethics journals have therefore frequently devoted attention to leadership. However, this does not mean that the ethics of leadership phenomena are also discussed. Business ethicists agree, of course, that leaders should behave ethically, but as business ethics professor Joanne B. Ciulla notes, 'few have delved into what this means'.[1] This is also part of what we shall argue in this chapter: the importance of ethics and morality is often emphasized within business ethics, but there is little engagement with the question of what ethical leadership would entail. Leadership scholars, for their part, have always taken an interest in the moral aspects of leadership. It is in this sense that they stand in a long tradition that goes back at least as far as Plato. If there would be a distinction between leadership studies and business ethics on leadership, then it would be that leadership scholars generally produce all sorts of beautiful images of leadership, whereas business ethicists tend to take more interest in the practical aspects of moral leadership. In this chapter, we discuss both streams and attempt to shed more light on what the difference between them might be. We will argue that the Slovenian philosopher, Slavoj Zizek, makes it clear that business ethics might also benefit from a certain kind of aesthetic representation of leadership.

This chapter starts with a discussion of the way leadership scholars and business ethicists have discussed moral and immoral aspects of leadership. We will argue that seemingly descriptive research on leadership is often normative in nature. In other words, what some leadership scholars portray as leadership is rarely a description of the way business leaders actually behave. Instead, it offers images of the way leadership *ought to* look. Drawing on Zizek, we will then go on to suggest that this confusion between what leadership is and should be tells us something about the nature of leadership itself: for leadership to exist, we must believe that it is good, even when it is not.

The embellishment of leadership

The idea that 'there are almost as many definitions of leadership as there are persons who have attempted to define it', has become a cliché among leadership researchers.[2] For some researchers, such as Joseph C. Rost, this is a nuisance that prevents the study of leadership from reaching its full potential. Nobody seems to know exactly what people are talking about when leadership is the issue. Nevertheless, attraction to the topic is enormous. Business scholars have probably published more about leadership than about any other topic and they often emphasize that much is at stake. For example, one of the most authoritative books in the field, Bass and Stogdill's *Handbook of Leadership*, notes that leadership 'is often regarded as the single most critical factor in the success or failure of institutions'.[3] The way to read this is that leadership is habitually regarded as *the* critical factor for success, and a *lack of* leadership *the* critical factor for failure. In fact, leadership is even seen as a solution to solve what has been labelled the problem of management. 'The problem with many organizations', two distinctive scholars wrote almost twenty-five years ago, 'especially the failing ones, is that they tend to be over-managed and under-led'.[4] This implies that whenever an organization is in trouble, financially, morally, or otherwise, the cause of this is a lack of leadership and probably too much management.

The debate is not so much whether or not leadership can save us in times of crisis. Most leadership scholars have great faith in leadership, and many make some extra money by selling their leadership recommendations to companies. The question is rather which *form* of leadership is supposed to provide the solution. Since the 1980s, leadership theorists have been proposing many different images of leadership, one even more attractive than the other. So, for example, 'transformational leaders', proponents say, are people who are charismatic, inspirational, considerate, and stimulate their followers intellectually;[5] 'servant leaders' are great for organizations because they put their followers first;[6] 'self-leaders' manage their inner life as a basis for leading others;[7] and the 'distributed leadership' approach argues that organizations are better led when every person acts as a leader, and not just one single individual at the top (see also Box 8.1).[8] What these images have in common is that they invariably portray leadership as something great, as an unconditional good for organizations. But these images bespeak a certain skepticism towards other images of leadership, and are often a direct response to them. For example, distributed leadership theorists portray transformational leadership as something that is potentially bad or dangerous for organizations because too much power rests with one person. Transformational leadership theorists respond that therefore only transformational leaders with a spotless moral character deserve the label transformational, all others are only 'pseudo-transformational'.[9] This is a good example of how leadership scholars defend their own concept of leadership by in fact assuming the characteristics they purport to argue for.

As a consequence, many leadership scholars think that leaders are the solution to all sorts of problems in organizations. Like most clichés, however, this is not as true as one might think. One of the reasons why so many people wager on leadership when it comes to solving problems is that leadership is an incredibly fuzzy issue. Management fads and hypes can be seen as panaceas exactly because they resist clear-cut definitions. The danger is that if a concept such as leadership can mean anything, it also implies that it can function in any way whatsoever. The vagueness of a concept engenders its own kind of irrefutability. As we said in our introduction: the assumption is that leadership must be something good. And in the event that it turns out to be bad, one might always argue that one did not witness the *true* concept of, let us say, 'transformational' or 'authentic' leadership. The concept is never to blame. Its beauty is always conceptually guaranteed because it is self-referentially true.

Many of these concepts of leadership and their miraculous powers can be seen as variations of what Andrew Huczynski a long time ago referred to as 'the great man theory of leadership', sometimes also known as 'heroic leadership theories'.[10] The great man theory of leadership refers to Thomas Carlyle's

Box 8.1	Popular leadership approaches

Trait approach. This approach to the study of leadership was especially popular from the 1920s until the 1940s. The assumption was that certain mental and physical traits (like intelligence, height, fluency of speech, or physical attractiveness) would make people especially fit to lead. Trait research attempts to isolate these traits and to see to what extent they predict leadership behaviour.

Transformational leadership. This approach to leadership has been popular since the mid-1980s. It emphasizes that transformational leaders move beyond exchange relations with their subordinates (for example 'I pay your salary and in exchange you do this and that task for me'). They are said to create a common purpose for the organization through charisma, inspiration, personal consideration, and intellectual stimulation.

Self-leadership. This approach emphasizes that organizations benefit if all members lead themselves first. This means that organizational members should develop their potential and take responsibility even when they are not high up in the organizational hierarchy.

Super-leadership. A super-leader is a leader that leads self-leaders. In other words, a super-leader inspires people to lead themselves.

Distributed leadership. This is a leadership approach that advocates the dispersion of leadership activities among different members of the organization. The responsibility should not lie with one single individual, but should be distributed over many. This avoids the danger of one person becoming too powerful.

Shared leadership. This is sometimes used as a synonym for distributed leadership, but sometimes also refers to the more specific idea of the rotation of the leadership role: when the leadership role is shared, all group members perform the role for a limited period.

Servant leadership. This refers to the idea that the ideal leader puts his or her followers first. Servant leaders are not primarily concerned with their own interests, but with the opportunities for growth of their subordinates.

Heroic leadership. This term refers to approaches to leadership that celebrate extraordinary qualities of certain people as the basis for leadership. The term is mostly used in a somewhat condescending way by scholars who promote so-called 'post-heroic' leadership approaches, and normally refers to approaches like transformational leadership, charismatic leadership, trait theory, and Carlyle's 'great man' theory of leadership.

Post-heroic leadership. This term refers to approaches that don't put their faith in the extraordinary qualities of one individual, and includes approaches like distributed leadership and shared leadership.

Value-based leadership. This leadership approach emphasizes the importance of values, like integrity and fairness, for leaders. The best leaders are the leaders with the most desirable values.

famous essay on heroism in history (first published in 1840). In this essay, Carlyle offers the following description of the great man:

> He is the living light-fountain, which is good and pleasant to be near. The light which enlightens, which has enlightened the darkness of the world; and this is not a kindled lamp only, but rather a natural luminary shining by the gift of Heaven; a flowing light-fountain, as I say, of native original insight, of manhood and heroic nobleness in whose radiance all souls feel that it is well with them.[11]

The point that we would like to alert you to is that Carlyle produces, just as much as contemporary commentators, a beautiful image of leadership. That these images may vary widely is not our concern here. We are rather interested in what we like to refer to as the embellishment of leadership. In other words, what we see in leadership studies is a plethora of images, but they all have in common that they portray leadership as something quintessentially beautiful and good. We will see below that business ethicists generally do not indulge in this kind of imagery, but have by and large offered a more down to earth approach to leadership. But before we enter the field of business ethics, we would like to draw your attention to a few problems relating to what we referred to as the great man theory of leadership. We will treat this theory as just an example of how leadership can be rendered as something beautiful.

Four types of imagery are particularly problematic about the great man:

(1) **Masculine imagery**. The first problem with the great man is that he is a man and not a woman. Hence, the theory seems to assume that women do not or cannot have the 'gift of Heaven' of which Carlyle speaks (which we now call 'charisma'). Indeed, much of leadership thinking is very masculine, often excluding women in more and less explicit ways.

(2) **Adventurous imagery**. The great man, in all his various guises, is routinely portrayed as a rule-breaking character, a daredevil, who, entirely aroused by a certain vision, goes where no one else dares to go. This is part and parcel of a tradition which seeks to emphasize that leadership or enterprise are all about breaking through certain more or less deeply ingrained habits.

(3) **Powerful imagery**. His influence on organizational performance is routinely overestimated. The pragmatist philosopher, Sidney Hook, has rightly pointed out that much thinking about heroic leadership falls prey to the logical fallacy of *post hoc ergo propter hoc* (after this therefore because of this).[12] This means that the leader is praised when an organization prospers and blamed when the organization is in trouble, irrespective of the real causes of success and failure. The same applies also to theories of heroic leadership: the impact of leaders on organizations is often assumed by heroic leadership theorists rather than explained.

(4) **Protective imagery**. There is always a sense that great men reduce the anxiety of their followers.[13] This could easily lead to a situation that followers surrender their critical attitude and thus give way to forms of moral

blindness. The leader is lionized to such an extent that dissent has become virtually impossible. Captured by the leader's shining light, followers surrender their own capacity to make moral judgements.

With these critiques in mind, many leadership scholars and business ethicists try to move away from great man theories of leadership. They suggest that the spurious moral character of the great man, whether he really exists or not, is a danger for organizations. Instead, we'd better search for alternative forms of leadership, which are truly morally commendable. But as we will soon see, these counter-images indulge in their own particular forms of imagery that we deem to be problematic as well. For example, a counter-image like distributed leadership may sidestep the problems above by imagining leadership without individual leaders and authority relationships. But one may wonder whether leadership without authority can actually exist.

Business ethicists on leadership

Joanne Ciulla is an example of a business ethicist with an interest in leadership. Contrary to many leadership scholars, she does not simply imagine leaders to be morally perfect. Instead, she is interested in what might amount to be practices of good leadership:

> We are not confused about what leaders do, but we would like to know the best way to do it. The whole point about studying leadership is to answer the question, what is good leadership? The use good here has two senses: ethical and effective.[14]

Ciulla continues by arguing that leadership scholars too often assume that moral leadership and effective leadership go together. Instead we must realize that some effective leaders were, in fact, immoral, whereas there are instances of moral leadership that are hopelessly ineffective. Instead of assuming that leadership and morality always go together, Ciulla argues that we must learn to keep them separated, so that we can see more clearly what good leadership, in both senses of the term 'good', would look like.

Ciulla's work is emblematic of the normative approach in business ethics literature.[15] She wants leaders to be good in both senses of the word: morally and effectively. Philosophically speaking, her work draws on utilitarian and deontological thought: effective behaviour is only laudable if it is directed at attaining the greatest possible good and if it is infused with a sense of moral duty. In this context Ciulla emphatically warns against the dangers of charismatic leadership. For her, the very fact that charismatics can do so much good and so much harm demonstrates how important it is to conceive of leadership in ethical rather than religious terms (see Box 8.2). One way to circumvent the danger

Box 8.2	Leadership and religion

The vocabulary we use to describe leadership is often permeated with 'religious' terms. Words that are often used in combination with 'leadership' have religious or spiritual connotations: 'charismatic leadership', 'visionary leadership', 'inspirational leadership', 'servant leadership', 'missionary leadership', and so on. Most people accept these kinds of notions whereas they would not easily accept notions such as 'intellectual leadership', 'scientific leadership', or 'learned leadership'. The eminent American historian, Richard Hofstadter, has pointed out that intellectualism is, at least in the US, but also elsewhere, widely considered to be a danger for good leadership since it allegedly undermines what he refers to as 'character'. Intellectual people have doubts, waver between different options, and display a proclivity towards inertia when it comes to decision-making. The 'active mind', or so the argument goes, tends to be distracted by the trivial and the ridiculous rather than by important affairs. What really matters for most people is livelihood and work. Thoughtful procrastination is of no interest here.

According to Hofstadter, part of the problem with popular thinking about leadership in the US is that it has long been suffering from an excessive 'devotion to practicality'. Given the fact that the US was founded by intellectual leaders (Washington, Jefferson, Madison, and others), this is a rather strange situation. The egalitarianism that underlies the American dream – every single person should be able to become a president or a business leader – has been an important aspect of the widespread turn to practice. Hofstadter quotes an orator at Yale in 1844:

> The age of philosophy has passed, and left few memorials of its existence. That of glory has vanished, and nothing but a painful tradition of human suffering remains. That of utility has commenced, and it requires little warmth of imagination to anticipate for it a reign lasting of time, and radiant with the wonders of unveiled nature.[16]

This practical bias emphasizes not so much the brain but the heart. In other words, a profound irrationalism sets in, and with it comes a plethora of religious imagery. This means, if we are to believe Hofstadter, that values and purposes become more important than reasoning and thought. In 1936, the immensely popular 'inspirational writer', Henry C. Link, wrote that 'reason is not an end in itself but a tool for the individual to use in adjusting himself to the values and purposes of living which are beyond reason'. And he adds:

> Just as the teeth are intended to chew with, not to chew themselves, so the mind is intended to think with, not to worry about. The mind is an instrument to live with, not to live for.

The privileging of value and purpose over thought and reason explains why character is deemed to be more important than wisdom and intellect. Important business people like Andrew Carnegie or Henry Ford had nothing but contempt for the liberal education in America. This kind of education, they believed, merely leads to demoralization, which is rooted in a profound 'distaste of practical life'.

Small wonder, then, that religious values rather than intellectual nimbleness come to dominate the field of leadership. 'Charisma' is the concept that has perhaps played the most important role. The word itself finds its root in the Bible. In several passages of the Bible, we see that God favours people who are righteous and faithful (see, for example, Psalms 5:12 or Lucas 2:52). The Greek word for favour is *charis*. When you get this divine gift, a positive radiation will sooner or later be yours. Compared to this, it is needless to say, excelling in the sciences or in literature does not count at all.

This kind of quasi-religious anti-intellectualism plays a pivotal role in the literature on leadership. Even though business ethics, as we will soon see in the chapter, has become suspicious of charisma (albeit, as we will see as well, for the wrong reasons), it still shares not only the practical bias of this literature but also the emphasis on values, goodness, and normativity. In this chapter, we ask a few critical questions about these tendencies. But perhaps, before continuing, you may want to ponder the question of whether the age of philosophy, as this orator at Yale once had it, has really passed. Did we all really succumb to the insuperable attractions of utility?

of charisma is, of course, to deny that it exists. So, some scholars have argued that the primacy afforded to charisma in leadership studies is problematic.[17]

A long time ago, the German sociologist, Max Weber, pointed out that one cannot formally designate a charismatic person. Charisma does not obey a 'form', it does not come into being thanks to 'a well-ordered procedure of appointment or dismissal'. It is not a matter of 'career', 'income', or 'professional education' (*Fachbildung*).[18] A person who 'carries' charisma, Weber argues, only knows 'internal determinations and limits': he or she takes up a certain task and requires obedient followers who recognize the importance of this task. If this recognition does not occur, the charismatic pretension will fall to pieces. In this sense, charismatic leadership should not be subsumed under the so-called traits approach of leadership that tries to establish essential psychological or physical characteristics of putatively charismatic leaders (see Box 8.1). Nothing seems to be further away from Weber's view of charisma. For him, charisma signals a certain relationship between leaders and followers. In a sense, the followers allow charismatics to come into being. Put differently, followers constitute charisma, not rules, not formal procedure, and definitely not intelligence or intellectual background. Some in business ethics, such as Robert Solomon, have also emphasized the importance of the relationship between leaders and followers in the emergence of charisma.[19]

The problem with leadership ethics is not so much related to the idea that great men are actually a moral danger as to a sobering insight that great men – and women, we would like to add at this point – refrain from working in a bureaucratic environment. Perhaps organizations need good managers rather than good, honourable, or charismatic leaders. Such at least was the upshot of a comment in *The Economist* in 2003 about the financial scandals that have plagued international business so much: corporate managers might have been captivated a little bit too much by the 'cult of the charismatic leader', and perhaps we should reimpose old and dull managerial virtues such as 'attention to detail and the capacity to follow through'. *The Economist* prophecies that, as a consequence of the financial scandals, bureaucracy will be 'on the rise again'.[20]

Let us summarize what we have said so far. Firstly, we have argued that leadership studies portray leaders as someone beautiful and good. We then briefly discussed the image of the great man and some of the problems associated with this imagery. Secondly, we have noted that a business ethicist like Ciulla shies away from great man theories of leadership. She argues that the great man constitutes a moral risk and that charismatics in general should be treated with suspicion: they may be good, but they may also be bad. This is one reason why business ethicists have an interest in different concepts of leadership than individual leaders. More specifically, they turn to forms of leadership that are within reach of those who work in the business organizations that they study. Some recent images of such types of leadership include: 'distributed leadership', 'shared leadership', 'systemic leadership', or even 'democratic leadership'. The question that remains is whether these approaches do not also involve some kind of embellishment of the notion of leadership. We will now turn to what is known as 'the Hitler problem' in scholarly debate about the morality of leadership. We use this debate as an example of the way leadership scholars and business ethicists tend to embellish leadership.

The Hitler problem

We have seen that many scholars of leadership picture leadership as something good and beautiful. Leadership is good and will somehow never fail. Cases such as Enron and WorldCom can henceforward only be explained through a lack of 'transformational', 'authentic', or 'distributed' leadership. However, rather than dismissing the claim that leaders are always good from the outset, in this section we shall explore the question of *why* so many leadership authors postulate leadership as something good. In other words, why does leadership have to be good even when it so often clearly is not?

The most obvious case of a bad or evil leader is Hitler. But the idea that Hitler was a leader does, of course, not resonate very well with the expectation that all leaders are morally good. Ciulla describes this as 'the Hitler problem'.[21] At first sight, this problem might appear as something that reminds us of the problem of theodicy: how can one justify the existence of a benevolent God in a world that has many evils? Perhaps more accurately, how can something bad or evil come from something good? As we shall see, in most accounts the 'solution' to the Hitler problem is basically to sidestep it: Hitler cannot be a leader for he was bad. For example, according to James McGregor Burns, transforming leadership 'raises the level of human conduct and ethical aspiration of both leader and led'.[22] For this reason, Hitler was not a leader but 'a tyrant' and a 'terrible mis-leader'.[23] In other words, our common sense feelings about good and bad are quickly restored: good comes from good, bad comes from bad. The only difference is that leadership is now *defined* as good. But we would like you to reconsider the formula that *leadership = good*.[24]

To think of Hitler as a leadership problem is a relatively new phenomenon. For a very long time, people like Hitler or Stalin were seen as great examples of effective leadership, not only in the field of political theory but also in the field of organizational theory. Just after the second world war, in 1948, the well-known organizational theorist, Chester Bernard, wrote that:

> few can be unaffected by the violent energy with which Mussolini throws his arm in the Fascist salute, or by the vehemence of Hitler's speech, or by the strenuous life of Theodore Roosevelt. Similarly, we are impressed by the endurance of Franklin D. Roosevelt in campaign.[25]

The question we like to ask is, basically, what happened between 1948 and now that allowed people to start thinking that leadership *must* be good? Why do business ethicists like Ciulla reject what Barnard took completely for granted? Or, why was Bernard still able to put Mussolini and Hitler on a par with the Roosevelts?

The Hitler problem, in its basic form, can be traced down in many places. Jim Kouzes and Barry Posner, to mention just one example, argue that leadership is characterized by the following five elements: (1) leaders challenge the process; (2) they inspire people to a shared vision; (3) they enable others to act; (4) they model the way things need to be done; (5) they encourage people's hearts.[26] The assumption is that these are all *good* things and it is the presence of these good things that constitutes leadership. The big promise underlying Kouzes and Posner's theory is that leadership is not extraordinary at all: these are rather normal people who can, in a kind of collective effort, do extraordinary things. Types such as Hitler and Stalin clearly do not belong to this 'ordinary' or 'low profile' category of leadership. So the leadership problem, with its 'solution' that Hitler was not a leader, lurks in the background of many leadership texts. However, explicit explorations of the Hitler problem are quite rare. In the end, the typical argument for the moral nature of transformational leadership can be captured in the form of a simple syllogism, for example:

Major premise: all transformational leaders are moral.
Minor premise: Hitler was not moral.
Conclusion: Hitler was not a transformational leader.

Although the argument makes sense, the rather elementary mistake is that the conclusion is put forward to prove the major premise ('transformational leadership is moral'), which in the end is postulated but by no means proven.

Indeed, we have not come across one single account of transformational leadership that offers a conceptual argument as to why it would be morally good, nor have we come across statistical evidence that suggests that people who bring about transformations tend to do good.

We now turn to a direct defence against the earlier-mentioned critique that charismatics can turn out to be dangerous creatures. Instead of arguing that charismatic leadership is inherently good or bad, leadership professors Jane Howell and Bruce J. Avolio have attempted to carve out an ethical form of charismatic leadership. Their conclusion is very remarkable:

> Ethical charismatic leaders in the end deserve this label only if they create transformations in their organizations so that members are motivated to follow them and to seek organization objectives not only because they are ordered to do so, and not merely because they calculate that such compliance is in their self-interest, but because they voluntarily identify with the organization, its standards of conduct and willingly seek to fulfill its purpose.[27]

This conclusion overlooks the fact that organizations can also – and frequently do – exist for bad purposes. Howell and Avolio openly maintain that anyone who can talk someone into willingly following some organizational goal deserves to be called ethical. This is, we like to suggest, quite a disturbing idea. One of the most respected academic journals in management, *The Academy of Management Executive*, accepted the paper by Howell and Avolio and decided that this was a message worth spreading. However, we have every reason to be stunned, especially if we remind ourselves of the philosopher Hannah Arendt, who found what she referred to as 'the banality of *evil*' in willingly and unthoughtfully following organizational objectives.[28] This, she argued, was the evil of Adolf Eichmann, responsible for the deportation of hundreds of thousands of Jews in the Nazi Holocaust. Eichmann's evil, Arendt argued, could not be explained by a monstrous character (Eichmann was a rather 'normal' human being, she argued) but only through his ability to wilfully pursue the goals of the organization he was 'working' for. Of course, Howell and Avolio do not really see the creation of Eichmann-like employees in organizations as the ultimate proof of ethical leadership.

What to make of these examples and how representative are they for the way ethics enters discussions around leadership? We would like to suggest that it is no coincidence that discussions around Ciulla's Hitler problem appear around the same time as business ethicists and leadership scholars look for an alternative model of leadership, which is assumedly more moral, or less dangerous, than the great man theories of leadership that preceded it. Bass and Steidlmeier's argument for authentic transformational leadership is interesting in this regard because it bridges the transformational leadership fashion of the 1980s and 1990s with the authentic leadership fashion of the 1990s and 2000s. Business ethicists and leadership theorists now actively try to rescue the image of leadership from the various charges against the great man. Their attempts to 'solve' this problem – i.e. the Hitler problem – are attempts to sidestep the moral *aporias* (impasses) related to the question of leadership. This is part of the practical bias that permeates the history of leadership studies and business ethics alike.

The problem with the Hitler problem, we argue, is therefore not the Hitler problem itself. There is no Hitler problem in leadership studies. In fact, everybody seems to agree that the man was evil. There is hardly any room left for ambivalences here. The real problem is why leadership scholars pose the Hitler problem as a problem. In other words, why are they unwilling to accept the rather straightforward idea that Hitler was a bad or evil leader? The problem here is that most of us do not feel any need to contest the idea that there are bad teachers, bad doctors, or bad scientists. We take for granted that these people can fail, morally or technically. Why is such an assumption unacceptable when we talk about leaders? What makes the sheer possibility of a bad leader so horrifying that scholars of business leadership are at pains to convince their readership that Hitler was not a leader?

We have already seen that great man theories of leadership, as well as charismatic leadership, are looked upon with suspicion. The move away from heroic leadership starts to take flight in the 1990s. Even though charisma was considered to be one of the main elements of transformational leadership in the 1980s, Bass in 1999 warns:

> The immature, self-aggrandizing charismatic is pseudo-transformational. He or she may seem uplifting and responsible but on closer examination is found to be a false Messiah.[29]

The question we would like to consider now is what such a close examination would look like. Who can or should make the judgement whether a charismatic leader is ethical or not? Indeed, is it not by definition very difficult to make such a critical examination when you are under the spell of charisma?

Zizek on leadership

In the previous section we looked at some different ways in which leadership scholars have attempted to engage with the ethics of leadership. What we will argue here is that conflation between ethics and leadership is an attempt to avoid uncomfortable ethical questions in relation to leadership phenomena. Our suggestion is that the posing of the Hitler problem (as a problem) tells us something about the nature of leadership itself. In other words, the belief in the goodness of leadership is part of the phenomenon of leadership. The attribution of goodness enables leaders to lead in the way they do. Barack Obama is an interesting example: people attributed goodness to him before he, as an American president at least, actually had done something good. One needs only to think here of the Nobel Prize for peace that he won. The US president himself admitted he was surprised, and we will not claim here that this was an instance of false modesty. The point is that the attribution of goodness is more important than acts or decisions that may be deemed, after due deliberation, to be good.

To examine how this might work, we now turn to one of the most popular continental philosophers of our time: the Slovenian philosopher Slavoj Zizek. Leadership is a theme that one can find in many of Zizek's writings, but his focus is political leadership rather than business leadership. This interest is likely fuelled by Zizek's own political experiences. In the late 1980s, Zizek cofounded the Liberal Democratic Party in his country Slovenia and ran for a seat in the Presidential Committee in the first democratic elections of the country, in 1990. He came very close to being elected. In his writings on polit-ical leadership, Zizek focuses especially on communist leaders such as Lenin, Mao, and Trotsky. Of course, political leadership is not the same as business leadership. Nonetheless, much of what Zizek has to say about leadership is of direct interest for the question that guides us here: why is it that we tend to think of leadership as something that is good?

Drawing upon the French psychoanalyst, Jacques Lacan, Zizek maintains that a leader has two bodies. When we think of a leader we think firstly of an empirical human body: a real existing human being that takes on a role as leader. However, for Zizek this is not enough for leadership to exist. Next to the empirical human being, a leader also has a sublime body that is 'made of a special, immaterial stuff'.[30] Only followers see this sublime body intuitively: it cannot be made explicit in the language that we use. As we have seen, this body can be thought of as 'radiating', an essential notion not only in leadership but also in religious literature.

But what does it mean to have a sublime body? Coming back to the example of Obama winning the Nobel Prize, we might say that it has been awarded to the sublime body of Obama, rather than to the empirical person. Or rather, we should see it as a contribution to the sublime image of Obama: as a result of awarding him the Nobel Prize his 'natural luminary shining by the gift of Heaven', to go back to Carlyle's description of the great man, shines even brighter. What Zizek helps us to understand, very much in line with what Weber tells us about charisma, is that the empirical person is not really naturally gifted by charisma or other extraordinary qualities; we only *attribute* these qualities to leaders. Through these attributions the sublime body of the leader is constituted. And it is only because of the attribution of the extraordinary qualities that 'great' leadership is possible:

> The subjects think they treat a certain person as a king because he is already in himself a king, while in reality this person is king only insofar as the subjects treat him as one . . . But the crucial point is that it is a positive, necessary condition for the performative effect to take place that the king's charisma

be experienced precisely as an immediate property of the person-king. The moment the subject take cognizance of the fact that the king's charisma is a performative effect, the effect itself is aborted.[31]

In other words, the attribution of sublime qualities sustains the leadership phenomenon. Once we realize that this is in fact the case, leadership itself disappears. This happens, for example, when a CEO is found guilty of criminal conduct. Think, for example, of what happened to Enron's Ken Lay and Jeff Skilling (see Chapter 4). But it can also happen in far less dramatic circumstances, for example, when we learn too much about the empirical body of the leader:

> Imagine a dignified leader: if he is photographed in an 'undignified' situation (crying, throwing up, hugging the wrong women), this can ruin his career, although such situations are parts of the daily life of all of us.[32]

Because of this danger, leadership is very much an art of making sure that one does not become too visible, which could ruin the sublime body of leadership needed for its functioning:

> recall the high art of the skilled politicians who know how to make themselves absent when a humiliating decision was to be made; in this way, they are able to leave intact the unconscious belief of their followers in their omnipotence, sustaining the illusion that, if they were not accidentally prevented from being there, they would have been able to save the day.[33]

To summarize, Zizek shows us that leadership has a complex relationship with knowing. Leadership is strengthened by faith, but can be harmed by objective knowledge (see Box 8.2). We suggest that this realization also motivates the ways in which business ethicists and leadership scholars engage with leadership. In speaking of ethical leadership, their concern for actually existing misconduct in business life is intertwined with the faith in a sublime body that counters it. This sublime body, on a theoretical level, appears under many names. Some of them we have already mentioned: transformational leadership, authentic leadership, super-leadership, and so on.

The idolatry of leadership that one encounters in leadership studies works because it is simultaneously denied. Bruce Avolio, the aforementioned leadership scholar famous for his emphasis of the moral qualities of 'transformational' and 'authentic' leaders, is very explicit (but perhaps unaware) about this. He says:

> I am firmly against the idolization of leaders, and indeed chose the term *idealized* in our model of leadership to distinguish idealized vs. idolized leaders. The former are those who build people up to be leaders; the latter are those who expect unquestioning followers.[34]

Idolization is of course not a property or characteristic of a person, but something initiated by and deriving from followers. A leader is not born as an idol, but turned into one by followers. But Avolio makes it sound like idolized leaders *really* demand to be idolized. In other words, he assumes that 'being an idol' is an inherent property of the empirical leader.

In terms of Zizek, Avolio fails to separate the empirical body of the leader from the sublime. Avolio's dismissive remarks on idolized leaders is needed to idolize 'real' leadership, that is to say, the 'transformational' or 'authentic' leaders who are believed to lift the organization to higher moral grounds. In other words, he *strategically* 'misses' that all leadership necessarily needs idolization; precisely because the sublime object of leadership is constituted through idolization. This, then, is the reason why so much of academic studies of leadership is, in fact, better understood as uncritical idolizations of leadership, albeit for a 'good' purpose: they contribute to the possibility of leadership phenomena themselves.

To what extent is this also true for a post-heroic leadership concept like 'shared leadership', which attempts to rid itself from any idolization of an individual human being? We would like to suggest that most of what we have said still holds: 'shared leadership' is an attractive concept precisely because of the sublime qualities that we attribute to leadership. If the concept was called 'well-functioning group' or 'shared responsibility' we would, most likely, not get very excited. In other words, the term 'leadership' itself has a radiating effect, almost irrespective of the context in which it is used.

Conclusion

We started with the observation that leadership has fascinated people throughout the ages. We argued that for someone like Plato leadership comes with moral fortitude. One cannot be a leader or a statesman if one does not have the right moral character.

The question we have tried to raise throughout the chapter is whether this idea that leadership must of necessity be something good is not based on what we referred to as an embellishment. There is a danger that we transform leadership into something better than it actually is. This is a problem we saw that Zizek was acutely aware of. He argued that we attribute qualities to the 'sublime' bodies of leaders rather than to real existent human beings.

Interestingly, even Plato himself alerted us to this problem. In his book *Republic*, Socrates gives an outline of the best education for becoming a leader (which includes subjects such as astronomy and logic). Eventually this education will open the student up to 'the all-embracing source of light, which is goodness itself'.[35] Goodness itself provides the basis for leadership. When Socrates has finished his description of the ideal education of leaders, the following conversation takes place between Socrates and Plato's older brother, Glaucon:

'You've created an image of the rulers which make them as thoroughly attractive as a master sculptor makes his statues, Socrates.'

'And there are female rulers too, Glaucon', I said.[36]

According to Robin Waterfield, who has translated the edition of Plato's *Republic* that we have used, Socrates chooses to 'pedantically' sidestep Glaucon's remark by shifting the theme to women and leadership which was not raised as an issue at all! Rather than missing the point on leadership and gender, Plato's brother rightly highlights the complex relation between the ethical and the aesthetic (or beautiful) in leadership. Indeed, many of the leadership scholars discussed in this chapter are sculptors of beautiful images of leadership. So, we concur with Barker when he notes that modern leadership theory – and business ethics we'd like to add – is still captured by Plato's philosopher-king.[37] This shows itself in the beautiful way in which ethical leadership is portrayed, but rarely discussed. In the end business ethicists and leadership scholars tend to be uninterested in ethical theory precisely because it is interested in leadership. One cannot discuss ethics simultaneously with leadership. Not because leadership is by definition unethical, but because leadership needs to appear as ethical (which appears as beautiful, in Plato's view) in order to exist. This image, whatever it may be, would be put at stake if one engages in a discussion of the ethics of leadership, and thereby leadership itself, as Zizek reminds us.

We can now return to the distinction between leadership and management that we spoke about when discussing the idea that organizations are over-managed and under-led. The difference between 'good management' and 'good leadership' is that the first refers to good in its technical sense, whereas good leadership *also* refers to moral goodness and therefore becomes more beautiful. Scholars in business leadership studies have been both consistent and persistent in maintaining this fusion of the technical goodness and the moral goodness. This makes good sense: leadership cannot be understood when it is considered without its moral dimension because without it leadership simply ceases to exist *as leadership*. We therefore propose a slight modification to Ciulla's suggestion that ethics is 'the heart of leadership'.[38] In our minds, aesthetics may be the heart of leadership.

NOTES

1 J. B. Ciulla, 'The state of leadership ethics and the work that lies before us', *Business Ethics: a European Review* 14 (2005), 323–35, 334. A characteristic example of an article on the ethics of leadership, that does not engage with the nature of ethics at all, is: D. S. Carlson and P. L. Perrewe, 'Institutionalization of organizational ethics through transformational leadership', *Journal of Business Ethics* 14 (1995), 829–38.
2 The citation is from B. M. Bass, *Bass and Stogdill's Handbook of Leadership*, 3rd edn. New York: Free Press (1990), 11.
3 Bass, *Handbook of Leadership*, 8.

4 W. Bennis and B. Nanus, *Leaders: the Strategies for Taking Charge*. New York: Harper and Row (1985), 21. For a similar perspective, see J. Kotter, 'What leaders really do', *Harvard Business Review* (May/June) (1990), 103–11. The point we are making here is, of course, is that leaders very likely do not do what they really do, according to Kotter.

5 B. M. Bass, *Leadership and Performance Beyond Expectations*. New York: Free Press (1985).

6 R. K. Greenleaf, *Servant Leadership: a Journey into the Nature of Legitimate Power and Greatness*. New York: Paulist Press (2002).

7 C. E. Manz and H. P. Sims, *SuperLeadership: Leading Others to Lead Themselves*. New York: Prentice Hall (1990).

8 D. Goleman, *The New Leaders: Transforming the Art of Leadership into the Science of Results*. London: Little Brown (2002).

9 B. M. Bass and P. Steidlmeier, 'Ethics, character, and authentic transformational leadership behavior', *Leadership Quarterly* 10 (1999), 181–217.

10 A. Huczynski, *Management Gurus: What Makes Them and How to Become One*. London: Thomson Business Press (1993), 88.

11 T. Carlyle, *On Heroes, Hero-worship, and the Heroic in History*. Middlesex: Echo Library (2007), 4. This text is also available at: www.gutenberg.org/etext/1091, accessed 12 January 2010.

12 S. Hook, *The Hero in History: a Study in Limitation and Possibility*. London: Secker and Warburg (1945), 1.

13 G. Gemmil and J. Oakley, 'Leadership – an alienating social myth?', *Human Relations* 45 (1992), 113–29.

14 J. B. Ciulla, 'Ethics: the heart of leadership', in T. Maak and N. M. Pless (eds.), *Responsible Leadership*. London: Routledge (2006), 21.

15 See also: M. Painter-Morland, *Business Ethics as Practice*. Cambridge: Cambridge University Press (2009), 182.

16 Richard Hofstadter, *Anti-intellectualism in American Life*. New York: Vintage Press (1962), 145–8, 253–71 (emphasis in original).

17 R. Solomon, 'Ethical leadership, emotions, and trust beyond charisma', in J. B. Ciulla (ed.), *Ethics, the Heart of Leadership*. Westport, CT: Praeger (2004), 83–101.

18 M. Weber, *Wirtschaft und Gesellschaft. Fünfte Auflage*. Tübingen: Mohr Siebeck (1980), 655.

19 Solomon, 'Ethical leadership', 98.

20 The Economist Group, *The World in 2003*. London: *The Economist* (2002), 118. The passage is quoted in: P. du Gay, 'The values of bureaucracy: an introduction', in P. du Gay (ed.), *The Values of Bureaucracy*. Oxford: Oxford University Press (2005), 1–2. Two other texts that emphasize the importance of managerial virtues rather than leadership virtues are: P. du Gay, *In Praise of Bureaucracy. Weber, Organization, Ethics*. London: Sage (2000) and R. ten Bos, *Fashion and Utopia in Management Thinking*. Philadelphia, PA: John Benjamin (2000).

21 J. B. Ciulla, 'Leadership and the problem of bogus empowerment', in J. B. Ciulla (ed.), *Ethics, the Heart of Leadership*, 2nd edn. London: Praeger (2004), 53–82.

22 J. McGregor Burns, *Leadership*. New York: Harper and Row (1978), 20.

23 *Ibid.*, 3; J. McGregor Burns, 'Foreword', in Ciulla (ed.), *Ethics, the Heart of Leadership*, ix–xii.

24 Ciulla does not agree with the idea that Hitler wasn't a leader. She rather emphasizes that Hitler did not embody the right values as the basis for his leadership.

25 C. Barnard, 'The nature of leadership', in K. Grint (ed.), *Leadership. Classical, Contemporary, and Critical Approaches*. Oxford: Oxford University Press

(1998), 89–111; originally published in C. Barnard, *Organization and Management*. Cambridge, MA: Harvard University Press (1948).

26 J. Kouzes and B. Posner, *The Leadership Challenge: How to Get Extraordinary Things Done in Organizations*. San Francisco, CA: Jossey-Bass (1987).

27 J. Howell and B. J. Avolio, 'The ethics of charismatic leadership: submission or liberation', *Academy of Management Executive* 6 (1992), 43–54, 52.

28 H. Arendt, *Eichmann in Jerusalem: a Report on the Banality of Evil*. New York: Penguin (1963).

29 Bass, *Handbook of Leadership*, 15.

30 S. Zizek, *For They Do Not Know What They Do*. London: Verso (1991), 255.

31 S. Zizek, *Looking Awry: an Introduction to Jacques Lacan through Popular Culture*. Cambridge, MA: The MIT Press (1991), 33.

32 S. Zizek, 'How to live with catastrophes', in B. Aretxaga, D. Dworkin, J. Gabilondo, and J. Zulaika (eds.), *Empire and Terror: Nationalism/Postnationalism in the New Millennium*. Reno, NV: Center for Basque Studies (2004), 209–10.

33 Zizek, 'How to live with catastrophes', 210.

34 B. Avolio and E. E. Locke, 'Should leaders be selfish or altruistic? Letters on leader motivation', in Ciulla (ed.), *Ethics, the Heart of Leadership*, 105–29, 129.

35 Plato, *Republic*, R. Waterfield (trans.). Oxford: Oxford University Press (1993), 540a.

36 *Ibid.*, 540c.

37 R. A. Barker, 'The nature of leadership', *Human Relations* 54 (2001), 469–94, 483.

38 Ciulla, *Ethics, the Heart of Leadership*.

9

Whistle-blowing

MOLLIE PAINTER-MORLAND AND RENÉ TEN BOS

Goals of this chapter

After studying this chapter you will be able to:

- understand the moral ambiguity surrounding whistle-blowing practices;
- understand the differences in the way the US and Europe perceive and deal with whistle-blowing;
- understand Caputo's description of obligations;
- understand Bauman's description of the moral impulse;
- understand Jonas's idea of a shared ethics.

Introduction

Whistle-blowing has become an increasingly important issue in business ethics in recent years. In business ethics, as in sporting events, whistle-blowing is related to sounding an alert that the rules of the game have been broken. But unlike the referee in a football game, the person blowing the whistle in the case of corporations is not an objective, independent observer, but rather an employee or a stakeholder who reports the misconduct of a colleague or of the corporation as a whole. Whistleblowers are individuals who believe that there is a risk of grave harm if unethical behaviour is not brought to light. And in fact, the collapses of both Enron and WorldCom around the turn of the century made it quite clear what harm can result from unethical behaviour. In both the WorldCom and Enron cases, the whistleblowers were employees of the organization, and as it happens, they were both female. Sherron Watkins (Enron) and Cynthia Cooper (WorldCom) both did much to bring the dilemmas that whistleblowers face into the public realm. Though they could not prevent their corporations' collapse, both were hailed as public heroes for their attempts to blow the whistle internally and for their strength of character in exposing their corporations' misconduct. They both believed that in reporting their suspicions of misconduct, they acted in the interests of their corporations and their stakeholders.

In this chapter, we will see that there is a lot of controversy about the character of the whistleblower. Occasionally hailed as a hero, the whistleblower is also often maligned as a tattler or traitor. We will see in this chapter that especially in Europe, the whistleblower is generally not seen as a laudable person. Cultural sensitivities play an important role here, but we also argue that there are institutional reasons for this European skepticism towards the whistleblower.

In the second part of the chapter, we will first try to show, using work by John Caputo, that the actions of whistleblowers cannot easily be explained. Instead, it is a response to a situation in which an individual often has no recourse to a set of clear decision-making guidelines that would provide them with direction. Then, we enter into the work of Zygmunt Bauman and Hans Jonas to shed some light on what it might be that drives the whistleblower. Is it, in the line of Bauman, a response to a 'moral impulse'? Or is it, in the line of Jonas, a 'sense of responsibility' that guides their behaviour? What Bauman and Jonas have in common is that both stress the importance of emotion for moral behaviour. They differ, however, on issues of scope: where Bauman thinks that moral action is conditioned by a proximity between me and the Other, Jonas urges us to feel responsible as well for those who are – spatially and temporally – far away from us. Technological developments have created an unprecedented level of interconnectedness of people all over the planet and responding to this interconnected world requires, if we are to believe Jonas, an entirely different kind of ethics.

But where do these considerations leave the whistleblower? Are people like Watkins or Cooper driven by a moral impulse incited by those who are close to them, or are they assuming a sense of responsibility for a much broader group of stakeholders? Can one feel morally responsible for what in the literature on the topic is routinely referred to as 'the public'? We will see, over and over again, that it is very difficult to tell. The controversy about the whistleblower will therefore remain a point of contention in the field of business ethics.

Whistle-blowing: a controversial issue

It is the priority that is placed on preventing harm to others that serves as the moral high-ground for whistleblowers. Natalie Dandekar argues that the whistleblower sees a certain wrongful practice within the company or organization they are working for as 'a source of non-trivial public harm'.[1] It is the seriousness of possible harm that confronts whistleblowers with a strong moral duty to report misconduct. However, what makes whistle-blowing such an interesting issue in business ethics is that reporting violations is by no means the only duty that an employee has. Essentially, whistleblowers often experience how difficult it is to make a choice between loyalty to their organization and loyalty towards the public. Add to this the fact that they often face the risk of serious personal and occupational retribution, and we can see a very difficult moral dilemma unfolding.

Whistle-blowing is often seen as morally reprehensible because whistleblowers violate the bonds of trust and loyalty that develop when people work or live together. Loyalty is often linked to gratitude. As Richard De George makes clear, biting the hand that feeds you can hardly be considered an 'admirable or praiseworthy action'.[2] However, if loyalty to the firm would be the highest moral obligation of every single employee, what would make this organization distinct from the Mafia? If silence would be the law that every single member of the organization would have to abide by, then there is no doubt that the whistleblower is in the same kind of predicament as any member of the Mafia. So we might argue that one way of putting a positive spin on the promotion of whistle-blowing practices is to describe it as a way of 'providing a safe alternative to silence'.[3] It allows employees to speak up in the case of wrongdoing without necessarily risking their own welfare or that of those around them.

Whistle-blowing in the US

Within business ethics there is a strong belief that loyalty towards the corporation need not be at odds with concern for the public. Corporations also have an interest in avoiding unethical behaviour, albeit just to avoid lawsuits, build reputational value, or attract and retain talented employees. Misconduct, if discovered in time, could in fact be resolved in ways that are in the interests of both the corporation and the public. This may be one reason why many business ethicists would claim that whistleblowers have a duty to report violations *internally* before seeking further recourse. In other words, they are expected to give their organizations the opportunity to remedy the situation *before* public disclosure will ensue. In some countries, like South Africa, whistleblowers cannot claim protection under whistle-blowing legislation if they do not report the unethical behaviour internally first. To make this possible, all organizations are encouraged or in some cases even legally obliged to put in place safe reporting mechanisms and to protect whistleblowers against occupational harm. The argument is that it is in their long-term interest to do so, because whistle-blowing serves both corporate and public interest. This is why US corporations are expected to establish whistle-blowing policies and environments of open communication, transparency, and trust. The Federal Sentencing Guidelines for Corporations in the US required of corporations to implement a safe reporting mechanism, or what is called a 'whistle-blowing line' or 'hotline' as part of a comprehensive ethics management programme. If corporations do so, they are entitled to a reduced fine in the case of prosecution for unethical conduct. They often even escape prosecution altogether if they bring the case forward and cooperate with the authorities. Whistle-blowing mechanisms have therefore become part of a kind of 'insurance policy' against legal penalties that corporations have to employ in the US.

Both legislation and regulation in the US encourage organizations to implement a whistle-blowing policy, which should include a clear statement of support for whistle-blowing from the organization and its leadership. It should guarantee that there will be no retaliation against whistleblowers who make *good faith* disclosures and follow the appropriate channels. A good faith disclosure is one that is in the interests of the public or others who may be affected, that can reasonably be expected to be true, and that is made without its primary motive being the self-interest of the whistleblower themselves. The organization should clearly state the appropriate avenues open to the whistleblower, which may include confidential whistle-blowing lines, hotlines, ethics officers, comments boxes, or an ombudsman. A confidential disclosure has to be distinguished from an anonymous disclosure, which could be made via a website or email address that allows whistleblowers to report unethical conduct without disclosing their identity, or via a physical drop-box where anonymous notes can be left.

Although anonymous reporting protects the whistleblower, it has its problems. It is for instance very difficult to follow-up the report and bring it towards disciplinary action if the person cannot be contacted to provide more information or substantiation of their claims. It also raises questions as to the veracity of the report and the motive of the whistleblower if they are not willing to disclose their identity. However, many whistle-blowing facilities make provision for anonymous reporting. Best practice dictates that the organization should indicate what kind of action is considered as wrongdoing that should be reported through this avenue. Many whistle-blowing lines fail because employees use the line, for example, to report their personal problems rather than unethical behaviour that could harm others. The organization should also make clear that disclosures must be made in good faith and that any malicious or false disclosure will be penalized.

The assumption behind all these directives and guidelines is that the organization has the ethical duty to create an atmosphere of trust and open communication. This entails that no retaliation against whistleblowers will be tolerated. Whistle-blowing mechanisms will not function properly if the organization has a culture of silence and retribution for speaking out. It is also important that the whistle-blowing policy should be linked to the organization's code of conduct, in order to make clear that all reports must be made out of a concern for protecting the values of the organization. The organization may even suggest possibilities for external disclosure. These are, needless to say, assumed to be only available after all internal reporting channels have been exhausted. Such external disclosures can be made by seeking recourse to relevant regulatory authorities, legal counsel, or public whistle-blowing mechanisms.

In the US, various pieces of legislation exist to afford whistleblowers some protection against retaliation after making their disclosures. The first important piece of legislation is the Whistleblowers Protection Act (1989) that protects whistleblowers working in government who report ethical misconduct or violation of the law. In 2002 Sarbanes-Oxley (SOX) legislation was passed, which has been influential in trying to further whistle-blowing in publicly held corporations. Section 301 of the Sarbanes-Oxley Act compelled all organizations to institutionalize whistleblower protections. It also describes concrete measures for the protection of whistleblowers. For example, they are protected against discharge, layoff, demotion, blacklisting, disciplining, or the refusal of overtime, promotion, and benefits.[4]

This does by no means solve all problems. Having a whistle-blowing line is one thing, but to get people to use it is quite another. According to Near and Micelli, there are both individual and situational factors that play a role in people's willingness to blow the whistle.[5] Individual factors include the personal characteristics of the whistleblower, the person to whom the disclosure is addressed, and the wrongdoer. In each case, the individual's credibility and position of power *vis-à-vis* other people in the organization play an important role. Individuals will more likely report misconduct if whistle-blowing is perceived to be part of their role within an organization.[6] Rothwell and Baldwin inferred that supervisory status was the most consistent predictor of whistle-blowing, while the existence of a policy that encouraged whistle-blowing also seemed to play a role.[7] This suggests that people are generally more likely to report misconduct if they feel that it is their professional or managerial responsibility to do so. There are also situational factors that influence whistle-blowing. For instance, the nature of the transgression, the extent to which an organization's fortunes are likely to be affected by it, the availability of evidence, and the legal basis for the complaint all play an important role. The specific characteristics of the organization seem to matter as well.[8] Whistle-blowing may, for instance, be affected by the way in which an organization is structured. A less rigid bureaucratic structure is believed to encourage more open communication. If an organization succeeds in establishing clear and proper channels for the internal disclosure of unethical behaviour, there may be no need for a whistle-blowing line.[9]

Finally, research has also shown that individual propensities with respect to whistle-blowing may not be consistent over time. Willingness to report misconduct varies across mood states and is often influenced by relatively minor events.[10] It was also found that people with a negative view of the world were less likely to report misconduct. These findings suggest that belief structures and emotions may play a significant role in how people interpret their personal ethical responsibilities in, and towards, an organizational system.[11] What all of this research seems to indicate is that it is pretty difficult to figure out what exactly motivates people to blow the whistle.

Whistle-blowing in Europe

The uncertainty about the acceptability and effectiveness of whistle-blowing becomes even more pronounced when one looks elsewhere in the world. Here, we will, for the sake of brevity, restrict ourselves to European experiences. Legislative frameworks and everyday practices in some countries in Europe seem to display a very different understanding of whistle-blowing. In Europe, the acceptability of whistle-blowing practices such as hotlines is deemed to be problematical. In 2005, the French National Commission for Data Protection (CNIL) decided that anonymous hotlines that companies like MacDonald's wanted to implement as part of their corporate code of conduct were deemed to be illegal for they violate laws regarding data protection. There was also a widespread sentiment among the French that the possibility of anonymous reporting was considered to be unfair. How can one, after all, defend oneself against anonymous complaints? Other American companies like Wal-Mart faced similar problems in Germany, even though here the hotlines were not considered to be illegal. The problem was rather that hotlines were deemed to be a poor alternative for the organization's work council, which is apparently supposed to be able to effectively handle all the problems that employees may have with whatever is going on in the organization.

Why do Europeans have so many doubts about whistle-blowing? In the US and the UK, people seem to think that whistle-blowing is a useful instrument to keep companies on the right moral track. Even though there are, as we have seen, qualms about the moral ambivalence of whistle-blowing, it is generally considered to be a practice which is morally praiseworthy. The overall European feeling stands in sharp contrast with this. Some commentators have argued that there might be historical and cultural reasons for this. Laura Hartman *et al.* argue that in countries like Germany the term 'whistleblower' immediately brings about associations with the national-socialists who encouraged and compelled people to tattle on everybody else in their neighbourhood.[12] Likewise, the French do not like the *dénonciateur* either because the person reminds them of the Vichy regime which collaborated with the Nazis during the second world war. Hartman *et al.* also offer other examples of cultural sensitivities towards whistle-blowing, but the problem with this kind of analysis is that it glosses over more institutional reasons to have doubts about the practice. Claiming that doubts about it are based on a particular culture's prejudice misapprehends the fact that in Europe the need for whistle-blowing may not be as obvious as in Anglophone countries. European companies display certain institutional characteristics that might render whistle-blowing rather superfluous.

More specifically: we list four reasons why Europeans are highly skeptical about this practice.

(1) Legislation on whistle-blowing is considered to be very expensive. Where the Americans generally seem to think that whistle-blowing is a fairly cheap alternative to other forms of regulation, there have been doubts in Europe about what the costs will be if people working in organizations are in constant danger of being exposed or disclosed. In other words, it has been argued that strict regulation on whistle-blowing – especially when it is not only encouraged but actually proscribed – poses unacceptable restrictions on freedom of action.

(2) It is also pointed out that there are many cases where whistleblowers simply misjudged particular actions of their organizations or of certain people who hold dominant positions. The number of 'unsubstantiated' disclosures is worrying. People do not always have complete information and may misjudge situations. There have been quite a few instances of directors and chief executive officers (CEOs) who had to leave their company because of allegations that in the end turned out to be wrong or at least unsubstantiated.[13]

(3) Europeans generally think that the interest of society cannot or should not affect the duty of loyalty. The latter duty of course requires of the whistleblower that any concern will be raised internally. It is taken for granted in Europe that this should not lead to their dismissal. Legislation to protect whistleblowers is therefore deemed to be unnecessary. In Europe, employees enjoy much more statutory protection than in Anglophone countries. Given the opportunity to report misconduct without immediately running the risk of losing one's job, whistle-blowing is frowned upon.

(4) Generally speaking, dissent within a company is in Europe much more taken for granted than in America. As we already saw with the experiences of Wal-Mart in Germany, most complaints are dealt with by the work council and will only in rare cases lead to dismissal. There are therefore structural provisions that make (external) whistle-blowing a much less plausible option. One might also put this somewhat differently: in Europe, trust in institutions and companies is bigger than in America. Europeans generally do not see the need why individuals require special protections against these institutions.

In face of all this, we need not to wonder why whistle-blowing has by and large been an issue which – perhaps with the sole exception of the Netherlands – has never been understood as very relevant. It is, for example, characteristic that the Germans do not even have a proper equivalent for the word 'whistleblower'. The need for legislation in Europe has never been seen as very urgent. Hassink *et al.* discuss a series of corporate codes from several European countries and claim that nowhere is there a special provision for whistle-blowing. The issue is considered to be irrelevant because institutions and companies are supposed to be capable of coping with this kind of dissent. In the words of Hassink and his colleagues:

> The recent trouble with the implementation of SOX [about the whistleblowers hotlines] in France suggests that the 'American way' of whistle-blowing might be incompatible with the part of Europe that does not employ the Anglo-Saxon business model.[14]

However, even in Europe, attitudes towards whistleblowers might change. Politicians in the European Parliament have tried to provide more legislation as far as whistleblowers are concerned.[15] Some notorious cases in the Netherlands have put the issue on the political agenda as well. The differences in sensitivities towards whistle-blowing are never constant and there is a likelihood that Europe will slowly adopt more and more American ideas. Nevertheless, at the time of writing it is fair to say that most Europeans would consider whistle-blowing as at best permissible rather than obligatory.

The lives of whistleblowers

The personal costs of whistle-blowing are certainly high. Not all whistleblowers eventually go on to become public heroes like Watkins and Cooper mentioned above. In fact, the vast majority lose their jobs and sometimes even their livelihoods for long periods of time, suffer from stress and stress-related diseases, marital break-up, and sometimes even become the victims of violent retaliation. Even more uncanny than all this is that organizations may erase any memory or record of the person who blew the whistle. See here what the daughter of a whistleblower has to say about her mother's experiences:

> you know, after a while I realized that they did want to kill her. Not really, but they wanted to make it as if she had never existed, that everything she said had never happened. That's a type of murder too.[16]

Whistleblowers can undergo nightmarish experiences that one would only expect to occur in novels by Kafka or Orwell. A case in point is what happened to Cynthia Brzak, a secretary working for the main United Nations (UN) refugee agency, who raised a complaint about sexual harassment by Ruud Lubbers, the former head of her organization. Even though there was hardly any doubt that there had been wrongdoing, Lubbers got away with it. The story by B. and other women was not without contradictions and Lubbers, being the former prime minister of the Netherlands, was held in such high repute that his position was simply unimpeachable. As Dandekar puts it eloquently: 'The wrongdoing is real, yet the wrongdoer is not *ipso facto* morally flawed'.[17]

Fred Alford has used the term 'scapegoat' to denote what a whistleblower might become. Scapegoats are not so much the victims of character assassination (either by colleagues, top managers, politicians, or media) but are, after having blown the whistle, entering a completely different world in which they are rendered as strangers. The most common reaction to the whistleblower,

Alford maintains, is not the accusation of being a betrayer but rather bafflement or bemusement: who is this strange person who washes the dirty linen in public? What makes them tick? Why would they do that?

It is precisely this reaction that causes a crisis of meaning in the life of the whistleblower. It is not simply iniquity or hostility that the whistleblower has to cope with but rather the fact that they are banned from the moral order of the universe. And from this outside world, they look back into the world they once belonged to, and find themselves to be completely incapable of making sense of it. There is no trust in legal or public institutions anymore, in leadership, or in other human beings. 'To be a whistleblower is to step outside the Great Chain of Being, to join not just another religion, but another world.'[18] Alford uses the stories of whistleblowers to reveal something rather unsettling about organizations. Following Bauman, Alford claims that 'every organization is dedicated to the destruction of its members' individuality, defined as the ability to think seriously about what one is doing'.[19] But it is not only reflection that is systematically discouraged but also the ability to speak out. What Foucault used to refer to as *parrheisia*, the old Greek word for fearless speech, is something that needs to be discouraged in the 'benighted worlds' of the organization. This is, if we are to believe Alford, the basic problem of the whistleblower. No matter what his or her motives are, the whistleblower will be condemned in organizational settings because he or she appeared as a flesh-and-blood individual. To retain any sense of organizational coherence and loyalty, the whistleblower must be made the scapegoat. In other words, the organization can only be cleansed if it bans the very person who did not only signal dirtiness but also dared to speak about it.[20]

Paradoxically, however, the scapegoat might eventually become the hero in the end. In Hollywood films, the whistleblower is routinely revered as the individual hero who was initially ostracized or excoriated but who in the end turned out to be the person who was capable of bringing redemption. An example of such a film is Michael Mann's *The Insider*, in which Russel Crowe plays a whistleblower who is persuaded by a television maker (played by Al Pacino) to bring to the public that the tobacco company he has worked for had always kept back its knowledge about the addictive properties of its core product. The story that is unfolded in the film is classical: the whistleblower loses his status, brings his family in serious jeopardy, and is eventually threatened with murder. Many people around him, including the members of his own family, do not understand why he wants to undergo all this. He experiences the shifts in meaning Alford is referring to, but in the end the crisis is overcome and the hero is redeemed.

However, the real world of most whistleblowers is much less redemptive than is suggested in contemporary myths. More often than not, their lives are, in words of Alford, broken. This raises all sorts of questions. Are whistleblowers led by a secret drive to attain legendary status? Are they simply following up their sense of responsibility and accept the consequences? Or is it simply a moral urge rather than a fully fledged awareness of responsibility? Again this question comes to the fore: what makes the whistleblower tick? Some business ethicists, like Tom Beauchamp and Norman Bowie, claim that it might be wise not to fight all evil in the world:

> often, to be sure, we are in a position where we cannot prevent evil or can prevent it only at a disproportionate price. In such a situation, we may be excused temporarily.[21]

This statement would make it seem as if whistle-blowing is merely a matter of costs and gains. But as we will come to see in the next section, explaining the actions of whistleblowers in such a straightforward way is very problematical.

Rethinking the challenge of whistle-blowing

Can we ever do the right thing?

One of the central assumptions that is made in the literature on whistle-blowing is that people engage in disclosure to protect the public or other stakeholders from significant harm. Whistleblowers should be able to calculate and anticipate significant harm and weigh this against the costs that reporting the misconduct would have for those who are involved, for the organization and for the whistleblowers themselves. Apparently, whistleblowers are assumed to have the clarity of thought and perspective that helps them to easily resolve the dilemma caused by the conflict of loyalties we discussed above.

It is this ability to calculate and weigh outcomes as well as to clearly understand one's moral duty that continental scholars may question. For instance, the American philosopher and theologian, John Caputo, would argue that moral obligations typically arise in cases of disaster.[22] He traces the concept of disaster back to its etymological roots: '*dis-astrum*' indicates that you have lost your star. In other words, you are without some kind of guiding light that tells you which direction to take. Caputo argues that any real moral dilemma is disastrous in this sense. You cannot hope to resolve the problem by arguing that more good will come out of doing the right thing amid the difficulties that you face in a specific situation. It is just a sheer loss, which throws reason and calculation into chaos.

The situations that whistleblowers face often have the character of a disaster. In many cases, the harm done to the organization has gone so far as to be unrecoverable. Take again the case of Sherron Watkins and Enron. Her disclosure could not prevent thousands of people losing their jobs and pensions, investors losing their money, and the executives ending up in jail, or even losing their lives, in some cases. Watkins herself suffered greatly through all of this, and even the respect and public status that she eventually recovered cannot make up for her ordeal. This is by no means an argument to say that Watkins should not have blown the whistle. It is rather an acknowledgement of the difficulties she faced after having decided to blow the whistle.

What we learn from Caputo is that questions about our moral duties do not find an easy answer. In the end, we may have to acknowledge that it is not possible to make a simple case for the moral duty to blow the whistle. It is an extremely complex issue. However, this does not mean that there are not very strong moral motivations behind blowing the whistle. In fact, Caputo would argue that the moral obligation that faces whistleblowers cannot be shirked *precisely* because it is not calculable. Obligation overcomes you, you cannot explain it, it is a fact that cannot be denied. As Caputo explains it:

> Obligations do not ask for my consent. Obligation is not like a contract I have signed after having had a chance to first review it carefully and to have consulted my lawyer. It is not anything I have agreed to be party to. It binds me. It comes over me and binds me.[23]

This perspective may help us understand why some whistleblowers would feel obliged to go forward with their disclosure despite the fact that family members, friends, and colleagues urge them not to do so, and even though it may involve huge personal costs. Caputo explains it as a feeling of being bound, being caught up, so much so that one feels one has lost one's autonomy in the situation and become blinded to anything but the obligation.

It is interesting that Caputo argues that obligations ring out like bells, they sound alarms, they cry out for a response and for redress. There is much in this metaphor to explore to get a perspective on what happens in the case of whistle-blowing. One may even argue that the alarm that a whistleblower sounds (in Dutch, they are literally 'bell-ringers') is the necessary and inevitable echo that results from the sounding of obligation. Another important insight that Caputo offers us is the fact that moral obligation tends to arise between good and evil.[24] He argues that life does not take us beyond good and evil, as Nietzsche would have claimed, but rather gets us stuck inbetween. We cannot simply argue that the whistleblower did the right thing, because the 'right thing' is never unitary and homogenous. Rather, Caputo argues, the good is always plural, always multiple, and open to variation. There are always multiple options available to do good, and whistle-blowing may be one of them.

The moral impulse of the whistleblower

But given multiple options, why would one ever choose what seems to be *the* most difficult option, to wit, to blow the whistle? The British-Polish sociologist and philosopher, Zygmunt Bauman, addresses this question. What he suggests, however, may not satisfy those who seek to find firm foundations to establish whistle-blowing as a moral and even as a legal duty. Bauman argues that 'moral *practice* can have only *impractical* foundations'.[25] What he means by this is that a moral practice must always set itself standards that it cannot reach. We can never rest assured that the moral standard has been satisfied, we must always wonder whether we could not have done more, sooner, or differently. Moral duty cannot be exhausted. It is what constantly haunts our decisions.

Given this perspective, it may become possible for us to accept the moral ambiguity that is part and parcel of the act of blowing the whistle. It is something that always comes too late, or in some cases too early. It is what brings the whistleblowers to do what is in their minds clearly 'the right thing', but often at incalculable cost to themselves and their families. Yet the whistleblower felt it must be done, regardless of all these considerations.

Bauman points out another paradox when it comes to morality: 'I am free only insofar as I am a hostage'. In Bauman's words: 'I am I in as far as I am for the Other'. What we tend to do with this paradox is to cover it over, to hide it behind notions of 'altruism', or to argue that self-interest should be set aside for the sake of the public weal or some established ethical norms. Bauman believes that we lose something in the process. He argues that we should not try to get rid of the paradox by establishing binary oppositions like self and other, or weigh up conflicting interests. In Bauman's opinion, this kind of orderly system of conflicting interests and clear moral principles hides the complexity of life. And it makes it very hard for us to understand the messiness of something as morally ambivalent as whistle-blowing.

Whistleblowers feel obliged to leave behind the comforts of conventions and to abandon the safe sense of togetherness that loyalties and mutual social duties and roles dictate. They refuse to keep quiet just because 'everyone does it'. Bauman describes this kind of behaviour as crucial in being truly morally responsive. If one is merely following convention, social rules, or even role-dictated duties, one refuses the individual moral demand that is responsible in the real sense of the word ('response-able', to be capable of a response). Whistleblowers take up their specific moral duty by giving their own, individual response to the situation, even if it is socially uncomfortable to do so.

What complicates the process of understanding how someone becomes convinced that whistle-blowing is the 'right' response to the situation that faces them, is the fact that the moral demand often remains *unspoken*. Bauman refers to this as the 'unbearable silence of responsibility'.[26] He draws on Knud Løgstrup's notion of 'the ethical demand' to explain that moral demands are unspoken, and precisely because they are unspoken, they are radical. They cannot be evaded, because they are directed at the single individual who receives them, and at no-one else. This demand comes from the Other, who has no right to demand and who often does not even deliberately express a demand, but yet this demand arrives. In terms of whistle-blowing, this moral demand comes from an Other who is often hard to identify in real terms. Assuming that they act in good faith, whistleblowers typically have the interests of the public at heart. 'The public' is often without a clear voice. They do not demand by decree, and hence it is sometimes difficult to interpret the demand correctly.

Vagueness and confusion are characteristic of the moral impulse, in the sense that it cannot be delineated as an explicit rule for all cases. This 'confused and confusing' character of a demand is characteristic of the moral impulse precisely because it is a demand made only to the individual in the situation. If the Other's demand is made explicit in terms of a right, an obligation, or a social norm or rule, it would lose its moral force, because it would become a generalized transaction within which we lose our unique moral responsiveness.

This may make one think twice about making something like blowing the whistle a legal duty. For instance, some corruption prevention legislation makes blowing the whistle a legal duty, and if one refrains from doing so, one becomes guilty of the crime oneself.[27] However, most legislation is not necessarily concerned with making blowing the whistle a legal duty, but rather with protecting the whistleblower against occupational detriment. This seems important in terms of mitigating the possible harm that could come to whistleblowers. Bauman's perspectives precipitate the insight that the law can merely provide a space within which an individual can receive the moral demand to whistle-blow – the duty to do so should not be legalized.

It seems the least one could do to give support to whistleblowers, but this can by no means alleviate the kind of anxiety that lies at the heart of any truly moral act. Bauman explains that moral anxiety is the only substance that the moral self could ever have. He argues that it is this moral urge to do something, without knowing exactly what the right thing to do is, that makes an act moral. A moral self is characterized by the urge to do, by recognizing an unfulfilled task, and not by a duty correctly performed. The moral self is therefore never without anxiety – it always wonders whether it could not have done more, and that what has been done is not at all moral enough.[28]

Bauman explains that all morality is *aporetic*. As we have seen in Chapter 5, this means that it is essentially impossible to find a way out of a moral dilemma. The reason for this is that most moral choices are not unambiguously good.[29] They are often made between contradictory impulses that leave the decision-maker uncertain as to what to do. Yet the moral *urge* remains. Caputo showed us that it is something that cannot be rationalized by employing a cost–benefit analysis. Bauman takes this insight one step further by arguing that morality is not something that can be organized by means of policies or pieces of legislation. It is an impulse that is by no means 'impulsive', in the sense of fleeting. It persists and drives the individual towards an individual moral response. The mistake that we tend to make in societal structures, like organizations, is to attempt to organize and tame this drive, this impulse, by means of technologies and policies. Paradoxically, in the process, we may disable precisely that moral urge, drive, and impulse, which brings someone to blow the whistle.

The functioning of many whistle-blowing lines seems to illustrate the way in which the moral urge can be undermined. Most large organizations in the US outsource their whistle-blowing lines to call centres, where reporting takes place via a highly mechanized system. Alice Petersen, founder of a unique whistle-blowing service called Listen-up, has identified a few basic problems with how these lines typically function, which her organization steers clear of.[30] According to her, whistleblowers generally respond very negatively to the scripted responses that are used in call centres. Call centres usually serve a wide variety of clients with divergent needs. It is for this reason that pre-prepared scripts are employed. They are designed to ensure that consultants respond to calls in a consistent way, and they address all necessary and relevant issues in an appropriate way during the course of a consultation. Call centre consultants are rarely capable of being spontaneously responsive, or of establishing a relationship of trust with callers who have sensitive information. Instead, scripted responses are used to identify, as quickly as possible, the issue at stake and offer a standard solution or response. Whistleblowers typically tend to take this as evidence that the organization does not take their unique situation seriously, or that it simply seeks as expedient a solution as possible to the problems that they raise. By sanctioning, or insisting on, the use of such standardized procedures, companies create the impression that they do not consider themselves accountable *to* the caller or the various other stakeholders who may be involved, but rather seek to limit their own liability *for* anything that might have gone wrong. This does precisely what Bauman objects to – it gives a standardized, general response to a moral urge that is highly individual and specific. It makes it a question of law and duty rather than a moral urge and desire to grapple with what is right, even when it constantly eludes you.

Further negative effects include the fact that whistle-blowing practices can create an environment in which individuals feel as though they are constantly being watched by their colleagues and superiors. In such an environment, colleagues may find it hard to trust one another or to be responsive towards one another. In some cases, employees may internalize the fear of being constantly watched by others to such an extent that they begin to police themselves. This is what Foucault referred to as the 'panopticon effect'.[31] Managers, who are interested in exercising control over their subordinates, may welcome this effect, but it is not conducive to a healthy organization environment. Studies into the effects of social monitoring mechanisms, such as email monitoring, have shown that this form of internalized control may have all sorts of counterproductive side-effects.[32] The feeling of 'being watched', for instance, may breed paranoia, which has a disempowering effect on an individual. The 'anticipatory conformity' that it induces also hampers creativity and causes a loss of autonomy.[33] In general, various forms of monitoring, of which whistle-blowing can be one, convey the message to employees that they are not trusted. In consequence, some of the basic elements of healthy organizational relationships, like respect for others' privacy and trust among colleagues, may be sacrificed.

Despite of all these concerns, whistle-blowing practices remain an important part of the ethics management practices of many organizations, especially in the US. And regardless of the problems that we mentioned, whistleblowers seem to still come forward and find the courage to report misconduct and other ethical violations. As we have argued so far, no clear reason can be found for why someone would still be motivated to do so. We now turn towards further explorations of the moral sense that drives whistleblowers.

A sense of responsibility

If one were to ask the question 'what ultimately drives the whistleblower?', the German philosopher Hans Jonas would undoubtedly argue that it must be a *sense of responsibility*. He understands this as an emotion. It is, we will see, a necessary condition for morality.[34] We feel responsible when the existence of something or someone is at stake. When we see an unknown child in a dangerous situation most people immediately want to save him or her. They will do so before making any cost–benefit calculation or before considering a certain rule. Their act is based on a moral impulse.

This is no doubt not far away from what Bauman is suggesting. Yet, there are a few important differences. For Bauman, responsibility is always bigger than obedience to rules or norms. If you were to express your responsibility as a rule, then it is undoubtedly a rule that would be a rule only for yourself, a rule that only you would be capable of hearing. Bauman refers to this as a *singular* obligation that has been spelled out for you alone because it is for your ears only.[35] Since you are the only person who understands this rule, there is no way of making it into a standardized rule. Standardization, as we have seen, undermines the moral impulse and hence responsibility for Bauman. But for Jonas, rules are not entirely bad if they serve to broaden our sense of moral responsibility. Even though we see in both Bauman and Jonas an emphasis on emotion and otherness, the latter is much less averse to rules than the former. For Jonas, the matter of singularity is not very important. The sense of responsibility he talks about is something that is not only there for me or for you but is essentially shared. Our time, he argues, calls for a 'collective' or even 'planetary' sense of responsibility. And if necessary, we need power and rules to make this collective sense of responsibility effective in the world.

The possibility of a moral existence

Jonas has a much broader understanding of responsibility than Bauman. He claims that everything in the world has only one purpose: it wants to be there. A rock resists its destruction, a certain species of animal does not want to die, human beings also lay claim to their existence. In this sense, Jonas argues that nothing can be *indifferent* towards its own existence. The absence of this indifference is what Jonas refers to as 'the good'. Our world, he argues, would become incomprehensible if we were not to accept that things *do* make a difference. It is the claim of things to existence, Jonas reminds us, that constantly appeals to moral beings. Existence is, by definition, vulnerable. That is why it has a value. This holds for objects, for animals, for human beings. It also holds for corporations as every single employee of Enron or WorldCom can attest. It is the vulnerability of every single being that stirs a sense of responsibility in us.

Jonas provides us with two key understandings when it comes to morality or ethics. Firstly, he jettisons the idea that there is a gap between fact and value – a gap that most business ethicists assume exists. He rejects the idea that certain things are just facts. This would imply that they do not make a difference. In the chapter on sustainability, we will see that for a very long time business people have understood the earth as something which is just a given, and it does not necessarily elicit a moral concern. The way that the mining industry has treated the planet or the environment is a case in point: whatever might be extracted from the mine, it is just there to make money. It has mere instrumental value. Jonas fiercely opposes this mentality and argues for the vulnerability of all existing entities – organic and anorganic, natural and artificial – and thinks they should be assigned a certain inherent value that must be proactively protected.

Secondly, Jonas claims that whatever is good in the world, that is to say, whatever makes a difference, is not determined by our wishes or desires. When something is merely the object of your will, he continues, it lacks the authority of the good. In other words, whatever makes a difference is not determined by your will or desire. For example, if we argue that stakeholders should make a difference to a responsible corporation, then we should never forget that this corporation does not choose its stakeholders. Stakeholders appear and are not the object of, let us say, a managerial will. The good, Jonas would point out, cannot coerce free will into making it a purpose, but it can make clear that there are indeed duties which are more profound than any will. If this *sense of duty* makes clear one thing, then it is that we always owe something to whatever is good. In this sense, a company who takes its stakeholders seriously might be argued to behave in a similar kind of way as the whistleblower. In both cases, there is something that becomes more important than whatever it is that people wish or desire.

That we can allow this to happen, that we can dominate our will and desire, is in the end what makes a moral existence (*sittliches Sein*) possible. For Jonas, morality implies selflessness. For a whistleblower, the matter of concern is more important than any self-concern, including happiness or love. That the lives of many whistleblowers are, in terms of Alford, 'broken', tells us indeed something about what Jonas understands as the *paradox* of morality: the self often yields to something else that is good. Whatever is deemed to be good, must be a matter (*Sache*) of the world and not a matter of the self. There is a second, even deeper paradox as well. Above, we noticed that the whistleblower stands out as an individual. If we link this understanding to the idea that morality overrides self-concern, then we may argue that it is exactly the selflessness that gives the whistleblower a certain kind of individuality. It is by dint of the fact that one hears the call of the other that individuality becomes a possibility. But it is an individuality that is, somewhat paradoxically, based on the ability to share with others. The point of all these considerations is that even though morality is always related to goals, it cannot be related to your or my own goal.

Jonas would agree with Bauman that emotion is crucial for morality, but he claims that this does not entirely rule out reason. The latter is what makes you understand that there is something wrong in the world. Emotion is especially psychologically important because it moves the will into the direction of a duty. This duty presupposes that you hear a call. You are, as we have seen, a moral being exactly because your will can be stirred apart from your own vital interests. We submit that this holds for whistleblowers as well. The fact that they hear the call from some being who is in distress, exceeds the 'indifferent freedom' characteristic of human reason.[36] What matters for a whistleblower is not their own will but rather a particular situation in the world. Law and duty do not inspire awe in the whistleblower, but this situation. In the sense that they understand the situation in a way that law or calculation does not, they might be argued to have developed a very specific kind of reasonability. After all, why would we wish to argue that a concern for the public weal would be unreasonable?

A shared ethics

Bauman argues that it is the distress of the Other that allows you to take up responsibility and he describes this as the 'unfounded foundation' of morality.[37] Jonas does not disagree, but he is more specific about what the foundation of morality might be: it is, as we have seen, the fact that being cannot be indifferent towards itself. What would it mean to act irresponsibly? 'To do nothing and let things simply happen' is the quite sobering answer we get. Jonas provides us with the example of the player in a casino. When he stakes all of his money, he acts frivolously. When this money is not his, he perhaps acts criminally. But when he is a father, he acts irresponsibly, no matter whether he has won or lost and no matter whether the capital was his or not. 'Only he who has responsibilities', Jonas claims, 'can act irresponsibly'.[38] It is therefore the 'situation' in which a person finds themselves which creates this responsibility. In the case of the father, the responsibility is not reciprocal: his children are not responsible for his behaviour. This seems to suggest that responsibility is also intricately bound up with authority or power. You can, Jonas suggests, only assume responsibility if you are in a powerful position. If a five-year-old child claims responsibility for your gambling behaviour, you would probably not take this claim all too seriously.

The relationship between power and responsibility is where the shoe pinches when it comes to whistle-blowing. Perhaps the ambivalent attitude that many people have towards whistleblowers is related to the fact that those who report misconduct have specific interests that may influence their decisions and actions. For instance, a whistleblower's sense of responsibility may also be influenced by their position. We saw earlier in the chapter that people are more inclined to blow the whistle when they view it as a duty that is part of their supervisory role in the organization. Yet, there are often personal interests and situational dynamics at stake too. These questions shed some light on why there are always doubts about the motives of the whistleblower. As Alford made clear, most people simply do not understand what drives him or her. What we have stressed in this chapter is that whistle-blowing is not always a reasonable act and yet at the same time it is not entirely unreasonable either.

But do we now really understand what drives the whistleblower? To us, it seems that their plight can only be understood if one understands one's own moral urges and the way in which they come into being. The certainty that a particular state of affairs, a *situation* is just unacceptable, and that you need to do something about it, is derived from living with others over time. Such urges are not irrational, but neither can they be completely rationalized. They emerge in and through our connections with others. Bauman argues that these connections can only be maintained if we remain close to others. Jonas wants us to believe that this sense of responsibility should apply even to distant others, and that certain societal structures are necessary to facilitate this.

Perhaps Bauman is aware of this as well. In several places in his work he discusses the work of Jonas in very positive terms. Here is how he summarizes Jonas's key insights:

> Since what we do affects other people, and what we do with the increased powers of technology has a still more powerful effect on people and on more people than ever before – the ethical significance of our actions reaches now unprecedented heights. But the moral tools we possess to absorb and control it remain the same as they were at the 'cottage industry' stage . . . Morality which has always guided us and still guides us today has powerful, but short hands. It now needs very, very long hands indeed. What chance of growing them?[39]

If Bauman is not optimistic about the possibility that we will be afforded the help of 'the long hands' of morality, it is because he believes that our modern system of orderly rules and regulations makes us morally unresponsive. It keeps morality at arm's length, and manages it by means of long-distance perspectives and high-tech mechanized responses. According to Jonas, we need to develop a sense of purpose that binds us to each other, and that guarantees our survival, despite technological advances that seem to lead to an even more impersonal world.

We saw the relevance of this danger when we discussed the mechanization of whistle-blowing practices. It makes acting on a moral obligation impersonal and distant. Though technology can create the means for us to respond to our moral obligations, it cannot recreate the moral impulse that drives us. Sometimes it makes bearing moral responsibility even more difficult. Jonas is keenly aware of the dangers of technology, and here again, he and Bauman find some common ground. In response to the dangers of technology, Bauman argues for an ethics of self-limitation. He believes that the only way to do this would be to visualize the others that may be involved in our action or inaction in order to reestablish the proximity that is required for a moral obligation to arise. Jonas would argue that this should always be coupled with what he calls a 'heuristics of fear'; if we cannot anticipate the consequences of our technological impact on our world, we should steer clear of it. More importantly, we should consider the mutual dependence of all people on the planet in thinking about our responsibilities. It is the emphasis on a global sense of responsibility that sets Jonas apart from Bauman.

Humanity as such has unprecedented powers and this is what requires a new sense of responsibility. Jonas describes it as future-oriented, unreciprocal, and continuous. When it comes to responsibility, he famously claims, you cannot go on holiday.[40] It is impossible to lay off responsibility once one has assumed it. He also thinks of responsibility and ethics in terms of conservation, preservation, and prevention rather than progress or perfection. In this, his ideas are very anti-utopian. And, again, he is adamant about the role of power: responsibility of human beings for one another is not to be taken for granted. It should be seen as a *potential* relationship that becomes *actual* only in accordance with a real advantage in power.

Conclusion

In this chapter, it became clear that whistle-blowing is a controversial topic in business ethics. Not only are there vast differences between how various countries deal with the issue of whistle-blowing, but it also remains a practice that is morally ambiguous. Some whistleblowers are hailed as heroes, whereas others are made scapegoats or treated as traitors. In many cases, whistleblowers suffer huge personal costs as a result of making their disclosures. In trying to understand why whistleblowers would still be willing to report unethical behaviour, we argued that it cannot be explained by means of a simple cost–benefit analysis. Whistleblowers often blow the whistle despite huge costs to themselves, their colleagues, and their companies. Sometimes, the public does not even see the immediate benefit of whistleblowers' disclosures.

We have tried to shed light on whistle-blowing by drawing on the thoughts of Caputo, Bauman, and Jonas. It is important to realize that these thinkers do not explicitly mention the whistleblower. However, they provide us with some perspectives on why people have a strong sense of moral obligation and why they may decide to act on them. Both Caputo and Bauman make it clear that a deliberate cost–benefit analysis is not employed in making these decisions. Instead, the whistleblower has a sense of responsibility that cannot be shirked, even by 'rational' reasons. But in understanding this moral urge we may want to understand the context within which these urges arise. For Jonas, it is the context of being a human being among other human beings. Being part of a healthy community cultivates the right kind of emotions that spur one into action, that urge one to act at the right time. We may even call these urges 'reasonable emotions', which steer clear of excesses in a way that Aristotle would have condoned. It is in this respect that Jonas provides us with a supplement to what Bauman has to say. There is a complicated relation between emotion and reason and also between your individual moral self and the social texture in which you find yourself.[41] The affective urge that drives the whistleblower is something that exists because as human beings we live with one another in society, and as such it is not irrational or unreasonable. In fact, it is a very important part of the relational fabric that makes our lives meaningful.

NOTES

1 N. Dandekar, 'Can whistleblowing be fully legitimated? A theoretical discussion', *Business and Professional Ethics Journal* 10 (1) (1990), 89–108.

2 R. De George, 'Whistle blowing', in R. De George (ed.), *Business Ethics, 3rd edn.* New York: MacMillan (1990), 200–16.

3 P. Omtzigt, *The Protection of Whistleblowers*, see http://74.125.77.132/ search?q=cache:ki33Tjpa4QIJ:fairwhistleblower.ca/docs/ti/Council_of_Europe_ Draft_WB_Resolution.pdf+whistleblowing+pentiti&cd=3&hl&=nl&ct=clnk& gl=nl, accessed 25 August 2009.

4 Anonymous, 'Companies must act soon to meet whistle-blower protection deadline', *Investor Relations Business* (22 December 2003).

5 J. P. Near and M. P. Miceli, 'Effective whistle-blowing', *Academy of Management Review* 20 (3) (1995), 679–708.

6 M. P. Miceli and J. P. Near. 'What makes whistle-blowers effective? Three case studies,' *Human Relations* 55 (4) (2002), 455–79.

7 G. R. Rothwell and J. N. Baldwin, 'Ethical climates and contextual predictors of whistle-blowing', *Review of Public Administration* 26 (3) (2006), 216–44.

8 G. King, 'The implications of an organization's structure on whistle-blowing', *Journal of Business Ethics* 20 (1999), 315–26.

9 King, 'Implications of organizational structure', 324.

10 M. B. Curtis, 'Are audit-related ethical decisions dependent upon mood?', *Journal of Business Ethics* 68 (2006), 191–209.

11 Curtis, 'Audit-related ethical decisions', 206.

12 L. Hartman, D. Elm, T. Radin, and K. Pope, 'Translating corporate culture around the world: a cross-cultural analysis of whistleblowing as an example of how to say and do the right thing', *Notizie di Politeia* XXV (93) (2009), 255–72.

13 For a brief discussion on this problem, see H. Hassink, M. de Vries, and L. Bollen, 'A content analysis of whistleblowing policies of leading European companies', *Journal of Business Ethics* 75 (2007), 25–44.

14 Hassink *et al.*, 'Content analysis of whistleblowing policies', 42.

15 Omtzigt, *The Protection of Whistleblowers*.

16 F. Alford, *Whistleblowers. Broken Lives and Organizational Power*. New York: Cornell University Press (2001), 54.

17 Dandekar, 'Can whistleblowing be legitimated?', 105. See also C. Calhoun, 'Responsibility and reproach', *Ethics* 99 (1998), 396–7.

18 Alford, *Broken Lives*, 6.

19 *Ibid.*, 116.

20 *Ibid.*, 128.

21 T. Beauchamp and N. Bowie, *Ethical Theory and Business*. Englewood Cliffs, NJ: Prentice Hall (1988), 5.

22 J. Caputo, *Against Ethics*. Bloomington, IN: Indiana University Press (1993), 5–6.

23 *Ibid.*, 7.

24 *Ibid.*, 33.

25 Z. Bauman, *Postmodern Ethics*. Oxford: Blackwell (1993), 81.

26 *Ibid.*, 78.

27 See South Africa's Prevention and Combating of Corrupt Activities Act 12 of 2004.

28 Bauman, *Postmodern Ethics*, 80.

29 *Ibid.*, 11.

30 Interview with A. Petersen at the Listen-up head offices, Chicago, January 2005. See also: Rothwell and Baldwin, 'Ethical climates and contextual predictors'.

31 See M. Foucault, *Discipline and Punish. The Birth of Prison*. London: Penguin (1970), 195–228.

32 C. Sprinkle, 'Surveillance in America. An interview with Christian Parenti', *American Behavioral Scientist* 48 (10) (2005), 1,375–82.

33 K. Martin and E. R. Freeman, 'Some problems with email monitoring, part 1', *Journal of Business Ethics* 43 (4) (2003), 353–61.

34 H. Jonas, *Das Prinzip Verantwortung*. Frankfurt: Suhrkamp (2003), 166.

35 Bauman, *Postmodern Ethics*, 52.

36 Jonas, *Prinzip Verantwortung*, 398.

37 Bauman, *Postmodern Ethics*, 75.

38 Jonas, *Prinzip Verantwortung*, 176.

39 Bauman, *Postmodern Ethics*, 218.

40 Jonas, *Prinzip Verantwortung*, 196.

41 For an extensive discussion on the relation between emotion and reason, see R. ten Bos and H. Willmott, 'Towards a critical business ethics: interweaving reason and emotion in working life', *Journal of Management Studies* 38 (5) (2001), 769–93.

10

Marketing, bad faith, and responsibility

JANET BORGERSON

Goals of this chapter

After studying this chapter you will be able to:

- understand some of ethical dilemmas relating to marketing and, more specifically, to the use of marketing images;
- understand what 'representational practices' are and how they can become a matter of moral concern;
- understand why and how business ethics could have ignored this area of research;
- understand some basic themes in existential phenomenology;
- understand Sartre's concept of 'bad faith'.

Introduction

This chapter deepens the sense of marketing's potential realm of influence, and thus broadens the territory for ethical issues in marketing. Marketing activities go beyond simplistic notions of promotion, persuasion, or selling 'stuff'. From prenatal testing and political candidates to personal ads, little remains untouched by marketing. Indeed, researchers and practitioners in the field of marketing seek to understand, but also cocreate, modes of knowing and being. For example, how we come to think about travel destinations, and moreover what we think about the identities of the people who live there, may be largely the result of marketing communications, whether popular travel websites, television specials, or the latest beer and wine promotions.

Marketing, simply understood, focuses on four areas of concern known as 'the four Ps': product, price, promotion, and place. These 'four Ps', the marketing mix, inspire basic marketing questions. For example, what type of product – and this includes services, experiences, and ideas generally – might be conceived and developed? Marketers might investigate how a caramel-coloured carbonated beverage could move beyond quenching thirst to spurring feelings of fun, comfort, and being with friends. These considerations might lead to innovations, such as creating a unique red label, recognizable bottle shape, and distinctive taste. Marketing also concerns the prices customers might be willing to pay for products, services, or experiences, as well as the ways in which aspects of these products, services, and experiences could be communicated and, moreover, to which specific target market. Marketing managers also decide where, or in what places and spaces, their products, services, and experiences could be promoted and distributed. Perhaps, during certain holidays, this red-labelled drink could be sold in celebratory, special-sized packaging and be consistently pictured as part of any festive gathering.

Ethical concerns intersect with the four Ps. For example, promoting soft drinks containing high percentages of corn syrup may not be a good thing to do if consuming these beverages damages human health. In creating marketing campaigns and designing retail layouts, have marketing managers overlooked the potential harms of placing attractive cans of sugary drinks at children's eye level next to store check-out lines? Marketing ethics has inquired into marketers' decision-making processes, and devised various checklists to provide criteria for judging, but also for guiding and directing, decisions deemed to have ethical content. Other standard conceptions of problems and solutions in marketing-related ethics promote turning to a code of conduct or implementing voluntary regulation of business practices.

Whereas much work in marketing ethics may focus upon misinformation, manipulation, and the consequences of all-consuming materialism, the approach offered in this chapter encourages an awareness of marketing's often unexamined constructive role in everyday life – from contributions to consumer identity creation to visualizing notions of responsible tourism. One experiences marketing activities, whether engaging with advertising images, deciding on a particular holiday vacation, or simply living through a typical day. Indeed, marketing processes and practices aim to generate, reveal, and cocreate, possible, and profitable, relationships between producers and consumers. The resulting scope of ethical concern and philosophical exploration is vast, including multiple stakeholders. Acknowledging these complexities will hopefully inspire thinking and investigation that surpasses the boundaries of business ethics typically understood.

Firstly, this chapter calls attention to a range of marketing activities and prevalent responses from business ethics, and, further, indicates a gap between the complexity of ethical issues that arises in marketing contexts and the resources offered, for example, via checklists or models for ethical decision-making. A key drawback is that typical ethical decision-making checklists and guidelines offer little context and few tools for recognizing and evaluating ethical issues that address various stakeholders' interests, including societal or employee welfare, or international relations. For a field such as marketing, that has relationships at its core, this is a problem. In short, the lack of conceptual frameworks for comprehending the ethical concerns at hand appears not only to foster incompetent decisions, but also to undermine the potential of marketing ethics.

We then turn to Jean-Paul Sartre and Lewis R. Gordon for conceptual resources, specifically around *bad faith* – explored here as a lie to oneself regarding the open and undetermined nature of human life and activity. Living and acting as though questions of knowing (epistemological questions) and questions of being (ontological questions) are already answered invariably leads to a closing down of possible understandings, and moreover a closing down of investigations into alternative ways of knowing and being. The final sections return to ethical issues in marketing, reconceived given these philosophical openings. However, to begin an investigation of ethical issues in marketing, one might ask a basic question. Why does marketing create ethical concerns?

Marketing beyond the four Ps: emotions, brands, and culture

As marketing theories and strategies change, particularly regarding relationships between the company, or producer, and the customer or consumer, understandings of what constitutes the ethical issues in marketing change as well. In other words, the need for new and varied tools emerges. Marketing managers and marketing researchers are interested in diverse aspects of human engagement with the world. Indeed, the ways in which consumption practices and consumer activity contribute to human relationships and social identity provide a foundation for contemporary marketing practices. For example, daily life relationships of knowing and being may emphasize intellectual, emotional, or sensual experiences. Perhaps, when you read Shakespeare, you increase your command of the English language, but at the same time you miss the opportunity to meet friends for coffee, or sit in the warm sunshine. Marketing research has noted, and marketing practice has utilized, the permeable boundaries and blurred distinctions between apparently distinct realms of consumer desires and satisfactions. Thus, your favourite coffee shop now includes an outside garden with areas for reading, but also for meeting and talking in groups.

Whereas earlier marketing research and marketing techniques followed dominant paradigms that ruthlessly distinguished between rational, functional, emotional, or pleasure-based marketing appeals, much recent work finds these concepts, and implied realms, less discernible, or at least intimately intertwined. For example, studies have explored the way in which a response that first seems rational may quickly expose an underlying emotional foundation.[1] Indeed, marketing excels at promoting emotional associations to products, brands, and services. Often the apparent boundaries, and relationships, between the human subject and the consumption object shift, revealing diverse possibilities for meaning and identity creation, as when a childhood toy, or favourite car, comes to feel like more than a 'thing'.[2] Perhaps, whenever you wear a particular cotton

T-shirt acquired at a summer music festival years ago, you feel more carefree, as if warm sunny days have arrived, and this triggers a confident feeling that helps you get on with your work. Indeed, you may find yourself seeking out this T-shirt when you desire that confident, carefree feeling.

Moreover, brands – whether for clothing, cars, or soft drinks – may draw upon stories rich in emotional or sensual detail that ground aspects of what consumers value. For example, stories around the historical heritage of a type of leather bag made for centuries in an Italian village may add to a consumer's enjoyment in owning and carrying the bag. In this way, brands cocreate value, legitimacy, and meaning for products, services, ideas, and experiences in relation to consumers. In other words, brands and branding processes are core to marketing concerns. Further, brands' ability to facilitate engagement with consumers has been explored through the lens of 'brand culture'.[3] Having a strong brand to which consumers relate and refer can be a powerful tool in brand extensions, or in launching new products – explaining in familiar brand imagery and terminology how and why the new reinforces and carries forward the venerable. Furthermore, brands do not only draw upon aspects of culture to communicate desirable qualities, rather brands cocreate culture. As well, relevant research reveals the ways in which consumers produce, or cocreate, identities, 'tribes', and communities that form around brands, such as Harley Davidson motorcycles, the BMW Mini, or festival gatherings such as Glastonbury.

Thus, crucial marketing practices often require psychological, anthropological, and cultural theories, and consumer data, as well. In short, any attempt to comprehend ethics in marketing must engage intersections, cocreations, and relationships: of production and consumption, of producers and consumers, of subjects and objects, and of selves and others. This sea change in marketing logic revolves around fundamental shifts in the understandings of the relationships between producers and consumers, and some of these reformulations have been spurred by insights from continental thought, and insights into identity and value cocreation as a vital part of the marketing field.

These insights emphasize the contribution of consumer agency – whether in pausing over a cup of coffee, trekking up Mount Everest, perusing fashion's advertising images, or 'consuming' one's own employee identity. In the past, marketing may have emphasized production – of agricultural crops, mass market automobiles, or functional refrigerators – including how to 'push' products and services into markets, and furthermore buyers' mind space. However, with more recent investigations into market realities, such as visual consumption, brand communities, and consumption's cocreative processes, marketing has been forced to recognize more fully formed consumer entities, capable of production in their own right.[4]

It is not surprising, then, that marketing should spark complex ethical thinking, as fundamental areas of philosophical inquiry intersect with marketing practice and research. For example, marketing practices require understandings regarding the ways in which time and space do impact upon human perception. These issues of time and space (metaphysical issues) include concerns for the precise lighting and layout of a retail environment, alleviating negative feelings towards long waits for Disneyland rides, or relating the historical gold-rush origins of Levi's denim jeans. Furthermore, key marketing concerns around consumer identity, or how consumers become who they are in relation to consumer products and experiences, drive investigation in ontology, or the study of being and relations. This includes inquiry into the fragmentation of consumer subjects. Moreover, epistemological investigations – focussed upon issues of knowing – might indicate strategies to encourage confidence in buyers through the use of visual images in marketing communications. As well, aesthetic questions around notions of beauty, desire, and engagement of the senses, generally, animate many aspects of marketing practice. By recognizing the range of basic philosophical issues that emerge in marketing concerns, this chapter aims to expand the range of possible ethical questions those in marketing ethics have the inclination to ask. Not all approaches to marketing ethics take such a broad view of the field of concern, however. Some standard approaches to marketing ethics are discussed next.

Ethical issues beyond decision-making

Marketing concerns include economic analysis, logistics, product development, and advertising design, linked with research and implementation that seeks to promote effective marketing communications, expand market share, and improve competitive advantage. These goals and strategic dilemmas, mobilized in a wide range of contexts, also engage culture, historical circumstance, and geographical location. In short, related practices and processes open a wide range of opportunities, tensions, and conflicts that constitute fundamental territory for marketing and the ethical concerns that arise in turn. Related investigations in marketing ethics involve unfair pricing, product safety, bribery at different levels of distribution, aspects of branding, sales 'techniques', and environmental sustainability.

Approaches to marketing ethics generally adopt an information-based model of decision-making in which perceived ethical problems, consequences, and alternatives are fed through an analysis of ethical judgements and intentions, and balanced by personal characteristics that impact on ethical perceptiveness and evaluation.[5] Of course, if one does not perceive certain ethical problems, or one does not understand the intentions of particular courses of action, not to mention the consequences of these, most models of ethical decision-making lose their power to guide and direct. Moreover, models and guidelines for decision-making processes are often framed by legal concerns, with false claims, misleading statements, improper labelling, and deceptive pricing

(1) Have you identified the problem accurately?

(2) How would you define the problem if you took a different position in the dilemma?

(3) Who could your decision or action injure?

(4) Could you reveal without qualm your decision or action to your boss, your co-workers, your family? [6]

elaborated for ethical review.[7] Such attempts to engage marketing ethics often lack a conceptual framework for recognizing and understanding ethical issues. Furthermore, a bias towards legality may lead to the avoidance of ethical considerations. In other words, that some processes, practices, and problems in marketing could be deemed unethical, yet still legal, highlights some of the most complex territory to be explored in business ethics generally, involving not only issues of corporate governance and social responsibility, but the particularities of global political systems in their current forms, as well.

Elements of an ethical decision-making process can be offered for marketing-related business decision-making.[8] Such a process might go as follows: firstly, identify the dilemma; secondly, obtain unbiased facts; thirdly, identify a variety of choices; fourthly, identify stakeholders; and finally, identify the impact of each alternative on each stakeholder and the stakeholders' resulting impacts on you and your firm.[9] Responses to such a set of requirements, which also might be specified in an ethical code of conduct, may provide ethical guidance.

Nevertheless, some difficulty remains in accounting for diverse ranges of perception, knowledge, and bias that influence comprehension of the scope of questions, such as those listed in Box 10.1, and alter understandings, for example, of 'the problem' and relevant stakeholders.

An example of ethical checklists from marketing communications might specify a category of 'image appropriateness' in relation to images or pictured representations in marketing messages. Assuring image appropriateness might require evaluation of sexual innuendos or ethnic stereotypes that are considered inappropriate for a particular audience. Yet, as suggested above, these ethical checklists provide few criteria by which to judge what constitutes 'sexual innuendos which are considered inappropriate', or by which to recognize, contextualize, or evaluate notions of 'appropriateness' generally. Evincing the lack of ethical analysis in marketing communications, a typical textbook may acknowledge that stereotypes are problematic, but focus, for example, only on the ways that product endorsers are meant to function, and give little advice about how to recognize and morally evaluate advertisements for stereotypes.[10]

Consider a voice from business ethics that exemplifies this lack of ethical concern. Robert Solomon has discussed contentious advertising images in the context of 'consumer intelligence and responsibility', which includes advertising-based problems.[11] In his line of argument, good sense and intelligence guides the consumer, or perhaps the corporate ethicist, to disregard any unfortunate, but perhaps unavoidable, instances of undermining representations, or as he calls them 'portrayals'. The use of 'sex' to lend appeal to products, and further, 'the offensive portrayals of women and minorities', manifests what he calls a 'lack of taste'. He is not sure, however, that this is an 'ethical issue'.[12] His use of the word 'sex', apparently referring to a displayed or evocative sexuality, stringently limits the possibility of acknowledging broader concerns with exploitative image-based representations. If a bikini-clad young woman clutching a large leather handbag is pictured laid out on a litter-covered street, legs splayed, eyes wide, staring, and circled with bruise-like eyeliner, this frightening scenario, arguably made attractive by fashion photography, represents a 'lack of taste' according to Solomon, not a serious ethical concern, let alone something about which marketing ethicists should worry.

Thus, Solomon's approach to ethics in marketing communications allows him to utterly neglect marketing's taken for granted role in cocreating the everyday worlds in which we live, in short, an understanding of marketing beyond basic notions of appeal, information, and persuasion. Moreover, damaging representations, endlessly repeated, fail to even qualify as ethical problems. Such an approach misjudges the power of perpetual representations that arguably provoke negative consequences for those pictured that are equivalent to, and as 'serious' as, more commonly acknowledged ethical concerns, such as misinformation or outright lying in advertising. One wonders if the dilemma or problem has been identified at all, or even could be identified given some people's worldviews.

Alternatively, consider practices of target marketing, or marketing segmentation, in which small groups, or even particular consumers, are vetted and pursued based upon idiosyncratic patterns and characteristics of consumption that may translate into knowable consumer desires. Ethical concerns might emerge regarding the kinds of psychological traits or personal habits that marketing researchers track, study, and draw upon in segmenting, or targeting, consumers. Marketing and consumer research distinguishes and mobilizes particular age, geographical location, race, class, or gender groupings for marketing purposes. Those who are addressed by target marketing will be distinguished by characteristic ways of being and knowing that have been observed in research, and that are seen as impacting desires, behaviour, and ways of interpreting products, experiences, lifestyles and, furthermore, the marketing images of these.

These groups – identified as 'tribes', 'brand communities', or perhaps 'virile females' – become ever more specified as consumer cultures emerge around surfing, Facebook, or adolescent cigarette smoking. Ethical concerns around target marketing frequently have focussed upon vulnerable consumers such as children. Particular vulnerabilities might be specifically mentioned in a marketing code of conduct or ethics checklist as needing attention. For example, one might suggest that persons known to be vulnerable to addictions should not be pursued with offers for high credit card limits, gambling casino holidays, or alcohol-related pleasures. Clearly claims for 'consumer intelligence and responsibility', as well as differing opinions on the 'sovereignty', or independence, of the consumer, mitigate corporate responsibilities to refrain from related marketing practices.

Moreover, consumer 'segments' are perceived to engage, and respond differently to, different types of marketing communication, or modes of address – for example provocative billboards in New York City, pop-up offers on Yahoo, product-based children's television programming, or 'word of mouth' marketing at music festivals such as Glastonbury. Segmentation and targeting may be guided by in-depth psychological or sociological research, some of which takes place through on-line networks, such as Facebook. One could interrogate potential ethical issues, beyond intrusions of privacy, involved in these research activities that seek to explore, expose, and arguably exploit, aspects of human lives relevant to marketing goals.

Related investigative research – not philosophy *per se* – could form fields of inquiry in their own right. However, by animating the breadth of marketing's engagement with the lived world, including concerns with relationships, responsibility and identity, this chapter develops marketing ethics as a realm of investigation that concerns approaches to being and knowing generally. In the next section, Sartre's notion of bad faith will be developed in order to provide a context for marketing ethics. We will also address how bad faith results in epistemological and ontological closures. These closures may be precisely the reasons for the blind spots we encounter within business ethics.

Continental perspectives

Bad faith and epistemic closure

Jean-Paul Sartre has argued that 'l'existence précède l'essence' (existence precedes essence).[13] To put this differently, doing comes before being. Human beings are not born into the world with fixed destinies, set choices, and determined selves. There are instead always alternatives, accidents, and the potential for change. Furthermore, human agency, or human action that transcends material conditions, defeats notions of predetermination and stasis, confronting human beings with responsibilities for choosing among diverse paths of action that inform who we become.

Bad faith, the failure to face the openness of human existence, fosters a lie of predetermined being, thus closing down the importance of choice. Moreover, bad faith blocks motivation to take responsibility for what we do, and thus who we are in the process of becoming, by denying the importance of action, attitudes, change, and even innovation. Fully setting the theoretical stage for

Sartre's ideas cannot be accomplished here. Rather, Sartre's notion of bad faith and the resulting awareness of epistemic and ontological closures, particularly as developed in Lewis Gordon's work, will offer insights for marketing ethics.[14]

Existential phenomenology

Sartre and Gordon work in the tradition of existential phenomenology. In order to explain what this means, we will first briefly describe what *phenomenology* and *existentialism* are, and then address *existential phenomenology*.

Phenomenology is the study of phenomena, in other words, the appearance or manifestation of things. Lived experience is thus an important concern of phenomenologists. For the phenomenologist, everyone lives at first with a naïve acceptance of things that, upon reflection, we must not take for granted if we adopt a critical, theoretical, and philosophical perspective. 'Existentialism' is an umbrella term used to describe philosophy that focuses on the human experience of existence, of standing out as a lived, individuated reality and the anxiety occasioned by that experience. Sartre, an important thinker and writer in existential philosophy, argued that anxiety included fear of freedom, which made human beings seek an essential or determined version of the self on which to anchor our experiences and actions. In short, human beings should accept that there is no essential self that precedes their actions. After he published *Being and Nothingness* (*L'être et le néant*) in 1943, the major statement of his early philosophy, Sartre became perhaps the single most important philosopher in post-war France for nearly three decades. The work of other existential philosophers such as Søren Kierkegaard, who is generally credited as the founder of existentialism, and Friedrich Nietzsche, is still an important source of inspiration for many continental philosophers.

Phenomenology is not simply a description of appearances and experiences, however. Instead, the manner in which something appears is treated as a problem in itself, and the distinction that emerges here is reflected upon for its own sake.[15] Existential phenomenology is 'oriented', in the sense that descriptive analyses take place from a particular position. Certain organizing concepts or pathways may be privileged in investigating possible relations between the self and others. In what follows, we will elaborate on three central themes which emerged in existential phenomenology: the owned body, freedom, and the other. In so doing, we should bear in mind that different positions and intentions render a different sense for particular instances of these themes.

The 'owned body' emphasizes the concrete particularity of the subject's position or perspective in the world, the placing of oneself in a situation, and does away with 'standpointless thinking'. But what possibilities are lost 'if man is so completely identified with his insertion into his field of perception, action, and life?' asks Ricoeur.[16] This question leads to the second existential phenomenological theme: freedom. Being is active, verbal, not simply in the sense of voicing one's subjectivity, but also in relation to activities and experiences in the world, with other human beings. Human beings consist in human existing, and freedom plays out in experiences and intentions that are not yet decided. Everything is opened up to uncertainty and possibility. The third theme is the other. Sartre has argued that the human self, or the human experience of being a subject, occurs with others. Indeed, the human self comes into being through the other's gaze in which this act of vision, this seeing, captures or creates an object. In this way, existential phenomenology places relationships, visual and otherwise, between the self and others at the core of human identity and experience. Relationships inform the world in which we live. Moreover, choices and actions impact not only on one's own existence, but on other people's existences as well. Thus, explorations in existential phenomenology concern ontological notions of being and identity, who one is and who one is not, including how relationships form and function.

Contingency and bad faith

Some philosophers have attempted to designate the necessary features of being, including the essential activities or qualities of animate and human life. However, assumptions of a necessary or fixed nature may obscure the accidental, or contingent, aspects of being and the undetermined social and historical contexts. Sartre focuses as much on the possibilities that the incomplete, the not-yet-known, and the unavailable may offer human subjects in becoming who they are as he does on what is decided, known, or currently present to us. He emphasizes the possibilities of *not* being identified with a completed self, or a set notion of 'who I am'. Contingency and incompleteness in relation to oneself and others raise epistemological and ontological questions, such as who certain human beings are and what we can know about them.

Drawing upon these insights, Gordon explored the intersections of existential phenomenology and concerns about racism.[17] He investigated conflicts between human contingency and the oppressive repercussions of designating essential qualities that carry, in particular, negative meanings. In considering the confusion involved in notions of racial difference, he writes:

> eventually, blackness and whiteness take on certain meanings that apply to certain groups of people in such a way that makes it difficult not to think of those people without certain affectively charged associations. Their blackness and their whiteness become regarded, by people who take their associations too seriously, as their essential features – as, in fact, material features of their being.[18]

In other words, Gordon notes the way that blackness and whiteness can become essential features serving to limit notions of human being, particularly in racist contexts. Bringing contingency into understandings of human existence disrupts these limits or closures around possibility and potential.

To consider these concerns more generally, one might think of an advertisement that pictures a person in a particular context – say a tourism website marketing the Hawaiian islands as a holiday destination. The advertising image uses a person's appearance in a landscape to infer something about who he or she *is*, as a person from that place, as well as suggesting something about the place from which such a person would be. This may seem innocuous enough, yet these impressions, derived from a glance at what marketing managers believe to be advertising features necessary to communicate the attractive and desirable aspects of Hawaii and its people, may impact one's expectations of the 'locals', how they dress, for example, or whether their lives are relevantly similar to one's own. Gordon writes, 'If one group of people is determined by its differences from another group of people, what characteristics count as major differences versus minor differences become a matter of evaluative determinations'.[19] In other words, in determining my difference from the person in the advertisement, skin colour or gender may become relevant in racist or sexist, or simply arrogant, ways.

Gordon notes that from a Sartrean perspective we seek our own identity, our sense of self, by way of negating, or 'freezing' that of others. The attempt to escape the freedom of human existence emerges in this solidifying of the other's nature, this completing of the other's being, that makes the other, and sometimes oneself, into an object. Indeed, these attempts to deny human contingency crystallize in Sartre's analysis of *bad faith*. Gordon explores the mechanism of bad faith – this attempt to flee responsibility for the open nature of human being and human projects, resulting in the diminishment of human being – in relation to anti-black racism.

Bad faith presses us to freeze and incarnate both the self and the other. One looks at the other, seeing an object. In this guise, the one in bad faith tries to appropriate the other's contingency. In Gordon's view, this diminishment marks a closing down upon the fullness, uniqueness, and potential of human being. This is not to claim that everything is possible for each human being. We all are born into ongoing history, various aspects of which become salient; and with particular starting points and conditions – including our bodies – that position us, however contingently, among others. In this context, Sartre insists that human beings acknowledge that they are 'free with respect to constituting the meaning' of their situations.[20]

Yet, processes of epistemic and ontological closures lead one to believe that one knows the other's being completely, and this assumption of knowledge denies the other status as a human being and erases the possibility for human relationships. These closures tend towards creation of a recognizable identity while knowing next to nothing 'about the typical Other beyond her or his typicality'.[21] Knowing the other as *typical* refers to an abstracting and condensing of characteristics that create a familiar identity or pattern for beings and occurrences of a kind. In short, the contingency of human existence is lost.

Gordon argues for a critical ontological role for the concept of bad faith, allowing understandings of 'human *beings* in the face of the rejection of human *nature* and a reductive view of history'.[22] Paying attention to bad faith allows us to interpret contingency, and denial of contingency, in human existence, and moreover to recognize the potential impact of closures in varied scenarios. Attending to epistemic and ontological closures may reveal the danger of typified representations of identity that increase the probability of human subjects interpreting what they experience, or have represented to them, as typical.[23] One might recognize epistemic and ontological closures in marketing communications, for example, in relation to a Hawaiian tourism advertisement's picturing of a 'typical' native; in a segmented and targeted consumer; or in an idealized employee 'living the brand' for a marketing campaign. In each case, marketing creates an *ethos*, through which particular relations and understandings of responsibility emerge. In each case, bad faith raises the concern of taking responsibility for actions, choices and attitudes, and it is to this we turn next.

Bad faith and responsibility

Responsibility in an active sense requires attentiveness to aspects of our own knowing and being that may damage others and ourselves. As we have seen, for Sartre, actions, attitudes, choices, and decisions create who we are and who we become. Moreover, each person participates in diverse, often 'given', relationships and forms of responsibility that are part of ethical human lives. What Sartre, and Gordon, seem to be asking for is 'having a true and lucid consciousness of the situation, in assuming the responsibilities and risks that it involves, in accepting it in pride or humiliation, sometimes in horror or hate'.[24] Furthermore, the reach of our relationships and the realms of responsibility may be extended by media and technology to which we have access in our everyday lives.

In the next section, the emerging ethical analysis does attend to the implications, or consequences, of representational conventions within marketing communication, but also emphasizes the ethical context from which such representational conventions emerge. Crucially, then, we turn to the distinction between having and taking responsibility.

Responsibility: the challenge of taking versus having

Our discussion of bad faith has raised questions around modes of responsibility. If we consider bad faith responses to responsibility, a key example relevant to this chapter might involve choices, activities, and attitudes that close down knowing and being in the face of human contingency. Additionally, one might refuse to take responsibility, and this could include the sense of refusing to act upon responsibility we already 'have'. In this sense, we want to consider implications for 'having' versus 'taking' responsibility.

The American philosopher Claudia Card argues that whereas someone or something may *have* responsibility for a set of situations or actions, *taking* responsibility requires a centre of agency, a choosing to act or follow through in a certain way.[25] She writes: 'We may be given responsibility, assigned it, inherit it, and then accept or refuse it'.[26] However, Card suggests that taking responsibility shows more initiative, and therefore those who take responsibility would seem to be more responsible. Tracing 'initiative', and hence forms of responsibility, particularly in groups, requires attention to the realms in which shared actions take place and attitudes and values are transformed.[27] This is particularly true when thinking about business organizations and the processes and practices involved in marketing.

Some people may not be willing to 'take' responsibility if as a result they incur more burdens or blame than they would have had otherwise. Indeed, there is, then, a potential flight from responsibility, or bad faith, that remains troubling. Responsibility-taking ethical concerns emerge beyond group and individual decision-making. These include, simply put, the possibilities of creating knowing and being that may be outcomes of marketing initiatives. Card designates four different senses of taking responsibility, each with its own related accomplishments.[28] Each resonates differently with various levels of business organization that relate to marketing processes and practices.

(1) *Administrative* or *managerial* – estimation and organization of possibilities, deciding which should be realized and how.
(2) *Accountability* – being answerable or accountable, either because someone has agreed to accept this or because someone 'finds' themselves accountable for something and accepts the consequences of this.
(3) *Care-taking* – a commitment of support or backing of something or someone, and holding to the commitment.
(4) *Credit* – taking the credit or blame for something that did or did not happen, 'owning up'.

Administrative or managerial responsibility clearly involves decision-making, setting out boundaries, and suggesting the form that various organizational processes will take. This might involve a marketing manager recommending that certain forms of marketing appeals or marketing research should not be used.

Being responsible in the sense of being 'accountable' reflects the position to which others will turn when decisions have been made, outcomes are under scrutiny, or results are in. Care-taking here invokes a commitment, perhaps a promise, to put resources or support behind a person, project, or way of seeing the world. In other words, one does not withdraw expected support, even if perceived outcomes have changed. This might require an ongoing awareness of potentially damaging closures, or a commitment to avoid developing profitable supply chains that exploit vulnerable populations. Taking responsibility in the sense of taking credit or blame may evoke not the decision-making process or supporting a specific end goal; but rather credit or blame may fall outside the general workings of organizational or institutional processes. In other words, individuals or groups might see themselves as a part of broader conditions they did not directly create. For example Kate Moss, as a fashion model and celebrity with certain qualities, might be credited, or blamed, for extending the attractiveness and market share of the Burberry brand. Yet, it is unlikely she would be held 'accountable' for resulting marketing problems, such as potential loss of exclusivity and brand loyal consumers. Nevertheless, even this sense of responsibility demands an active 'taking' if one is not to deny one's involvement in creating situations – some of ethical concern and some not – in everyday life.

For Card, 'having' responsibility cannot generate the same sense of agency as 'taking' it. Perhaps, from this perspective 'having' responsibility could undermine the very means by which responsible actions are produced. In other words, you may be perceived as having diminished agency if you have not chosen, or taken, your responsibilities, but rather have had responsibilities thrust upon you. Thus, being in a position that does not require, or moreover does not allow, you to choose your responsibilities may have ontological implications. Over time certain groups may be perceived as typically unable to 'take' responsibility. Furthermore, should marketing managers, and others working in business organizations, become such groups, it may be difficult to hold them responsible in any of Card's senses.

In this way, contexts that encourage 'having' rather than 'taking' responsibility may provide support for bad faith choices and attitudes. Taking responsibility evokes an active willingness, and what kind of agent manifests such willingness becomes an issue for investigation. Taking responsibility for the way in which actions, attitudes, and choices – for example as manifested through marketing communications or employee identity-based marketing campaigns – support damaging closures towards human beings and the world, may require strong notions of mediated relationships. The potential for bad faith representations in marketing communications is explored further in the following section.

Bad faith in marketing communications

Within business and management research, ethically motivated criticisms of marketing communication are often simplistically understood as generalized criticisms of capitalism and related excessive consumption.[29] By contrast, the approach of this chapter does not criticize consumption *per se*, nor take a moralistic stance against materialism. Instead, focus falls upon representations of identity. The fact that represented identities profess to express something true or essential about those represented is something that should concern us.

Those people and places represented in marketing communications – including models in common advertisements and CEOs in annual reports, but also more broadly, for example, a country's 'natives' or a country's iconic sights pictured in tourism marketing and travel guides – may appear characterized by manageable, strategically stereotypical cultural and personal traits. Indeed, they often stand in for others of their 'kind'. These often visually communicated characterizations or representations may have a significant impact on how related people and places are interpreted, recognized, and treated. Moreover, the opportunities that are considered relevant for them and the possibilities offered to them for the future may be decided in relation to who they are perceived to be.[30]

Margaret Urban Walker, an American philosopher, has argued that traditional philosophical approaches lack sufficient conceptual strength to handle representations that characteristically manipulate and damage the identity of various groups. Indeed, philosophers concerned with ethical norms and behaviour have traditionally proceeded as though all problematic situations of moral recognition could be countered through constructive definitions of personhood, through formal requirements of universality or universalizability, and through substantive demands for impartial or equal consideration.[31] These three prescriptions, maintains Walker, fail to provide sufficiently complex considerations to deal with problems of representation, and worse – as in Solomon's earlier arguments – damaging representations even fail to qualify as ethical problems.

Mobilizing understandings of bad faith and modes of closure helps to further Walker's concern that *representational practices* propagate and create assumptions that people are a *kind* or *type*. She contends that representational practices 'are among those that construct socially salient identities for people'.[32] Recalling Gordon's concern with typicality, we further grasp potential damage emerging from these practices. Typified representations, especially those that are racist or sexist, for example, may undermine a group's dignity and historical integrity and cast a demeaning light upon their physical habits and intellectual potential. In this way, the representations disrupt their ontological status and may have implications for the seriousness with which their concerns, or needs, are met.

For decades the natives of the Hawaiian islands were represented in travel brochures, Hollywood movies, and through images such as the Hula girl connected to so-called Hawaiian music. Aimed at marketing Hawaii as a tourist destination, and as a part of the US, these representations were often all a US mainlander knew of the people who lived on these Pacific islands. Images of smiling brown-skinned women and men dressed in little more than 'grass skirts' and flowers shown paddling outrigger canoes or dancing at the ocean's edge did little to reveal the social and political realities of the people who actually lived there. Nor could tourists, their heads filled with pleasurable, colourful images and strains of steel guitar, understand an often less than warm welcome as they struck out to discover Hawaiian paradise.[33]

In cases such as these, an intended or unintended audience reads or interprets the representation within a field broadly determined by cultural meanings and categories. Marketing images are certainly read in different ways by different people, but creating a successful marketing communication often relies upon typified representations. Further, consumers, or viewers generally, may have an 'investment' in responding in certain predictable ways: 'What makes one take up a position in a certain discourse rather than another is an "investment", something between an emotional commitment and a vested interest in the relative power (satisfaction, reward, pay-off) which that position promises (but does not necessarily fulfill)'.[34] Insights around the existential phenomenological workings of bad faith can strengthen understanding of this analysis.

Moreover, Walker argues, if practices of representation 'affect some people's morally significant perceptions of and interactions with other people, and if they can contribute to those perceptions or interactions going seriously wrong, these activities have bearing on fundamental ethical questions'.[35] In short, Walker implies that a person influenced by images and representations – developed in marketing practices and visualized through marketing communications – may treat members of the represented group as less than human and undeserving of moral recognition. In other words, these representational practices motivate bad faith, freezing the other as an object.

Drawing upon and developing such insights allows marketing communications scholars to articulate the way in which representations are part of lived experience. Representations from advertising, film, and the Internet, inform and cocreate notions of reality. Mobilizing an understanding of bad faith for an ethics of representation can sensitize marketing managers, for example in relation to international campaigns, and moreover can highlight interactions with, and impact upon, cultural difference, global relations, and the constitution of the consuming subjects.[36] In short, linking marketing communication to bad faith dilemmas in visual representation enables researchers to engage a global communication system in which images provide resources for, and hence shape, our understandings of the world – including the identities of people and places.

At times, image creation in marketing communication draws upon and reinforces simplified, even subordinating, representations of cultural difference, group identity, and geographic specificity. That such representations, harnessed in the attempt to create a product image, potentially undermine the full human status of represented groups and individuals, is of great concern.[37] Representations of identities that are exoticized, sexist, or racist may damage the reputation of represented groups, and associated group members, and manipulate their being for consumption by others. The claim is not that some advertising, as well as other forms of marketing communication, might offend the damaged group or its members, but that associated groups and individuals, and their opportunities for the future, may be damaged by certain forms of representation. Moreover, the use of demeaning or stereotypical images is especially misleading in the global marketplace, where kaleidoscopic cultural contexts already complicate communication.

One of the most serious outcomes of representational practices is that people's perceptions, even misinformed perceptions, often have the weight of established facts.[38] Indeed, ontological categories presented by representations in marketing communication are not confined to the context of being a particular case in a given society in a particular historical moment. Rather, they are presented as what *is* the case about particular individuals or groups.

Some scholars have argued that representation in marketing communications is an improvement over racist and sexist days gone by, when most marginalized groups were not represented at all. Indeed, exclusion functions in different modes. To put this another way, there exists a phenomenon of absence through presence that is manifested in an *invisibility* or *anonymity* through which anyone might stand in for anyone else of a certain kind or type.[39] This is unlikely to be undone by bad faith marketing representations. In other words, 'bad faith' marketing creates a paradox, for even as more diverse human subjects are being represented in marketing communication and advertising images, their human existence suffers from erasure. One might think that simply including images of under-represented or marginalized cultural groups in marketing communication would help, but this strategy often leads to exoticized images, images informed by a distorted typicality, and 'token' images. In short, through the ease of epistemic and ontological closures and the lie that allows the typical to stand in for the human, bad faith emerges within representational practices.

Evaluations of contexts for 'image appropriateness' must be informed by an awareness of the ethical relationships between marketing communications, representations, and ontology. The point made here is not the naïve one that consumers believe that the artificial, stereotypical, or idealized realms of marketing communications do or can exist. Nor is it the case that consumers consume advertising images from a single unitary or predetermined perspective. Rather, marketing communications are part of lived experience: they contribute to the realities into which contemporary consumers are socialized, influencing lives and relationships with friends, loved ones, and strangers, as well. Moreover, such omnipresent resources for being and knowing often evade apparent possibilities for creative interpretation and critical resistance touted by image apologists, leaving much to be done in this realm of marketing ethics.

Epistemically closed representations of identity harnessed in the attempt to create brand images, or corporate identity, potentially undermine full human status of represented groups and individuals. The following section interrogates related processes in the flesh of employees. In the real case discussed, marketing campaigns require embodiment of brand qualities.

Marketing bad faith in the flesh

One of Sartre's examples of bad faith focused upon café waiters who in their taking of orders, table clearing and related movements and gestures seemed to express an essential 'waiter-being'. This is a case of taking one's identity too seriously, an attempt to realize a frozen or completed version of the café waiter. Sartre writes: 'As if from the very fact that I sustain this role in existence I did not transcend it on every side, as if I did not constitute myself as one *beyond* my condition'.[40] Once again, avoiding bad faith requires an awareness of contingency and incompleteness of human existence, even here as a waiter.

To push this into a marketing or retail realm, waiters in bad faith might identify with the atmosphere and values of a particular type of restaurant and embody this diminished version of human existence in their interactions and relationships with others. Indeed, employees generally may intensify this experience and become living brand marketers, especially retail staff and other employees that are often at the front line of contact with consumers and play the role of 'face of the brand'. For example, certain restaurants require employees to speak predetermined words of greeting, wear a uniform, or sit down at customers' tables to take their order. Other retail outlets, such as fashion clothing stores, may hire only salespeople that 'fit' the look of the brand, perhaps preferring blonde women and clean-shaven men. A person working in this environment could begin to feel their identity altered and constrained as they attempt to become the being that the employer requires. This is also an issue, of course, when the employee feels that the company or brand truly reflects them, and they happily adopt the look or style demanded. Obviously, in these roles employees can resonate with, but also undermine, a brand's marketed characteristics and values if, for instance, a woman working at Hooters usually dressed in a tiny T-shirt arrives at work in a suit and tie.

Corporations, at least those that want to be visible at all, build identities, often in the form of a brand, to differentiate themselves from competing firms. Moreover, corporate brand-building activities associate a recognizable set of values and characteristics with the brand, communicating outward to targeted consumers, but also inward, for example to employees. In other words, corporate branding processes lay a foundation that informs employee identity, and in certain circumstances a corporation may require employees to represent, embody, or otherwise live the brand during marketing efforts.

For example, in one case, university students taking on part-time work were hired for a major credit card's public corporate branding exercise, the goal of which was to make consumers more aware of a new credit card. The students accepted the notion that as employees embodying marketing communications they could be considered part owners of a brand. Moreover, they could impact how the brand was perceived, and thus be partly responsible for delivery of the brand values. This may sound strange, but again consider the clothing or lifestyle companies that hire sales personnel to match – in terms of hair colour, height, and physical attractiveness – the desired image of who wears the brand's jeans, scarves, and blazers. As Bell writes:

> To the extent that society demands such identification from individuals in these roles, however, there is something tantamount to bad faith in society's very structuring of the roles. This may make it extremely difficult for anyone in these roles to escape bad faith.[41]

Such identification between a person and the role inhabited conflicts with the 'nothingness' or incompleteness of human self and existence. It attempts to freeze human being, if only for the space of a workday, creating contexts for bad faith scenarios. The principle of identity, that is to say the project of being-the-same-as, is applicable only to what Sartre calls the 'in-itself', a functional object that one can exhaustively characterize. In the credit card employee case, human being embodies the non-contingency of a role in a way that denies human existence with ethical implications.

The students described above had two days of training in identifying with the brand values. They were dressed in relevantly styled uniforms of matching cargo pants and T-shirts, and – already screened and hired based on appearances and personality traits representative of the brand – told to 'be themselves' in delivering their scripted lines of dialogue. However, when face to face with consumers, the students found that their marketing efforts of embodying the corporation's brand identity felt 'fake'. Thus the students experienced what has been called 'enactment without authorship'.[42] While they did attempt to connect with the brand's desired image and qualities, they ultimately found themselves resisting, feeling cynical, or, as one keenly said, 'as if I'd sold my soul'. Adopting attitudes and roles in these circumstances may be common enough, and many people accept this adapting of their own identity to brand or workplace requirements. However, in the sense that living out these roles may give one the sense of having a 'fake' or frozen identity that is not related to one's self, or make one feel less responsible for carrying out actions that are part of this role, concerns around accountability and blame certainly arise.

Conclusion

If the field of marketing ethics continues to promote a focus on information processing and decision-making models, many key ethical issues arising in marketing contexts will remain invisible and thus unaddressed. Marketing practitioners in bad faith and bad faith practices in marketing contribute to epistemic and ontological closures that suggest a broad range of ethical issues in marketing. These investigations help us begin to conceive of the way in which issues of responsibility, relationships, and identity form core ethical components, and inform ethical contexts, in business and marketing. Explorations, descriptions, and interpretations of bad faith call attention to closures that may result in a process of self deception regarding the contingency of human existence and undermine responsibility in the face of this contingency. Such closures, whether created through advertising representations or in the bodies of retail marketing employees, serve as potential bases for understanding crucial contexts from which might emerge deeper, more fully ethical, guidance in marketing activity.

Moreover, in much ethical discourse, notions of having responsibility typically function in reference to fulfilling, usually abstract, duties and obligations such as those that might be referred to in common renditions of codes of conduct and ethical guidelines. Such an approach provokes scarce investigation into responsibility's more comprehensive and insightful modes – as a context for choice and agency based in relationships that defy bad faith, and developed and borne out in conjunction with others. Nevertheless, the argument of this chapter maintains that taking responsibility in diverse modes of relation that remain open to contingency lies at the core of ethical business organization and practices, including marketing.

The generally limited resources of marketing ethics call attention to the delineation of philosophical questions, including the kinds of questions philosophically informed business ethics has the potential, or inclination, to ask. Perhaps if marketing ethics is to flourish and continental philosophy is to play a part, then turning to notions such as bad faith and, moreover, remaining open to the potential of an existential phenomenological perspective, generally offer opportunities for understanding as the impact of global business and international marketing relationships expand.

NOTES

1 A. Venkatesh and L. A. Meamber, 'The aesthetics of consumption and the consumer as an aesthetic subject', *Consumption, Markets and Culture* 11, (2008), 45–70.
2 D. Miller, *Material Culture and Mass Consumption*. Oxford: Berg (1987).
3 J. E. Schroeder and M. Salzer-Mörling, *Brand Culture*. London: Routledge (2006).
4 J. L. Borgerson, 'Materiality, agency, and the constitution of consuming subjects: insights for consumer research', *Advances in Consumer Research* 32 (2005), 439–43; A. M. Muñiz, Jr. and T. C. O'Guinn, 'Brand community', *Journal of Consumer Research* 27 (2001), 412–32; J. E. Schroeder, *Visual Consumption*. London and New York: Routledge (2002).
5 N. C. Smith and J. A. Quelch, *Ethics in Marketing*. Homewood, IL: Irwin (1993).
6 Adapted from L. L. Nash, 'Ethics without the sermon', in K. R. Andrews (ed.), *Ethics in Practice: Managing the Moral Corporation*. Boston, MA: Harvard Business School Press (1989), 246, cited in N. C. Smith and J. A. Quelch (eds.), *Ethics in Marketing*. Boston, MA: Irwin Press (1993), 18.
7 A. Crane and D. Matten, *Business Ethics: a European Perspective*, 2nd edn. Oxford: Oxford University Press (2007).
8 L. Hartman, 'Technology and ethics: privacy in the workplace', *Business and Society Review* 106 (1) (2001), 1–27.
9 *Ibid.*, 6.

10 J. E. Schroeder and J. L. Borgerson, 'An ethics of representation for international marketing communication', *International Marketing Review* 22 (5) (2005), 578–600; G. J. Tellis, *Effective Advertising: Understanding When, How, and Why Advertising Works*. Thousand Oaks, CA: Sage (2004).

11 R. Solomon, 'Business ethics', in P. Singer (ed.), *A Companion to Ethics*. Oxford: Blackwell (1993), 354–65.

12 *Ibid.*, 362.

13 J. P. Sartre, *L'existentialisme est un Humanisme*. France: Gallimard (1996), 26.

14 L. Gordon, *Bad Faith and Antiblack Racism*. Atlantic Highlands, NJ: Humanities Press (1995); J. P. Sartre, *Being and Nothingness: a Phenomenological Essay on Ontology*, H. Barnes (trans.). New York: Washington Square Press (1973).

15 P. Ricoeur, *Husserl: an Analysis of his Phenomenology*. Evanston, IL: Northwestern University Press (1967), 210.

16 *Ibid.*

17 Gordon, *Bad Faith*.

18 *Ibid.*, 95.

19 *Ibid.*

20 L. Bell, *Sartre's Ethics of Authenticity*. Tuscaloosa and London: The University of Alabama Press (1989), 39.

21 L. Gordon, *Her Majesty's Other Children: Sketches of Racism from a Neocolonial Age*. Lanham, MD: Rowman and Littlefield (1997), 81.

22 Gordon, *Bad Faith*, 136.

23 Gordon, *Her Majesty's Other Children*; M. Natanson, *Anonymity: a Study in the Philosophy of Alfred Schutz*. Bloomington, IN: Indiana University Press (1986).

24 Sartre, cited in Bell, *Sartre's Ethics*, 46.

25 C. Card, *The Unnatural Lottery: Character and Moral Luck*. Philadelphia, NJ: Temple University Press (1996).

26 *Ibid.*, 29.

27 L. May, *Sharing Responsibility*. Chicago, IL: University of Chicago Press (1992).

28 Card, *Unnatural Lottery*, 28.

29 Crane and Matten, *Business Ethics*; C. J. Thompson, 'A critical reader-response analysis of the mytho-ideologies encoded in natural health advertisements', in K. Ekström and H. Bembreck (eds.), *Elusive Consumption*. Oxford: Berg (2004), 175–204.

30 J. L. Borgerson and J. E. Schroeder, 'Ethical issues of global marketing: avoiding bad faith in visual representation', *European Journal of Marketing* 36 (5/6) (2002), 570–94; Schroeder and Borgerson, 'An ethics of representation'.

31 M. U. Walker, *Moral Understandings: Feminist Studies in Ethics*. New York: Routledge (1998).

32 *Ibid.*, 178.

33 Borgerson and Schroeder, 'Ethical issues of global marketing'.

34 T. De Lauretis, 'The technology of gender', in T. De Lauretis (ed.), *Technologies of Gender: Essays on Theory, Film and Fiction*. Bloomington, IN: Indiana University Press (1987), 16.

35 Walker, *Moral Understandings*, 179.

36 L. Chouliaraki, 'The aestheticization of suffering on television', *Visual Communication* 5 (3) (2006), 261–85; Schroeder and Borgerson, 'An ethics of representation'.

37 J. L. Borgerson and J. E. Schroeder, 'Building an ethics of visual representation: contesting epistemic closure', in M. Painter-Morland and P. Werhane (eds.), *Cutting Edge Issues in Business Ethics*. New York: Springer (2008), 89–110.

38 Gordon, *Bad Faith*, 203.

39 Gordon, *Her Majesty's Other Children*, 80; Natanson, *Anonymity*.

40 Sartre, *Being and Nothingness*, 103.

41 Bell, *Sartre's Ethics*, 38.

42 E. Arnould and L. Price, 'Authenticating acts and authoritative performances: questing for self and community', in S. Rattneshwar, D. Mick, and C. Huffman (eds.), *The Why of Consumption*. New York: Routledge (2003), 158.

11

Corporate social responsibility

RENÉ TEN BOS AND STEPHEN DUNNE

Goals of this chapter

After studying this chapter you will be able to:

- describe how the meaning of corporate social responsibility (CSR) has been historically contested;
- appreciate the productive role which questioning can play within the CSR debate;
- illustrate how Martin Heidegger's work delineates just such a manner of destructive questioning;
- offer an understanding of how established research traditions, in this case the tradition that questions CSR, can have the unintended effect of concealing the very thing they strive to reveal;
- understand how complex discussions about responsibility are, both in theory and in practice.

Introduction

The acronym 'CSR' conventionally refers to corporate representatives' voluntary integration of social and environmental concerns into their business decisions. There is perhaps no other acronym that has become more prevalent within contemporary business ethics debates. Not a day goes by, it seems, where corporations and/or their representatives aren't routinely commended *and/or* condemned for demonstrating either too much, or else too little, CSR. The discussion over the appropriate level of CSR isn't only topical, of course: it is also an inherently controversial discussion defined by very little by way of consensus. And yet, for all of its inherent topicality and controversy, the nature of CSR is by no means something initially easy to grasp, despite its having been defined almost as many times as it has been mentioned. On the contrary, as will be demonstrated within this chapter, the very fact that CSR is both topical and controversial is a fact that makes its very meaning ever more fleeting and enigmatic.

To show that this is the case not only in theory but also in practice, we will first briefly discuss the way that oil companies have treated CSR. More particularly, we will shed some light on the problems that British Petroleum (BP), and more particularly its chief executive officer (CEO), Tony Hayward, had with assuming responsibility for the disastrous oil spill in the Gulf of Mexico during spring 2010. While reading the more theoretical parts of the chapter, the questions that we will ask about Hayward and BP should make you wonder about what responsibility might mean when companies – and BP was surely one of them – are talking about corporate social responsibility.

The chapter will then turn to more theoretical concerns. We will first summarize some of the key theoretical positions that have been taken on the question of CSR over time. This will be done with recourse to the manner in which the corporate social performance (CSP) framework has been constructed out of a series of concerns over the extent to which CSR *should* become practical. This brief historical overview will then serve as something akin to a diagnosis of why CSR has gradually become a central aspect of contemporary corporate strategy, whereas for many authors it had originally represented something of a fundamental threat to a corporation's very reason for being.

We will finally turn towards the work of Martin Heidegger for the sake of attempting to find another way into the CSR debate. Our necessarily preliminary discussion of Heidegger's work will take us through a consideration of how to ask questions about what CSR is, as well as underlining the manner in which we should relate our questions to an ongoing debate. We will eventually find, through such a brief encounter with Heidegger's work, that a concern over how to ask a question is entirely inseparable from a concern with how that question *has been asked* within a particular tradition. We will end the chapter by asking how these reflections might impinge on both business ethics and on the BP case.

Beyond promises

BP is an international oil and gas company operating in more than eighty countries. It provides its customers with fuel for transportation, energy for heat and light, retail services, and petrochemical products. Its turnover in 2009 was $253 billion and its profit in the same year $23.5 billion. To give you an impression of the size of the company, its annual turnover more or less equals the gross domestic product (GDP) of countries such as Finland or South Africa.

This huge organization consists of two segments. The first is exploration and production, which is engaged in activities such as oil and natural gas exploration, field development, and production. The second is refining and marketing, which engages in the supply and trading, refining, manufacturing, marketing, and transportation of crude oil, petroleum, and petrochemical products.

BP is one of the first oil companies which seemed to have embraced, in the context of an overarching CSR programme, an environmental agenda. During the 1980s, and especially during the 1990s, it invested more money than its competitors in exploring possibilities for alternative energy such as solar power or wind energy. At a given point BP became so self-confident about its 'green' reputation that it rebranded itself as 'Beyond Petroleum'. This had caused a lot of irritation, not only among critics of the oil industry, but also among competitors. In the end, however, it was incidents in the company itself that undermined BP's image as a 'green' company. A number of incidents, ranging from a refinery explosion in Texas in 2005, killing fifteen workers, to pipeline leaks at several other places in the world, gave ammunition to the cynics. The company, which used to be in British–Iranian hands for a long time, also has a contestable reputation of doing business in and with rogue states where human rights are systematically violated.

Yet, all these incidents and circumstances, which are, unfortunately, not uncommon in the oil industry at large, were completely overshadowed by the oil spill in the Gulf of Mexico, which was caused by an explosion in a drilling rig that BP was leasing from a company called Transocean. We cannot go into the technical details here, but the incident, which took place on 20 April 2010 and killed eleven workers, caused a leak in an oil well at a depth of 1,100 metres that turned out to be unstoppable for a significant period of time. Commentators agreed that this could be considered one of the biggest oil disasters in history. Thousands of fishing communities in the southern states of the US were threatened, not to mention their very vulnerable natural environment. BP spent billions of dollars to solve the problem and also offered compensation payments, but this has hardly helped the company to restore its reputation. On the contrary, its shares plummeted spectacularly and some analysts argued that the catastrophe was so bad that even BP's very existence might be at stake.

To show how complex discussions about responsibility are, we will now turn to the very interesting role played by BP's CEO, Tony Hayward, a self-acclaimed family man and a rig geologist who holds an honorary doctorate of science at the University of Edinburgh. Since his appointment in 2007, Hayward has stressed the importance of human capital in his organization. He claimed, for example, that top executives at BP did not listen to the bottom of the organization. In an interview, he also referred to the catastrophe in Texas and claimed that his top priority was to improve 'the safety of our operations everywhere in the world'. However, there was another side to the new leader as well. One of the first things he did after being appointed in 2007 was to rephrase the idea that BP was an acronym of 'Beyond Petroleum'. 'Our aim', he wrote in the preface of *BP Sustainability Report 2007*, 'is not to abandon fossil fuels, but to produce them more efficiently, while scaling up and investing significant resources in the new technologies we need for the transition to a low carbon future. This is what we mean by "going beyond petroleum".' Critics immediately argued that BP might as well mean 'Beyond Promises', but industrial analysts praised

Hayward for bringing in a certain kind of business realism that would allow the company to be truly competitive. This realism was also manifested in massive lay-offs and other forms of cost cutting, which transformed BP into a serious profit machine.

After the explosion in the Gulf of Mexico, Hayward systematically tried to downplay the full extent of the damage. In the first week, he argued that the oil spill was 'very very modest' and 'relatively tiny'. But on 28 April the *New York Times* claimed that the spill was bigger than initially thought: not 1,000, but 5,000 barrels a day were leaking into the sea. With hindsight, we can observe that BP, but also the other parties involved – the American government, the British government, academics from universities in the US, consultancy firms, environmental organizations, and so on – have been juggling with and bickering about the figures. As a consequence, no-one had any real idea about the extent of the damage. Two months after the explosion, on 11 June to be more precise, the media reported that there might be 40,000 barrels a day gushing into the Gulf of Mexico. This equals about 1.7 million gallons, or 6.5 million litres a day.

Sensing that the catastrophe might have truly ominous proportions, Hayward initially tried to dodge responsibility by arguing that safety on the drilling rig was not BP's major responsibility, but Transocean's, the company with which BP had a leasing contract. 'It is their rig, their equipment, their people, their system, their safety processes . . .'. Yet, no-one took this claim seriously. On 10 May, the *Wall Street Journal* published an article in which it was claimed that there had been doubts about the quality and performance of safety systems on the oil rig for a long time, suggesting that BP chose to neglect these out of financial reasons. The US president, Barack Obama, expressed his frustration about this in unequivocal terms, but there were misgivings among the American public in general about whether his administration was doing enough to meet the challenge. It would take Hayward till 27 May before he finally acknowledged that there was something very big going on. In order to cope with the critique that he had dodged responsibility by systematically underestimating the extent of the disaster, he claimed, on 30 May, that there was no-one who wanted 'this thing' to be over more than he. But when he, in a gesture of sham despondency, added that he wanted 'his life back', he became the butt of jokes and slander. Who, after all, is going to give the lives back to the fishing communities and the plants and fauna in the area, not to mention the workers who lost their lives?

It is not our intention here to scapegoat a particular business leader or the company he is working for. We rather want to ask some questions about this case. For example, can one truly assume responsibility for something that is so big? Can we not understand Hayward's clumsy remarks as a sign that he had been truly overwhelmed by the extent of the disaster? What is the precise relationship between his managerial style and the disaster? Is there such a relationship? Is, for example, cost cutting, directly related to the oil spill? These kinds of questions are, needless to say, very complex. For example, one might also wonder what the role of other oil giants is. Did they offer help because they feel a sense of shared responsibility for the oil industry as such? Or did they remain silent, surreptitiously enjoying the problems of a competitor? What we have heard so far at press conferences is that competitors do not think it is plausible that such a tragedy might happen to them. They did not, unlike BP, engage in cost cutting as far as safety measures are concerned. Needless to say, such reassurances hardly seem to be convincing, especially given the fact that the entire industry is looking for oil in deeper and deeper undersea locations.

But it is not only the increasingly risky methods used to obtain 'the black gold' that are disquieting. What about the roles of the American and British governments? Do they monitor or supervise activities of oil companies such as BP? Did they respond quickly enough to the exigencies relating to the catastrophe? For example, if President Obama argues that BP is solely responsible for the catastrophe and threatens to sue those who are involved in all this, does he then acknowledge the true extent of the problem? How quick was his administration to accept help by countries such as the UK or the Netherlands, who have arguably more expertise with these disasters than the Americans? Finally, what about our own responsibility as consumers of petroleum and other oil-related products? Entire economies depend completely on the oil industry and most of us hardly have any sense, at least not on a day-to-day basis, of the risks involved.

All these questions are very difficult indeed. We cannot answer them here, but would suggest that they form the backdrop of the discussion about CSR that we will start in the next section. We will see that much of the debate in business ethics about CSR is actually about avoiding tangled questions, and that this is going on in the name of practicality.

Social responsibility, responsiveness, and performance

In the world of business ethics, discussions of CSR have been routinely guided by the notion that there has been a progression from CSR onto CSP. On this reading, CSR is best understood as an early moment along the way towards CSP, something of a preliminary forerunner. Archie Carroll, for instance, argues that CSP can be seen as an 'extension of the concept of CSR that focuses on actual results achieved rather than the general notion of businesses' accountability or responsibility to society ... CSP is a natural consequence or follow-on to CSR'.[1] He goes on to claim that 'if CSR does not lead to CSP then it is vacuous or powerless'.[2] Within this first section of the paper we will challenge this notion that the development of CSP out of CSR has been a singularly positive one. In order to do so, we will trace three key moments of CSP's development out of CSR, with particular emphasis being placed upon the question of what is supposed to have been gained at each step.

Step 1: from responsibility to responsiveness

Might CSR eventually become a notion informing behaviour, a concept suggesting procedure, an idea directing action? In the late 1960s and the early 1970s, the very idea of CSR was challenged for a variety of reasons. One of the most important allegations made against it was, quite simply, that it was too impractical.[3] The very idea of CSR was seen by such critics to place needless constraints upon action, to offer abstract ideas when practical initiatives were required, to think when doing was the order of the day. Most authors agreed that too much deliberation was a bad thing.[4] The time for thinking and talking had passed; the time for acting had arrived.

Out of such practically oriented misgivings, a practically oriented response was derived. Where critics bemoaned CSR's lack of practical resonance, advocates began to place increasing emphasis upon the notion of corporate social respons*iveness*, as distinct from that of corporate social respons*ibility*.[5] Too much thinking, it was regularly argued, resulted in too little doing. Too much theory, it was frequently protested, amounted to too little practice. The very distinction between responsibility and responsiveness therefore made it possible to assimilate the pragmatic complaints against the discipline of CSR *within* the discipline of CSR. In this sense, the most severe complaints against CSR were embraced by its most notable protagonists.

The by now doctrinal separation between corporate social responsibility and corporate social responsiveness, for its part, was initially solidified within William C. Frederick's distinction between CSR_1 and CSR_2.[6] The epoch of CSR_1 (corporate social responsibility), Frederick argued, was being gradually replaced by that of CSR_2 (corporate social responsiveness). This very evolution, Frederick continued, was of profound importance. No longer were CSR's concerns of an abstract and impractical nature as was the case with CSR_1. They were, in the spirit of CSR_2, becoming increasingly focussed upon the real issues at hand. The guiding question, in other words, was no longer 'what is CSR?', but rather 'how can CSR be done?'. The essence of the improvements that should be made in the name of CSR was no longer a topic for debate: the more pressing task was one of demonstrating how such improvements were to be made.

Frederick outlines four basic objections against CSR_1. Firstly, he claims that the content or substance or the 'operational meaning' of CSR_1 is extremely vague.[7] Secondly, he argues that it isn't at all clear whether there are any 'institutional mechanisms through which the idea of "Corporate Social Responsibility" could be made to work, assuming that its essential meaning could be clarified'.[8] Thirdly, he makes the point that another 'unresolved issue in the corporate social responsibility debate is that the tradeoff between economic goals and costs, on the one hand, and social goals and costs, on the other hand, cannot be stated with any acceptable degree of precision'.[9] The final objection Frederick makes to CSR_1 is that 'the moral underpinnings of the idea are neither clear nor agreed upon. One searches in vain for any clear and generally accepted moral principle that would impose on business an obligation to work for social betterment'.[10]

As the title of Frederick's article itself insists, the evolution from the abstract procedures of CSR_1 towards the concrete activities of CSR_2 signifies nothing less than the maturing of business and society itself. Frederick heralds the new era of CSR_2; an era in which the capacity of corporations to respond to social pressures will be constantly discussed. As he points out, the key questions are:

> Can the company respond? Will it? Does it? How does it? To what extent? And with what effect? One searches the organization for mechanisms, procedures, arrangements, and behavioural patterns that, taken collectively, would make the organization more or less capable of responding to social pressures.[11]

A terminology is consequentially established whereby the apparent separation between a *theory* of CSR and a *practice* thereof is named. This terminology sets the terms for all the debates that were to follow on the problem of unifying theory with practice in the name of CSR. And yet, Frederick had his doubts about CSR_2. In the conclusion to his article, he writes that 'it is not unlikely that social values will stand at the core of all business-and-society concerns'.[12] Those working towards *responsiveness without responsibility* will probably run into a new series of problems. Frederick never saw CSR_2 as some sort of universal panacea. He therefore goes on to suggest that each side of the CSR divide might one day resolve the shortcomings of the other, forming a general synthesis of particular contradictions that would henceforth be referred to as CSR_3. The era of CSR_3, Frederick argues, 'will clarify both the moral dimensions implied by CSR_1 and the managerial dimensions of CSR_2'.[13] Frederick thereby readily acknowledges that when it comes to the question of CSR, action cannot be completely devoid of reflection, doing cannot be rigorously distinguished from thinking, and practice cannot be understood as absolutely autonomous from theory. And it was precisely this insight that is more or less routinely ignored within the work of his successors, as we will now see.

Step 2: from responsiveness to performance

The distinction between responsibility and responsiveness served an important purpose in the sense that it placed the concerns of practice firmly upon the CSR agenda. But without having arrived upon a solution to the problem of what it would mean to fully synthesize the demands of CSR with those of corporate social responsiveness, a proper account of what practice *is* remained wholly absent. This lack of a resolution to the problem of practice became a characteristic concern for CSR as such, not least of all on account of the fact that the quest for it had hitherto failed. Out of this failure, another apparent solution emerged in the form of CSP.

One of the earliest archetypes of CSP was an article proposed by Archie Carroll.[14] What is significant about his work was the manner in which it offered a summary of what CSP is, while simultaneously constructing a framework for so much of what was to follow. Carroll's model, like Frederick's before it, hence played a monumental role in solidifying the terms of engagement for future scholars of CSP. This emerging body of researchers would, after Carroll, labour under the auspices of a three-dimensional conceptual model, a model which synthesized:

(1) A *basic definition* of social responsibility. An all-important question here is whether corporate responsibility goes beyond economic and legal concerns.
(2) An enumeration of the *issues* for which social responsibility exists. More specifically, what are the social areas – environment, product safety, discrimination, etc. – in which corporations do have a responsibility?
(3) A specification of the *philosophy of response*. In other words, do we develop a proactive or reactive stance towards these issues?[15]

Carroll explicitly credits Frederick's work with having 'articulated the responsiveness view'.[16] He even goes so far as to claim that Frederick prepared groundwork for his own model of CSP, especially when it comes to the latter's emphasis on the importance of practice. What Carroll fails to consider in the rolling out of his model of CSP, however, is the already discussed emphasis Frederick placed upon the necessity of synthesizing the theoretical concerns characteristic of the era of CSR_1 with the practical concerns characteristic of the era of CSR_2. A fundamental aspect of Frederick's work is, in fact, deprioritized by Carroll to the point of erasure. Carroll simplistically synthesizes the theoretical concerns of CSR_1 with the practical concerns of CSR_2, thereby performing a synthesis that Frederick himself insisted upon being anything *but* simplistic.

By a sleight of hand, therefore, the inherent difficulty Frederick recognized in merging reflection with action is more or less written away. Carroll's reading of Frederick ignores the very concern that Frederick's early work so succinctly articulated. The problem is that Carroll's work manages to underplay the very concern that Frederick was at pains to emphasize. That his work gets away with having underplayed such a crucial matter is worrying, more worrying still on account of the fact that it represents no obvious discussion point for any of his successors. Let us take just one influential example. Introducing their own contribution to the CSP discussion, Wartick and Cochran make the following statement:

> In scholarly inquiry, new models do not appear suddenly. They evolve through a process of analysis, debate, and modification. The value of a model therefore is as much a function of its past as its future. In his 1979 work Carroll covered much of the background literature of his CSP model. However, his review failed to capture the model's dynamic evolution.[17]

The project of CSP is therefore cast as a story of incremental progression, our concerns regarding the fidelity of Carroll's reading of his acknowledged predecessor notwithstanding. This means Frederick's work is merely constituted as a step that needs to be overcome. Wartick and Cochran invite themselves to go one step further. And yet, in so doing, they make observations against Frederick, on the basis of Carroll's rendering of his work, which were nothing but Frederick's own insights, insights which both Carroll and Wartick and Cochran failed to acknowledge! Wartick and Cochran argue, for example, that to replace social responsibility with social responsiveness simply eliminates the need to theorize the ethics of business or rather the lack thereof.[18] As we have seen, Frederick made precisely the same point, anticipating the era of CSR_3 as the eventual resolution to this very problem.

Nevertheless, Wartick and Cochran unapologetically proceed to cast CSP as the 'synthesis of the challenges' made to CSR, telling its story along progressive, even heroic, lines.[19] The many positives of the era of CSP culminate in the assertion made by the authors that 'the past, healthy discourse that led the development of the CSP model makes its future very promising'.[20] And yet, as we have seen, in order to tell such a positive and uplifting story, Wartick and Cochran somewhat disingenuously cast Frederick as an outright advocate of the corporate social responsiveness view.

The misreading of Frederick's work is illustrative of how the question of CSR has come to be understood. Only when the fundamental incompatibility of the challenges which the eras of CSR_1 and CSR_2 posed to one another became assimilated into a broader framework, namely the framework of CSP, did it become possible to leave Frederick's difficult problem about the relationship between theory and practice behind, and focus attention elsewhere.

Step 3: from performance back to responsibility

At this point, a discussion of the significance of Donna Wood's hugely influential revisitation of CSP becomes indispensible.[21] Wood's article has become something of a cornerstone within the entire CSP debate, recently hailed as 'one of the most influential, helpful, parsimonious yet comprehensive conceptualisations of Corporate Social Performance'.[22] As with the work of her predecessors, Wood's central concern was with the history of CSP and its tendency towards an as yet unrealized synthesis. Her project was to establish, once and for all, *how* the phenomenon of CSP could become a determinate, measurable entity. Her analysis eventually arrives at a definition of CSP as 'a business organization's configuration of principles of social responsibility, processes of social responsiveness, and policies, programmes, and observable outcomes as they relate to the firm's societal relationships'.[23]

Wood thereby constitutes CSP as an analytical framework with no less than *nine* basic and fundamentally interrelated parts. She works through each of these interrelated parts in turn, discussing their various histories while simultaneously demonstrating the manner in which each principle should be understood as fully integrated within the wider framework of CSP.[24] Having attempted such an ambitious synthesis, Wood then claims that her work 'gives management researchers a more useful framework, or template, for organizing their research and theory on corporate social performance'.[25] Hers is a framework which, she insists, is a construct for evaluating business outputs that must be used in conjunction with explicit values about what kind of relationships between business and society are appropriate.[26] To understand the essence of CSP along these lines is to understand a particular business organization as a compound of nine parts. It is also to make it possible to distinguish any particular compound from any other particular compound similarly constituted. Once CSP becomes an analyzable object, then it can be compared, assessed, and ranked.

But if CSP does indeed become a measurable phenomenon, towards what and in the name of what might such measurement be undertaken? Of what significance is such an analytic framework if not to be put towards some sort of end? Wood suggests that if business and society researchers reorient themselves towards the predicates of CSP, they may be able to stop asking so many tangled questions about responsibility (for example: what is responsibility? How are we to conceive of our responsibilities? What kinds of responsibilities are there?). According to Wood, it would be much better if business people such as Tony Hayward start asking questions about outcomes; questions such as: who is harmed and who benefits from corporate actions? Is it right or just that these harms and benefits should occur? What can be done to reduce the harms and increase the benefits of corporate behaviour? It is only by answering these kinds of concrete questions that business people, if we are to believe Wood, shall move closer to *doing* something like CSR. And in the process, Wood adds, a move will be made towards 'the good society', indeed, towards a better world.[27]

But would asking these questions have helped Hayward to create a better world? How are people like him to know this better world? Upon what basis? This is where the work of Diane Swanson comes in, arguing that Wood's framework of CSP makes it impossible to offer consistent moral arguments and, furthermore, that it offers inadequate normative criteria for the assessment of both corporate social responsiveness *and* the outcomes of responsive processes.[28] Swanson's solution to the dilemma is a broadening out of the CSP model, beyond the manner in which Wood had constructed it, so that it can more successfully embrace its normative underpinnings. Only when the questioning convention explicitly recognizes its inherently normative nature, argues Swanson, will it be possible to set Wood's quest for the good society in motion.[29] Her adaptation of Wood's model hence respects the 'assertion that the CSR principles are analytical forms to be filled with value content that is operationalized'.[30] In other words, businesses should have a normative orientation for what good business practices should be like and scholars should be responsible for delineating what these norms are. Rather than erecting a frame-work that would deny or neglect the existence of normative presuppositions, Swanson instead offers a research strategy for CSP on the basis of what she calls *value attunement*.[31] This strategy, she argues, would make a normatively poised theory of CSP possible.[32] Throughout her work, Swanson is at pains to underline and emphasize the absolute centrality of adopting normative evaluative positions for anybody concerned with understanding what CSP is. And it is in this light that the supposed significance of a *value attuned* CSP framework is portrayed by her.

Nevertheless, for all the talk of value necessity that proliferates throughout her work, Swanson does not seem to offer any *particular* values of her own. She instead argues that because relativism is 'more realistic' than formalism, business and society scholars must adopt a relativist stance to all matters of corporate social policy.[33] Insisting upon the inherent plurality and sociality of all normative values, Swanson underlines the need for a communicative ethic which would, in turn, make an expansive notion of value attunement possible. However, it is also clear that she brings a privileged set of certain values into the discussion. Her apparent openness to the relativity of all values clearly prioritizes values such as plurality, openness, communication, dialogue, consensus, respect, and toleration. If Swanson were to take her own relativism seriously, she should not prohibit anything in the terrain of norms and values since, if ethical relativism were truly the case, then literally anything would go.

We are hence entitled to be somewhat suspicious of the extent to which value attunement is actually attuned to the disparity of values she writes in the name of. Her openness to the plurality of values, on closer inspection, looks very much like a manifesto for liberalism. The problem here, however, is not only that the good society we all want is deemed to be of the liberal variety, but also, and perhaps more importantly, that it remains unclear how this good society should be brought about. On the one hand, the will for a better society is offered. On the other hand, the possibility of achieving suchlike is renounced. The logic seems to run as follows: we all want a good society; we all have different ideas as to what that good society would be like; let us all go and create a good society on the basis of the fact that we all have different ideas as to what a good society would be like. It is as if the reader is given a destination but no map. Or rather, it is as if every reader is given a different destination and a different map and told to make their way to wherever it is they want to go, all the while assuming that those places will all be the same! Swanson's value attuned model of CSP therefore announces a goal while simultaneously withdrawing the possibility of its achievement.

This failure of CSP's advocates to posit any particular norms has put a lot of wind in the sails of a much more conservative project, the project of attempting to connect CSP to something called corporate financial performance (CFP). And it is for this reason that people such as Michael Porter have recently jumped on the bandwagon. As he writes in a recent coauthored article:

> Corporations are not responsible for all the world's problems, nor do they have the resources to solve them all. Each company can identify the particular set of societal problems that it is best equipped to help resolve and from which it can gain the greatest competitive benefit. Addressing social issues by creating shared value will lead to self-sustaining solutions that do not depend on private or government subsidies. When a well-run business applies its vast resources, expertise, and management talent to problems that it understands and in which it has a stake, it can have a greater impact on social good than any other institution or philanthropic organization.[34]

Porter and Kramer are essentially arguing that if the practising of CSR can be harmonized with the more general competitive concerns which define corporations, then corporations have good reason to pursue CSR. To put it somewhat differently, they should implement CSR practices only if it is in their financial interest. Or, more specifically, they should act in their own interests, or rather in the interests of their shareholders, at all times. CSR thereby functions as a legitimating foil for 'business as usual' – pursue CSR, by all means, but only if it leads towards CFP.

For most advocates of CSR, however, CSR must amount to a lot more than business as usual. And yet, it is not at all clear how an avowedly *pragmatic* understanding of CSR can bring about anything other than this normative husk. To put it somewhat differently, it is very difficult to see how even pragmatic understandings of CSR might help our protagonist Tony Hayward. It is as if for him responsibility means nothing less and nothing more than a burden. Remember the exasperation with which he said that he wanted his life back! For Hayward, the issue of responsibility surely did not come as the somewhat aloof kind of reflection about a better world that people like Wood and Swanson have in mind. It came as a challenge which seemed to be too big to handle.

What is then the status of these normative ideals and values? BP has made itself conspicuous by explicitly espousing them. One needs only to consult their website. Yet, this did not prevent the disaster. Of course, this is more than we might reasonably expect from CSR and business ethics. The point, however, is that espousing all the proper ideals and values did not prevent BP from initially dodging responsibility for the disaster. This should make us wonder how important these reflections about ideals and values are. The contemporary advocate of CSR, we may surmise, is therefore in something akin to a Catch-22 position: if they want to be practically relevant, then they will have to abandon any form of moralizing idealism: to be practical seemingly means to be without ideals. But what is CSR without just such a set of ideas as to what business should be doing? What might CSR mean, other than business as usual, once it subjects itself to the demands of practical relevance?

Heidegger and the question of CSR

> Whoever ponders the necessity, the genealogy and therefore also the limits of the concept of responsibility cannot fail to wonder at some point what is meant by 'respond', and '*responsiveness*', a precious word for which I can find no strict equivalent in my language. And to wonder whether to 'respond' has an opposite, which would consist, if commonsense is to be believed, in not responding. Is it possible to make a decision on the subject of 'responding' and of 'responsiveness'?[35]

While it is perhaps quite difficult to be against CSR, it is, by the very same token, also quite difficult to be for CSR. This ambiguity is itself produced by the fact that it is not at all clear what being for or against CSR amounts to today. We know this on the basis of what has been outlined in the previous section, particularly in terms of how to be for CSR, now means both to be for, as well as to be against, business as usual (whatever *that* is). We have also argued that it is difficult to see how CSR makes practical sense in concrete circumstances where something has gone terribly wrong. It is very difficult to see how practitioners might maintain high moral standards when they are driven into a tight corner.

In this section, we will resort to the work of Martin Heidegger in order to understand how the CSR tradition has brought itself into contradiction with itself by ignoring the nuances of its very own tradition. So, our focus in this section will be mainly theoretical. The encounter with Heidegger will show us how we might question the way in which questions are asked within a certain tradition, in this case the tradition of CSR. More particularly, why did this tradition not ask what social responsibility for corporations, not only in theoretical but also in practical contexts, might actually mean?

Heidegger on questioning

What does it mean to question? What does it mean to put yourself in a position where you open answers up to the possibility of further questioning? So far, we have been asking questions about CSR precisely in terms of how an ongoing tradition has asked them. In other words, we have been asking questions about what CSR might mean in daily practice or about what or whether CSR can contribute to a better world. For example, would CSR have helped to prevent the oil spill in the Gulf of Mexico? But before getting back to this disaster, we want to ask what it means to ask questions in the first place. Heidegger writes:

> Questioning builds a way. We would be advised, therefore, above all to pay heed to the way, and not to fix our attention on isolated sentences and topics. The way is one of thinking. All ways of thinking, more or less perceptibly, lead through language in a manner that is extraordinary.[36]

This means that to be guided by questioning in this manner requires us to consider how a particular question has been *asked* rather than answered. To do this is by no means a straightforwardly undertaken endeavour. On the contrary, it demands *both* a familiarity with the abstract nature of questioning itself *as well as* the capacity to bring this abstract familiarity to bear upon a particular, concrete questioning tradition. Pairing a notion of the basics of questioning with a sense for the particularities of a specific questioning tradition, Heidegger suggests, is to ask questions *destructively*. We have considered how the question of CSR has been asked in a variety of ways already. So what are the basic components of questioning, insofar as destructive questioning is concerned?

Destructive questioning

With respect to any question, what is first of all required, as far as Heidegger is concerned, is a deliberate attempt 'to reawaken an understanding for the meaning of this question'.[37] In other words, for Heidegger, we need to understand what we are asking even before we can go about the business of asking. And all of this before we can even consider getting to the business of answering. For whether it is a question about a very complicated philosophical issue, as it was for Heidegger, or an investigation into the question of CSR, as it is for us, there exists the need to acknowledge a variety of prejudices which may trivialize the question itself. As we have seen, one of the prejudices characterizing the ongoing questioning of CSR is the idea that business people long for practical solutions to their problems. This amounts to an *anti-inquisitive* prejudice encircling CSR.

Once we have understood these prejudices, we must then turn towards the task of question formulation. If a question is to be formulated, according to Heidegger, the act of formulation must be done with an eye towards a set of 'structural items' which characterize all questions.[38] But just what are these so-called structural items? Heidegger makes a distinction between three of them:

(1) Each inquiry is about something. We may refer to this as the inquiry's subject. Heidegger refers to this as 'that which is asked about' (*das Gefragte*).
(2) But when you are engaging in an inquiry about something, you somehow question it. In this sense, *you* do not only ask questions about CSR, but CSR as such is being interrogated. This is what is referred to as 'that which is interrogated' (*das Befragtes*).
(3) When you ask questions about something and when this something is being interrogated in this way, you will always discover something. This is referred to as 'that which is to be found out by the asking' (*das Erfragte*).

For the sake of simplicity, we will maintain that each questioning is structured around a subject or topic (that which is asked about), the interrogated (that which is contested), and a discovery (that which is found out). For Heidegger, these structural items determine the inquirer's behaviour. Their goal is to discover something. The discovery completes the inquiry.[39] The task of formulating a question, for Heidegger, becomes one of a questioner putting these three structural components together in such a way as to make it possible to launch an inquiry. The question of CSR can similarly be formulated with an eye towards this set of structural items. We can, in other words, take from Heidegger *a way of questioning*. What matters in this regard is that a robust attempt is made to understand what is asked for in the asking of any question. So what does this mean with respect to CSR? What did we do in this chapter so far?

With respect to what is being asked about in our question (the subject), we can speak of CSR. The guiding question asks about CSR, it asks what CSR is. For example, we have seen that CSR refers to a corporation's voluntary engagement with societal concerns. We have also seen that promulgators of CSR think that this might amount to nothing less than striving for a better world. Our questioning therefore has turned towards CSR. We want to know what it is.

Secondly, regarding that which gets interrogated within the question of CSR (the interrogated), the parallel is not to be so readily drawn. In Heidegger's case, we are interrogated as human beings. We are, one might say, questioned with respect to our being. Heidegger therefore focuses on the entity that he calls *Dasein*, the concept he uses to describe our being in the world. So it is the *human* being that is interrogated throughout Heidegger's *Being and Time*. But where does all of this leave us with respect to 'the interrogated' of CSR? If CSR is indeed the 'subject' of our question, that which gets asked about within it, then what is going to be 'the interrogated' of CSR? What, in fact, did we interrogate when we started asking questions? What we have done so far in this chapter is to *interrogate* the tradition by asking questions about the way in which it has treated CSR. We have done this in two ways. We have asked what CSR might be about in a company which is, for a variety of reasons, in a lot of trouble. Did BP govern the situation after the oil explosion in a way that defenders of CSR would condone? We have explained why we think that this is very improbable. But if this is the case, then we may wonder what CSR might probably mean for a company such as BP. We do not wish to suggest that it is just a case of window dressing. On the other hand, given the way it handles the oil disaster, we may sympathize a bit with the cynics who have always harboured misgivings about how substantial BP's claims about CSR were.

Later in the chapter, we have also asked questions about the more theoretical and idealistic underpinnings of CSR. And in so doing, we have interrogated some people working in the tradition of CSR about what it means to be a defender of CSR. Who and what have they become through their engagement with this tradition? Who and what have *we* become? Could it be that we have been naïve about what CSR is capable of? Is talking and dreaming about a better world not just silly when we take into account the BP case? Could it even be that in doing so we have become handmaidens of profit-interested business?

Is this not exactly what is suggested by the whole 'performance' discourse we have discussed in section two?

Finally, Heidegger urges us to rethink what is discovered by the question, by our investigation. We have found out many things during the chapter. We have found out that the meaning of CSR has been constantly shifting. Part of this was related to the concerns theoreticians of CSR have about the practicality of the concept. But we have, following the BP case, also found out how difficult it is to abide by whatever it is that CSR promises to deliver when things are at their worst. Heidegger suggests that once a questioner has achieved clarity about his or her discovery, the questioning procedure has reached its terminus. However, did we achieve such clarity? Are we satisfied when we conclude that the meaning of CSR has been shifting and that daily practice may be more difficult than theory?

What drives destructive questioning?

What does it mean to ask questions destructively? The driving issue of *destruction* is one of wondering, better still demonstrating, how openness towards what lies beyond your own tradition had fallen away. The Ancient Greeks asked questions about the world that we do not ask anymore. For Heidegger, it became all-important to understand how this could have happened. Heidegger's destructive questioning attempts to open up a tradition in such a way that it might confront its own prejudices as constitutive of itself.

This *destruction*, however, suggests nothing at all like an incitement towards violence, or an invitation towards any sort of starting afresh. On the contrary, *destruction* has a quite precise, technical meaning within Heidegger's work. It refers to a very particular way in which a tradition, in Heidegger's case the Western philosophical tradition, is to be approached and subsequently engaged. In this chapter, we have not tried to dismiss the tradition of CSR. Instead, we have tried to shed light upon how this tradition develops tendencies over time, delimits what can and cannot be asked, and hones in upon certain aspects of the question at the expense of others. For example, we have argued that the focus on practicality might have been at the expense of the effort to theoretically substantiate CSR. We have more importantly, also tried to show that, in spite of all the concerns about practicality, CSR is easier said than done. In order to give you a feeling for this, we have asked you to imagine yourself to be in Tony Hayward's position. Something inconceivable happened to the company of which he is the CEO, not to mention the fishing communities in the region. Media, environmentalists, and politicians were very eager to pass the buck to BP and to its CEO in particular. But can we, given the complexity of the situation, assign responsibility for a disaster to an individual? Even though Hayward may have made mistakes, it seems unfair to blame him personally for what happened. But if this is the case, then we should ask ourselves what CSR might mean if it somehow does not touch the personal realm.

The case of BP at least shows us what might in practice become of CSR when a company is in serious distress. We have suggested that it would be very simplistic to just blame certain individuals or even individual companies for disasters such as the one in the Gulf of Mexico. The fact that BP's competitors feign to be on the safe side is disconcerting in the sense that it bespeaks an unawareness of – or even a disdain for – the *systemic* nature of the problem. You may think here of our dependency on oil, the ever-growing demand for it, the risks we are willing to run in order to obtain it, or the inefficiency or dangers of alternative forms of energy. In the chapter on whistle-blowing we briefly discussed, in relation to Hans Jonas, the idea of a 'heuristics of fear'. If we cannot anticipate the consequences of our technology for the world, Jonas argued, we should refrain from using this technology. The idea that fear should guide us is not a very attractive one. In his inaugural address in 1932, Franklin Rooseveldt claimed that 'the only thing we have to fear is fear itself'. Yet we suggest that we should heed the idea that fear might occasionally be useful. We can imagine that it is a useful corrective to the relentless technological optimism or enterpreneurial recklessness that prevails not only in the oil industry, but also elsewhere (the food industry, the medical industry, the world of finance, etc.).

When we wished, following what Heidegger did with the tradition of Western thought, to question the tradition of CSR, it was not to dismiss it, but rather to open it up to new questions, new ideas, and new ways to envisage a responsible corporate future. We surmise that indeed an understanding of the systemic nature of our problems or a discussion about risk and fear might help us to achieve such an opening.

Conclusion

> When tradition thus becomes master, it does so in such a way that what it 'transmits' is made so inaccessible, proximally and for the most part, that it rather becomes concealed. Tradition takes what has come down to us and delivers it over to self-evidence . . . Indeed it makes us forget that they have had such an origin, and makes us suppose that the necessity of going back to these sources is something which we need not even understand.[40]

We started our discussion by reflecting upon what will no doubt become a typical business ethics case: the oil disaster in the Gulf of Mexico and the way that BP, most notably its CEO Tony Hayward, responded to it. We have argued that much of what has been going on so far shows how problematic it can be to implement something called CSR. The question of responsibility – which is, we have suggested, a question we *should* ask if we are talking about the social responsibility of corporations – is exceedingly complex. BP can take responsibility, but there are many more parties involved, including Transocean, the Obama administration, the fishing communities, and, indeed, the general public. Moreover, nobody seems to be agreeing about what exactly CSR in the oil business might be.

Again, the vicissitudes of one single company can be, as we have seen, dramatic, but the real question is bigger than that. Critics and analysts agree that what could happen to BP might as well happen to Exxon or Shell. Jedrzej George Frynas, a British professor of CSR who has specialized in the oil industry, has argued that there is 'mounting evidence of a gap between the stated intentions of business leaders and their actual behaviour and impact in the real world'.[41] He points out that people working in the business are increasingly irritated by the discourse on CSR. Some consider it a waste of time while others argue it is just a way of making feel people good about themselves, something which disappears as soon as one becomes more realistic. In this sense, CSR is just a way to keep employees in the oil business happy. Catastrophes such as the one we have discussed in this chapter and the public criticisms that ensue have 'demoralizing effects on . . . staff'.[42]

Another problem with the implementation of CSR is that companies such as BP – where many people work who have, like Hayward himself, a background in exact sciences or technology – are inclined to reduce the question of responsibility to a mere technical matter. That CSR might be a matter of social value and therefore also of social attitudes is often overlooked. In the past this lack of social skill has led oil industries such as BP to neglect responsibilities with respect to local communities or to the environment at large. See here what Frynas writes:

> When BP initiated a course to teach its managers about issues such as biodiversity and global warming, they typically turned to a business school (the Judge Management Institute at Cambridge University) rather than a developmental institution. Furthermore, staff often spend very little time in the field and lack understanding of specific local problems.[43]

This quote should make us aware that oil companies such as BP tend to recast the question of CSR as a mere technical or managerial challenge that can be reduced to metrics, indicators, or guidelines. However, many problems in the oil industry – and the catastrophe in the Gulf of Mexico is no exception – are indelibly social or developmental as well.

This all serves to show you how difficult CSR might be in practice. Whatever it is, it must have dimensions that reach way beyond the turn to practicality that has been suggested by so many CSR-theoreticians operating in the field of business ethics. We suggested that there is a need to raise the question of what CSR might be in the midst of all this complexity and confusion. And we are pretty confident that it is not something that, in the name of an alleged practicality, can be implemented very easily. Indeed, we have tried to unmask this as one of the prejudices that have come to dominate the CSR-tradition. In light of our reflection upon the structure of questioning, we learned, in the name of destruction, that we must interrogate how this prejudice was constituted within an ongoing questioning tradition. This is exactly what we have been doing in the second section of the chapter.

Much of our discussion in this section has centred upon various transitions in the way in which CSR has been interrogated. What has been foreclosed during the interrogation is, indeed, the endless complexity in which companies such as BP find themselves. While academics are asking how, in the name of practicality, CSR can be made palatable for business practitioners and can indeed contribute to a 'better' world, we have shown you something of the messiness that the debate tends to overlook. Again, we do not wish to claim that the idea of CSR practice is ridiculous, far from it in fact. The issue we wish to draw your attention to is rather that the meaning of CSR practice has not yet been secured by anybody. And because of this, nobody, neither practitioners nor eminent theorists, has yet spoken with absolute authority on the topic of CSR in practice. Hence its essential meaning remains contentious in itself. This is not a task from which theorists should shy away. It is rather a challenge that must be directly confronted. Neither is this a task from which practitioners should scurry. It is rather a question that is of immense practical significance.

NOTES

1 A. Carroll, 'Corporate social responsibility (CSR) and corporate social performance (CSP)', in R. W. Kolb (ed.), *Encyclopedia of Business Ethics and Society*. London: Sage (2008), 508–17, 508.

2 *Ibid.*

3 D. Votaw and S. P. Sethi, 'Do we need a new corporate response to a changing environment? Part I', *California Management Review* 12 (1) (1969), 3–16; S. P. Sethi and D. Votaw, 'Do we need a new corporate response to a changing Environment? Part II', *California Management Review* 12 (1) (1969), 17–31.

4 Ian Wilson, for example, argued for the need to embed the preachings of corporate social responsibility within the practical needs of businesses while Keith Davis considered the arguments for and against corporate social responsibility from the clear-eyed perspective of the corporate strategist. See I. Wilson, 'Reforming the strategic planning process: integration of social responsibility and business needs', *Long Term Planning* 7 (5) (1974), 121–40; K. Davis, 'The case for and against business assumptions of social responsibility', *Academy of Management Journal* 16 (1973), 312–22. Henry Eilbirt and Robert Parkett argued that corporations could not simply ignore the demands for social responsibility, while Peter Challen underlined the practical difficulties involved in the delivery of corporate social responsibility programmes. See H. Eilbirt and R. Parkett, 'The current status of corporate social responsibility', *Business Horizons* 16 (4) (1973), 5–14; P. Challen, 'Corporate planning for social responsibility', *Long Range Planning* 7 (3) (1974), 38–44. Elsewhere, Robert Ackerman reviewed the ways in which corporations could actually respond to demands for corporate social responsibility: see R. Ackerman, 'How companies respond to social demands', *Harvard Business Review* 51 (4) (1973), 88–98. Edward Bowman and Mason Haire advocated a strategic orientation towards demands for corporate social responsibility: see E. Bowman and M. Haire, 'A strategic posture towards corporate social responsibility', *California Management Review* 28 (2) (1975), 49–58.

Vernon Buehler and Y. K. Shetty wrote of the need to manage social responsibility as if it were a corporate function: see V. Buehler and Y. K. Shetty, 'Managing corporate social responsibility', *Management Review* 64 (8) (1975), 4–17. Meyer Feldberg attempted to reevaluate the practical role that is to be played by businesses within society: see M. Feldberg, 'Defining corporate social responsibility', *Long Range Planning* 7 (4) (1974), 39–44. Archie Carroll outlined a way in which corporate social responsibility programmes could be strategically operationalized: see A. Carroll, 'Setting operational goals for corporate social responsibility', *Long Range Planning* 11 (1) (1978), 35–8.

5   R. Ackerman and R. Bauer, *Corporate Social Responsiveness: the Modern Dilemma*. Reston, VA: Reston Publishing (1976).

6   W. Frederick, 'From CSR$_1$ to CSR$_2$ – the maturing of business-and-society thought', *Business and Society* 33 (2) (1994), 150–64.

7   Frederick, 'From CSR$_1$ to CSR$_2$', 152. In making this observation, Frederick explicitly acknowledges his debt to S. P. Sethi, 'Dimensions of corporate social performance: an analytical framework', *California Management Review* 17 (3) (1975), 58–64.

8   Frederick, 'From CSR$_1$ to CSR$_2$', 153.

9   *Ibid.*

10   *Ibid.*, 153–4.

11   *Ibid.*, 154–5.

12   *Ibid.*, 161.

13   *Ibid.*, 162.

14   A. Carroll, 'A three-dimensional conceptual model of corporate performance', *Academy of Management Review* 4 (1979), 497–505. Other exemplary articles published at the time include, for example: R. Aldag and K. Bartol, 'Empirical studies of corporate social performance and policy: a survey of problems and results', *Research in Corporate Social Performance and Policy* 1 (1978), 165–99; B. Spicer, 'Investors, corporate social performance and information disclosure: an empirical study', *The Accounting Review* 53 (1) (1978), 94–111; L. Preston (ed.), *Research in Corporate Social Performance and Policy, Vol. I.* Greenwich, CT: JAI Press (1978).

15   Carroll, 'A three-dimensional conceptual model', 499.

16   *Ibid.*, 501.

17   Stephen Wartick and Philip Cochran, 'The evolution of the corporate social performance model', *Academy of Management Review* 10 (4) (1958), 758–69.

18   *Ibid.*, 763.

19   *Ibid.*

20   *Ibid.*, 768.

21   D. Wood, 'Corporate social performance revisited', *Academy of Management Review* 16 (4) (1991), 691–718.

22   M. Orlitzky, F. Schmidt, and S. Rynes, 'Corporate social and financial performance: a meta-analysis', *Organization Studies* 24 (3) (2003), 403–41, 411.

23   Wood, 'Corporate social performance', 693.

24   The framework synthesizes insights from literatures as diverse as institutional legitimacy theory (see K. Davis, 'The case for and against business assumptions'); public policy (e.g. L. Preston and J. Post, *Private Management and Public Policy: the Principle of Public Responsibility.* Englewood Cliffs, NJ: Prentice Hall (1975)); moral discretion (e.g. A. Carroll 'A three-dimensional conceptual model'), strategic environment analysis (e.g. L. J. Bourgeois III, 'Strategy and environment: a conceptual integration', *Academy of Management Review* 5 (1) (1980), 25–39); stakeholder theory (e.g. R. E. Freeman, *Strategic Management: a Stakeholder Approach.* Boston,

MA: Pitman (1984)); and issues management (e.g. J. Brown, *This Business of Issues: Coping with the Company's Environments*. New York: New York Conference Board (1979)).

25 Wood, 'Corporate social performance', 713.

26 *Ibid.*, 693–4.

27 D. Wood, 'Toward improving corporate social performance', *Business Horizons* 34 (4) (1991), 66–73, 66.

28 D. Swanson, 'Addressing a theoretical problem by reorienting the corporate social performance model', *Academy of Management Review* 20 (3) (1995), 43–64.

29 *Ibid.*, 52.

30 *Ibid.*, 60.

31 D. Swanson 'Toward an integrative theory of business and society: a research strategy for corporate social performance', *Academy of Management Review* 24 (3) (1999), 506–21.

32 *Ibid.*, 519.

33 *Ibid.*, 518.

34 M. Porter and M. Kramer 'Strategy and society: the link between competitive advantage and corporate social responsibility', *Harvard Business Review* 84 (12) (2006), 13–14.

35 J. Derrida, 'Passions: an oblique offering', in J. Derrida (ed.), *On the Name*. Stanford, CA: Stanford University Press (1995), 3–34, 13.

36 Martin Heidegger, 'The question concerning technology', in D. F. Krell (ed.), *Martin Heidegger: Basic Writings*. London: Routledge (1978), 283–317, 311.

37 Martin Heidegger, *Being and Time*. Oxford: Blackwell Publishing (2005), 20.

38 *Ibid.*, 25.

39 *Ibid.*, 24–5.

40 *Ibid.*, 43.

41 J. G. Frynas, 'The false developmental promise of corporate social responsibility: evidence from multinational oil companies', *International Affairs* 81 (3) (2005), 581–98.

42 *Ibid.*, 586.

43 *Ibid.*, 591.

12

Corporate responsibility standards

ANDREAS RASCHE

Goals of this chapter

After studying this chapter you will be able to:

- understand the emerging standard infrastructure of corporate responsibility;
- distinguish auditing, reporting, and principle-based initiatives;
- develop insights into key selected standards;
- understand the criticisms of corporate responsibility standards based on Derridian philosophy;
- learn about the aporia of rule-following and the aporia of decision-making in relation to corporate responsibility standards;
- develop insights into how to apply standards despite their aporetic nature.

Introduction

Despite its enormous success as a concept, corporate responsibility always faces the challenge of implementation on the ground. Waddock, for instance, defines corporate responsibility as 'the strategy and operating practices a company develops in operationalizing its relationships with and impacts on societies, stakeholders, and the natural environment'.[1] Inevitably, such definitions beg the question of how do we change corporations' strategies and operational practices? What are the relevant issues and how are these issues addressed? While each company needs to find its own way in 'managing' its responsibilities, guidance is also provided by so-called corporate responsibility standards (e.g., the Global Reporting Initiative, Social Accountability 8000, the Fair Labor Association Workplace Code, and the UN Global Compact). Although these initiatives differ very much in their aim, scope, and operational procedures, they all recognize the essential role that business plays in building sustainable societies.

In their most general sense, we define such standards as predefined rules and procedures for organizational behaviour with regard to social and/or environmental issues that are usually not required by law. Standards differ from codes of conduct insofar as companies do not develop them 'internally'. Codes of conduct are developed by the very same company, which later on uses the code internally and/or imposes the code on its suppliers. In 1991, Levi-Strauss pioneered responsible global sourcing through a code of conduct. By contrast, standards are developed by third parties (often non-governmental organizations, or NGOs) and thus externally imposed on corporations. Although not required by law, a variety of companies have adopted corporate responsibility standards over the last decade. For instance, the United Nations (UN) Global Compact moved from just fifty business participants in 2000 to over 5,300 signatories in 2010 (data as of February 2010).

There are a variety of reasons why managers find it attractive to use these standards. Firstly, standards provide a level playing field when it comes to corporate responsibility. They offer orientation while managing the often unspecific (and sometimes contradictory) demands which are placed on corporations. Secondly, stakeholders pressure corporations to adopt standards to live up to their responsibilities. Corporations, in turn, respond to this pressure by using standards as signalling devices to consumers and other stakeholders to distinguish themselves from competitors. Thirdly, there is also isomorphic behaviour between businesses. If one key actor in an industry starts to use a standard, other companies join in because they fear competitive disadvantages. Fourthly, although heavily debated in terms of its ethical dimension, some companies have also signed up to standards because of business benefits. For instance, there is increasing evidence that financial markets are valuing firms' participation in standards, largely because standards help to anticipate business risks.[2] It should be noted, however, that the relation between corporations' social and financial performance is contested and remains subject to further debate.[3]

Differentiating corporate responsibility standards – a framework

By now, the overall number of different standards is hard to oversee and even harder to classify and structure in a comprehensive way. Hence, our remarks in this chapter are necessarily selective and based on exemplary initiatives rather than a full overview. We distinguish between three different types of corporate responsibility standards:

(1) principle-based standards, which outline broadly defined principles that are supposed to provide firms guidance while reflecting on corporate responsibility issues;
(2) reporting-based standards, which outline comparable performance indicators corporations can report on; and

(3) certification standards, which predefine compliance targets and assess a company's performance against these targets through audits.[4]

Principle-based standards (example: the UN Global Compact)

Principle-based standards do not certify or accredit but are designed to offer corporations guidance on acceptable and unacceptable practices.[5] Prominent examples of principle-based standards are the UN Global Compact, the Principles for Responsible Investment, the Organization for Economic Cooperation and Development (OECD) Guidelines for Multinational Enterprises, and the Caux Roundtable Principles for Business. Principles can be imagined as a 'moral compass' for corporations.[6] They are supposed to give guidance and foster discussions about a corporation's responsibilities. The idea is to help managers develop an internal corporate responsibility agenda for their corporations. Principle-based standards support such agenda-setting because they require managers to reflect their current strategies and operating practices against the background of the principles.

One of the most widely used principle-based standards is the UN Global Compact.[7] When the then Secretary-General, Kofi Annan, went to the World Economic Forum in Davos, in January 1999, he challenged the business leaders of the world to help fill the governance voids that the rise of the global economy had brought about. Based on the conviction that the goals of the UN and those of business can be mutually supportive, Annan declared: 'I propose that you, the business leaders gathered here in Davos, and we, the United Nations, initiate a global compact of shared values and principles, which will give a human face to the global market'.[8] This speech would mark the birth of the UN Global Compact, which was formally launched on 26 July 2000 at UN headquarters in New York. Historically speaking, the launch of the UN Global Compact marks a move in the UN's attitude towards business actors, a move from confrontation to collaboration.[9] This move, of course, remained not without critique. Critics argue that the establishment of the UN Global Compact leads to the privatization of the UN system in the sense that private enterprises 'capture' its agenda.[10]

The UN Global Compact is a call to companies to *voluntarily* align their operations with ten universal principles in the areas of human rights, labour standards, the environment, and anti-corruption (see Box 12.1 for a list of the ten principles). By participating in the Global Compact, businesses are expected to contribute to the fulfilments of the initiative's two major objectives: (1) to mainstream the ten principles in business activities around the world; and (2) to catalyze actions in support of broader UN goals (including the Millennium Development Goals, or MDGs). The ten principles are designed as *universal* principles and are based on conventions and declarations, which are endorsed by the 192 UN member states: the Universal Declaration of Human Rights, the International Labour Organization's Declaration on Fundamental Principles

Box 12.1	The ten principles of the UN Global Compact

The Global Compact asks companies to embrace, support, and enact, within their sphere of influence, a set of core values in the areas of human rights, labour standards, the environment, and anti-corruption:

Human rights

Principle 1: Businesses should support and respect the protection of internationally proclaimed human rights.
Principle 2: Make sure that they are not complicit in human rights abuses.

Labour standards

Principle 3: Businesses should uphold the freedom of association and the effective recognition of the right to collective bargaining.
Principle 4: The elimination of all forms of forced and compulsory labour.
Principle 5: The effective abolition of child labour.
Principle 6: The elimination of discrimination in respect of employment and occupation.

Environment

Principle 7: Businesses should support a precautionary approach to environmental challenges.
Principle 8: Undertake initiatives to promote greater environmental responsibility.
Principle 9: Encourage the development and diffusion of environmentally friendly technologies.

Anti-corruption

Principle 10: Businesses should work against corruption in all its forms, including extortion and bribery.[11]

and Rights at Work, the Rio Declaration on Environment and Development, and the United Nations Convention against Corruption.

In the spirit of principle-based standards, the UN Global Compact is neither a compliance-based tool to measure and benchmark firms' performance with regard to the ten principles, nor a seal of approval for participating companies. Rather, the idea is that companies make a principle-based commitment to corporate responsibility and report annually on the progress they make in implementing the ten principles. Although the UN Global Compact recommends using the Global Reporting Initiative (GRI) guidelines (see Box 12.2), there is still a lack of standardization when looking at how reports are created as many signatories do not use the GRI framework. The UN Global Compact delists all signatories which fail to submit an annual Communication on Progress report. So far, more than 1,800 companies have been delisted for failure to meet the reporting requirement (as of February 2010). While delisted corporations are permanently removed from the Global Compact database, they can rejoin the Global Compact if they make a new commitment to the initiative and start reporting on progress. Implementation of the ten principles is supposed to be based on dialogue and partnership between businesses and NGOs, unions, academia, and other stakeholders. All these stakeholders can also join the UN Global Compact and are asked to participate in multi-stakeholder discussions to develop, refine, and exchange tools and best practices to align business practices with the ten principles.

Reporting standards (example: Global Reporting Initiative, or GRI)

While principle-based standards focus on changing the practices of corporations, reporting standards aim at helping firms to communicate information on their social and environmental impact in a comparable way. Reporting standards provide indicators on social and environmental issues that corporations have to disclose information on. The first reporting initiatives were created in Western Europe throughout the 1970s – most notably the legal requirement in France to present a *bilan social* and the efforts of some German companies to publish a *Sozialbilanz*.[13] Nowadays, the GRI sets the most influential standards for social and environmental reporting.

KPMG's 2008 survey on corporate responsibility reporting revealed that reporting has gone mainstream. Nearly 80 per cent of the 250 largest corporations worldwide issue reports on non-financial information (up from around 50 per cent in 2005).[14] While reporting was started by companies in industries that had a particularly strong social and environmental profile (e.g., mining, textiles, oil and gas, chemicals), it is nowadays widely used throughout most sectors. The KPMG survey also revealed that a large majority of those corporations engaged in non-financial reporting are using the GRI guidelines as a reference point to select report content. This wide-ranging uptake of the GRI guidelines creates several advantages: (1) corporations can better benchmark their performance regarding non-financial issues; (2) stakeholders can better compare corporate reports and are given reliable and quantifiable data, avoiding documents that purely rely on non-integrated case stories and corporate 'spin'; and (3) assurance providers can better verify report content (about 40 per cent of all companies surveyed by KPMG used third-party assurance to check on report quality).

Although reporting on social and environmental issues is supposed to serve stakeholders by providing them accurate, timely, and relevant information, corporate reporting practices are still criticized for not considering and responding enough to the concerns of stakeholders. Owen *et al.*, for instance, find that

Box 12.2   **Summary of the Global Reporting Initiative's G3 guidelines**

The GRI G3 guidelines consist of *principles*, giving guidance on how to prepare a report (e.g., how to define report content and how to ensure quality), and *standard disclosures*, determining specific performance indicators, which elicit comparable information.

Principles for reporting

- Principles for defining report content. Reports should be (1) responsive to stakeholder expectations and interests; (2) give relevant information; (3) present performance in relation to the context the company operates in; and (4) offer complete information regarding a company's activities.
- Principles for defining report quality. Reports should (1) reflect positive and negative aspects of an organization's performance; (2) allow for comparisons over time and with other organizations; (3) contain accurate, reliable, timely, and detailed information; and (4) present all information in an understandable manner.
- Principles for setting the boundaries of reporting. The report should include entities (e.g., subsidiaries, joint ventures, etc.) whose financial and operating policies can be either controlled and/or significantly influenced by the reporting organization.

Standard disclosures (report content)

GRI G3 asks corporations, considering the principles mentioned above, to (1) describe key impacts, risks, and opportunities; (2) give an organizational profile; (3) comment on the report scope and boundary; (4) discuss corporate governance, engagement in external initiatives (e.g. the UN Global Compact), and stakeholder engagement; and (5) give information on performance indicators such as (selection):

- economic category: direct economic value created, financial implications for the organization's activities due to climate change, significant financial assistance received from government;
- environmental category: percentage of recycled materials used, direct energy consumption by primary energy source, total water withdrawal by source, total direct and indirect greenhouse gas emissions by weight; and
- social category: percentage of employees covered by collective bargaining agreements, total number of incidents of discrimination, actions taken in response to incidents of corruption.[12]

'despite its claims of promoting stakeholder dialogue, engagement and inclusivity, much current SEAAR [social and environmental accounting, auditing and reporting] practice is likely to amount to little more than empty rhetoric'.[15] Even a quick look at most firms' corporate responsibility reports confirms this criticism. Often, reports fail to present detailed and quantifiable data about a corporation's impact on social and environmental issues. Instead, many reports focus on unconnected case stories about philanthropic activities.

Considering this shortcoming and recognizing the need for more standardization in the field of corporate responsibility reporting, the GRI released its first guidelines in 2000.[16] Based on deliberations between a variety of stakeholders, the GRI issued improved guidelines in 2002 (the so-called G2 guidelines) and in 2006 (the so-called G3 guidelines). The GRI's emphasis on multi-stakeholder engagement is vital as it gives legitimacy to the guidelines and allows for a structured feedback process and, as a consequence, a consideration of a variety of perspectives while improving the reporting framework.

The GRI guidelines ask corporations to report on indicators in three core dimensions: economic, environmental, and social (see Box 12.2).[17] It should be noted that the GRI guidelines are not a simple summary of a variety of performance indicators. A considerable part of the guidelines is devoted to selected principles defining *how* the report is supposed to be compiled. For instance, a corporation that chooses to report in accordance with the GRI guidelines has to be responsive to stakeholder expectations and interests (see Box 12.2). The consideration of the process-dimension of corporate responsibility reporting (How do we prepare our report?) is a specific strength of the GRI guidelines since it allows managers to deliberately reflect on the way the report is constructed over time. Currently, more than 750 firms use the GRI's G3 guidelines while creating their corporate responsibility reports (as of November 2009). This number is likely to increase with more governments asking corporations to create reports on non-financial information. For instance, the Danish government recently mandated corporate responsibility reporting for all large corporations. While there is no requirement to use the GRI standard under Danish legislation, but only an obligation to come up with a report, it can be expected that many firms will turn towards the GRI guidelines to seek orientation.

Certification-based standards (example: Social Accountability 8000)

Many certification initiatives are based on the idea of social and environmental auditing and accounting. The underlying idea of accounting and auditing is to 'assure' the public that corporations are actually doing what they are claiming to do. Unlike principle-based initiatives, certification standards predefine more narrow performance measures against which corporations are certified. Usually, certification is limited to single production facilities and does not cover entire corporations or even supply chains. Widely used examples of certification standards for social issues include Social Accountability (SA) 8000, the Fair Labor Association Workplace Code, and the Base Code of the Ethical Trading Initiative, while environmental issues are covered by the Forest Stewardship Council, the Marine Stewardship Council, and the ISO 14001 standard.

The rich literature on social and environmental accounting and auditing defines accounting as the process of gathering and analyzing information on relevant issues, while auditing refers to the external (i.e. independent) verification of the account.[18] The main purpose of auditing is to enhance transparency by offering credible information to stakeholders about a firm's social and environmental performance. Transparency, in general, is about a firm's willingness to publicly disclose information about its business policies and performance regarding financial and non-financial issues.[19] Corporations around the world use certification standards because they offer clear guidance on what issues businesses should be transparent about and how transparency is supposed to be achieved.

The uptake and proliferation of certification-based initiatives is inevitably linked to the rapid globalization of supply chains and the resulting proliferation of governance gaps. Enabled through decreases in logistics and communication costs and liberal trade agreements, many multinational corporations (MNCs) have shifted their manufacturing activities to places where production factors are cheap, tax burdens low, and regulations weakly enforced or non-existent. This so-called 'race to the bottom' has increased the need for MNCs to be transparent about how their supplier factories and/or subsidiaries handle social and environmental problems.[20] By requiring certifications from suppliers and subsidiaries, which are often located in countries where social and environmental standards are low, MNCs use standards to make their global sourcing practices more responsible.

One of the most widespread certification standards for social issues is SA 8000.[21] While participants in principle-based initiatives are typically entire corporations, SA 8000 only certifies single production facilities. Currently, there are over 2,000 certified production facilities in sixty-four countries (data as of September 2009).[22] Audited production facilities are often suppliers for big MNCs, which in turn require certification. In this sense, MNCs act as catalysts for certification and can sign up to a corporate programme to publicly show their support for SA 8000. Prominent companies supporting SA 8000 certifications include Chiquita, Carrefour, Toys 'R' Us, and Disney.

SA 8000 claims to be a universal standard, applicable to a wide range of industry sectors, geographic locations, and sizes of production facilities. SA 8000 defines minimum requirements for workplace conditions that need to be met by production facilities and their suppliers. Independent audits are based on the behavioural rules defined by SA 8000. These rules cover eight essential areas: child labour, forced labour, health and safety, freedom of association, and right to collective bargaining, discrimination, discipline, working hours, and compensation (see Box 12.3). In addition to these rules, SA 8000 provides a definition of key terms that plays a significant role in the scope of certification. For instance, a child is defined as 'any person less than 15 years of age, unless the minimum age for work or mandatory schooling is stipulated as being higher by local law, in which case the stipulated higher age applies in that locality'.[23]

Box 12.3   Summary of SA 8000's social accountability requirements

Child labour: no workers under the age of 15; remediation of any child found to be working (including provision of adequate support to enable children to attend school).

Forced labour: no forced or compulsory labour; no lodging of deposits or identity papers by employers or outside recruiters; no withholding of salary and benefits.

Health and safety: provide a safe and healthy work environment; take steps to prevent injuries; regular health and safety training; system to detect threats to health and safety; access to bathrooms and potable water.

Freedom of association and right to collective bargaining: respect the right to form and join trade unions and bargain collectively; where law prohibits these freedoms, facilitate parallel means of association and bargaining.

Discrimination: no discrimination based on race, caste, origin, religion, disability, gender, sexual orientation, union or political affiliation, or age; no behaviour which is abusive, exploitative, or sexually coercive.

Discipline: no corporal punishment, mental or physical coercion, or verbal abuse.

Working hours: comply with the applicable law but, in any event, no more than forty-eight hours per week with at least one day off for every seven-day period; voluntary overtime paid at a premium rate and not to exceed twelve hours per week on a regular basis; overtime may be mandatory if part of a collective bargaining agreement.

Remuneration: respect of right for a living wage; wages paid for a standard work week must meet the legal and industry standards and be sufficient to meet the basic needs of workers and their families; no disciplinary deductions.[24]

SA 8000 asks facilities seeking certification to go beyond a simple compliance approach and integrate the standard into existing management systems. Practically, this can mean a variety of things, for example: (1) management has to 'translate' the standard into a policy document which is continuously reviewed and made available to all workers; (2) dialogue between workers and management through representatives; (3) periodic training and awareness-raising for all personnel; and (4) provision of confidential means to report non-compliance with the standard.

The responsible body for SA 8000 – the NGO Social Accountability International (SAI) – has set up a special organization to accredit and monitor those organizations which act as certification bodies for SA 8000. Once a certification body has been accredited by SAI it can carry out audit visits and award the SA 8000 seal to a production facility for a period of three years. To increase the reliability of the auditing process itself, each factory audit is followed by a series of unannounced mandatory surveillance audits. Certification costs vary depending on the size of the production facility and its location. Although SAI has not fixed a specific amount for the costs of the certification process, it is reasonable to estimate total costs (for the certification audit and the surveil-lance audits) of about $11,500 when assuming a production facility with around 1,000 workers.[25]

Complementarities among standards

Our characterization of corporate responsibility standards shows that there is certainly no shortage of 'tools'. Today, managers rather complain that there are too many standards and that a comprehensive internationally agreed framework for corporate responsibility is still missing and also not likely to emerge in the near future.[26] What is needed, then, is to explore complementarities among existing standards. Although each of the discussed initiatives exists, by and large, as an independent organization, there are a variety of connections that are usually not much acknowledged.

For instance, there is an obvious relationship between principle-based and reporting standards. Some firms already use the GRI G3 guidelines to fulfil the Global Compact's annual Communication on Progress reporting requirement. Equally, the GRI recommends the UN Global Compact to those corporations looking for guidance about how to best align their existing business strategy with universally recognized principles. There is also overlap between principle-based initiatives and auditing standards. Corporations that sign up to the UN Global Compact and look for guidance on how to improve labour standards in their supply chain can refer to SA 8000 (or related standards). Making this con-nection allows firms to put the Global Compact principles into action because SA 8000 certifications directly address the issues listed in the Global Com-pact's four labour principles (compare Box 12.1 and 12.3). Last but not least, businesses reporting in accordance to the GRI guidelines can use certification standards like SA 8000 to obtain the necessary information required under the GRI's 'social performance indicator' category. For example, the GRI requires information on incidents of discrimination that is also a requirement during SA 8000 certifications.

While there is no overarching global standard for corporate responsibility yet, it is important to recognize the potential for cross-fertilization among the different initiatives. Using them in isolation makes it hard to unravel their full potential. Although the discussed complementarities are obvious, further collaboration between the discussed initiatives is required to develop a robust standard architecture for corporate responsibility. Within the business ethics discourse, some scholars have questioned the legitimacy and effectiveness of corporate responsibility standards. For instance, there are concerns that, because standards are voluntary and management can decide which standard to adopt, the scope of resulting changes in business practices remains limited.[27] Our philosophical discussion complements and extends these critiques insofar as it critically reflects the very possibility to standardize corporations' social and environmental behaviour.

Continental responses to corporate responsibility standards

Derrida, deconstruction and the necessity of aporias

The literature on business ethics has primarily aimed at: (1) describing the different corporate responsibility standards; and/or (2) presenting evaluations of the standards from a variety of perspectives.[28] While such discussions are clearly necessary (especially when considering that many of the standards are pretty recent phenomena), there is almost no reflection on the very idea of *standardizing* a concept like corporate responsibility. Continental philosophy can help us to challenge the very idea of standardization. This challenge is affirmative in the sense that it does *not* conclude the absolute ineffectiveness of corporate responsibility standards. Even this affirmative challenge remains a challenge as it explores the limits of standardizing an organization's response to social and environmental issues. It asks: what can we not expect from standards? Approaching the limits of standards is necessary because it reveals what we can meaningfully expect from their application. Considering and discussing the limits of standards is productive since it allows us to take a look 'behind the curtain' to problematize the very idea of standardizing corporate responsibility – an idea which we would otherwise accept as given.

We approach the limits of standards by discussing selected parts of the philosophy of Jacques Derrida (1930–2004). Often, Derrida's philosophy is referred to as deconstruction. While corporate responsibility standards reflect managerial tools, Derrida's deconstruction is not a tool or technique. As Derrida suggests: 'Deconstruction is not a method and cannot be transformed into one'.[29] Rather, deconstruction would be the awareness of the internal contradictions and tensions that are always at work in any standard. Although we do not aim at introducing deconstruction in this chapter, we should recognize that deconstructive philosophy is, among other things, about questioning the existence of hierarchical oppositions.[30] A good example for such an opposition would be rule/action. Usually, we conceive of the rule as being the origin for action; first there is a rule and then action 'according to the rule' follows. Derrida would question this order by claiming that there is no 'pure' origin (i.e. a pure rule which could define its own application perfectly well). Deconstruction allows us to become aware of the dismantling of hierarchical oppositions which are always already at work within our thinking. Dismantling does not mean destroying the oppositions, but recognizing that there is a supplementary logic between the two poles of an opposition. The supplement, which is the formerly suppressed pole of the opposition, is something that gives rise to the other pole that is apparently thought of as the origin. Think of the following example. The tenth principle of the Global Compact – 'business should work against corruption in all its forms, including extortion and bribery' – represents a regulative rule. However, for this rule to gain contextual meaning it needs to be applied to a context. Hence, 'action' (i.e. the supplement) defines the 'rule' (i.e. the origin) *in situ*.

According to Derrida, every apparent origin remains caught up in an aporia. On the one hand, the supplement is necessary for the origin to mean anything at all. On the other hand, we cannot have both, origin and supplement (see above), at the same time. Hence, the simultaneous occurrence of origin and supplement is impossible. That is why Derrida talks about the 'aporetic supplement'.[31] For Derrida, any aporia refers to the contradictions we face when trying to justify the pureness of an origin. An aporia describes an undecidable situation in which we cannot turn to or justify one side of the opposition as being pure and self-defining.[32] To stick to our example: no rule could ever define its own conditions of application. Hence, the *perfect* iteration of a rule in different contexts remains impossible. The impasse, which any aporia aims to uncover, is not destructive or paralyzing.

Aporia I – the rules of corporate responsibility standards

Corporate responsibility standards consist of rules. Here, we are interested in regulative rules – i.e. rules which regulate the behaviour of corporations.[33] For instance, SA 8000 has fixed the following rule: 'the company shall provide a healthy and safe workplace environment and shall take effective steps to prevent potential accidents and injury to workers' health'.[34] Derrida would question the pureness and easy applicability of such a rule. Of course, strictly speaking, this rule needs to mean *the same* every time it is applied during a social audit; it not only needs to mean the same throughout multiple applications over time, but also in different social and economic contexts, as SA 8000 claims to be a universal standard applicable to corporations in all parts of the world. Derrida would ask us to consider that rules cannot possess a pure/metaphysical meaning which could be iterated easily. Rather, every rule gains meaning *in and through* its own application. The supplement (application) is constitutive for the origin (standards' rules) to acquire contextualized meaning.

At the heart of corporate responsibility standards rests an aporia which Derrida describes as follows: 'So, *at the same time*, you have to follow the rule and to invent a new rule, a new norm, a new criterion, a new law.'[35] In order to really apply a standard, managers must do two conflicting things at the same time. They must enforce the rules of the standard and, at the same time, respect the individual, unique context, which makes each case of standard application different. In other words, the universality of a standard is, and needs to be, always already bound up with the particularities of the context in which one operates.

No rule can regulate its own conditions of application. The contextualized application of corporate responsibility standards always adds new meaning to standards' rules. The necessary contextualization of standards is thus intertwined with a 'deviation' from the rules – deviations which are indispensable and which should, ideally, be in the spirit of the standard. DeRuisseau's first-hand experiences during social audits reflect this very well:

> What exactly constitutes forced labor? When is a dormitory sufficiently clean to satisfy the requirements for adequate housing? How much should a factory be allowed to charge a worker for a dormitory room and how many women are allowed to live in the same room? . . . These are but a few examples of the perplexing issues that arise in a factory or farm assessment and that must be evaluated, and accepted or rejected by the assessor.[36]

In other words, we cannot simply fix the meaning of a standard to then lean back and watch its implementation. Applying corporate responsibility standards is 'hard work' – it involves coming to grips with the underlying aporia, reflecting on standards' rules, and embedding them in a particular, unique social context.

To follow a rule is not as simple as we might think. When iterated during applications in different contexts, standards' rules gain new meaning *and*, in a sense, also preserve their 'original' meaning. Derrida describes this interplay of sameness and alteration with the term *iterability*.[37] In and through its repetition each standard gains new meaning but still remains identifiable. The content of a standard is in some way preserved when it is iterated, while at the same time the contextualized standard also differs from the 'original'. Acknowledging the iterability of corporate responsibility standards implies to recognize that exceptions to the rule have to be reflected carefully since a different context can 'force' a rule to adopt a different meaning. For instance, Leipziger points out that in some Muslim countries religious norms require that men and women work separately.[38] Strictly speaking, this is against the SA 8000 standard as it would be considered a discriminatory practice. A serious consideration of the context of application, however, requires us to rethink and reflect on what is in the spirit of the standard. Often, social auditors face the challenging situation of distinguishing between those exceptions that are necessary to acknowledge the local context of application and those exceptions which undermine the standard.

We can sharpen our understanding of the aporia of rule-following when looking at two other discussions by Derrida. Firstly, there is the question of why the meaning of a rule cannot be simply stabilized. According to Derrida, the meaning of language is not simply 'present'; the complete/full meaning of words is continuously postponed and thus remains 'to come'. For instance, we cannot simply refer to a fixed and forever complete meaning of the term 'discrimination'. Barthes uses the examples of a dictionary to illustrate this point.[39] If we look up 'discrimination' in the dictionary, we do not end up with the complete/full meaning of the term. Instead, we find other terms describing what 'discrimination' means (e.g., 'differential treatment'). These terms, however, are also not full of meaning. They face the same problem of being reliant on yet other terms. Hence, meaning rests on differences and, at the same time, is constantly deferred. To describe this combination of differing and deferring effects, Derrida comes up with the term *différance*, uniting the verbs 'to differ' and 'to defer'.[40]

Secondly, the aporia of rule-following also relates to Derrida's discussion of the 'openness' of contexts. As discussed above, the regulative rules of corporate responsibility standards need to be embedded into a specific context. Naturally, these contexts look very different. For instance, signatories of the UN Global Compact face very different contexts of implementation which are influenced by: their country of operation, their size, their legal structure, the sector they operate in, etc. Of course, the Global Compact has produced a variety of documents/frameworks explaining what the ten principles mean in these different contexts. But how far can we fix/predefine a context for the application of a standard? Derrida emphasizes on several occasions the openness of contexts and asks his readers to recognize that the 'finiteness of a context is never secured or simple, there is an indefinite openness of every context, an essential nontotalization'.[41] Contexts are always open to further description, as there is no predefined limit of what should be included. Every firm is different and faces an idiosyncratic context that cannot be fully accounted for by a predefined rule. This, then, is a serious call to not accept corporate responsibility standards as a given, but to reflect on how their rules need to be adapted to the context at hand. It highlights the necessity of a 'fresh judgement' every time we turn to a standard for guidance on social and environmental matters.[42] Each application of a corporate responsibility standard, then, has to conserve the spirit of the standard and, at the same time, destroy its rules insofar as a recontextualization is inevitable.

Aporia II – the undecidable nature of corporate responsibility standards

To apply a standard and to follow its rules involves decisions. For instance, the decision to comply with the standard in the first place; the decisions involved in taking corrective actions in order to be 'in line' with the rules of the standard; and the decisions involved while embedding the standard into ongoing management practices (e.g. to assign a budget). Derrida's reflections on the nature of decisions expose yet another aporia: decisions are only possible if they are impossible.[43] In other words, only when we do not know what to expect from a decision, the decision will become 'real'. If we know exactly how to proceed and what to expect from a decision, there is no need for a decision because the outcome is fixed and programmable and we could leave the task of deciding to a computer. Derrida discusses this in detail in 'Force of law' by stating that:

> In short, for a decision to be just and responsible, it must, in its proper moment if there is one, be both regulated and without regulation: it must conserve the law and also destroy it or suspend it enough to have to reinvent it in each case, rejustify it, at least reinvent it in the reaffirmation and the new and free confirmation of its principle. Each case is other, each decision is different

and requires an absolutely unique interpretation, which no existing, coded rule can or ought to guarantee absolutely.[44]

Only the undecidable nature of decisions gives us something to decide. Traditionally, economists disagree with such a conception of decision as they see decisions as an outcome of a rational calculation. James Coleman, for instance, refers to the decision of whether or not to trust someone as a rational calculation. Rational actors will only trust if the 'pay off' from trusting someone else is higher than the eventual 'loss' from being betrayed. But, if we already know whether it is worth trusting someone *before* the decision, where, then, is the decision?[45]

Let's turn to a specific example. It is widely acknowledged that most suppliers of large MNCs are not themselves interested in signing up to certification standards like SA 8000. Usually, MNCs put a lot of pressure on suppliers and ask them to obtain the necessary certifications.[46] Hence, the decision to comply is, strictly speaking, not a decision, because the supplier either complies or loses its contract. For a supplier, the aporia of not-knowing-what-to-do (and still having to do something) is not relevant in this case because there is no decision. In this case, the application of a standard rests on a programmable procedure. To make a decision 'real', the decision needs to be impossible as for any straightforward/quick/calculable/programmable decision there is no moment of undecidability. We can conclude from this that undecidability is the condition of possibility of any real decision.[47]

What our reflections on undecidability show is that standards should not be treated as ways to reduce or neglect the undecidable moments of decisions. If, for instance, a company just uses the guidelines of the GRI to not have to reflect on what information should be passed on to stakeholders, it not only faces no decision but also, and maybe even more importantly, accepts no responsibility. Accepting responsibility, as Jones *et al.* argue, is about *not* knowing exactly what to do.[48] Corporate responsibility standards are not supposed to make ethics 'easier' or more 'manageable', but instead they should give guidance in asking tough questions about what it means to be responsible. Responsibility entails undecidability because being fully responsible requires us to accept the 'uncomfortable' nature of the experience of not knowing precisely who and how to respond to a claim. So, from a Derridian perspective, we have to accept that corporate responsibility standards cannot tell us exactly what to do. We might adopt the GRI guidelines, but we cannot (and should not) expect that the standard will do the work for us in the sense that the guidelines will tell us exactly what to do.

Undecidability does not imply paralysis or an inability to act; it does not neutralize the need for decisions while adopting or implementing standards. Quite contrary, undecidability reflects the most serious and urgent requirement to make a decision in the light of uncertainty. In the context of corporate responsibility standards, we could even claim that without undecidability there would be no possibility to bring a standard close to its context of application. The case for standard implementation does not rest on very general reflections about 'human rights' or 'the environment'. By contrast, it requires getting our hands dirty by reflecting the various involved decisions in light of the idiosyncratic, yet open, context of a corporation and its supply chain. Without such reflections we risk that standards turn into ineffective tools for acknowledging and responding to a firm's responsibilities.

Implications – reflecting on corporate responsibility standards

The necessary and dispensable nature of standards

Our discussion reveals the two-edged nature of standardization in the field of corporate responsibility. On the one hand, standards are necessary because they allude to universally accepted rules for corporate behaviour. In the absence of weak national regulations and enforceable international law, standards fill an important governance void. On the other hand, standards are also dispensable because their serious implementation requires that we reflect the standard in the context of application and perform a 'fresh judgement' which cannot be included in the standard itself. This, of course, points to yet another aporia: standards are (and need to be) necessary and dispensable at the same time.

This insight calls mostly for a shift in attitude. So far, standards are often perceived as practical tools/instruments/means to implement a concept – i.e. corporate responsibility – that often lacks precision. Many firms find standards attractive because they provide guidance while navigating through the variety of demands placed upon them. In this sense, the list of regulations, which are provided by a standard, gives orientation. However, and at the same time, this list also excludes topics and keeps them off the corporate agenda and thus undermines responsibility. Corporate responsibility can only be achieved if the focus moves from the standard itself to the uncomfortable task of reflecting on the diverse nature of responsibilities a firm has to address. A simple 'ticking the boxes' approach not only runs against the very idea of responding to stakeholder needs, but also exposes the firm to a variety of risks. Unacknowledged responsibilities are at least as dangerous as poorly addressed ones.

The emptiness and fullness of standards

The discussion of the two aporias of corporate responsibility standards implies that each standard faces a *necessary* contextual 'emptiness' which can only be 'filled' with meaning through action (i.e. the supplement in Derrida's terminology) and the belonging reflections about the context in which action takes place.[49] It is vital to point out that this emptiness is *not* a shortcoming of corporate responsibility standards. Rather, it is a direct consequence of the aporias that standards have to cope with. The inevitable emptiness of standards forces managers to accept that the ground on which they base standard implementation is often not clearly defined. Ironically, it is this missing precision which enables us to accept real responsibility while applying standards. A fixed (i.e. 'non-empty') ground would make standard implementation a programmable procedure, which, as Derrida argues, does not involve any responsibility at all.

How, then, do managers cope with the necessary emptiness of standards? First of all, there is a need to become aware of standards' emptiness and to not think that the standard 'will do the work'. Similar to the implementation of strategic concepts (e.g. the 'balanced scorecard' or 'lean management'), it is less the standard itself that counts but rather the time that managers and employees spend thinking about it. Faced with the 'empty' nature of standards and the discussed impasses, managers have to establish an *as if*: 'Let us act as if the standard gives us something to rely upon, even though we know that its rules are not contextualized yet'. Such fictions are often not explicitly recognized (but still existent). They provide internal legitimation to 'go ahead' with the standard, to start discussions about the meaning of its rules, and to get internal approval for budgets and resources.

The 'empty' nature of standards always extends responsibility. The singularity of each decision, for which there is no predefined rule, asks us to consider those stakes for which we are not prepared, for which we do not have ready-made answers. Derrida speaks about the 'monstrous' nature of the future, because a non-monstrous future would not be a future.[50] The imagination which is necessary to 'fill' a standard via an *as if* asks us to consider this radical uncertainty about which stakes need to be addressed (and also to take into account that we can never arrive at a final list of responsibilities). Imagination also means to think about a corporation's influence on the future state of the world and to acknowledge the interaction effects among problems. For instance, climate change will affect water scarcity (e.g. because populations living near snowmelt-fed rivers will experience a decrease in the volume of natural water storage), while water scarcity will also affect food security (e.g. because water scarcity makes food prices more volatile).

The inevitable need for filling a standard is also at the heart of many of the critical assessments of standards.[51] Rules' interpretative flexibility has to be used responsibly but can also be misused. Hence, we need to distinguish between: (1) filling the rules of a standard responsibly to match the idiosyncrasies of a specific local context; and (2) the deliberate circumvention of standards. Often, the difference between both scenarios is blurry and requires in-depth assessments and discussion. Some participants of the UN Global Compact, for instance, have been criticized for not living up to the ten principles.

Usually, these accusations are based on disagreements about what the ten principles mean in practice and what corporations are expected to do *in their context*.[52] While some critiques argue that the problems of the Global Compact are related to its broad principles, there is also plenty of evidence that even the more precisely defined rules of certification standards leave room for interpretation. For instance, in the context of labour standard certifications there is the question of whether overtime should be recorded on handwritten timecards since falsification of such documents is easy. The bottom line is that the *necessary* contextual emptiness of standards can potentially be misused, especially when the standard is seen as a 'tool' and not as a way to foster reflections about a firm's multiple responsibilities.

Implementing standards – reflection versus urgency

As emphasized above, the need for 'filling' a standard requires reflection. Any reflection takes time and managers are often asked to proceed slowly to really reflect on what the standard requires *them* to do. However, how much time do we have when considering the scale and scope of the problems corporate responsibility is concerned with? For instance, the number of people living in extreme poverty worldwide is expected to be 55 million to 90 million higher than before the global economic crisis.[53] Although Derrida calls for in-depth reflections when making decisions, he also recognizes that there is a sense of urgency when making decisions and implementing rules.[54] Decisions do not wait, justice does not wait, corporate responsibility does not wait. This, of course, points to another aporia: we have to reflect in order to not blindly follow a standard, while, at the same time, we cannot reflect too long as the problems which are addressed by standards are pressing problems.

For Derrida, every moment of decision 'remains a finite moment of urgency and precipitation'.[55] Implementing corporate responsibility standards means to balance the need for reflection and the urgency of acknowledging corporate responsibility. Quick and non-reflected solutions are just as bad as no solution at all. This final aporia points to understanding standard implementation as a reflected management process which, like any other management process, needs to balance deliberations about the meaning and applicability of standards' rules with achieving specific outcomes. Such a balance implies most of all to create an internal firm-specific infrastructure for communication to discuss the meaning behind the words. One very practical way of doing this would be to set up a cross-departmental steering committee. Too often, standards are not known beyond the borders of the CSR department. Embedding a standard into a corporation and reflecting on its content requires raising awareness and capacity in different departments. If a standard is perceived as something 'imposed from the outside' or understood to be a 'flux idea of top management', there is little chance that reflection and urgency can be balanced.

The reflection/urgency aporia specifically relates to social auditing, which has been criticized for following a quick and superficial approach during certification visits.[56] A key critique is that during audits interviews with workers are carried out in a superficial way (typically under enormous time pressure) so that many important questions are overlooked or actively ignored. O'Rourke, for instance, reports that 'interviews lasted 7–10 minutes per worker. By the end of the 3.5 hours of interviewing, the PwC [PricewaterhouseCoopers] auditor was extremely tired and asked the questions in a rote fashion'.[57] Rushing through the audit without even the slightest reflection makes certification standards ineffective. A different approach to social auditing, one that realizes the reflection/urgency aporia, does not have to be overly lengthy. What is needed is a serious involvement of workers. Such involvement can be based on interviews which are conducted without time pressure and under the recognition of anonymous complaints procedures.

Conclusion

In this chapter, we reviewed and discussed the role of corporate responsibility standards. We distinguished between principle-based standards (e.g. the UN Global Compact), reporting standards (e.g. the Global Reporting Initiative), and certification standards (e.g. SA 8000). Our discussion showed that there are important differences among these standards – e.g. in terms of their scope, the specificity of their rules, their overall objective and institutional design, and also regarding their levels of uptake. We also highlighted the complementary nature of some standards and discussed why further strengthening of such complementarities is essential.

We started to respond to the generally uncritical discussion of the foundation of corporate responsibility standards by highlighting that behavioural standards in general consist of regulative rules. Referring to Derridian philosophy we exposed two aporias related to: (1) the difficulties of acknowledging the regulative character of a standard while, at the same time, distancing oneself from its rules to account for the singular context of implementation; and (2) the difficulties of not letting the decisions involved in standard implementation become predefined. We concluded that there is a need to think about standards differently; to not perceive them as 'quick fixes' and to stress their 'filling' in and through action. Such a filling emphasizes that ful*filing* a firm's responsibilities depends more on those who implement the standard than the standard itself.

Standards themselves cannot be the sole solution to social and environmental problems. However, in the absence of enforceable national regulations (e.g. the government of Bangladesh employs only sixty-three inspectors for social audits for the *entire* country), and weak or non-ratified international regulations (e.g.

India has not yet ratified International Labour Organization [ILO] Convention 182 prohibiting the worst forms of child labour), corporate responsibility standards are an important element of global economic governance.[58] Currently, it is unclear whether standards will make a substantial contribution to address social inequalities and the multiple environmental challenges. Their scale in terms of number of participants is not sufficient to justify any considerable impact. Considering this, it is obvious that standards' future will depend on both the quantity of participants and the quality of implementation.

NOTES

1 S. Waddock, 'Corporate responsibility/corporate citizenship: the development of a construct', in G. Palazzo and A. G. Scherer (eds.), *Handbook of Research on Global Corporate Citizenship*. Cheltenham: Edward Elgar (2008), 50–73, 52.

2 Goldman Sachs, *Introducing GS Sustain*. London: The Goldman Sachs Group (2007).

3 For an overview see M. Orlitzky, F. L. Schmidt, and S. Rynes, 'Corporate social and financial performance: a meta-analysis', *Organization Studies* 24 (2003), 403–41.

4 See also A. Rasche, 'Toward a model to compare and analyze accountability standards: the case of the UN Global Compact', *Corporate Social Responsibility and Environmental Management* 16 (2009), 192–205.

5 S. Waddock, 'Building a new institutional infrastructure for corporate responsibility', *Academy of Management Perspectives* 22 (3) (2008), 87–108, 90.

6 G. Kell, 'The Global Compact: origins, operations, progress, challenges', *Journal of Corporate Citizenship* 11 (2003), 35–49.

7 See www.unglobalcompact.org. For a comprehensive overview of the first decade of the Global Compact, see: A. Rasche and G. Kell, *The United Nations Global Compact: Achievements, Trends and Challenges*. Cambridge: Cambridge University Press (2010).

8 United Nations, Secretary-general Address to the World Economic Forum in Davos, SG/SM/6881. UN press release (1999), 1.

9 See also the detailed historical analysis by T. Sagafi-Nejad, *The UN and Transnational Corporations: from Code of Conduct to Global Compact*. Bloomington, IN: Indiana University Press (2007).

10 See, for instance, the discussion by J. Nolan, 'The United Nations Global Compact with business: hindering or helping the protection of human rights?', *University of Queensland Law Journal* 24 (2005), 445–66. For a response, see A. Rasche, 'A necessary supplement: what the United Nations Global Compact is and is not', *Business and Society* 48 (2009), 511–37.

11 UN Global Compact, available at www.unglobalcompact.org.

12 GRI G3 Guidelines.

13 D. L. Owen and B. O'Dwyer, 'Corporate social responsibility: the reporting and assurance dimension', in A. Crane, A. McWilliams, D. Matten, J. Moon, and D. Siegel (eds.), *The Oxford Handbook of Corporate Social Responsibility*. Oxford: Oxford University Press (2009), 384–409, 386.

14 KPMG, *KPMG International Survey of Corporate Responsibility Reporting 2008*. London: KPMG (2009).

15 D. L. Owen, T. A. Swift, and K. Hunt, 'Questioning the role of stakeholder engagement in social and ethical accounting, auditing, and reporting', *Accounting Forum* 25 (3) (2001), 264–82.

16 Global Reporting Initiative (GRI) G3 Guidelines, available at www.globalreporting.org.

17 These three dimensions are often summarized as the triple-bottom line of business. See also Chapter 13 in this book on sustainability by David Bevan and René ten Bos.

18 M. R. Matthews, 'Twenty-five years of social and environmental accounting research. Is there a jubilee to celebrate?', *Accounting, Auditing, and Accountability* 10 (4) (1997), 481–531.

19 H. J. van Buren, 'Transparency', in R. W. Kolb, *SAGE Encyclopedia on Business Ethics and Society*. London: SAGE (2009), 2,101–4, 2,102.

20 A. G. Scherer and G. Palazzo, 'Introduction: corporate citizenship in a globalized world', in Palazzo and Scherer, *Handbook of Research*, 1–24.

21 Social Accountability International (SAI), *SA 8000 Standard Document*. New York: SAI (2008), 5, available at www.sa-intl.org.

22 See www.saasaccreditation.org/certfacilitieslist.htm, accessed 11 October 2010.

23 SAI, *SA 8000 Standard Document*.

24 *Ibid.*

25 I. Stigzelius and C. Mark-Herbert, 'Tailoring corporate responsibility to suppliers. Managing SA 8000 in Indian garment manufacturing', *Scandinavian Journal of Management* 25 (1) (2008), 46–56.

26 Considering this criticism, the International Organization for Standardization (ISO) has recently released a new standard, ISO 26000, which is supposed to provide an integrating framework for many of the existing initiatives. See www.iso.org/sr, accessed 8 April 2011.

27 A. Rasche and D. E. Esser, 'From stakeholder management to stakeholder accountability. Applying Habermasian discourse ethics to accountability research', *Journal of Business Ethics* 65 (3) (2006), 251–67.

28 D. Leipziger, *The Corporate Responsibility Code Book*. Sheffield: Greenleaf (2003); M. Goebbels and J. Jonker, 'AA1000 and SA8000 compared: a systematic comparison of contemporary accountability standards', *Managerial Auditing Journal* 18 (1) (2003), 54–8.

29 J. Derrida, 'Letter to a Japanese friend', in D. Wood and R. Bernasconi (eds.), *Derrida and Difference*. Warwick, CT: Parousia Press (1985), 1–5, 2.

30 Faced with the question of what is deconstruction, Derrida replies: 'I have no simple and formalizable response to this question'. See Derrida, 'Letter to a Japanese friend', 4.

31 J. Derrida, *Aporias: Dying – Awaiting (One Another at) the 'Limits of Truth'*. Stanford, CA: Stanford University Press (1993), 67.

32 Derrida, *Aporias*, 12.

33 For a discussion of different notions of rules (including regulative rules), see A. Giddens, *The Constitution of Society*. Cambridge: Polity (1984), 17–23.

34 SIA, *SA 8000 Standard Document*, 6.

35 J. Derrida, 'The Villanova roundtable', in J. D. Caputo (ed.), *Deconstruction in a Nutshell: a Conversation with Jacques Derrida*. New York: Fordham University Press (1997), 1–30, 6 (emphasis added).

36 D. DeRuisseau, 'Social auditing – an auditor's perspective', in A. G. Scherer, K.-H. Blickle, D. Dietzfelbinger, and G. Hütter (eds.), *Globalisierung und Sozialstandards*. Munich: Hampp (2002), 223–34, 226.

37 J. Derrida, *Limited Inc*. Evanston, IL: Northwestern University Press (1995), 53.

38 D. Leipziger, *SA 8000. The Definitive Guide to the New Social Standard*. London: Prentice Hall (2001), 108.

39 R. Barthes, 'The death of the author', *Aspen* 5–6 (Fall-Winter 1967), section 3.

40 The term 'différance' appears in many of Derrida writings. A good explanation is given in the following collection of interviews: J. Derrida, *Positions*. London: Continuum (2002).

41 Derrida, *Limited Inc.*, 137.

42 J. Derrida, 'Force of law – the mystical foundation of authority', in D. Cornell, M. Rosenfeld, and D. G. Carlson (eds.), *Deconstruction and the Possibility of Justice*. London: Routledge (1992), 3–67, 23.

43 *Ibid.*

44 *Ibid.*

45 J. Coleman, *Foundations of Social Theory*. Cambridge, MA: Harvard University Press (1991), 99.

46 D. Gilbert and A. Rasche, 'Discourse ethics and social accountability. The ethics of SA 8000', *Business Ethics Quarterly* 17 (2) (2007), 187–216.

47 J. D. Caputo, 'Commentary: deconstruction in a nutshell', in J. D. Caputo (ed.), *Deconstruction in a Nutshell: a Conversation with Jacques Derrida*. New York: Fordham University Press (1997), 31–203, 137.

48 C. Jones, M. Parker, and R. ten Bos, *For Business Ethics*. London: Routledge (2005), 121–4.

49 The analogy of 'emptiness' and 'fullness' was first used in: G. Ortmann and H. Salzman, 'Stumbling giants: the emptiness, fullness and recursiveness of strategic management', *Soziale Systeme* 8 (2) (2002), 205–30, see especially 213–14.

50 J. Derrida, *Points – Interviews, 1974–1994*. Stanford, CA: Stanford University Press (1995), 386.

51 J. Nolan, 'The United Nations Global Compact with business: hindering or helping the protection of human rights?', *University of Queensland Law Journal* 24 (2005), 445–66; S. Deva, 'Global Compact: a critique of the UN's "public-private" partnership for promoting corporate citizenship', *Syracuse Journal of International Law and Communication* 34 (2006), 107–51.

52 For some of the critiques see http://globalcompactcritics.blogspot.com, last accessed 12 October 2010.

53 United Nations, *The Millennium Development Goals Report* (2009). Available at www.un.org/millenniumgoals/pdf/MDG_Report_2009_ENG.pdf, accessed 12 October 2010.

54 Derrida, 'Force of law', 26.

55 *Ibid.*

56 Clean Clothes Campaign, *Looking for a Quick Fix*? Amsterdam: Clean Clothes Campaign (2005); A. Fung, D. O'Rourke, and C. Sabel, *Can we Put an End to Sweatshops?* Boston, MA: Beacon (2001).

57 D. O'Rourke, *Monitoring the Monitors: a Critique of PricewaterhouseCoopers (PwC) Labor Monitoring* (2003). Available at http://web.mit.edu/dorourke/www/PDF/pwc.pdf, accessed 12 October 2010.

58 Federation Internationale des Ligues des Droits de l'Homme (FIDH), *Bangladesh: Labour Rights in the Supply Chain and Corporate Social Responsibility*. Paris: FIDH (2008), 6.

13

Sustainability

RENÉ TEN BOS AND DAVID BEVAN

Goals of the chapter

After studying this chapter you will be able to:

- understand why sustainable development has become an important issue for business corporations;
- understand the skepticism that mainstream approaches towards sustainability have generated;
- understand how discussions about sustainability impact on the variety of ways we have come to understand 'nature' as opposed to 'culture';
- understand how these discussions might change the way we think about the role that scientists play in our society;
- understand Latour's distinction between 'matters of fact' and 'matters of concern'.

Introduction

Why is 'sustainability' or 'sustainable development' important to business? A standard argument goes like this: when we say that economies grow, we imply that they become 'bigger', but 'bigger' does not mean 'better' and 'better' is what should matter more than 'bigger'. We might refer to an economy that is becoming better as a 'developing' economy. A growing economy is not the same as a developing economy, because no economy can grow indefinitely whereas all economies can develop indefinitely. To make economies better rather than to make them grow is therefore a primary ethical obligation for business. To put it differently, one cannot speak of sustainable growth but one can speak of sustainable development. In the end, all businesses will benefit from it, and not just a few.

We leave you to consider whether this argument is fallacious or not, but it seems to be true that businesses all over the world have indeed recognized the importance of something called sustainable development. Just visit a website of any major firm you can think of and you will see that businesses do at least pay lip-service to it. And since sustainability is generally perceived as beneficial, it became an important issue in business ethics as well. Business activity, the business ethicist argues, is the paradigm which dominates the organization of our contemporary lives. Whatever business we are doing, doing it sustainably suggests it is longer-lasting, cleaner, more efficient, less wasteful, kinder, less smelly, less toxic, and has better value. Because the implicit message of sustainability is thus a beneficial one, we naturally think of it as somehow moral. Sustainability is a concern for business ethics because it seems to fall into the 'ethics zone'.

In the first section of this chapter, we will briefly present a view of sustainability such as we might find in a conventional business ethics textbook. In this literature, it is generally taken for granted that sustainability and sustainable development constitute an ethical concern. While it is not our intention to contest this, we would like to take issue with the underlying optimism that is typical of conventional approaches. Therefore, we end the first section with some highly critical remarks on sustainability and sustainable development. This will pave the way for the next section in which we will first present a typical case of how corporations in the oil industry have dealt with sustainability issues. This serves as a reminder that we should not be too optimistic. Then we will present the ideas of continental authors such as Michel Serres, Bruno Latour, and Peter Sloterdijk. The overall message of the chapter is that, even though there are many things commendable about sustainability, the concept as it is discussed in business ethics and the practices it incites are rife with difficulties. The philosophers we discuss in this chapter provide us with novel ideas about how to render the discussion on sustainability more convincing.

Mainstream view of sustainability

Most business ethicists prefer to talk about sustainable development rather than about sustainability. Sustainable development can be seen as a set of managerial practices that should make something like sustainability possible. These practices are guided by a relentless optimism. Sustainable development is routinely presented as the solution to sustainability problems.

It is important to note that most other texts on sustainability, whether they originated in the field of sociology, economics, or critical management studies, do not share this optimism. This is not to say that they do not address issues that are related to what is discussed under the name of 'sustainability'. Someone like Ulrich Beck, a German sociologist, argues that our way of life implies certain risks for the environment, for communities, for mankind as such. He also makes clear that perceptions of risk can only arise against the ethical or normative background of security which, according to him, can never be 'calculated or experimented away'.[1] What he means by this is that you cannot simply go on living any longer as you have been without questioning the moral acceptability of your way of life. According to Beck, this is an unprecedented situation in the history of mankind: we have become a species that can no longer take for granted the way it lives. To put it differently, we need to ask ourselves the question of how we want to live given the context of risk. This is an entirely new question. The old ethical question was: how do we want to live? In the new reality of precariousness, this question must reflect a perspective of risk and insecurity. Our point here is that arguments from authors such as Beck appear implicitly and explicitly in business ethics as well, especially when it is concerned with sustainability. The central question about sustainability is: how can we do things better? And we surmise that in the business context 'better' means 'less risky' or 'less insecure'.

That something needs to be done is a key assumption in business ethics. The difficulty, of course, is that talking is easier than doing. The problems are so complex and the opinions are so diverse or even contradictory that all good ideas get bogged down in what seems to be a collective shiftlessness and inertia. Part of the problem seems to be that nobody is agreeing about what each country or each organization should do in order to make sustainable development possible. Early in December 2009, a big conference on the theme of sustainability was held in Copenhagen, Denmark. Everybody who had a say on the topic – political leaders and scientists alike – turned up, but the conference, like so many other conferences on the same topic before it (e.g. Rio, Kyoto), was widely believed to be a sad failure. Again it turned out that we do not lack the words to discuss sustainability, but implementation is an entirely different matter. Business ethicists, however, claim that they are generally more interested in implementation. Is it that the world does not listen to the ideas propounded by them? Let us turn therefore to these ideas.

The triple bottom line

The most popular theorization of sustainability among business ethics has been the so-called 'triple bottom line' (3BL). While now fading away from its prominence as a management fashion, the triple bottom line held business ethicists, consultants, and their clients in thrall for about a decade. It is a simple and therefore probably deceptive model that allows one to keep, initially at least, the complexity of sustainability issues at bay.

The concept of 3BL dates back to the early 1990s when consulting firms such as the British organization AccountAbility began to think about ways to interest business companies in more than just the financial bottom line. Originally theorized in a PhD thesis by Braden Allenby, a professor of environmental studies at Arizona State University, 3BL was renovated in 1998 by John Elkington in a popular management textbook, *Cannibals with Forks*.[2] The 'bottom line', as we all know, is economic. But the *triple* bottom line is divided across three dimensions: economics, environment, and society. 3BL became better known as the

Figure 13.1

The triple bottom line (3BL)

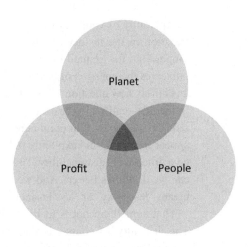

three Ps: profit, planet, and people. Sustainability, it is assumed, is achieved at the point where all three dimensions are in balance (see Figure 13.1).

On the basis of this simple formulation, a rash of initiatives broke out in corporate reports starting from the late 1990s and lasted for almost a decade. It is still employed as a theoretical lens for considering sustainability issues. In Box 13.1, we have outlined not only what supporters of 3BL believe but also what critics think about it.

It is perhaps its simplicity that allowed 3BL to strike at least some sympathetic chords in the corporate world. While we can look back wistfully upon early environmentalists as instigating the groundswell of support for sustainability in the 1950s and 1960s, it was not until the 1990s or even later that major corporations and also governments showed signs of taking sustainability a bit more seriously. 3BL has undoubtedly played an important role in this process. Its message is hopeful and contests the rather gloomy visions of earlier decades. So, finally, the Stern report (2006) and the Geo4 report (2007) to the United Nations Environment Programme (UNEP) became compulsory reading for all those chief executive officers (CEOs) who had been telling us for the last forty years or so that we could not afford sustainability. For CEOs too, the crisis concerning sustainability has become much more compelling. But as we will soon see, reading is not the same as acting.

Three factors are most often cited to explain and justify the need for a model of economic development that stresses sustainability rather than growth. *Firstly*, billions of human beings live in severe poverty and daily face real challenges due to the lack of food, water, healthcare, and shelter. Addressing these challenges will require significant economic activity. *Secondly*, the world population continues to grow at a disturbing rate, with projections of an increase from 6 billion people in 1998 to 7 billion shortly after 2010 and 8 billion before 2030. Most of this population growth will occur within the world's poorest regions, thereby only intensifying the first challenge. Even more economic

Box 13.1   **3BL supporters and critics**

What do 3BL supporters believe?

(1) Businesses have more than simply financial goals.

(2) In addition to financial goals, social and environmental goals can be objectively measured.

(3) Businesses have the obligation to report how well they perform to all stakeholders.

What do critics say about 3BL?

(1) This is nothing new. It is just a version of what is already known as the 'stakeholder approach'.

(2) Quantitative assessments of how good or bad an organization performs are very difficult to obtain. A radical version of this criticism goes like this: moral performance is never measurable.

(3) 3BL supporters assume that moral performance equals wealth maximization and environmental friendliness, but this is a fairly dubious assumption. Other ethical duties may well override duties of wealth maximization and environmental friendliness.

(4) 3BL is vague: The concept of a triple bottom line in fact turns out to be a 'good old-fashioned single bottom line plus vague commitments to social and environmental concerns'.[3]

activity will be needed to address the needs of this growing population. *Thirdly*, all of this economic activity must rely on the productive capacity of the earth's biosphere. Unfortunately, there is ample evidence that the type and amount of economic activity practised by the world's economies has already approached if not overshot the limit of the planet's ability to support human life.

Given these realities, citizens within developed economies have three available paths. Firstly, we can believe that developing economies in places such as China, India, and Indonesia either cannot, will not, or should not strive for the type of economic prosperity enjoyed in developed economies. Secondly, we can believe, optimistically, that present models of business and economic growth can be extended across the globe to an expanding population without degrading the natural environment beyond its limits. In this context, we will suggest that liberal politics and business corporations everywhere in the world have so far focussed on this second option. However, there is an emerging third option: we can search for new models of economic and business activity that provide for the needs of the world's population without further degrading the biosphere. It is a moot question where we should locate sustainable development and all the models that were, in its name, developed. More particularly, can it be done while continuing with business as usual or should we seriously develop new business models?

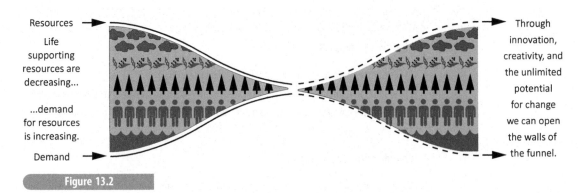

Resources →
Life supporting resources are decreasing...

...demand for resources is increasing.

Demand →

Through innovation, creativity, and the unlimited potential for change we can open the walls of the funnel.

Figure 13.2

The Natural Step

The Natural Step

Most discussions in business ethics about sustainable development clearly assume that there is nothing wrong with the way business is currently practised. Indeed, it seems that the very idea of 'sustainable development' has been developed to carry on with business as usual. There is not a scarcity of business-friendly approaches. Apart from 3BL, we encounter the 'Natural Step', 'cradle to cradle', and various international standards like BS8900 and ISO 26000. Other popular instruments are the aforementioned 'triple bottom line accounting', the 'balanced scorecard', and versions of bio-effectiveness. We leave you to read widely among these to see what instructions they offer. Basically, they all have a positive take on sustainability and sustainable development as a means to a better future, both for the world and for businesses.

However, to provide you with a flavour of the business-friendliness that all these models assume, we will have to say something about one of these exemplary approaches, to wit, the 'Natural Step'. Whereas regulatory and compliance models tend to interpret environmental responsibilities as constraints upon business, the sustainability model is more forward-looking and may present business organizations with greater opportunities than burdens. Indeed, it offers a vision of future business that many entrepreneurial and creative businesses are believed to be pursuing already.

Founded in 1989 in Sweden, the environmental research and consulting group, the Natural Step, uses the image of a funnel with two converging lines to help business understand these opportunities. The resources necessary to sustain life are on a downward slope. While there is disagreement about the angle of the slope, there is widespread consensus that available resources are in decline. The second line represents aggregate worldwide demand, accounting for both population growth and the increasing demand of consumerist lifestyles. Barring an environmental catastrophe, many but not all industries will emerge through the narrowing funnel into an era of sustainable living. Businesses unable to envision that sustainable future will hit the narrowing wall. Innovative and entrepreneurial businesses will find their way through (see Figure 13.2).

The Natural Step then challenges business to 'backcast' a path towards sustainability. We are all familiar with forecasting, in which we examine present data and predict the future. 'Backcasting' examines what the future will be when we emerge through the funnel. Knowing what the future must be, creative businesses then look backwards to the present and determine what must be done in order for them to arrive at that future.

Reasons for business to embrace sustainability

Why should businesses pursue a strategy of sustainability? At least five reasons establish a persuasive case for concluding that it is in business's self-interest to pursue a strategy of sustainability:

(1) *Sustainability is a prudent long-term strategy.* As the Natural Step's funnel image suggests, business will need to adopt sustainable practices in order to ensure long-term survival. Firms that fail to adapt to the converging lines of decreasing availability of resources and increasing demand risk their own survival. One can look to the ocean fishing industry as a case in point. Fishing technologies have become so sophisticated that many species of fish – for example, cod, tuna, shark – run the risk of becoming extinct. This also means that on a global scale especially smaller fishing companies go bankrupt.

(2) *There is a huge unmet market potential among the world's developing economies that can only be met in sustainable ways.* Enormous business opportunities exist in serving the billions of people who need and are demanding economic goods and services. The base of the economic pyramid represents the largest and fastest-growing economic market in human history. Yet, the sheer size of these markets alone makes it impossible to meet this demand with the environmentally damaging industrial practices of the nineteenth and twentieth centuries. For example, if China were to consume oil at the same rate as the US, it alone would consume more than the entire world's daily production and would more than triple the emission of atmospheric carbon dioxide. It is obvious that new sustainable technologies and products will be required to meet China's demand.

(3) *Costs can be significantly minimized through sustainable practices.* Business stands to save significant costs in moves towards eco-efficiency. Savings on energy use and materials will reduce not only environmental wastes, but spending wastes as well. Minimizing waste makes sense on financial grounds as well as on environmental grounds.

(4) *Competitive advantages exist for sustainable businesses.* Firms that are ahead of the sustainability curve will have an advantage serving environmentally conscious consumers, as well as enjoying a competitive advantage attracting workers who will take pride and satisfaction in working for progressive firms.

(5) *Sustainability is a good risk management strategy.* There are many down-
sides in refusing to move towards sustainability that will be avoided by
innovative firms. Avoiding future government regulation is one obvious
benefit. Firms that take the initiative in moving towards sustainability will
also likely be the firms who set the standards of best practices in the field.
Thus, when regulation does come, these firms will likely play a role in
determining what those regulations ought to be. Avoiding legal liability for
unsustainable products is another potential benefit. As social consciousness changes, the legal system may soon begin punishing those firms who
are now negligent in failing to foresee harms caused by their unsustainable
practices. Consumer demand and consumer boycotts of unsustainable firms
are also a risk to be avoided.

Criticizing optimism

The optimism underlying initiatives such as the Natural Step has been much
criticized. Some of the criticisms point out that nobody really knows what
sustainability might mean. To some skeptics, it seems at best an idealized
chimera. Consider what is perhaps the most common definition of sustainable
development:

> Sustainable development is development which meets the needs of the present
> without compromising the ability of future generations to meet their own
> needs.[4]

If we take this frequently repeated and familiar definition as our starting
point, we begin to develop a sense of what is unsettling in the discussion. It is
assumed that we are taking care of the needs of the present. This is, however,
quite clearly a blatant falsehood – we are not taking care of the needs of the
present across the greater part of human activity. It also suggests that we are
able to anticipate the needs of the future, but as Martinez-Alier has pointed
out, 'individuals not yet born have . . . difficulties in making their presence felt
in today's market for exhaustible resources'.[5] Whatever sustainability is, it
is demonstrably not based on what is assumed in the Brundtland definition.
Many debates on sustainability and sustainable development are fallacious in
the sense that they are way too optimistic about the problems that we all face.
The conventional theory of sustainability is, as the French philosopher Derrida
might have pointed out, a screen for 'non-concepts' such as 3BL or Natural
Step which simply serve the project of business as usual.[6] Critics claim that
managerial solutions will not work. The only positive conclusion we can come
to from a reflective reading of conventional sustainability is that, given the
purported state of ecology and the economy, the best we can hope for is *less
unsustainability.* What we have tried to argue so far is that in corporate practice
sustainability is, in fact, a highly contestable subject that has to be rendered
innocuous by focussing on sustainable development, which critics consider to

be a practice that allows us to carry on with business as usual. In fact, this is a process that can be observed with other popular concepts in business ethics as well (see, for example, Chapter 11 on corporate social responsibility).

Critics like Bobby Banerjee have argued that the discourse on sustainable development in the corporate world and in business ethics leaves one dejected, if not downright cynical, as far as sustainability is concerned.[7] Underlying this discourse is still the Western heroic construction of human beings who will, in the end, be capable of solving all problems.[8] This optimism is, of course, hardly realistic or plausible. As Jacques Derrida once reasoned:

> If there were continual stability, there would be no need for politics, and it is to the extent that stability is not natural, essential or substantial, that politics exists and ethics is possible.[9]

In the discussion on sustainability, there is often a utopian trend: one day, if we work hard enough and if we are able to lay aside our cynicism, everything will be perfect. A perfect world, however, would mean the end of politics and ethics. For Hans Jonas, whose work we already discussed in the chapter on whistle-blowing, most debates in ethics – and we surmise that business ethics is not an exception to the rule here – are under the spell of the 'starry-eyed ethics of perfectibility'.[10] What we need, in contrast, is an ethics of responsibility that responds to reality; an ethics that is contextual and contingent; an ethics that purports to protect anything that is vulnerable or fragile; an ethics that calls for personal action.

With this in mind, we will now discuss Michel Serres and Bruno Latour. We do not have the space here to discuss their work in great detail and will therefore focus on two elements that are generally neglected in most literature on sustainability: (1) should we not reconceive well-entrenched dichotomies such as nature vs. culture?; and (2) should we not reconceive the roles that are played by the public, politics, and science? Serres and Latour have made radical propositions as far as both of these questions are concerned.

Continental views of sustainability

Is a more responsible and less cynical attitude towards sustainability possible? One of the worries that critics have about sustainability is that the concept was so easily embraced by the very multinational corporations that have a long history of environmental damage. A concept like this, they seem to realize only too well, remains obligation-free.

As we saw in the first section of this chapter, business ethicists generally take for granted that sustainability is something good. However, not everybody is in agreement with this. Some people, especially intellectuals from the third world, have argued that sustainability is simply a Western ideology that serves to mask the devastating nature of capitalism. Others have joined these critical voices and claim that sustainability is a token of a new ecological 'bourgeois' mentality that simply functions, as the Slovenian philosopher Slavoj Zizek once put it, as 'an opiate for the masses' that allows us to consume more and more with a 'warm conscience'. *The paradox of sustainability is that it incites us to change practices in order to keep things going as they always did.* The concept as such suggests that the forces which we have unleashed can somehow be controlled. But consider what the British economist, Paul Seabright, has to say:

> A larger, more affluent, and industrially more inventive world population may well create such threats faster than the tunnel vision of its individual members will allow them to respond.[11]

Sustainability becomes a problem when it functions as a kind of moral tranquillizer that allows us to go to sleep as if nothing is wrong with what we do. A related kind of critique, finally, is that sustainability has become a powerful moral tool used immorally to pester or even blackmail local governments or business people. There have been, for example, a lot of occasions where financial aid was withdrawn when it was felt that standards for sustainability were not reached.

The point of these criticisms is, in fact, that by and large our engagement with sustainability is not serious enough. It is even suspected that the elusiveness of the very concept itself prevents us from pondering the right questions. Perhaps business ethics stands accused as well. Does it reflect the problems on our planet seriously enough when it simply resorts to instrumentalism? In this section, we will discuss some ways in which continental philosophers have rethought the question of sustainability. Serres has argued that we should indeed rethink the very relationship between nature and culture; Bruno Latour agrees with Serres in this and comes up with the outline of a new 'political ecology' that seems to dispense with the very idea of 'nature'; finally, in our conclusion, we will refer to Peter Sloterdijk, who has argued that a new 'hyper-politics' is called for, a politics which is credible enough to make sustainability into something which is more than just a rather conservative moral ideology. All three authors that we will discuss in this chapter share a cautiously positive attitude towards sustainability even though they argue that contemporary policies fail completely. It is not a surprise then that these philosophers focus on ways to change the nature of politics as we know it today.

Anthropocentric environmentalism and business realism

On 17 June 1991, the well-known American essayist and columnist Charles Krauthammer wrote in *Time*:

> sane environmentalism begins by unashamedly declaring that nature is here to serve man. Nature is not our ward. It is not our master . . . It is man's world.

Nature will have to accommodate. Man should accommodate only when his
fate and that of nature are inextricably bound up.[12]

One argument that Krauthammer advances is that you cannot always conserve
species and gain economic advantage. He solemnly states that he is not the
enemy of the spotted owl in California or of calving caribou in Alaska but if he
has to choose between the interests of the wood or oil industry on the one hand
and the interests of animals on the other, he would definitely opt for the industry.
Krauthammer's position stands in a long tradition of Western philosophy. Man
is the measure of all things and nature stands at the disposal of his industrious
activities. Environmentalism needs to be entirely anthropocentric if it is to make
sense to a commentator like Krauthammer, who exemplifies what the French
philosopher and sinologist, François Jullien, refers to as Western man's tragic
appropriation of nature.[13]

On 14 August 2009, *Los Angeles Times* and *Dallas Business Journal* reported
that Exxon-Mobil agreed to a US district court in Denver to pay a $600,000
fine for the violation of a federal act that is designed to protect birds. Due to
its drilling activities and the contaminants that were subsequently spilled into
the environment, the company was believed to have killed eighty-five birds.
However, Exxon-Mobil promised to mend its ways and reported that it had
already spent more than $2.5 million for the protection of migratory birds in
particular. It was heralded that the company would henceforth work in close
collaboration with the Departments of Justice and the US Fish and Wildlife
Service.

One wonders what Krauthammer might have made of this news. The example
of Exxon-Mobil somehow makes clear that the kind of environmentalism he
promulgated – one which entirely serves the interests of man – has not remained
uncontested. All over the world companies like Exxon-Mobil have been taken
to task for the detrimental effects of their activities. However, what does it mean
when a district court somewhere in the US decides that a bird's life is to be
estimated at $7,000? What does it mean if one realizes that the annual personal
security costs alone of Exxon-Mobil's Chairman and CEO, Ray Tillerson – we
do not dare to mention his annual income here – are estimated at $2.3 million?[14]
Does this mean that the life of a renowned CEO has a price which is 320 times
higher than the life of a bird? Tillerson has a firm reputation among shareholders
for his unwillingness to embark on the search for alternative fuels. As late as
May 2009, he assured the shareholders that fossil fuels still have the future:
depletion of the world's resources will not ensue earlier than in the next century.
Exxon-Mobil's CEO considers himself to be a realist and has always believed
that shareholders are principally uninterested in the search for alternative and
sustainable fuels. It is simply not a competitive market.

Is this to say that behind the lip-service being paid to the issue of sustainability
and the small victories occasionally won by environmental organizations there is
still the old, unshakeable philosophical dogma on which Krauthammer seemed

to rely? One of Exxon-Mobil's competitors, Shell, has clearly opted for a different kind of attitude towards the issue of alternative fuels. On the occasion of his retirement, Shell's former CEO, Jeroen van der Veer, claimed that the search for alternative fuels was inevitable: 'Alternative energies will come. We are absolutely convinced'.[15] But, like Tillerson, van der Veer warns against unrealistic expectations. First of all, the alternative energies will not be very cheap and affordability of energy is for most people in the world a crucially important issue. Second, even if we become less reliant on fossil fuels – today they supply about 90 per cent of the total energy used – and are capable of reducing this figure to about 70 per cent, we will not use *less* of it, because the need for energy will have doubled by the year 2050.

Rethinking nature and culture

Behind this discussion lurks a sobering awareness that, as the French philosopher Michel Serres claims, man and world are still very dependent upon each other.[16] This is not an insight CEOs of big companies would probably disagree with, even though they do not understand its consequences. Serres urges us to think through the interdependence of man and world. He goes on to claim that the relationship between man and world has always been antagonistic. While it appears as if humanity finally won the battle against nature, this victory has created its own problems. It is as if nature strikes back and shows us that we cannot get away with plundering her endlessly. The more she loses terrain, the more she becomes an issue.

Serres argues that 'worldwide nature' is the only decisive factor nowadays. What he means is not nature on a local level, let us say, the forest in your neighbourhood or the river in your city. We are increasingly troubled by a nature that encompasses the entire world: the rise of the sea-level, global warming, the ozone layer, and so on. Serres suggests that the battle between man and nature has reached unprecedented levels of intensity. He visualizes this as a giant struggle going on between 'the big animal that all of us are forming' and this worldwide nature. Serres uses this expression – 'the big animal' – to remind us that mankind as such has become a physical entity. We are animals who have become so powerful and energetic that nature is no longer a superior force that is indifferent to what living creatures are doing. This is, of course, not to say that we control the planet, even though heroic thinking allows us to think that we do: 'This idea recalls a bygone era when the Earth placed in the centre of the world reflected our narcissism, the humanism that makes us the exact midpoint or excellent culmination of all things'.[17]

But we *do* have an actual physical impact on the earth. It is this situation, Serres argues, that requires us to make a sort of contract with nature. People have always assumed that there is a necessity for a social contract: the conflict potential between human beings calls for such a contract. Now that mankind impacts nature as much as nature impacts mankind, we need a natural contract as well. We have focussed so much on the necessity of a social contract that we completely forgot that it is not social antagonisms alone that haunt us. As Serres puts it, when the social contract has been made, 'nature is only there for a lonesome dreamer'. Nature, he complains, disappears in politics and science: both domains are completely 'a-cosmic'.[18] This is a folly, for the earth can perfectly well exist without us *whereas we cannot exist without it*.[19]

But there is a different element in the contract that requires our attention. In one of the most famous passages in the history of philosophy, Jean-Jacques Rousseau wrote that '[t]he first person who, having fenced off a plot of ground, took it into his head to say this is mine and found people simple enough to believe him, was the true founder of civil society'.[20] The point here is that the act of taking possession will only be completed and legitimized when two parties enter into an agreement: the first party takes possession of a plot of ground and another party approves this claim. The parties enter into a contract and it is their willingness to abide by it which makes civilization possible. Serres, however, draws our attention to the fact that any contractual activity is by definition exclusionary. A contract between two partners necessarily implies that others are excluded.[21] In this sense, a contract is always local, or as Serres repeatedly emphasizes, 'a-cosmic'. Insofar as it is constitutive for civil society, we have to acknowledge the fact that its citizens only develop a local rather than a global or worldwide awareness.

Serres's entire philosophical work urges us 'to get out into the world' and to develop a global consciousness.[22] Only such a consciousness allows us to see the necessity of a contract with planet Earth as such: a contract with nature. As is clear from the examples we gave in this chapter, nature has rarely been seen as a partner and it is this exclusion which makes possible an unequalled 'parasitism':

> The parasite takes all, and gives nothing; the host gives all, and takes nothing. Rights of mastery and property come down to parasitism. Conversely, rights of symbiosis are defined by reciprocity: however much nature gives man, man must give that much back to nature, now a legal subject.[23]

The idea that nature is a legal persona or entity is no doubt controversial. Human beings or organizations have a legal status in our society, not nature. But this is, according to Serres, exactly where the shoe pinches. The problem in our culture, he argues, is that it still thinks in terms of locality rather than globality. Here is a theme that we encountered in other chapters of this book as well: the developments of the world become dangerous as long as we stick to old modes of thinking.[24] The way we think about law and right is obsolete since it does not acknowledge globality and cosmos. We will see below that the sciences made a similar mistake and it should therefore not surprise us that science and right are very intimately connected: they are based on a contractual and therefore exclusionary view of the world. The globality of our culture must overcome such partiality. Its task is to truly 'meet' the globe if we and nature are to survive. There should be equality between 'the force of our global interventions and the globality of the world'. To acknowledge this can only be done by a non-exclusionary mind and the capacity to think in this way is what Serres refers to as 'reason'. It is a reason that is willing to place its immense power at the service of the earth.

This search for a balance between nature and culture is also present in Latour, who explicitly states that he extends Serres's analysis, as it appears in the latter's seminal book, *The Natural Contract*.[25] One of the fears he expresses, however, is that the concept of nature as such is problematic since it seems to make possible the kind of exclusionary or hierarchical thinking that is typical of our culture. More specifically, it has allowed politics, science, and business to be very clear about what has no value and it has served ecological movements to invent a reverse and equally damaging hierarchy, one in which culture is subjected to nature. Like Serres, Latour argues that the problem with both approaches is that they still separate politics and nature, or culture and nature. We act as if there are '*two* distinct arenas' that allow us to 'totalize the hierarchy of beings'.[26] The notion of plurality plays an important role here: there are many cultures and just one single nature. We easily use words such as multiculturalism but refrain from using words such as 'multinaturalism'. And all these different cultures are supposed, in one way or the other, to ride roughshod on the big passive one-ness we refer to as nature.

So, in this 'bi-cameralist' worldview, both arenas are distinct from one another, but we can also see how strongly (and, one might add, perversely) they are related. The metaphor Latour uses is that of a seesaw: when politics goes down, nature comes up, and vice versa. So, the proposal is to remove one-self from nature and society, and to convoke 'a single collective whose role it is precisely to debate the said hierarchy – and to arrive at an acceptable solution'.[27] Approaching the world as one singularity is the only way to make a political ecology and an ecological politics possible. But before taking on the practical issue of politics, we will first consider the role of science.

A new science

In discussions about sustainability, scientists have always played a very important role. The problems that are often associated with sustainability – climate change, CO_2 emissions, bio-safety and biohazard, or environmental pollution – were first addressed by experts with a scientific background. It was biologists, physicists, or geologists who first addressed the deleterious consequences of human enterprise. In contemporary democracies, these experts are supposed to enlighten not only the general public but, more specifically, the politicians who are representing the public. However, there are many difficulties here: the chain of communication between the parties involved is hardly ever clear. The public and politicians do not always wish to hear the expert messages about the

Box 13.2	Sustainability problems in the meat industry

Let us tell you some facts about the meat industry. The numbers here are simply unimaginable. It is expected that in 2027, humanity will consume about 330 million tonnes of meat, which is more than twice as much as it was in 1983. The increase in meat consumption is strongly related to economic growth in the third world. In Western countries, it is expected that meat consumption will remain more or less on the same level. Of all the populations in the world, the Americans eat by far the most meat: while they make up only 5 per cent of the world population, they consume 15 per cent of the entire world's meat production. It is expected that between 2027 and 2050 meat consumption will have tripled.

Now, it is not our intention to talk you into vegetarianism, but consider just a few facts that are related to countries such as China and India: a serious increase in meat production will lead there to an enormous slurry problem; the people there can expect acid rain and greenhouse effects; there will be a scarcity of water since the production of one kilogram of meat uses 12,000 litres of water. These and similar kinds of numbers are, however, always contested. Even if they were not contested, we might wonder whether the public would want to hear them. People all over the world do not only wish to eat meat, they want lots of it. Especially problematic is that the production of all this meat will lead to an increase in scale in the industry: chickens and pigs would especially be destined for mass slaughter around the world. This has led health experts to wonder not only about the health effects for the meat consumers themselves, but also about broader, unforeseen effects such as pandemic diseases caused by viral infections: SARS and bird flu have already been connected with poultry. Another problem with the increase in scale is that smaller farms will lose the battle in the meat markets, if only because they cannot engage in price competition with the bigger industries.[28]

current state of the world. Moreover, many of the experts themselves do not seem to agree about particular developments (see Box 13.2).

In our society, people no longer rely on experts or even trust authority figures as far as their lives are concerned. There are many good reasons for this. Scientists have, of course, been complicit in creating the problems we have now. They have a long-standing and rather scary tradition of being involved with industry, indeed of making the kind of industry possible that incites people on the planet to live more and more '*un*sustainably'. Unfortunately, scientists have not always acted with academic integrity. At the time of writing this chapter, there is a huge debate going on about the world famous Dutch virologist Ab Osterhaus. In his country, he has persistently warned against the dangers of a pandemic. He repeatedly tried to persuade politicians that they should develop or purchase vaccines on a massive scale. Yet, his authority received a blow when it turned out that he not only held several positions on advisory boards for the medical industry but also had shares in a few of the companies involved.

These kinds of conflicts of interest have haunted scientific experts for a long time. How objective is what they say? How reliable are their research programmes? The problem that plays an all-important role here is that scientists have always been capable of relating to industries or powerful politicians but hardly ever to the public. In the chapter on whistle-blowing, we saw how difficult our organizations can make it for a person to be seriously concerned for the public weal. What counts for employees who think about blowing the whistle counts for scientists as well: they too are involved in social situations that do not make this concern for the public weal an easy option. Moreover, there seems to be a certain antagonism between science and democracy. To put it straightforwardly, is there a way in which the public can control the kind of expert knowledge that people like Osterhaus have?[29]

The role of science and scientists, some commentators argue, has to change. Karin Backstränd, a Swedish political theorist and environmentalist, has identified three interrelated problems with science as it is currently practised: (1) it lacks public trust; (2) it has deteriorated into specialist self-indulgence; and (3) it is not properly controlled and governed. To gain back public trust, it is crucially important that science revamps itself. One of the major things to be done for scientists is to cope with complexity and the only way to do that is to start thinking about how to get out of the specialist box into which they have been coerced by contemporary academic organization. The 'civic' science about which Backstränd muses is transparent, interdisciplinary, and accessible.[30]

Latour has similar ideas. He argues that science should activate rather than paralyze public and politics since these are the only forces in the contemporary world that enable action. But science has deteriorated into a 'political science', that is, a science that paralyzes public and politics. In our society, science functions as 'curare' basically because it is still hooked on rigour and objectivity.[31] The problem with this is that the world does not need more objectivity but more concern. Latour therefore proposes to make a distinction between 'matters of fact' and 'matters of concern' and he claims that for a very long time science has only taken interest in the former.[32] In Box 13.3, we have listed a few differences between matters of fact and matters of concern. Latour's point is that many discussions related to sustainability do not have the clear-cut objective status that indisputable facts have. Global warming, climate change, the human genome, CO_2 emissions, and cloned animals or otherwise genetically modified organisms are all examples. They are capable of agitating people even before they start to understand the consequences. Nobody seems to remain unaffected. They are therefore not only a concern for scientists but for bureaucrats, managers, pressure groups, politicians, and citizens as well. And the discussion is badly served if scientists, basing themselves on rigidity and objectivity, remain aloof and distanced. Matters of concern show us that old distinctions such as fact/value, objective/subjective, or nature/culture are not as clear-cut as previously supposed.

| Box 13.3 | Matters of fact and matters of concern (Latour) |

Matters of fact

- Objects have clear boundaries, a well-defined essence, and well-recognized properties; objects are 'things' with a hard kernel that is rigorously separated from their environment.
- Scientists, researchers, and experts disappear behind these objects; this is what scientific objectivity is all about: bring your 'objects' to the market and render yourself invisible and immune; this is why Latour speaks of 'risk-free objects'.
- These objects are incontestable and as such they plunge from one universe (nature) into an entirely different universe (society); it is expected that they make an indelible impression in this different universe.
- The definition of these objects cannot be changed no matter how they impact society: matters of fact always remain what they are; as such they remain detached from the consequences they may have.
- Examples are: trees, the sun, a distant planet, an animal, a chair, the normal objects that make up your landscape.

Matters of concern

- 'Objects' have no clear boundaries and no hard kernel; they are 'tangled beings' or 'quasi objects' that belong to a world of networks and rhizomes.
- Those who speak and write about these non-objects are very visible and therefore also contestable, controversial, complicated, and so on; the actors who bring these facts to the fore are running certain risks.
- They do not belong to a different universe; they blur the old distinctions between objectivity/profitability on the one hand and the political/social on the other; they also blur the distinction between nature and society.
- These can all but be detached from their unexpected consequences; they already agitate everybody well before they start having consequences.
- Examples are: stem cells, genetically modified animals, global warming, the rise in sea levels.[33]

This all implies that science is no longer an isolated domain. In a few publications, Michel Serres has elaborated extensively upon this.[34] He argues that for a very long time scientists have tried to impose their findings on us more or less in the way that the judge imposes his or her verdict on a criminal. But scientists have lost their privileged position: they should constantly legitimate their knowledge, which is no longer taken for granted. The time of apodictic truths is over. Everyone is involved in science these days. It has become part of ordinary life and does not stand outside of it.

This may not be to the liking of the initiated few who still hope for aloofness and objectivity, but Serres wagers on what he refers to as 'a house of laicism', where the people who dwell there accept science as a part of their lives and who would not accept any privileges for people who claim to know what others do not know. The desacralization of science is what Serres aims for and he describes it as a process of forgetting. In *Les Cinq Sens*, he offers us a marvellous image: you can only swim if you forget how to swim. In other words, you will very likely not be a good swimmer if you think about how to proceed in water. Analogously, you can only speak a language if you forget what you are in fact doing when speaking it. In the way that swimming or language can be in us, as a forgotten presence, science should be in all of us. 'This is what I have labored for with passion: that in my books knowledge and science would plunge into forgetfulness, so that their very loss may work towards new objects and bear a new subject'.[35]

We can perhaps make these ideas a bit clearer by referring to a famous story by Edgar Allen Poe. In his *The Purloined Letter*, the police are simply unable to retrieve the letter because they work too systematically and methodically. System and method have always been the hallmarks of science. The same holds for jargon and aloofness. All these aspects have allowed science to occupy a place alongside culture in a quasi-sacred domain. Nowadays, the matters that really concern us all do not require system, method, jargon, and aloofness. We submit that the entire discussion on sustainability gains much more force if we leave managerialism and scientism behind and think, like Serres and Latour, about new roles for science in our society.

Conclusion

In this chapter, we have developed a critical perspective on sustainability. There are many problems with the concept. Critics have argued that it is too vague and therefore does not have any real effect on what business organizations are doing. Moreover, underlying the discussion on sustainability is often a belief in the malleability and measurability of the world. But the world is probably not a place where everything can be fixed or measured. The world is not a perfectible place.

Rather than thinking of sustainability in instrumental or managerial terms, we have tried to redirect our focus to two problems that often remain ignored in many discussions: the concept of nature on the one hand and the role of the sciences on the other. Using ideas by Serres and Latour, we have argued that a reconceptualization of what we understand by nature and by science is important. Nature has been thought of for a long time as representing all that where culture is absent. When scientists claimed to have special knowledge about this realm, they located themselves as it were beyond culture too. This has indeed been understood as a requirement for scientific objectivity and rigour but it has catapulted science away into an area where politics and the public are painfully absent.

However, if we are to work on issues of sustainability, we cannot only rely on a monstrous alliance between science and business but we need to involve the public and politics. The idea of a contract with nature and the idea of a lay science are important here. Moreover, we have seen that the issues surrounding sustainability can hardly ever be seen as hard facts. They are 'matters of concern' and as such they will be addressed not only in business and science but also by politicians and by the public. This is, we believe, where the discussion should take place in a democratic society.

One of the problems with the discussion so far is that no participant seems to be convincing enough. We suggest that there are three reasons for this: cynicism, consumer indifference, and a lack of political credibility. There is, to be sure, a lot of cynicism among corporations. We have already discussed the cases of Exxon-Mobil and Shell. Many companies only pay lip service to sustainability. A perhaps even worse example of this cynicism would be Japanese fishing companies. While publicly endorsing the idea of sustainable fishery, their technologies are more and more damaging to the population of fish in our seas. The blue fin tuna, one of the most valued delicacies among Japanese consumers, has been nearly driven to extinction. However, there are reports of companies who respond to this news by increasing rather than reducing their fishing activities. The idea is to store excess tuna in freezers so that it can be sold a long time after the animal has actually become extinct! The longer it will be extinct, or so the calculation goes, the more money it will bring.

Cynicism is hard to counteract, especially since by and large consumers do not seem to mind too much what might happen to, for example, a blue fin tuna. Cynicism and consumer indifference foster each other. The only way out is a politics of credibility, but how do politicians become credible in an age of consumerism, that is to say, in an age that values consumption more than anything else? The German philosopher Peter Sloterdijk has argued that politics should no longer be based on principles for it is the principles that have lost their credibility more than anything else.[36] They stem from a time when politics was still linked to nation states and empires, entities that nowadays have lost most of their significance. He argues that politicians seem to be more and more incompetent in the face of the problems of our planet. One of the reasons is that politicians nowadays shamelessly act in what they perceive as the interests of the public, no matter how uninformed the public might be. Unpopular measures, no matter how necessary, are increasingly difficult to take. Electoral damage is often the inevitable consequence. This is precisely one of the reasons why Serres and Latour think so much about ways to infuse politics and the public with science, something which can only be achieved when science itself abandons its ivory tower. Sloterdijk opts for a 'hyper-politics', a politics that understands that 'the art of belonging' has become more and more difficult, a politics that understands that risk and catastrophe make up the context of contemporary life, a politics that functions as a bridge between science and the general public because it refuses to accept that any practice, let alone science, should take place in isolated circumstances.

Where does this leave business? Business will not disappear:

> The hyperpolitical society is still a community of people who will wager too on the betterment of the world in the future; what they need to learn is a process that allows for the possibility of winners who themselves allow for the possibility of winners after them.[37]

We surmise that this may be an interesting way of recasting the attraction of sustainability for business companies: are they willing to bridge the gap between ancestry and posterity?

NOTES

1 U. Beck, *Risk Society: Toward a New Modernity*. London: Sage (1992), 37.

2 J. Elkington, *Cannibals with Forks. The Triple Bottom Line of 21st Century Business*. Stony Creek, CT: New Society Publishers (1998).

3 This is loosely based on Wayne Norman and Chris MacDonald, 'Getting to the bottom of the triple bottom line', in *Business Ethics Quarterly* 14 (2) (2003), 243–62.

4 This famous and eloquent description stems from 'Our common future', the report written by the Brundtlandt Commission in 1987. See www.un-documents.net/wced-ocf.htm, accessed 8 April 2011.

5 J. Martinez-Alier, *Ecological Economics: Energy, Environment and Society*. Oxford: Blackwell (1987), 17.

6 J. Derrida, 'Politics and friendship: a discussion with Jacques Derrida', in G. Bennington (ed.), *Centre for Modern French Thought*. Brighton: University of Sussex Press (1997).

7 B. S. Banerjee, *Corporate Social Responsibility: the Good, the Bad and the Ugly*. Cheltenham: Edward Elgar (2007).

8 F. Jullien, *Vital Nourishment: Departing from Happiness*. New York: Zone Books (2007).

9 J. Derrida, 'Remarks on deconstruction and pragmatism', in C. Mouffe (ed.), *Deconstruction and Pragmatism*. London: Routledge (1997), 84.

10 H. Jonas, *The Imperative of Responsibility: in Search of an Ethics for the Technological Age*. Chicago, IL: University of Chicago Press (1984), 201.

11 P. Seabright, *The Company of Strangers. A Natural History of Economic Life*. Princeton, NJ: Princeton University Press (2004), 119.

12 C. Krauthammer, 'Saving nature, but only for man', *Time* (17 June 1991), 82.

13 Jullien, *Vital Nourishment*, 25.

14 See www.networkworld.com/slideshows/2009/080209-ceo-perks.html?t51hb#top, accessed 15 August 2009. But we can mention Tillerson's annual income in an endnote: it is estimated at $22.5 million. When he retires at the age of 65, he is believed to get a package worth about $600 million. Exxon-Mobil's turnover in 2008 was $45.2 billion. This means that Exxon-Mobil spent 0.0001 per cent of its turnover in 2008 on the protection of birds. See http://chrisy58.wordpress.com/2009/05/29/

exxon-mobil-ceo-tells-shareholders-that-fossil-fuels-have-long-future, accessed 15 August 2009.

15 See www.algemene-energieraad.nl/newsitem.asp?pageid=14100, accessed 15 August 2009.

16 M. Serres, *The Natural Contract*. Ann Arbor, MI: University of Michigan Press (1995), 34.

17 *Ibid.*, 33.

18 *Ibid.*, 110.

19 *Ibid.*, 33.

20 J.-J. Rousseau, *Discours sur l'Origine et les Fondements de l'Inégalité Parmi des Hommes*. Paris: Gallimard (1965), 87.

21 Serres, *The Natural Contract*, 38–9.

22 See, for example: M. Serres, *Atlas.* Paris: Julliard (1994).

23 Serres, *The Natural Contract*, 38.

24 See especially Chapter 9 in this book on whistle-blowing and Chapter 14 on globalization.

25 B. Latour, *The Politics of Nature. How to Bring the Sciences into Democracy.* Cambridge, MA: Harvard University Press (2004), 251.

26 *Ibid.*, 29.

27 *Ibid.*

28 Based on R. ten Bos, *Het Geniale Dier.* Amsterdam: Boom (2009), 69–70.

29 S. Turner, 'What is the problem with experts?', in E. Selinger and R. P. Crease (eds.), *The Philosophy of Expertise.* New York: Columbia University Press (2006), 158–86.

30 K. Backstränd, 'Civic science for sustainability: reframing the role of experts, policy makers, and the citizens in environmental governance', *Global Environment Politics* 3 (4) (2003), 24–41.

31 Latour, *The Politics of Nature*, 202. Curare is a paralyzing poison used by indigenous people in South America for hunting.

32 Latour, *The Politics of Nature*, 22–3.

33 Based on Latour, *The Politics of Nature*, 22–5.

34 See especially the last chapter of M. Serres, *Les Cinq Sens. Philosophie des Corps Mêlés.* Paris: Grasset (1985), 371–5. Another important text in which laicism is discussed is M. Serres, *Le Tiers-instruit.* Paris: Gallimard (1991). The latter text has been translated into English as M. Serres, *The Troubadour of Knowledge.* Ann Arbor, MI: The University of Michigan Press (1997).

35 Serres, *Les Cinq Sens*, 324.

36 P. Sloterdijk, *Eurotaoismus. Zur Kritik der Politischen Kinetik.* Frankfurt: Suhrkamp (1989), 172–8.

37 P. Sloterdijk, *Im Selben Boot. Versuch über die Hyperpolitik.* Frankfurt: Suhrkamp (1993), 80.

14

Globalization

RENÉ TEN BOS

Goals of this chapter

After studying this chapter you will be able to:

- understand the difficulty in defining globalization;
- understand how business ethicists engage with globalization;
- understand how the issue of relativism has dominated the discussion about globalization in business ethics;
- understand how continental philosophers have tried to reframe the discussion on globalization;
- understand that globalization is much more than just an *economic* issue.

Introduction

Globalization is a challenging issue not only because there is hardly any agreement about what it is, but also because it raises so much moral and political dispute. Take the protests of anti-globalists during the G8 conferences, which were organized in cities like Seattle, Genoa, and Gleneagles. The protesters rallied against what they considered to be unfair trade, environmental pollution, or the exclusion of people from economic processes. They also took issue with the role that institutions such as the World Bank or International Monetary Fund play. These institutions stand accused of being the servants of multinational corporations (MNCs) rather than helping poor people around the world. Many protesters argue that MNCs have had a bad influence, especially in the poorer parts of the world. These companies are not just upsetting local economies but also sustaining corrupt regimes and plundering natural resources. It is no exaggeration to say that companies working on a global scale have the protesters, as it were, on their doorstep.

It is no surprise, therefore, that business ethics has a strong interest in globalization and the problems that it raises. In this chapter, we will see that much of this interest is indeed focussed on MNCs. Practitioners and academics have tried to develop corporate codes that would lead to improved moral performance, but skepticism about MNCs has not waned. The financial crisis, obscene rewards for managers, and ongoing environmental destruction are just some factors that kindle this skepticism. The question, therefore, is how business ethics should respond to this widespread discontent. It is exactly this question that we will discuss in this chapter. But before answering this question, we will first describe what globalization might be.

What is globalization?

We have just seen that there are people against globalization. What does it mean to be against globalization? Can one really be against globalization if one is able to travel around the world in order to protest against it? And if people who are against globalization blame corporations or international institutions for almost anything that is wrong in the world, does this then imply that these corporations are *for* globalization? But what does it mean to be *for* globalization?

There are many definitions of globalization circulating but here we will, initially at least, resist the temptation to provide one of them. For the moment, it suffices to note that the word 'globalization' as such is an indication that at least quite a few observers feel that something very big is taking place, something that they routinely describe in terms of 'growing interdependencies of markets and economies', 'an explosive growth of international trade', or 'rapid industrialization of the world'. Underlying all these and many other ideas is the belief that *the* world is becoming 'one', that there are no isolated communities anymore, and that the opportunities and problems that many people in the world have are somehow related to this 'one-ness'. To put it simply: if the economy of the US is in bad shape, then many other economies will suffer. If it is in good shape, then most other economies will profit.

Controversies about globalization

However, for those who long for conceptual and empirical clarity there is bad news. There is disagreement on basic questions such as: (1) When did globalization start? (2) Does it actually take place? (3) Is it a process the significance of which should be narrowed down to the economic realm? In this section, we will discuss these three questions.

In order to shed some light on question (1), we would first like you to compare the following two quotes:

(1) 'The need of a constantly expanding market for its products chases the bourgeoisie over the whole surface of the globe...The bourgeoisie has through its exploitation of the world market given a cosmopolitan character to production and consumption in every country.'

(2) 'From a corporate perspective the dominant feature of today's world econ-
    omy is the increased globalisation of market competition. Formerly isolated
    geographically bounded markets are being transformed, if not always into
    a global market, then into a set of interconnected markets.'

At face value, there is not much difference between both quotes. Their authors
stress that markets are expanding and increasingly becoming interconnected.
The first quote, however, is from the *Manifesto of the Communist Party*, which
was written in 1848 by Karl Marx and Friedrich Engels. Quote 2, on the other
hand, is from a chapter in an edited textbook about *Strategic Human Resource
Management* that appeared in 1984.[1] When one reads these quotes, it seems as
if there is not a big difference between the nineteenth century and the end of the
twentieth century. Is the concept of globalization then the umpteenth example
of old wine in new bottles?

Question (2) – does a process called 'globalization' actually take place? –
has also raised controversy. In a now classic text on the topic, the English geog-
rapher Peter Dicken distinguishes between the *hyperglobalist* and the *skeptical*
position.[2] Hyperglobalists argue that globalization is a hard fact that cannot be
denied: this means that we live in a borderless world where concepts such as
'culture', 'nation state', or 'citizen' have become virtually obsolete. What we
witness now is indeed a one-ness that has homogenized consumer taste and
that allows companies to deliver standardized products and services all over
the globe. Rather paradoxically, one might argue that anti-globalists take this
hyperglobalist position: there is no doubt among them that globalization is an
empirical fact, which has detrimental consequences all over the world. It is,
after all, rather silly to protest against the 'cultural imperialism' that is believed
to be the outcome of the homogenization of consumer taste if you really do
not believe it exists. Hyperglobalism is therefore not a matter of being for or
against globalization.

There are, however, quite a few people who contest the claims of the hyperglobalists and who would argue that these are grossly exaggerated. We still have
distinct cultures, distinct nation states, and even though many human beings
can be seen as consumers there is no doubt that, for example, the concept of
the 'citizen' has not lost its significance. One of the hot issues in the debates
between hyperglobalists and skeptics is the degree of *openness* that pervades
the world economy. The skeptics claim that the world economy is much less
open now than it was around 1900: at this time, prior to the first world war,
companies all over the world had to cope with much less regulation and law.

The changing international division of labour: Shell in Nigeria

Dicken steers a middle course and claims that although there are 'undoubtedly
globalizing forces at work, we do not have a fully *globalized* world economy'.[3]

We barely understand the impact of the *processes* we are now witnessing, let alone their end results. However, a distinction can be made between *internationalizing* processes and *globalizing* processes. In the first case we refer to the simple extension of economic activities across national boundaries whereas in the second case there is a complete landslide in the way that the international division of labour is taking place. During the age of internationalization – and this has been typical of the period prior to the first world war – there was still a clear dichotomy between the periphery of the world and its centre in the sense that the former delivered the raw materials to the latter and that the latter took care of the manufacturing of end products.

Nowadays, in the age of *globalizing* processes, we see that this has profoundly changed and that more and more the formerly peripheral states produce end products that are subsequently exported to what used to be the centre of the world economy. Today, it hardly makes sense anymore to talk in terms of 'periphery' and 'centre', although, as we will see, this is not to say that there are no 'excluded' people. Indeed, one of the problems with the changing international division of labour is that MNCs increasingly locate themselves in what used to be the periphery. This has led to all sorts of problems: MNCs have not only morally or financially supported corrupt regimes but also delivered weapons to these regimes in order to allow them to suppress any form of resistance against the way they conduct business.

A case in point is Shell and Nigeria. Members of the Ogoni tribe in that country have a long history of vehement opposition against what they see as the plundering of their country by oil companies. One of the spokesmen of the Ogoni was Ken Saro-Wiwa, a famous poet and novelist. The Nigerian regime arrested and killed him. Shell has always been accused of being complicit in the murder. At the time of writing, more than ten years after Saro-Wiwa's demise and after a juridical verdict, Shell has finally agreed to pay compensation to the family members of the poet. In this way, they implicitly acknowledge responsibility. But at a press conference, the chief executive officer (CEO) of the company, Jeroen van der Veer, insisted that Shell had nothing to do with Saro-Wiwa's murder, and that Shell paid for humanitarian reasons.

It is not difficult to describe many more of these cases where, from a moral perspective, something went terribly wrong. The Shell case at least shows that the changing international division of labour that seems to be an effect of globalization has more than just economic ramifications. Many MNCs have become involved in politics: they have used corrupt regimes all over the world to boost their economic performance, they have taken advantage of gaps in local law, and they have plundered natural resources. So, it seems that question (3) – is globalization an economic process? – can only be answered negatively. The Shell case makes this abundantly clear. Globalization is definitely not just an economic issue.

Business ethics and globalization

Business ethics has always had an international focus. In journals such as *The Journal of Business Ethics*, which was founded in the early 1980s, there was from the beginning an interest in cases such as Shell. A central question that business ethicists have in mind is what practitioners in MNCs can learn from these and other notorious moral failures.

It took, however, quite a long time before the field started to notice that these problems might be related to processes of globalization. Perhaps it is that globalization as such raises problems of unprecedented moral dimensions. One of the first business ethicists who recognized the novelty of the situation was Tom Donaldson, who raised new issues for the field.[4] Due to globalizing processes, business organizations were supposed to think about cultural relativism, human rights, international law, politics, and many more issues that do not belong to the natural field of business people's interests. Here, we will only briefly focus on one of these issues: *cultural relativism*. This is not to say that the other issues are less important. The point is rather to show how business ethicists typically respond to one of the problems that come with globalization.

Relativism

Here is how Norman Bowie, a renowned business ethicist, defines cultural relativism:

> it is a descriptive claim that ethical practices differ among cultures; that, as a matter of fact, what is considered right in one culture may be considered wrong in another culture.[5]

The argument here is not difficult to follow. All our moral judgements are culturally determined. They are based on our own particular experiences, but what we experience is by and large determined by the culture in which we find ourselves. This implies that no-one is qualified to judge about certain features of other cultures since this would only mirror the prejudices of the person's own culture. *Moral relativism* or *value relativism* is a specific version of cultural relativism in which we are not qualified to judge moral habits or values in other cultures. Even though people live on the same planet, they all live in different worlds and the gaps between these worlds are sometimes unbridgeable. As Bowie points out, 'one has to abide by the ethical norms of the culture where one is located'.[6]

Business ethicists often assume that relativism is one of the big problems for multinational business, for it by definition bridges these different worlds. If two companies working in different countries encounter each other in the market place, there should be some mutual understanding about what is morally acceptable or not. In other words, they should find a way to bridge the cultural gap that might exist between their respective cultures. Here is another suggestion by Bowie:

> If Romans are to do business with Japanese, then whether in Rome or Tokyo, there is a morality to which members of the business community in both Rome and Tokyo must subscribe – even if the Japanese and Romans differ on other issues of morality.[7]

The idea is that there will always be some point of mutual agreement that will then make profitable *and* good business possible. What should this mutual agreement be about? For example, about what counts as corruption and what does not, what is contract breaking and what is not, or what is theft and what is not?

Even though it is well-known that people belonging to different cultures have different opinions about these matters, it is always claimed that some sort of agreement should be in place in order to make business possible. Donaldson goes so far as to claim that there is an 'ethical algorithm' that might allow business people to establish a common understanding on moral issues. Later he would come to refer to this in terms of universally acknowledged 'hypernorms', something to which we will return soon.

Bowie does not see any problems at all since a 'great deal of morality has already been internationalized, either explicitly, by treaty or by belonging to the UN; or implicitly, through language or conduct'.[8] People all over the world know what is moral or not. And they agree about it. This pertains especially to business people. The only thing that business people all over the world have to agree about, Donaldson claims, is what constitutes fairness and what is deemed to be extremely important or valuable.[9] In other words, people like Donaldson or Bowie remain entirely practically oriented: relativism is a problem for management practitioners that business ethicists can help to resolve.

Hypernorms

Business ethicists are hardly interested in theoretical issues. They prefer to focus on practice. This leads scholars to formulate a set of rules or guidelines that can help business people to cope with the dilemmas globalization imposes. See Box 14.1, which offers an example of the guidelines for MNCs proposed by Richard De George.

Of course, the relativist can easily take issue with at least some of these guidelines. They ignore value relativism in the sense that not every culture would agree about what constitutes a violation of norms. In many countries in the world, for example, there are, compared to what people in Europe or America might think, completely different ideas about what is corruption and what is not. By and large, De George's guidelines are based on an 'Anglophone' or 'utilitarian' kind of ethics, that is to say, on an ethics which is by itself embedded in a particular culture. But De George simply sweeps these kinds of

Box 14.1	Business ethics guidelines for multinational corporations

(1) MNCs should not inflict direct harm intentionally.
(2) MNCs should produce more good than bad for the host country.
(3) MNCs should contribute by their activities to the host country's development.
(4) MNCs should respect the human rights of employees.
(5) MNCs should pay their fair share of taxes.
(6) To the extent that local culture does not violate norms, MNCs should respect the local culture and work with it, and not against it.
(7) MNCs should cooperate with the local government in the development and enforcement of just background institutions.[10]

arguments under the carpet. His rather straightforward claim is that following these guidelines might somehow help most companies to escape most 'legitimate criticisms'. Again, the interest is basically practical: MNCs are in need of ethical guidance when it comes to globalization.

Tom Donaldson and Tom Dunfee have gone much further in this and argued for a unique, systematic, and universal approach that might help businesses to cope with the challenges of globalization.[11] Their 'integrative social contract theory' offers procedural guidelines to MNCs, but also explicit normative content in the form of 'hypernorms'. In his work with Dunfee, Donaldson replaced the idea of the 'ethical algorithm', which he developed in 1989, with this notion of 'hypernorms'. These hypernorms are 'principles so fundamental to society that they shape and inform all those "second-order" norms that are formulated to guide specific kinds of human behaviour'.[12] Again, the assumption is that globalization does not force us to resort to value relativism. Some sort of moral agreement is always possible in the sense that there are a number of normative principles that are allegedly shared by all cultures. One of these hypernorms, for example, is that one should respect the institutions of a particular society.

The problem with the hypernorms, as Mollie Painter-Morland has pointed out, is that they are too abstract and too universal to make sense in specific circumstances.[13] An example here would be the right of political participation or the requirement that a country's institutions are efficient in the sense that its citizens should be able to take advantage of them. This is also why Donaldson and Dunfee would allow for a 'moral free space' that enables all people involved to bring in local or cultural specificities without abandoning the possibility of universal consent. Donaldson and Dunfee want to have their cake and eat it too: they acknowledge value pluralism but they do not want to exclude the possibility of universal consent. So, they offer us a version of universally applicable and morally neutral contractarianism based on tolerance and pluralism. But here again, we see how difficult it is to match the requirements of universalism with the requirements that are tied to specific circumstances.

We can easily understand this as the conundrum of globalization: the attitude of pluralistic impartiality that some scholars exemplify seems to gloss over the fact that morality is also about responsiveness and relationality. In other words, even though no-one would disagree that neutrality is an important value in the age of globalization, there is something hopelessly detached about it. It is still a moot question: can we ever develop a morally neutral ethics that would be commendable to cultures and communities all over the world? The problem can be phrased in simple terms: value relativism is a fact, but we shy away from the moral consequences of this fact.

A new kind of ethics?

The discussion about these matters still continues. One of the most interesting recent contributions is by the Mexican organizational theorist Eduardo Ibarra-Colado.[14] He too struggles with what we might also refer to as the problem of universalism versus particularism. Like the business ethicists discussed so far, he wants to maintain notions such as 'liberty', 'justice', 'pluralism', or 'solidarity', but he also urges us to rethink what ethics might mean in the age of globalization. One of the problems with the work of Donaldson, Bowie, or De George is that they still stick to a certain ethical paradigm that assumes the possibility of a rational consensus. In this sense, the name of philosophers such as Immanuel Kant or John Rawls, who have both in their own ways tried to ground ethics in rationality, are never far away in the work of these business ethicists. There is a strong sense that reason and reason alone can solve the most important moral problems in business. We will see later in the chapter that this is, to the say the least, contestable.

Ibarra-Colado has argued for a 'new' kind of ethics.[15] Firstly, this ethics will be 'transmodern': it should be multicultural, poly-faceted, hybrid, postcolonial, tolerant, democratic, and ecological. Secondly, it will be radically material, that is to say, it should be rooted in the realization that we are all living human beings and that the protection of life should be essential to all ethics. This would imply that an MNC that causes unemployment or ecological damage is simply wrong because it impedes the efforts of all human beings to sustain their lives and the lives of those they care for. Thirdly, the new ethics will be inclusive: it should not only amount to a discussion between CEOs or managers. The idea is that those who are excluded and often live in devastating circumstances will be given a voice and be heard as well. Fourthly, the new ethics will always be critical in the sense that it will always recognize that human action produces negative effects and therefore at least some victims. This also implies a constant will, not only to reconsider ethical norms and practices, but also to constantly reorganize.

Departing from these ideas for a 'new' ethics, Ibarra-Colado phrases ten main proposals (see Box 14.2). These proposals clearly differ from the ones put forward by De George. They are less concerned with managerial practicality

Box 14.2	An alternative list of guidelines for multinational corporations

(1) The basis for ethics is the reflective protection of life.

(2) The substantive goal of life is the well-being of humankind.

(3) Participative dialogue and conversation based on reason are the foundations to building a new ethics.

(4) Human freedom, but not isolation or individualism, is a basic value of society; its unnegotiable limit is the protection of life.

(5) The well-being of humankind must be fulfilled by the exercise of free human action via cooperation and agreement.

(6) Wealth is only a means for preserving life and providing the conditions for a better existence for humankind, so the economy must be at the service of society.

(7) If corporations are a means to fulfil the well-being of humankind, then they are essentially social/public entities.

(8) Therefore, managers are at the service of the people under the principle of 'the best interests of society'.

(9) Society must regulate the economy and corporations, protecting life to build a free and diverse global society, trying to minimize the production of victims by its recursive reorganization.

(10) In a transmodern ethical world, there is space for everyone.

and sketch a sort of outline for a world that needs to be formed not only by MNCs but also by politicians, consultants, academics, workers, and, indeed, all citizens of the world. Globalization is everybody's concern. In this sense, these proposals differ from 'standard' business ethics: they are, for example, critical of typically Western values such as 'utility' or 'individualism'. They also cast doubt on the idea that globalization just requires rational solutions for the moral problems that it raises. And perhaps most importantly, they speak from the third world rather than from the first world. This implies that the language used by Ibarra-Colado is much less managerial than the language spoken by De George. The latter speaks on behalf of MNCs whereas the former stands for a voice that has something to offer to these MNCs and this offering comes from a domain that is morally internationalized in a somewhat different way than business.

In spite of their differences, however, both De George and Ibarra-Colado have a certain confidence in and optimism about their guidelines. They are more interested in what globalization means for the daily business of companies and people who experience the consequences of what these companies do, than in rather abstract philosophical speculations about the nature of globalization. However, in the sense that Ibarra-Colado is more interested in challenging certain ideas about globalization rather than in instrumentalizing them, we might see him as one of those thinkers who can bridge the gap between business ethics and the continental philosophers that we will address now.

Continental philosophy and globalization

In what follows, we will show how continental philosophers have tried to make sense of globalization. There are philosophers who have vented all sorts of social and political critiques about the process, and there are philosophers who apparently take a more neutral stance and try to philosophically analyze the concept of globalization. It is important to bear in mind that the philosophers we will discuss below have never addressed an audience of business ethics scholars. So, unlike business ethicists they are not primarily helping management practitioners of MNCs to deal with the problems of globalization. But there is a sense in their work that globalization is a process that raises all sorts of new moral problems.

More specifically, the ideas of these philosophers shed fresh light on how we are to think about the moral implications of the globalized world. In this sense, their work might indeed relate to Ibarra-Colado's effort to outline what might constitute an alternative capitalistic world, one in which social responsiveness is not an exception but the rule. However, we should also bear in mind that many continental philosophers clearly do not share Ibarra-Colado's optimism. We will first briefly discuss a few philosophers who try to frame questions about globalization in a more political way. Then we will enter into the work of arguably the most outspoken continental philosophers as far as globalization is concerned: Jean-Luc Nancy and Peter Sloterdijk. We will see that one of their major concerns is relativism and how to overcome it.

Rejecting global business

Many continental philosophers harbour all sorts of misgivings about what global capitalism has created: the gap between the rich and the poor is becoming bigger and bigger, more and more people in the world feel frustrated by what they perceive as the ongoing hegemony of the West, businesses all over the world have contributed to the financial crisis, governments have not been able in any way to guarantee social security, and, finally, on a worldwide scale millions and millions of people are on the move looking for a better life. Of course, this is just a small list of problems that might be related to globalization. For example, we did not mention issues such as global warming, the war on terror, the war on drugs, or the increasing scarcity of water. Sometimes, all these problems seem to be too big or too complex to handle.

Perhaps, the widespread frustration with the complexity of these problems has led to the moral outcry that we hear everywhere. We do not only think of the anti-globalization activists we spoke about earlier, but also of documents signed by renowned academics, politicians, or intellectuals who express their concerns about what is going on. Of course, no-one seriously thinks that corporations alone are responsible for all these problems; politicians, civilians, governmental organizations – they all seem to be involved as well. Nonetheless, there seems to be an understanding that the problems of globalization are strongly related to the way that business organizations are operating on a worldwide scale. The mentality of the 'bottom line' is as equally widespread as are the objections against it. Therefore, many people and not only philosophers have a feeling that business might, after all, be the root of all evil. The point to be made here is not that this is right; the point is rather that this is a widespread sentiment. MNCs such as Nike, Starbucks, Shell, or MacDonald's have been chastized for underpaying staff, busting union activities all over the world, undermining population health, violating animal rights, depleting rainforests, or colluding with unstable and repressive regimes.

Some continental philosophers are also discontented with these injustices and claim that globalization seems to have been 'hijacked' by what has been referred to as 'global capital'. Business and economics determine what we are supposed to understand by 'globalization' and this is the root of all problems. Michael Hardt and Antonio Negri, for example, are concerned about what such a completely business-driven kind of globalization might eventually imply for democracy. They offer two reasons for this concern:

(1) Globalization unmoors democracy from its traditional meanings and practices. It brings in 'a new scale' that gives concepts such as 'nation state', 'parliament', or 'elections' entirely different meanings or even renders them obsolete.
(2) As a consequence, most politicians have no clue about what democracy might mean in the age of globalization. Most of them simply assume that globalization nowadays implies liberty and nothing else. This in fact means that private property rules supreme. The problem, however, is that liberty – and especially this kind of liberty – is not the same as democracy.[16]

These misunderstandings about the nature of freedom and democracy, Hardt and Negri argue, are also the reason why so many politicians today think that something like democracy can be imposed on people all over the planet. The worldwide protests against these efforts simply show that this is wrong: in the age of globalization, democracy cannot be imposed by the privileged few on the repressed and ignored masses all over the world. Democracy can only spread around the world by means of *bottom-up* processes.

If this is right, then we may take issue with business ethicists' efforts to formulate global codes for MNCs. Firstly, such codes are generally phrased in the offices of CEOs and other powerful persons and then imposed upon people in or outside the organization. It is, for example, very easy to say that corruption is under no condition acceptable, but people working in the field know that business cannot always be done in a 'clean' way. Secondly, and more importantly, why should managers or CEOs be dictating what the world is supposed to look like? The task to create a better world, something that we may assume lies at the heart of business ethics, is in the hands of many more people than just business people.

These insights have led some philosophers to contest the idea that globalization is actually a process which is basically propelled by business capitalism. In fact, there may be other factors that are even more important. Today, business or capitalism, someone like Slavoj Zizek argues, are not the most important factors in globalization but rather what he describes as the 'destructured masses': the poor and the deprived who do not yet form a political class (like the labour class) and who live in semi-urban environments all over the world 'constitute the principal horizons of the politics to come'.[17] Zizek claims that these masses are even more fundamental than business and capitalism to whatever globalization might be. The most genuine form of globalization, he claims, would be an effort to politicize and organize these destructured masses.

People often complain that, from a cultural perspective, globalization generates a homogeneous culture all over the world: everywhere you see the same cellphones and the same fast-food restaurants. This is true, no doubt, but there is, according to Zizek, also a homogeneity that is much more relevant for future politics. He claims that life in the outskirts of Bamako or Shanghai is not different from life in the *banlieues* of Paris or the ghettos of Chicago. This offers possibilities for a worldwide solidarity among the poor and the deprived and this will sooner or later become a political force in its own right. Zizek argues that the signs of political consciousness-raising are already there and he goes so far as to applaud Hugo Chavez, the Venezuelan president, for having caused a political awakening in the slums of Caracas.[18] The point to bear in mind here is that Chavez is an example of what might happen if business organizations and international institutions were not able to appease the discontent among these destructured masses. For MNCs, Chavez is a reminder that a failure to address the burning issue of poverty and power disparity might eventually be very bad for their business. Business ethicists are, we believe, well-advised to address these kind of issues in their work.

In summary, there is a clear tendency among many continental philosophers to *politically* reclaim globalization. Not only the names of Hardt, Negri, or Zizek play an important role here but also Derrida, Agamben, or Balibar. All these thinkers claim that globalization should become a process that is not determined by economy and business but rather by poor and excluded people. The question for business ethics then becomes whether businesses can see these people – people who generally have no buying power and are not employed – as stakeholders. Perhaps, there is a task for business ethicists here. Indeed, if we do not take up this matter, we miss a unique opportunity to become politically and morally more relevant.

The philosophers we just mentioned do not hesitate to take a strong politico-ethical position. Perhaps, many business ethicists may feel that this position is too radical or too unrealistic. What, after all, are businesses all over the world supposed to do with these allegedly 'left-wing' insights? Perhaps, it might indeed be argued, they are morally compelled to invest much more in the destructured masses Zizek writes about. But this seems to be very difficult. Bolivia, Ecuador, and Venezuela are examples that illustrate the problems businesses have nowadays with countries where an 'awakening' of the masses has taken place. MNCs operating in these countries fear that the state will take them over and it is not a surprise therefore that many companies collude with governments and secret agencies to prevent this. This happened in the past in Chili, Haiti, and Honduras, and it will continue to happen in the future.[19]

Be this as it may, even in the philosophical literature discussed so far in this section, we hardly see any reflection on the concept of 'globalization' itself. It is generally assumed that globalization is there, out in the world, as it were, and that this has bad rather than good political and practical consequences. Here again, the focus is on consequences. But how are we to make sense of the concept itself? Can we somehow rethink it? Can we make sense of globalization in a different kind of way? In what follows, we will be concerned with two thinkers, Jean-Luc Nancy and Peter Sloterdijk, who have tried to understand globalization from a different kind of perspective: what does it mean for communities? We will see that Nancy forces us to rethink the homogeneity and 'oneness' that play such an important role in the debates about globalization. Sloterdijk contests the very idea of 'one-ness' and argues that globalization implies, if anything, a crisis of human communities. The question that will guide us throughout the discussion is how all of this might be related to business ethics.

Nancy and the world

A central theme running through the work of Nancy is the lack of an essence that is common to all men. Again and again he asks us to think about what this means. Contrary to Zizek, who claims that globalization makes the world homogeneous, Nancy writes that '[t]he unity of the world is not one [because] it is made of a diversity, and even disparity and opposition'.[20] The 'oneness' of the world that we discussed in the beginning of this chapter is in fact nothing else than its diversity. The world is one but it is one in its diversity. The world is therefore always a multiplicity of worlds. What does this mean? Is this the same position as the relativist position, which business ethicists, as we have seen, have been trying to overcome?

People who live in the age of globalization are, Nancy writes, more or less 'world-conscious'. Many people, not only business managers and academics, have transcended their own culture. This is a matter of fact. More than earlier generations, they have become aware that they are living on a planet, that what was once far has now become close, and that their lifestyle is influenced by people from all over the world. They belong to the world, and in some sense they *are* the world. This is why people nowadays routinely use expressions such as *world-class, world record, worldwide, world-famous, Miss World*, or *World Bank*.

That the word 'world' is occasionally misused is also obvious. Anti-globalists would argue that the World Bank is not a bank for the world but a bank for the rich. The Americans speak about the *World Series* when they are in fact talking about an all-American championship. The point is, however, that we do not pay sufficient attention to what this expression 'world' might mean. Increasingly, people live in *the* world, not in *a* world that is different from *other* worlds. This is why the relativist position is wrong. The relativist argues, as we have seen, that people live, as it were, in different worlds. Nancy begs to differ: people live in *the* world, but this world remains, as we will see, always a multiplicity.

Nancy takes up the question of the world in a number of texts.[21] Like so many other philosophers who are discussed in this book, he is heavily inspired by Martin Heidegger. In *Sein und Zeit (Being and Time)*, Heidegger distinguishes four different senses that we can give to 'world'.

(1) 'World' signifies everything that is, everything that is present in the world.
(2) 'World' signifies a subset of everything that is. We can, for example, use an expression like 'the mathematical world' to denote the kind of objects mathematicians take an interest in.
(3) 'World' signifies that *in* which human beings live. Human beings live *in-the-world*. But there are always a lot of possibilities here: a person can live in the world of soccer, in the world of fashion, in the public world, and so on.
(4) 'World' also denotes 'worldliness' (*Weltlichkeit*). This is an existential feature of human beings. We do not only live in the world (see 3), but this world is also in us. Human beings are open to the world in a way that animals or objects are not. This also implies that they are open to several possible worlds.[22]

After having made these distinctions, Heidegger goes on to claim that only (3) and (4) give a philosophically proper understanding of 'world'. This means that the worldliness of human beings allows them to be in-the-world and to actually *form* worlds. What does it mean if we say that human beings form worlds? It means that they create conditions for themselves in which they dwell. A farmer in the third world will do that in a different kind of way than a business manager working for an MNC. Even though they are in the same world, they live in entirely different conditions. This is not to imply that the farmer and the manager are complete masters of the worlds in which they live. It is rather the case that humanity's ability to be in-the-world gives them the possibility to appropriate and transform their worlds. With this in mind, we might argue that globalization is a process through which humanity has created for itself not many worlds but just one world, *the* world. And as human beings, whether we like it or not, we all dwell in this one world. For example, a farmer in Madagascar is, even though he may not be aware of it, affected by decisions made on Wall Street. On a worldwide scale, the effects of the financial crisis have not only been catastrophic for businesses all over the world but also, and even more so, for people like this farmer. The very fact that the manager of an MNC may be unaware of the way that her decisions have an effect on farmers in Madagascar then becomes a moral problem that is new in the world of business and that requires new sensitivities. It is as if farmers and managers are somehow *touching* each other.

The idea of touching is very important for Nancy's conceptualization of 'world'. In fact, he defines the world as a 'touching of everything with everything'.[23] This is *the* sense of the world and only if we know how to be touched by it will responsible behaviour with respect to the world become a possibility. The sense of the world does not therefore reside in some transcendence (God, Allah, a demiurge) or destiny (an idea such as a proletarian utopia). Sense is never outside the world. 'What is coming to us', Nancy writes, 'is a dense and serious world, a *world-wide* world, one that does not refer to another world'.[24] Perhaps this is also what Ibarra-Colado might have had in mind when he argued for an all-inclusive ethics. The moral scope of our actions, including the actions of MNCs, has dramatically increased as a consequence of globalization.

Nancy's point is that we can no longer act as if we do not coexist in the world or as if we are, as the relativist maintains, living in different worlds.[25] That people differ in various kinds of ways and can be very strange to each other – as the farmer in Madagascar and the manager probably would be – is not to suggest that they cannot share the same sense of the world. For the manager, this implies that it would be irresponsible to think that she can manipulate the world, in the name of the bottom line, at her own discretion. Nancy's idea of touching fiercely opposes the idea that we can objectify or rationalize the world. In the age of globalization, we need to overcome this idea and seriously think about the sense of the world. If we understand the world as *one* and if nothing is excluded from it, would we then really go on depleting rainforests or butchering animals the way we do now? Not to think these kinds of questions, Nancy claims, is tantamount to 'cowardice' or 'laziness'.[26]

To think the sense of the world *in* the world is what Nancy refers to as '*mondialization*': we have to make a world from the world and this implies, as we have seen, a radical rejection of transcendence and objectivation. The world is our political and moral horizon, not God, not an ideal, utility, or some other end. 'Mondialization' is carefully distinguished from two other concepts: '*modernization*' and '*globalization*'. 'Modernization' is the process of secularization and rationalization. Nancy's concern about this process is that it has led to a worldview in which the world is a passive object. 'Globalization' is used by Nancy to denote the worldwide exchange of people, goods, and services. This is a world of profit and utility. The historical claim is that modernization precedes globalization. And if there is such a thing as the age of globalization, then we are desperately in need of mondialization, which we might understand here as an ethical rephrasing of problems that haunt the community of the world. For MNCs, mondialization would imply that they understand that globalization is not so much about the possibility to do business more easily across the world, but understanding that doing this kind of business changes the world in profound ways.

This also means that MNCs must learn to understand human beings as beings who are constantly *exposed* to the various ways they conduct their businesses. What Nancy means by this is that people are affected and touched by the activities of these companies. To make his point clear, he uses an untranslatable pun: *expeausition*.[27] *Peau* is the French word for *skin*: it is the organ that makes touching possible. Touching is, of course, unlike the other senses: it acts upon the world and it registers the action of the world on you.[28] Nancy's response to the global age – an age in which diversity and unity are alternating rapidly – is a suggestion towards a 'mondialization' that renders the world so dense and mixed-up that the only proper moral attitude is not to escape from it and resort to relativism (people live in their own worlds) or objectification (there is a world out there and we can manipulate and use it), but to be *in touch* with it. One of the problems that MNCs have with the phrasing of global codes of conduct is that they know how to phrase them in a captivating way, but not how to embody them. Perhaps we can understand Nancy's idea about touching as a way to think about this embodiment. Can we expect people who are phrasing all sorts of ethical guidelines in the luxurious offices where they do their work to be in touch with the world? And can we subsequently expect them to embody what they purport to believe in? In other words, will the manager ever be touched by the farmer in Madagascar if all the manager sees is a computer screen, overhead sheets, and like-minded people?

Sloterdijk and the globe

Peter Sloterdijk has been referred to as *the* philosopher of globalization. Nowhere else do we find such an elaborate philosophical theory of globalization. Whereas Nancy still shies away from the use of the term 'globalization' in any philosophical sense and opts for 'mondialization', Sloterdijk reclaims the term for philosophy and does not only think through the moral consequences of globalization, but also offers a fully fledged historical account of it. In what follows, we will first conceptually define globalization, then briefly outline its history and end by discussing what Sloterdijk has to say about morality in the global age.[29]

In a colossal project called *Spheres*, Sloterdijk also starts with Heidegger's musings about the world.[30] Where Heidegger argued, as we have seen, that human being is always a being-in-the-world, Sloterdijk claims that human being is always being-in-a-sphere. What does this mean? Sloterdijk argues that we all live in an outside world that does not only offer opportunities but also threats. People are in need of protection against these threats.[31] They seek this protection by forming or constructing 'spaces' where they can feel at home, can feel safe, can cherish a certain kind of immunity. These communal spaces include houses, villages, cities, families, organizations, tribes, or sects. The word Sloterdijk uses for these kinds of sheltering places is 'sphere'.

He provides us with at least two definitions of this concept: (1) it is an interior, closed, and shared roundness in which people live as far as they succeed in becoming people;[32] and (2) it is from the start also a bipolar and differentiated roundness.[33] In spheres, intimacy and struggle, mutual inspiration and opposition, and solidarity and animosity go hand in hand. This state of affairs engenders an ongoing instability: spheres never last permanently. Like soap bubbles, they will sooner or later burst. Human beings who once lived in the comfort zone of the sphere and enjoyed its immunity are now in an outside world in the hope that there will be people – political leaders, for example – who can create new spheres or with whom they can create new ones. Sloterdijk defines human beings therefore as people who are capable of transcending the spheres in which they are dwelling. Simultaneously, however, they also want to be in spheres, for transcending them always implies risks. For example, it is difficult to think of families that are worthy of the name if they are not offering a protective environment for their members. Another example pertains to schools: the shoot-outs at schools in America and Europe are so morally shocking because people do not expect schools to be such dangerous places. Similarly, business organizations have always been seen as 'spheres' that should offer a protective environment to their staff. The bottom-line mentality that permeates global business has, some critics would argue, undermined the immunity function of organizations. Sweatshops all over the world do not so much protect staff members as threaten their well-being.

Sloterdijk always understands community in terms of roundness. His work teems with bubbles, circles, spheres, and globes. Perhaps, it is important to note here that organizations are generally not represented as round entities: the representation of the organizational structure is typically in the form of a tree, the branches of which connect squares rather than spheres. For Sloterdijk, this alone is sufficient to claim that globalization should not be in the hands of business organizations. Whatever globalization is, it must somehow be related to roundness. The imagery of bursting bubbles is used to alert us to the fact that no sphere in the real world – in contrast to mathematical spheres – is perfect. On the contrary, a crisis of spheres is always lurking, no matter whether it concerns the relationship between mother and child who will eventually lose their intimacy, between two lovers who will finally have to split up, or the Roman Empire, which in the end fell apart as well.

The problem with spheres is that there is always an outside world that threatens their immunity and permanence. But there are also destructive forces at work from the inside: children will take up an interest in other persons besides their mother, and previous lovers are tempted by new partners. People in a community are, to some extent at least, always curious to know what is outside the community. In other words, whatever community there is, be it a microsphere between mother and child or two lovers, *or* a macrosphere such as an entire empire, the outside world always threatens to enter into the inside world. The result is a crisis of spheres. This crisis of spheres, provided that it is restricted to macrospheres, is what Sloterdijk refers to as globalization. More precisely, *globalization is the process during which an outside world permeates an inside world*. It is the crisis of the round shape. And insofar as human beings are creatures who are in these round shapes, who are in spheres, globalization is, in this sense at least, what jeopardizes their very lives.

Perhaps surprisingly, the processes we are describing here are pertinent to organizational spheres as well. Many employees think that in times of globalization the company they are working for cannot guarantee their social security like it used to. They have experienced their companies being taken over by foreign investors or how international competition has made business tougher. Due to all these influences, employees become uneasy or discontented with their employers and they sometimes long for the past when things in business were not so complicated.

But organizations do not only experience that their own spheres are jeopardized, they also threaten non-organizational spheres. The Dutch company AKZO, one of the biggest producers of birth control pills, always used a particular herb from the Mexican rainforest to manufacture these pills. An indigenous community in Mexico became economically dependent on AKZO, to whom they had to deliver these herbs. However, after a while chemists working in AKZO's labs invented an artificial alternative for these herbs. The company clearly had no further need to get these herbs from southern Mexico, an area which all of a sudden was deemed to be politically unstable. We need not go into detail to explain what the consequences were for this particular indigenous community. It was only after public pressure that AKZO started to financially compensate them.

On a global scale, one might argue that more than ever before in history, people are on their way to spheres rather than in spheres. This implies that they are not 'at home anymore' and that widespread unease is the result. Sloterdijk offers us a historical explanation for this state of affairs. He makes a distinction between three kinds of globalization: the oldest kind of globalization is what he refers to as '*uranian*' or '*cosmological*' globalization. This is just the philosophical and mathematical reflection of old Greek thinkers about life *in* and *on* perfect rounds, globes, or spheres. We need not to be concerned with this here. It would take a long time before this intellectual version of globalization would be replaced by a much more practical one. As soon as some people were able to nautically chart the world and to empirically discover that Earth is not a place of mathematical perfection at all, the second age of globalization set in. Sloterdijk refers to this as '*terrestrial globalization*'. Basically, at this time there are at least some people who forget about mathematical perfection and discover the seven seas. These people displayed a range of moral virtues formerly unknown: they were risk-seeking, entrepreneurial, dare-devilish, profit-seeking, and adventurous. Even nowadays, these virtues are strongly valued in business life. This is probably also why so many business ethicists have tried to focus on an alternative set of virtues which might be related to ancient times: prudence, wisdom, and generosity are important examples here. This might be seen as a way to counteract the tendency towards recklessness that, according to Sloterdijk, set in during the age of terrestrial globalization.

European seafarers started to discover that the world is a place that offers opportunities to those who dare to transcend their communities and to go out. Globalization, Sloterdijk claims, became an affair for cartographers and seamen. It is no longer in the hands of intellectuals musing on spherical beauty and perfection, but in the hands of practitioners who experienced how imperfectly edgy the planet was.[34] This imperfection, however, became only a kind of moral problem when the impetus of terrestrial globalization was no longer in the hands of seafarers and cartographers, but in the hands of ecologists and biologists. They pointed out that this kind of globalization might actually jeopardize the world, a topic discussed in the chapter on sustainability.

During the age of cosmological globalization, it was only the contemplative mind that explored the globe. During the age of terrestrial globalization, it became also the body that explored the globe: people started to travel over the seas and endless mobility became a precondition for global capitalism as well. It implies, as we have seen, a 'crisis of form'.[35] Critics contend that this crisis is still going on nowadays. We live in a world which is formless and shapeless and where no sphere can encircle or surround us anymore. Churches, schools, and other institutions do not offer enough security anymore. The same holds for companies. As a consequence of globalization, Sloterdijk believes, nobody can feign to live safely within spheres anymore. There is a constant threat from the outside and unfortunately MNCs can be part of this threat as well.

This crisis has, of course, political, epistemological, and psychological ramifications. Sloterdijk uses the term 'foam' to describe what is going on in our time: it is a metaphor to indicate the third stage of globalization. *Foam* stands for a perversion of perfect substances, for a hollowing-out of the immunity structures that Sloterdijk referred to as spheres.[36] Nowadays, not only minds and bodies explore the world but also messages, signs, and so forth. We live in an era of immense communication, but does this imply that we can live together, that we can build spheres that offer shelter and security? For the 'destructured masses' who hope to find better spheres, the dream still remains unfulfilled. Others prefer a life in isolated or gated communities. They withdraw themselves on an island and prefer self-isolation. This is also one of the panic-stricken reactions to globalization. Like Nancy, Sloterdijk speaks about the 'density' of the world.[37] He defines this as the 'increasing likelihood of encounters between different action centres' which require 'far-reaching moral shifts' in the sense that reckless, univocal, and one-sided initiatives are increasingly deemed to be dangerous. He claims that the reckless virtues of terrestrial globalization are, by and large, obsolete. Density, Sloterdijk explains, requires an unprecedented moral reservation. The heyday of 'unilateral praxis', which was characteristic of the age of terrestrial globalization, is over now.

Compared to the recklessness of seafarers who once sailed the world, we nowadays are coerced to behave with moral inhibitions. Stakeholders everywhere in the world tell us what they think of our actions and we tell them what we think of theirs. The danger lurking here is that global initiatives – let us say on issues such as poverty, environment, or human rights – are increasingly difficult to carry out. The one-sidedness of financial measures proposed by the International Monetary Fund (IMF) are immediately corrected by resistance from local governments or the United Nations Educational, Scientific and Cultural Organization (UNESCO). But the problem is that this leads to a paralysis in decision-making. Politically and ideologically, we are condemned to what Sloterdijk, rather cynically, refers to as 'mass unemployment': many people work hard to improve the world but they achieve hardly anything.[38] This is, of course, a risk to which MNCs are not immune as well. Many promising initiatives are bogged down in the complexity of bureaucracy and institutions.

However, Sloterdijk suggests that at present individual or collective responsibility is not so much a moral category but something that is inherent to the human condition as such. We all live with the other and no matter how much we desire action that might help us to better the world, we have to respond to what they have to say to us. We cannot, like the relativist, allow ourselves to be locked up in our own world. Neither can we simply impose our worldviews upon the others. Of course, there are still people who act as if others are insignificant and do not really matter. Self-isolation is for them a most welcome option. But they opt for a strategy of regression. Sloterdijk also wants us to believe that global crime and global terror are following such regressive strategies. They are fed by an isolated, activist, and non-inhibited energy and are in this sense akin to what entrepreneurialism might have been in the terrestrial age of globalization.

For most inhabitants of our planet, however, life has become so dense that the activist and entrepreneurial dreams that once characterized the age of terrestrial globalization have become impossible. Business ethicists should take note of this: what has been referred to as the new world order might be at odds with values that used to be appreciated in business. 'Everything which pushes itself forward, which wants to get out, which wants to build has to mirror itself, long before the first spade breaks the ground, in protests, participation, counterproposals, postponements; whatever wants to be a measure will soon be overtaken by counter measures'.[39] This implies that the very notion of responsibility has become misleading or even false. It is not, as is often assumed, meant to inspire people to engage into action. It is rather meant to embark on a process of functional routines that provide us with perfect excuses to continue not doing anything at all. In the global age of foam and density, moral notions such as responsibility have lost the sense they once may have had.

Conclusion

In this chapter, we have seen that globalization is not a simple phenomenon that can be reduced to one single essence. This has allowed scholars from a variety of disciplines to shy away from conceptual definitions. It is generally assumed that globalization stands for a variety of economic and financial processes that somehow determine the contemporary world. What we have tried to do in this chapter is to wrest the term 'globalization' away from this focus on economy and finance. The concept has cultural, political, and philosophical significance as well, and this means that the problems caused by globalization are not only to be addressed by business people or economists.

In terms of culture, we discussed the problem of relativism. We saw that this problem is a major issue in the field of business ethics. How are business people to cope with a one-ness of the world that is also indelibly plural and diverse? We do not live in different worlds but we 'form' worlds in different ways and at the same time we threaten or even destroy these worlds. We saw that business ethics is not so much interested in the theatrical conundrum typical of relativism but prefers to offer straightforward practical advice to business people who transcend their cultural background. This advice often comes in the form of guidelines that are supposed to help, for example, MNCs. The assumption is that globalization – and especially the problem of multicultural variety and relativism – raises a whole range of challenges that need practical responses. In spite of the often idealistic character of these responses, substantial philosophical reflection is generally refrained from. Practicality and instrumentalism are offered as an alternative for more sustained reflection.

In terms of politics, we briefly discussed the problem of the destructured masses. This problem is raised by a variety of continental thinkers who argue that globalization should not be in the hands of business people and economists but in the hands of classless people all over the world who are in desperate need of politicization. We have presented these ideas as a counter-proposal about what the real global issues of the future will be. The issue, it is argued, is no longer relativism but rather the political exclusion of the masses, no matter whether they are slaving away their hours in sweatshops or starving on small vessels desperately hoping for better futures.

We ended by discussing the ideas of Nancy and Sloterdijk. We saw that Nancy does not so much theorize globalization, which for him is still a phenomenon related to economy and business, but he offers us some ideas about how we are to think the *world* in (what we refer to as) global circumstances. The concept of the world is understood by Nancy in terms of density and touch: even the most distant communities in the world have become so close to one another that a morality of mutual touching is necessary. This morality can be achieved by a thinking process Nancy refers to as 'mondialization': we need to address the problems not only with beautiful words, but also on a more affective or even physical level. Do we really believe CEOs or politicians when they talk about the betterment of the world if they have never ventured to actually see this world? The conditions of possibility for this mondialization lie in the essential openness of human beings to the world. We referred to this openness as 'worldliness'. It is this openness, Nancy believes, that undermines the argument of both the relativist who claims that people live in different worlds, and the objectivist who claims that the world is just out there and can be endlessly manipulated. A responsibility of touch is what Nancy offers as an alternative.

Finally, Sloterdijk was presented as a thinker who conceptualizes the notion of globalization. For him, the question about the world is also crucial. He argues that people are in spheres. The novelty of Sloterdijk's thought on globalization is that he urges us to take seriously the imagery of roundness: spheres, globes, and so on. He diagnoses the contemporary world in terms of a form crisis: people increasingly have difficulty feeling at home in encompassing spheres. Contrary to what relativism argues, people are constantly capable of transcending the spheres in which they once dwelled. Nowadays, people are not only in spheres but are also constantly on their way to particular, highly unstable, and impermanent spheres. This leads to all sorts of psychological and moral problems. Not only do many people feel tempted to construct isolated spheres for themselves and for kindred spirits, but also notions such as responsibility lose their original meaning. Sloterdijk seems to be especially relevant to business ethics since he allows us to understand that business under globalized circumstances requires new virtues. The reckless virtues that characterized yesterday's business values need to be replaced by values that exemplify more prudency.

NOTES

1 See V. Pucik, 'The international management of human resources', in C. Fombrun, N. Tichy, and M.-A. Devanna (eds.), *Strategic Human Resource Management*. New York: Wiley (1984), 403–21, 403. Both quotes are also in A. Mills and J. Hatfield, 'From imperialism to globalisation: internationalization and the management text', in S. Clegg, E. Ibarra-Colado, and L. Bueno-Rodriguez (eds.), *Global Management. Universal Theories and Local Realities*. London: Sage (1999), 37–67, 52.

2 P. Dicken, *Global Shift. Reshaping the Global Economic Map in the 21st Century*. London: Sage (2003), 10.

3 *Ibid.*, 12.

4 T. Donaldson, *The Ethics of International Business*. New York: Oxford University Press (1989). See also T. Donaldson, 'Multi-national decision-making', *Journal of*

Business Ethics 4 (1985), 357–66; T. Donaldson, 'Values in tensions: ethics away from home', *Harvard Business Review* 74 (5) (1996), 48–59.

5 N. Bowie, 'Relativism, cultural and moral', in P. Werhane and E. Freeman (eds.), *The Blackwell Encyclopaedia of Management. Second Edition*. Oxford: Blackwell (2005), 455–8, 455.

6 *Ibid.*

7 N. Bowie, 'Business ethics and cultural relativism', in P. Madsen and J. Shafritz (eds.), *Essentials of Business Ethics*. New York: Penguin (1990), 366–82, 378.

8 *Ibid.*, 376.

9 Donaldson, *Ethics of International Business*, 74–5.

10 R. De George, 'Ethical dilemmas for multinational enterprise: a philosophical overview', in M. Hoffmann, A. Lange, and D. Fedo (eds.), *Ethics and the Multinational Enterprise*. Washington, DC: University Press of America (1986), 39–46, 43.

11 T. Donaldson and T. Dunfee, *Ties that Bind: a Social Contracts Approach to Business Ethics*. Boston, MA: Harvard Business School Press (1999), 29.

12 M. Painter-Morland, *Business Ethics as Practice. Ethics as the Everyday Business of Business*. Cambridge: Cambridge University Press (2009), 71.

13 *Ibid.*, 72.

14 E. Ibarra-Colado, 'The ethics of globalisation', in S. Clegg and C. Rhodes (eds.), *Management Ethics. Contemporary Contexts*. London: Routledge (2006), 32–54.

15 *Ibid.*, 47.

16 M. Hardt and A. Negri, *Multitude. War and Democracy in the Age of the Empire*. New York: Penguin (2004), 236.

17 S. Zizek, *In Defense of Lost Causes*. London: Verso (2008), 426.

18 *Ibid.*, 427.

19 See, for example, W. Patalon III, *Venezuela says 'Adios' to Most Foreign Investment, making it a Stay-away Play for Investors* (2009), available at www.moneymorning.com/2007/06/29/venezuelasaysadios, accessed 14 May 2009.

20 J.-L. Nancy, *Being Singular Plural*. Stanford, CA: Stanford University Press (2000), 185.

21 What followed is based on J.-L. Nancy, *Le Sens du Monde*. Paris: Galilée (1993) and J.-L. Nancy, *La Création du Monde ou la Mondialisation*. Paris: Galilée (2002). These are just two texts in what has meanwhile become an impressive oeuvre with literally hundreds of titles. It goes without saying that 'the world' is just one theme in this oeuvre.

22 M. Heidegger, *Sein und Zeit*. Tübingen: Max Niemeyer (1979), 65.

23 Nancy, *Le Sens du Monde*, 184. In French: 'un attouchement de toutes choses'.

24 J.-L. Nancy, *Corpus*. New York: Fordham University Press (2008), 41.

25 J.-L. Nancy, *A Finite Thinking*. Stanford, CA: Stanford University Press (2003), 305.

26 *Ibid.*, 1.

27 Nancy, *Corpus*, 33.

28 S. Connor, *The Book of Skin*. London: Reaktion Books (2004), 263.

29 See for more details on this history: M.-E. Morin, 'Cohabitating in the globalized world: Peter Sloterdijk's global foams and Bruno Latour's cosmopolitics', *Environment and Planning D: Society and Space* 27 (1) (2009), 58–72. Also R. ten Bos, 'Towards an amphibious anthropology: water and Peter Sloterdijk', *Environment and Planning D: Society and Space* 27 (1) (2009), 73–86.

30 P. Sloterdijk, *Sphären I. Blasen*. Frankfurt: Suhrkamp (1998); P. Sloterdijk, *Sphären II. Globen*. Frankfurt: Suhrkamp (1999); P. Sloterdijk, *Sphären III. Schaum*. Frankfurt: Suhrkamp (2004).

31 Sloterdijk, *Sphären I. Blasen*, 28.
32 *Ibid.*
33 *Ibid.*, 45.
34 P. Sloterdijk, *Im Weltinnenraum des Kapitals*. Frankfurt: Suhrkamp (2005), 31.
35 Sloterdijk, *Sphären II: Globen*, 72.
36 Sloterdijk, *Sphären III: Schaum*, 28–30.
37 Sloterdijk, *Weltinnenraum des Kapitals*, 277.
38 *Ibid.*, 280.
39 *Ibid.*, 299.

Glossary

Absolutism – Absolutism refers to a belief that there is one set of moral values or principles that unequivocally constitute the right way of thinking and doing in all contexts and at all times. This kind of belief often leads to MORAL IMPERIALISM. The opposite of absolutism is RELATIVISM.

Agency – A term often used in philosophy and the social sciences to refer to the capacity of an agent to act in the WORLD on the basis of their own decisions. Agents can be individuals, but also non-individuals such as corporations, nation states, and so on.

Agency theory – This micro-economic theory concerns the contractual relationships between the principal (shareholder) and the agent of the principal (managers of the company). The relationship is typically characterized by information asymmetry which is the result of the fact that the principal delegates power to the agent. This implies a loss of control that is often referred to as 'agency loss'. Such a loss occurs when the agent takes actions that are not (entirely) consistent with the principal's interest. For example, managers may not always act in the interest of the shareholders. If this is the case in a particular company, then it has so-called 'agency problems'. Debates about agency theory often focus on the underlying assumption of human beings as calculative seekers of profit and advantage. Recently, much effort has been made to link agency theory to STAKEHOLDER THEORY, which argues that in some sense not only shareholders but also other stakeholders of the organization can be seen as principals for whom managers have a certain RESPONSIBILITY.

Analytical philosophy – A style of philosophy which emphasizes the importance of clarity and sound reasoning. As such it has always been inspired by those scientific disciplines that were argued to display the same characteristics, to wit, mathematics and the natural sciences. However, the focus was on language and not on mathematical or physical problems. Rigid linguistic analyses were supposed to replace the more poetic statements that characterized so much of CONTINENTAL PHILOSOPHY. Logical rigour and methodological accuracy were seen as all-important virtues for philosophers. Even though there are many different kinds of analytical philosophy, it is safe to say that it has dominated the English-speaking world. Since business ethics has its roots in this world too, it was profoundly influenced by philosophers and thinkers working in the analytical tradition.

Anthropomorphism – When people are ascribing human characteristics to non-human entities, they are often accused of being 'anthropomorphistic'. In business ethics, anthropomorphism has become an issue in the discussion about CORPORATE MORAL AGENCY. To ascribe moral qualities such as agency, intentionality, or conscience to business organizations is, some commentators argue, anthropomorphistic.

Aporia – Philosophical problems are deemed to be *aporetic* if they do not lend themselves to easy solutions. Literally, *aporia* means 'no' (*a*) 'passage' or 'opening' (*poros*). *Aporias* cause doubt, puzzlement, confusion, and even perplexity. One of the synonyms frequently used for 'aporetic' is 'undecidable'. *Aporias* are then theoretical situations in which one cannot make a decision. These situations are, philosophers argue, characterized by UNDECIDABILITY. The concept of *aporia* has been pivotal in the work of continental philosophers. It is often used by them to undermine the idea that words, concepts, sentences, or language as such have determinate meaning.

Assemblage – The English translation of the French word '*agencement*', which is used by Deleuze and Guattari to denote what they see as the intermingling of bodies in nature and society, including all the attractions and repulsions, sympathies and antipathies, amalgamations, penetrations, and expansions that might affect these bodies. This process of intermingling is seen as an emerging pattern that eventually produces AGENCY or IDENTITY. Important here is that one understands that according to Deleuze and Guattari it is not agencies or identities that cause action or productivity, but the assemblage as such. In other words, by using the word '*agencement*', they urge us to rethink the understanding that 'organizations', 'corporations', or 'individuals' act as AGENTS and thus determine the shape of our world. Yet, the concept of '*agencement*' emphasizes the importance of activity, action, or force. There is agency in the world, definitely, but there are no agents. So, 'organization' or 'individual' is the result of this agency, that is to say, the result of a multiplicity of underlying processes. There is no need to say that this idea takes issue with classical notions such as CORPORATE MORAL AGENCY. Finally, it should be remarked here that Deleuze and Guattari use a whole range of different concepts that are more or less synonymous with 'assemblage': 'plane of consistency', 'plane of immanence', 'rhizome', or 'body without organs'.

Bad conscience – Conscience is a person's awareness that their conduct has moral and ethical aspects. Generally, this is guided by a feeling and understanding that the good is preferable over the bad. Sometimes, however, this particular person understands that their actions do not meet the requirements for goodness. This may subsequently result in a bad conscience which can then be understood as a feeling of guilt. In philosophy, Nietzsche has developed the idea of 'bad conscience' into a fully fledged ethical concept that he uses to describe what he sees as collective feelings of guilt imposed upon us by a Christian morality that wants us to think of our natural inclinations as something bad and reprehensible.

Bad faith – This is a concept that became prominent in the philosophy of Jean-Paul Sartre. It is usually understood to be what causes people to deny their own freedom and to live inauthentically. More specifically, people who act in bad faith lie to themselves regarding the open and undetermined nature of their lives and activities. For example, a person may hate the job they are doing but refuses to look for something else because they fear the consequences (e.g. loss of income, loss of status). It is due to bad faith that people might in the end turn out to be resentful (see also: *RESSENTIMENT*).

Bicameralist view – The adjective '*bicameral*' literally means 'consisting of two chambers'. In this sense we can speak of a bicameral political system, but also of a bicameral organ (the heart). In a somewhat different context, scholars sometimes speak of a 'bicameralist view' in order to take issue with the widespread tendency to reduce complex issues to simple oppositions (good–bad, masculine–feminine, and so on) that are supposed to make easy decisions possible. An example of a bicameralist view would be former president Bush's (in)famous remark that 'You are either *for* or *against* us'.

Charisma – In common parlance, we attribute 'charisma' to people who are inspiring, attractive, and have a magnetic appeal. An artist, a sportsman, or a TV-star can have charisma. Literally, the word means 'the gift of God' or 'to stand in God's favour'. The term is nowadays often used to describe certain leaders to whom we may attribute the aforementioned qualities. In leadership studies and business ethics, scholars have linked the concept of charisma to THE GREAT MAN THEORY OF LEADERSHIP in order to express the sexist and pompous quality of the concept.

Codes of conduct – Documents adopted by various types of organizations to provide behavioural guidelines to those who belong to the organization. They are often lengthy and contain specific rules and directives.

Codes of ethics – Also referred to as 'values statements' or 'charters', these documents are more often than not shorter than codes of conduct, and they contain aspirational statements regarding the normative commitments of an organization.

Communitarianism – Communitarians argue against certain key tenets of liberal theory about the pivotal role of the individual in modern politics and society. Rather than highlighting the importance of the individual, they argue that: (1) such an individual can only be properly understood if we consider them as a member of a community rather than as an isolated self; and (2) tradition and social context are much more important for an understanding of people, politics, or even societies as such than notions such as free will or autonomy, which are prominent in liberal theory. Such claims are often guided by strongly normative understandings about the value of communal life. Philosophers such as Alasdair MacIntyre, Charles Taylor, or Michael Walzer have often been described as 'communitarian'.

Complex adaptive systems – This term refers to a dynamic network consisting of many agents or elements that constantly act and react to what other agents and elements do. Order within such systems emerges spontaneously and can therefore not be directed or controlled. It is complex because the system consists of a large number of interacting elements, which interact in a non-linear fashion. Feedback loops play an important role as well and allow for learning and adaptive behaviour. In business ethics, there has been some attention for complex adaptive systems in the sense that the multidirectional dynamics that operate within corporations allow certain behavioural patters to emerge. Within such complex systems, values function as 'strange attractors' and the resulting sense of 'how we do things around here' has been described by some authors as the emergence of organizational culture.

Continental philosophy – This notion refers to the kind of philosophy that emerged in continental Europe during the second half of the twentieth century. The name was coined by supporters of ANALYTICAL PHILOS- OPHY who felt a need to distance themselves from certain streams of philosophy that were popular in Europe. These streams were accused of being metaphysical, undisciplined, or even irrational. It is, however, important to bear in mind that in Europe, the distinction between analytical and continental philosophy is considered to be spurious. It is also important to note that there have been efforts, most notably by the American philosopher Richard Rorty, to blur the distinction between these two 'schools' of philosophy.

Contingency – In EXISTENTIALISM, this word refers to the absolute absence of necessity in life. In other words, each individual life is absolutely open and can therefore turn into many directions. Those who deny this behave inauthentically and act in BAD FAITH.

Contractarianism – In ethics, this is the claim that moral standards and principles in a given society derive their normative force from the idea of a mutual agreement among its citizens. This mutual agreement is often metaphorically depicted as a contract.

Corporate citizenship – This term refers to the idea that corporations have the same moral responsibilities as human citizens (e.g. paying taxes, abiding the law, philanthropic work). The idea, however, has severe limitations. Critics have pointed out that, unlike citizens, corporations cannot feel pain, cannot vote, etc. The problem of ANTHROPOMORPHIZATION may play a role here.

Corporate culture – In layman's terms, corporate culture is defined as 'the way we do things around here'. It refers to the shared beliefs, values, practices, rituals as well as artefacts that emerge as salient within a corporation. However, it is important to note that not all cultures are fully integrated around these shared values. Organizations often have SUB-CULTUREs which can be linked, for example, to the characteristics of certain professions. A department of philosophy at a university differs from a department of physics or business studies. These kinds of differences can also be linked to regions. A subsidiary company in South Africa will no doubt differ from one in the US or The Netherlands. Interestingly, it has been argued by critical scholars that business corporations as such should be seen as sub-cultures. Here the notion of 'sub-culture' is used dismissively. See also: SPHERE.

Corporate governance – Broadly speaking, this term refers to the processes by which corporations are directed and controlled. It provides normative guidelines for the functioning of corporations' governance structures, such as their board of directors, board committees, individual executives within the corporation, and their internal checks and balances. The need for governance resides in the idea of CORPORATE AGENCY. The governance systems of the corporation must assure that the corporation's principals are properly served by its agents. As such the term is very closely linked to STAKEHOLDER THEORY in the sense that it is widely acknowledged that corporate governance processes affect many more stakeholders than just the shareholders. In Europe, the term 'corporate governance' is also closely related to what is often referred to as the *Anglo-Saxon model* and the *Rhineland model*. The first model privileges the shareholder perspective and is believed to be prevalent in Anglo-Saxon countries. The second model aims at harmonization of different stakeholder interests and is believed to be prevalent in countries such as Germany, France, and The Netherlands. Ed Freeman, the famous promulgator of stakeholder theory, has himself acknowledged the affinity between his ideas and the *Rhineland* model.

Corporate moral agency – Two central questions have haunted business ethics since its early days: (1) does it make sense to hold corporations morally responsible for their actions? (2) Do corporations have moral duties which are not reducible to the duties of individuals? Both questions relate to the problem of corporate moral agency. It is important to understand that it does not go without saying that corporations can be held morally responsible for their actions. As such, the problem of corporate moral agency relates to a fundamental assumption of business ethics, to wit, that corporations and not just individuals can be held responsible. This long-standing discussion opens up to a plethora of different but related philosophical questions: do corporations have intentions? Can they make decisions in the way that individuals do? Do they have a conscience? Corporations can cause harm, and therefore need to be held accountable for harm. The fact that complex corporate decision structures, and not single individuals, cause harm or do good, seems to suggest that they do have some form of agency. Peter French was the most influential theorist in putting forward a defence of corporate agency based on his analysis of corporate decision structures.

Corporate social responsibility (CSR) – Broadly speaking, this refers to the way in which companies *voluntarily* integrate social and environmental concerns rather than just financial motives into their business decisions on the basis of their interaction with their stakeholders. Underlying the idea of CSR is an understanding that corporations have a much broader role to play in our society than just an economic one. Some commentators have suggested that corporations will become unduly politicized when they embark on CSR. Others claim that CSR can only become acceptable if economic concerns remain prevalent. No matter what position one takes in the debate, all participants seem to agree that CSR is potentially *critical* of at least certain corporate practices. How far this criticism should be carried through is a moot question.

Cultural relativism – Broadly speaking, this is the position that habits and practices differ across cultures. As such the position is entirely descriptive and only a few people would be willing to contest this. However, cultural relativism develops a normative dimension in the sense that it urges us not to morally judge habits and practices in different cultures than our own. When it leads to a statement that 'when in Rome, one should do as the Romans do', this is referred to as ethical relativism. This position is generally considered to be a massive problem for business ethics. If business as a practice takes place on a global scale and hence impacts on a variety of cultures, should it then still respect cultural diversity when it comes to certain practices, such as gift-giving? Much of business ethics tries to deal with this question by phrasing norms and principles that are universal (see also: HYPERNORMS).

Dasein – A philosophical concept used by the German philosopher Martin Heidegger to denote human being. More precisely, it is not just human being, but actually the possibilities of a human being. Heidegger always conceived of human beings in terms of openness. Such openness implies that life cannot be entirely controlled. There is always the possibility that something unexpected might happen to us. This essential openness is crucial not only in Heidegger's philosophy, but also in much other continental philosophy. Literally, *dasein* means 'to be in the open' or 'being there'.

Deconstruction – This concept, which is most often related to the work of Jacques Derrida, is a contamination of two key terms used by Martin Heidegger: 'construction' and 'destruction' (see: DESTRUCTIVE QUESTIONING). This should make clear that deconstruction, whatever it is, is not about destroying – which is a common misunderstanding. However, having said this, the fact remains that the concept is very difficult to define. Derrida himself has repeatedly argued that he did not know the precise meaning of this word, but to deny that meanings can be fixed and defined is perhaps what deconstruction might be all about. What is clear about the concept is that it came to play an all-important role in the kind of philosophy – often referred to as 'CONTINENTAL PHILOSOPHY' – that does not aim at a representation of reality or at the unearthing of unshakeable truths but rather at problematizing concepts such as 'reality' or 'truth'. The point here is not to simply *destroy* the idea that such concepts are useful and important to philosophy or to science. Nor is it the idea to *construct* deeper and newer meanings about them that might inspire philosophy or science to venture into new directions. The point is rather to show how ambivalent, complex, and *aporetical* these concepts are (see: APORIA). Take for example, the concept of 'reality'. Critics of 'deconstruction' often claim that it denies reality and therefore amounts to an extreme form of skepticism or relativism. Derrida's intentions, however, are not to deny reality but to show that our access to reality is fundamentally mediated by language and that (our understanding of) reality may therefore be just as transient as language is. For Derrida, the implications of this idea are profoundly ethical and political: that language and reality are constantly prone to change also means that they cannot be easily controlled or manipulated. It is therefore hardly a surprise that many politically engaged philosophers (left-wing philosophers, feminists, anti-globalization activists, and others) have resorted to deconstruction as a gateway to change.

Deontology – This term stems from the Greek words for 'duty' (*deon*) and logic or reason (*logos*). In moral theory, deontology is the position that the moral quality of an action does not depend on the outcomes it produces, but rather on whether the action has been carried out with a certain sense of duty. It is often assumed that this sense of duty is linked to the idea that some sort of rule or norm should be obeyed in order to judge that a particular action is morally praiseworthy. The gist of this theory can be described as follows: an action is to be considered as bad, no matter what the outcomes are, if it has not been carried out in compliance with moral law autonomously formulated by a rational person.

Desiring-production – A concept coined by the French philosophers Gilles Deleuze and Félix Guattari. Desire, they argue, is a productive and positive force which not only permeates the natural world but also the social world. As such it plays a crucial role in the creation and functioning of social practices and institutions. An example here would be the bureaucrat who loves the work they are doing out of a desire for accuracy, or the investor whose willingness to run certain financial risks is permeated with a desire too (albeit a different kind of desire). Desire is produced in the *fabric* of life, not by means of intention or individual will. Nevertheless, the conceptual apparatus that Deleuze and Guattari develop in their book *Anti-Oedipus* (1972) – desire, desiring-machines, desiring-production – still retains certain subjectivist or transcendental undertones. This is why it would be abandoned in *A Thousand Plateaus*, a book published eight years later. There, the notion of ASSEMBLAGE became all-important.

Destructive questioning – This is a key part of Martin Heidegger's philosophical methodology. To ask questions destructively is not the same as asking them in an aggressive or radical way. The precise technical meaning of destructive questioning is that one interrogates certain research or cultural traditions, especially those to which one belongs. We cannot take for granted, Heidegger argues, that the key concepts and ideas used in these traditions are permanently useful. The world changes, and so should the concepts we use to describe the world. Traditions can be harmful in the sense that they block off change. In philosophy, Heidegger emphasizes over and over again, there should always be openness towards what lies beyond our own tradition. It is in this spirit of openness that the idea of destructive questioning arises.

Différance – In the work of many continental thinkers (Derrida, Deleuze, Levinas, Serres, or Nancy), it is argued that we should not think in terms of absolute oppositions (man–beast, nature–culture, language–reality, etc.) but rather in terms of a *difference* that has many more shades than bipolar oppositions are capable of suggesting. Rather than focussing on the poles of these oppositions, these philosophers claim to be interested in what has been referred to as the '*supplementary interval*' between them. Derrida himself was primarily interested in the relationship between language and reality (and not in language and reality as such). He coined the word '*différance*' to describe the constant dynamics between these poles, something which eventually affects the poles as well. *Différance* relates to the French word for 'difference' ('*différence*') as a verb to a noun, and hence also has the meaning of deferring, i.e. postponing. Derrida describes meaning(s) as always different, and always deferred. Meanings are constantly flexible and slippery. See also: DECONSTRUCTION.

Dilemma – A moral dilemma occurs when one is confronted with two equally binding moral duties. It is a case of being 'damned if you do, and damned if you don't', or being 'between the devil and the deep-blue sea'. No matter what you chose, some moral objection could be raised against your decision. One example of how business life presents us with two or more equally justifiable moral injunctions is that of the whistleblower who seems to be caught up somewhere between loyalty towards their employer and concern about the public weal. The notion of dilemma is related to the APORIA, but in the case of an aporia, it is not necessarily the case of choosing between two equally morally valid options, but being uncertain, at an impasse. Dilemmas can be described as the way in which ethicists categorize opposing duties in order to get to a resolution. The *aporetic* does not lend itself to such resolution.

Distributive justice – The dimension of justice concerned with whether the various resources and rewards available through work are distributed fairly among employees. Most commonly this relates to the fair distribution of pay and other benefits on a principle of merit.

Egology – The French philosopher Emmanuel Levinas uses this concept to indicate a life form where the 'ego' just uses up the 'other' (with a small 'o'; in French: '*l'autre*'). The 'other' is reduced to the 'same', and this is then regarded as the source of his happiness and fulfilment. Levinas confronts this egology with an ethics that radically poses the centrality of the 'Other' (with a capital 'O'; in French: '*l'autrui*') which is never to be reduced to the same. As such, *ethics* always calls egology into question. See also: FACE.

Employment at will – This is, most notably in the US, a juridical notion which indicates that the relationship between employers and employees can be terminated by both parties whenever one of them deems that to be appropriate. The underlying idea is that both parties voluntarily engage in a working relationship. On this basis they are both allowed to step out of the relationship at any time. Critics of this idea have argued that this notion undermines the juridical protection of employees. They can be sacked at any time for any reason or for no reason at all.

Epistemology – The Greek roots of this term again help us to understand what it means. '*Episteme*' means 'knowledge' and again '*logos*' refers to word, reason, or logic. So epistemology refers to what we can say about how we come to know anything, and how we can say anything about what we know. The epistemic most often refers to what is accepted as scientific knowledge, and as such, epistemology allows us to reflect on the grounds of our knowledge, and what separates knowledge from what we would deem non-scientific.

Ethical climate – If we say that an organization has a certain ethical climate we refer to a set of shared perceptions of practices that are taking place there. These perceptions relate to the way decisions are made, the way power is being exercised, and the way people treat each other on a day-to-day basis. There is a lot of literature that uses this term to indicate a certain shared feeling about what is morally acceptable and not. In this sense, the term 'ethical climate' is very closely linked with CORPORATE CULTURE. But where corporate culture is seen as something that emerges over time and is more resilient, climate can be described as a more short-term perspective on a specific set of factors that is either conducive to ethical behaviour, or not.

Ethical culture – In business ethics, this term often refers to a kind of ideal moral environment that is created by shared beliefs about right and wrong in organizations. Such a situation implies that people are always conscious about the moral implications of their actions and take that into consideration when they make choices. The idea that moral excellence can be achieved in this way has been popular among at least some business ethicists. It is premised on an understanding that living according to principles and in line with one's virtues is superior to a life without principles and virtues. Typically, ethical culture is always seen as something that can be brought about if one only takes the right steps. In order words, the assumption is that an ethical culture can be designed and organized.

Ethical imperialism – This term refers to the efforts of a particular dominant culture to impose its own norms and principles upon another culture with different norms and principles. Doing this assumes the superiority of one's own norms and principles. The term is frequently used by scholars who are critical of the Western cultural hegemony. If Western governments actively seek to put an end to what they understand to be morally reprehensible, then they may be accused of ethical imperialism. The term is often juxtaposed to CULTURAL RELATIVISM.

Ethical subjectivism – This term refers to the belief that all ethical judgements, indeed all ethical thinking, are shaped by subjective perceptions. In other words, whatever you have to say on ethics, it is more an expression of your own feelings and preferences than an objective statement. Ethical subjectivism also holds that an individual need not justify or explain their moral position to anyone, since it is their subjective choice.

Ethos – This is a very difficult term to define, as its meaning seems to be constantly changing. Originally, the Greek word '*ethos*' meant 'home' or 'dwelling place'. Later, its meaning would shift to 'role', 'character', or 'habit'. Important in the discussion is that *ethos* often referred to what was bigger than an individual, for example, tradition, culture, or context. These elements were supposed to determine the kind of rules and principles the individual was expected to follow. In organizational theory, we encounter the term in expressions such as 'the ethos of the office' which indicates a certain set of moral standpoints and attitudes within organizations. Generally, one might say that the term reminds us of the fact that ethics never comes into being all out of itself, but that it is always culturally and socially embedded.

Existentialism – This is an umbrella term for a wide range of philosophical approaches interested in what individuality might mean for human being. This means that existentialists are not, unlike biologists or many social scientists, interested in the human being as an example of a particular species, but in the unicity of each single individual. The Danish philosopher Sören Kierkegaard (1813–55) is credited as the founding father of existentialism. He critiqued philosophers like Hegel for talking only in abstract terms about human being and forgetting about the concrete existence of individuals, real men and women. In the twentieth century, especially in the decades after the second world war, existentialism became immensely popular in CONTINENTAL PHILOSOPHY. This is not to suggest, however, that all existentialists are in agreement with each other. Among its most important representatives are Martin Heidegger, Karl Jaspers, Albert Camus, Jean-Paul Sartre, and Maurice Merleau-Ponty.

But someone like Heidegger was very critical of Sartre's version of existentialism.

Existential phenomenology – This kind of philosophy – which combines, needless to say, insights from existentialism and PHENOMENOLOGY – argues that human beings are situated in the world. At the same time, however, it never proposes that human beings are completely determined by their 'context'. Human beings are free and can give direction to their own lives. To accept this freedom is nothing less than the most important ethical burden.

Face – The concept of the 'face' has a pivotal role in the ethical system of the French philosopher Emmanuel Levinas. 'Face' stands for the human face, but here it is not thought of as a concrete physical or aesthetic object, but rather as the most concrete evidence of a living presence – the 'Other' – in one's vicinity. The 'Other' is exposed to me as an undeniable reality. The Other can speak, gesture, or has a complete physical presence, but the face, Levinas believes, is the most vulnerable and expressive aspect of the Other. The British-Polish sociologist Zygmunt Bauman has employed the concept of the 'face' to explain how organizations use all sorts of 'de-facing' strategies, that is, strategies that aim to deny the vulnerability of the other. Examples of such strategies can be found everywhere: bureaucracies reduce stakeholders to numbers or units to be processed. The point here is to deny any moral proximity. It is only distance that makes an individual immune to the call of the Other.

Fairness – Generally speaking, fairness refers to the quality of being honest and impartial, and treating people without prejudice or favouritism. Fairness and justice are often used synonymously although justice often infers the following of laws and rules, while fairness is a more personal virtue focussed on decision and actions that are equitable and unbiased.

Fallacy – This notion refers to a flawed piece of reasoning. ANALYTICAL PHILOSOPHY, with its insistence on logical and sound argumentation, understands fallacies as dangerous, and much of its efforts are dedicated to their elimination. However, the struggle against fallacious argumentation is very difficult. Philosophers distinguish many different kinds of fallacies. One of the most notorious examples is the naturalistic fallacy which presupposes that because something is the case in nature, it is good that it is the case. For example, because living creatures eat each other in nature, it is also permissible to eat meat. Many more examples of fallacies could be given here.

Fiduciary duties – There are duties which arise out of a special trust relationship that people have with each other. If someone trusts you, you will have a special kind of duty. In business ethics, the notion of a fiduciary relationship – which stems from juridical discourse – especially applies to the relationship between managers and shareholders. This means that shareholders are special stakeholders because they trust managers to perform a certain task (e.g. profit maximization).

Global Compact – A call by the United Nations (UN) to companies to *voluntarily* align their operations with ten universal principles in the areas of human rights, labour standards, the environment, and anti-corruption. By participating in the Global Compact, businesses are expected to contribute to the fulfilments of two major objectives: (1) to mainstream the aforementioned principles in business activities around the world; and (2) to catalyze actions in support of broader UN goals (including the Millennium Development Goals [MDGs]).

Globalization – A process that is very difficult to define, but which is characterized by an increasing interconnectedness of communities all over the world. It is generally conceded that globalization does not only have economic ramifications. It has a cultural, political, and social dimension as well. Philosophers such as Peter Sloterdijk argue that globalization jeopardizes the immunity of communities all over the world (see also: SPHERES). Others are much less pessimistic about it and argue that globalization is to the benefit of all these communities.

Golden parachutes – This part of an executive remuneration agreement refers to a severance package that includes substantial compensation for the possibility of lost earnings in the event of a change in company ownership or changes in, or the severance of, the employment contract.

Good faith – Good faith is a concept that is most frequently used in business ethics in the context of 'good faith disclosures' made by whistleblowers. A good faith disclosure is one that is made without ulterior motives, which could include personal financial gain, hiding the whistleblower's own complicity in wrongdoing, or character assassinations.

Governmentality – There are several ways in which this term, which was coined by Michel Foucault, might be understood. One of them is the way that governments try to render citizens 'governable'. This is important, because effective government requires citizens who accept to be governed. Later, Foucault seemed to have understood the term in a somewhat different kind of way. It does not only refer to how the self is governed, but also how it governs itself. More particularly, governmentality is about the self's relation to itself amid the power relations that we encounter in our multiple interactions with others. Here, Foucault talks about 'strategic games between liberties', i.e. the processes and strategies that we employ to navigate the various power dynamics of which we are part in order to maintain our sense of freedom within all the connections we have with others.

Great man theory of leadership – Even though this term can be traced back to the 1950s, it became really popular after organizational scholar Andrew Huczynski started to use it in 1993 to denote a particular kind of discourse which emphasizes certain qualities of the leader that turn *him* into a hero. Among these qualities are masculinity, a proneness to adventure, power, and the ability to protect followers. The *great man* theory of leadership, also referred to as *heroic* leadership, is now often denounced as sexist, unrealistic, and politically dangerous. It has never attracted business ethicists, but it has played a key role in leadership discourses.

Herd mentality – A term used by Friedrich Nietzsche to describe the way in which human beings uncritically adopt convenient truths devised by those in power of the group that they belong to, in order to preserve the peace. This makes it impossible for human beings to think for themselves and to critically reevaluate the values that are prescribed within the 'herd'. This ultimately leads to a meaningless existence devoid of creativity. According to Nietzsche, the best example of this 'herd mentality' is found in people's adherence to the Christian faith.

Heuristics of Fear – The German philosopher Hans Jonas uses this concept to describe his idea that if we cannot anticipate the consequences of what we are doing, we ought to steer clear from it. For him, this is a pivotal aspect of RESPONSIBILITY, for example with respect to posterity. Of old, 'heuristics' has been the term philosophers have used to describe a variety of practical and simple methods of problem-solving.

Hitler problem – A problem raised by Joanna Ciulla about the question of whether Adolf Hitler was a *real* leader or not. Important in the discussion is the more general question of whether leaders who turned out to be moral failures can be understood as veritable examples of leadership. If one answers this question negatively, one is likely to admit that leadership must of necessity be something *good*. If one answers the question affirmatively, then one would allow for the possibility of *bad* leadership.

Hyperglobalization – People who believe in this argue that globalization is a hard fact that cannot be denied. This position does not involve a judgement about whether globalization is 'good' or 'bad'.

Hypernorm – The famous business ethicists Tom Donaldson and Tom Dunfee introduced this concept. They define it as a principle which is so fundamental to a given society that it shapes and informs all 'second-order norms' that guide human behaviour. The underlying idea here is that different societies can be in agreement about certain hypernorms. In this way, the problem of CULTURAL RELATIVISM might be circumvented. An example of a hypernorm would be the obligation to respect a society's institutions.

Hyperpolitics – Peter Sloterdijk has pointed out that nowadays, under conditions of GLOBALIZATION, traditional politics does not work anymore. This kind of politics always used to be concerned with local or national communities. The problems in our WORLD, however, transcend the confines of these communities. What is called for is a 'hyperpolitics' that does not restrict itself to representing merely local or national interests. Such a politics is therefore in many senses the antithesis of politics: it should unite what is not united (different communities, different countries, and so on). Sloterdijk is skeptical not only about the possibility of such a politics but also about what it might actually be able to achieve. He argues that a hyperpolitics of the future should be permeated by what he refers to as an ETHOS of urgency, i.e. worldwide problems should become top priorities rather than side issues.

Identity – Identity refers to those aspects of a certain person or entity that allows us to identify them as distinct from other persons or entities. It has, however, become a very laden term in post-Enlightenment philosophy, since it tends to refer to a certain kind of human being with a fixed set of characteristics. The way in which certain identities, such as male and female, black and white, first world versus third world were defined, came to display the prejudices of male patriarchy and first world biases. It trapped individuals within categories that were not of their own making and often made it impossible to be all that they could and wanted to be. Hence certain philosophers, like Deleuze and Guattari, suggest that we give up our preoccupation with identity and embrace the multiplicities that are always part of each one of us.

Impression management – In the work of the famous Canadian sociologist, Erving Goffman, this term refers to the way in which people simultaneously form impressions of other people and manage impressions of themselves. The central idea here is that people always try to meet expectations of others and to do that, they may adopt a wide variety of different roles. The concept has become important in business ethics since corporations have become aware of how important it is to meet societal expectations. However, when applied to business ethics, 'impression management' often seems to imply a critical undertone in the sense that *the image* of being ethical becomes more important than being ethical.

Instrumentality – As the word suggests, instrumentality has to do with the fact that people, animals, and other entities can be used as means to an end, i.e. as instruments that serve the purposes of others. Many continental philosophers are critical of instrumental thinking, since it tends to measure someone or something's value only in terms of the usefulness that it may have for others. Instrumentality was famously opposed by Immanuel Kant's categorical imperative, which stipulated that human beings should be treated as ends in themselves.

Integrity – Having 'integrity' is commonly described as being consistent in one's application of one's beliefs, moral values, or principles. It is often related to honesty, i.e. it requires of a person to refrain from falsehood and to speak the truth. However, integrity can also be described using moral discretion in a way that displays a congruent character over time. This means displaying the kind of character in which one's values are evident, even if one treats specific cases in a different manner. It can also be related to displaying practical wisdom in the Aristotelian sense, which means doing the right, moral thing at the right moment.

Interactional justice – The dimension of justice concerned with whether people are treated fairly in terms of their interactions with other people in organizations and the nature of the communication involved in those interactions. The main focus here is on whether people in positions of authority, such as managers, communicate consistently with different people, share information equally with all, and treat people with respect.

Internationalization – This refers to the extension of economic activities across national borders. As such the concept is not to be confused with GLOBALIZATION which is much less narrowly defined since it also includes cultural, technological, or social activities.

Invisible hand – This term refers to Adam Smith's often misunderstood idea that the capitalist system has an in-built mechanism to distribute the gains of the hard work of all who participate in the system to all others in society. It is argued that this self-regulative mechanism only operates if the forces of self-interest, supply and demand, and competition are allowed to function freely. This idea has been appropriated by those within the capitalist system who defend a policy of non-interference and minimal government intervention in the economy. Smith's intention, however, was not to condone capitalist exploitation as long as it yields benefits only to some people. This has to be understood within the broader context of Smith's moral philosophy, in which the limits of the free market and the need for government parameters are well understood.

Iterability – This is a very central aspect of Jacques Derrida's philosophy. He makes us aware of the fact that an expression or a sentence only derives meaning from the fact that it can be repeated, i.e. reiterated. The idea behind this is that the same expression or sentence can be used in exactly the same way at different times or in different contexts. This implies that meaning is 'disseminated' in many unpredictable ways. Derrida alerts us to the essential uncontrollability of meaning, indeed of language.

Justice – The idea of justice relates primarily to how one relates to and interacts with other people and how those relations are practised among members of a community. To be just means treating people fairly and equitably and not seeking to take advantage of them for the purpose of self-interest. Justice also concerns the way that an attestation to this fairness and equity is enshrined in laws and rules designed to ensure that all members of a community are treated equally.

Laicism – This concept has a long history in French political thought and refers to the idea that the state should be exempt from all non-secular expression (such as religious symbols or apparel). It is often translated as SECULARISM. However, continental philosopher Michel Serres is not so much interested in this as the layman and the way that he is still alienated from developments in science and technology. The concept of 'laity' is invoked in order to think of a science that is not exclusive, i.e. not only for the initiated. He objects to the idea that science should take place in a sacred and enclosed space – *temple, church, academia* – from which the uninitiated are excluded. The idea of laicism is especially important, Serres argues, when we discuss matters that are relevant for the general public. For example, the cause for SUSTAINABILITY is not helped by scientists who only write for scientists and are incapable of addressing the general public. It should not be a surprise that, in his country, Serres has been and still is a well-known defender of Internet encyclopaedias such as Wikipedia.

Leadership – See: CHARISMA, GREAT MAN THEORY OF LEADERSHIP, TRANSFORMATIONAL LEADERSHIP, and VALUE-BASED LEADERSHIP.

Matters of fact/matters of concern – This distinction is made by Bruno Latour. Like so many other continental philosophers, he is worried about the role that politics and sciences play in our society. Generally, it is believed that politics pertains to the domain of value and sciences to the domain of facts. However, Latour casts doubt on these kinds of firmly entrenched distinctions. Why do we, he wonders, believe that values are subjective and facts are objective? He proposes that we should rather make a distinction between opinions that are uncontested and opinions that are contested. Nobody would, for example, take issue with the idea that the earth circles around the sun. This is a matter of fact. Latour argues that matters of fact are not problematical in our society, but he also argues that they only form a part of reality and we would be ill-advised if we would try to narrow the whole of reality down to matters of fact. So, he opposes matters of fact to matters of concern. These are facts that are contested, form a problem, put reputations at stake, and so forth. Examples of matters of fact are global warming, health risks of bio-industry, the depletion of fossil energy, or CO_2 emissions caused by man. Even though Latour is never willing to clearly define matters of concern, he argues that both politicians and scientists have a RESPONSIBILITY for them.

Metaphysics – The word 'metaphysics' derives from the word 'meta', which means 'beyond' or 'after', and physics, which we still know as the science of the physical realm. As such, metaphysics is an attempt to engage with those questions that transcend or go beyond science, and as such, it also deals with the conditions, assumptions and limitations of science itself. ONTOLOGY is a branch of metaphysics.

Mondialization – Mondialization can be described as 'world-forming'. Though the French term is translated as GLOBALIZATION, Nancy insists that the two terms should not be conflated.

Narcissism – Originating from the myth of Narcissus, this term designates the psychological state of someone who loves only themselves. It is also characteristic of the narcissist to be able to acknowledge only their own needs, perspectives and interests, and interpret the entire reality within these terms.

Normativity – Since David Hume, philosophers make a clear distinction between what *is* the case and what *ought* to be the case. To express what is the case, we use sentences such as 'people get rich at the expense of other people' or 'today, it is 44°F in Chicago'. These are referred to as *positive* sentences. They are to be distinguished from sentences which express a certain desire about what ought to be the case: 'It is very bad that people get rich at the expense of others'. These sentences are often referred to as normative sentences. Critics of business ethics often argue that it merely focuses on normativity, for example when it tries to help corporations to formulate CODES OF CONDUCT.

Ontology – A branch of philosophy which studies the most general question that we know: what does it mean to be? It originates from the Greek words for existence (*onto*), and word (*logos*). See also: EGOLOGY.

Organizational justice – Conventionally understood as the extent to which people at work perceive that they are treated fairly by their organizations, managers, and colleagues. The main dimensions of organizational justice that have been researched relate to whether people feel they are fairly rewarded (distributive justice), feel that procedures are applied equally (procedural justice), and feel that they are treated respectfully (interactional justice).

Panopticon – Originally, this was a type of prison constructed by social reformer and philosopher Jeremy Bentham in 1785. His idea was to construct a building that would make it possible that all (*pan*) inmates were observed (*opticon*). Vital to the construction, however, was a second idea: the incarcerated themselves should not be able to tell whether they were, at any given moment of the day, being watched or not. The French philosopher Michel Foucault has used Bentham's ideas to describe what he thinks is going on in contemporary Western society. He argues that a 'carceral continuum' permeates our society. What he means by this is that citizens in Western society are, very much like the inmates in a prison, increasingly rendered visible by a whole range of technologies and techniques. The problem is that these citizens hardly ever know whether and by whom they are being watched and monitored. The fact that we act as if we are being watched is what Foucault refers to as 'discipline'.

Parrheisia – In Ancient Greece, this term denoted a certain practice of candid or fearless speech. To engage in it implies a duty to speak the truth, even when this entails certain personal risks. The French philosopher Michel Foucault has alerted us to the pertinence of the concept for contemporary contexts as well. He points out that truthfulness is a crucial quality of those who engage in fearless speech, but he makes clear that this is not to say that there can be no doubt or criticism. On the contrary, it is only doubt and criticism that allow for fearless speech.

Phenomenology – Philosophical movement founded by the German philosopher Edmund Husserl (1859–1938). Supporters of this movement want to describe human experiences or phenomena in such a way that they 'speak' for themselves. They fiercely oppose the idea that human beings are observers of the world who stand outside this world. A human being is not an isolated entity detached from the world, and neither is the world something which is 'out' there. There is no world without a subject and no subject without a world. As such, phenomenology clearly takes issue with the 'objective' or 'scientific' worldview. As human beings we do not experience the world in the same way as scientists do. Phenomenology is interested in how the world appears to you and me. It purports to reflect systematically on these appearances. See also: EXISTENTIALISM, EXISTENTIAL PHENOMENOLOGY.

Pleonexia – This is a term used by Aristotle to refer to a particular type of greed that desires one to have more than one's fair share and hence to benefit personally at the expense of others.

Pluralism – This term is used for the worldview which acknowledges that there are multiple perspectives on truth and reality, which may all be equally valid. This, however, does not amount to RELATIVISM, but rather to a kind of *perspectivism*. Pluralists, for example, acknowledge that not all behaviour is right, but argue that behaviour should always be understood from a certain kind of perspective. This implies that we do not have access to any absolute truths. On the continuum between the extremes of ABSOLUTISM and RELATIVISM, pluralism lies somewhere in the middle.

Political ecology – Even though the origin of this term is not entirely clear, 'political ecology' is now generally understood as referring to a set of intellectual efforts to link the question of ecology – which is traditionally concerned with 'nature' as such – to politics and economics. So, if political ecology is a new kind of academic research area, it is profoundly interdisciplinary. Bruno Latour has argued that much of political ecology is still captivated by what he understands as worn-out dichotomies such as 'nature' versus 'society'. He has especially taken issue with the way that people use the concept of 'nature' as if it is an independent reality that is somewhere 'out there' and that calls for protection. For him, the idea to protect nature is just as 'hegemonic' as the idea to conquer it. Latour challenges political ecology to venture into new directions and has developed concepts to make this possible.

Practice(s) – In general laymen's language this term refers to the way in which professionals exercise their professional vocation. However, the American philosopher Alasdair MacIntyre goes one step further to argue that a 'practice' characteristically displays the rules of engagement that have to be followed for someone to engage in it. If these rules are broken, the practice will cease to exist. One of his most famous examples of a practice is that of chess.

Procedural justice – The dimension of justice concerned with whether the same rules and procedures are applied equally to all people in an organization. Key organizational procedures considered in relation to this form of justice are performance appraisals, pay allocation, recruitment and selection systems, employee retrenchments, and work allocation processes.

Relativism – Relativism is the belief that there is no one 'right' or 'wrong' set of moral norms. It argues that 'right' and 'wrong' depend on context, and that it is therefore useless to try to come to some kind of agreement regarding what constitutes morally acceptable decisions and actions. See also: ABSOLUTISM and PLURALISM.

Representational practices – In social science, this term is often used to indicate how visual images (film, photo) and language are used to represent individuals or groups. However, the focus is often on how these individuals and groups differ from what is generally seen as normal or accepted. *Stereotyping* (of gender, race, or culture) is a representational activity which causes many moral problems.

Responsibility – One of the most used and contested concepts in philosophy and business ethics. In common parlance, it means the state of being accountable or answerable, but in scholarly circles it has much more profound meanings as well. One of the big issues around responsibility is whether it is an entirely rational affair. Philosophers such as Emmanuel Levinas or Hans Jonas have argued that affect plays an important role as well. Responsibility is not only what you rationally acknowledge but also what you feel. There are many different kinds of responsibility and all imply a different position to the *reason vs. emotion*-issue: parental responsibility, collective responsibility, individual responsibility, ministerial responsibility, social responsibility, corporate responsibility, and so on. See also: CORPORATE SOCIAL RESPONSIBILITY.

Ressentiment – This term is found in Nietzsche's writings. Though it is close to the English term 'resentment' in that it describes a specific type of resentment, Nietzsche uses it to describe the jealousy that takes over someone's life as soon as they come to believe that someone else is to blame for their hardship. In order to deal with the jealousy, people who suffer from *ressentiment* have to devalue the person of whom they are jealous. Nietzsche argues that in the modern world, *ressentiment* lies at the heart of much morality, most notably Christian morality.

Re-valuation – This is also a Nietzschean concept, which refers to the capacity that at least some human beings should have to critically reconsider what society, or the 'herd', prescribes as valuable or normative. See also: HERD MENTALITY.

Scapegoating – A process during which certain individuals – for example, whistleblowers – are not only denounced but altogether excluded from the social SPHERE in which they once found themselves.

Secularism – The secular is normally defined as that which does not make reference to religious or transcendental explanations or worldviews. In business ethics, it has been important to find the kind of normative orientation that does not necessarily make reference to religious views.

Separation fallacy – Business ethicist Ed Freeman has accused those who advocate the separation of the economic realm from the social or cultural realm of succumbing to the seductions of this fallacy. His criticism of this fallacy has been a very important aspect of his STAKEHOLDER THEORY and determined how he came to think about CORPORATE SOCIAL RESPONSIBILITY. Moreover, it is not difficult to relate this to ideas of some continental philosophers. For example, Bruno Latour's work on POLITICAL ECOLOGY and Michel Serres's understanding of LAICISM seem to defy the logic of separation as well.

Spheres – A concept used by the German philosopher Peter Sloterdijk to describe the variety of ways in which human beings can be together. He distinguishes 'microspheres' from 'macrospheres'. Examples of microspheres are mother and child, a pair of lovers, twins, in short, all forms of intimate togetherness. Macrospheres, on the other hand, are 'bigger' associations of human beings. Examples are international organizations, cities, nations, and perhaps even the globe as such. Even though macrospheres lack the kind of intimacy typical of microspheres, they all have one aspect in common: they should offer their inhabitants some sort of semi-permanent shelter. Sloterdijk understands this as the immunity function that spheres ought to provide. GLOBALIZATION is understood as what threatens this immunity.

Stakeholder democracy – This notion refers to how corporations may engage in a reasonable deliberation with different stakeholder groups and then respond to the result of such a deliberation. The idea that a dialogue or conversation between people with different interests is possible is crucial here.

Stakeholder theory – This theory, which is generally ascribed to the work of business ethicist Ed Freeman, argues that there are many individuals or groups that are or might be affected by the activities of corporations. In this sense, the theory distances itself from the idea that corporations are merely accountable to shareholders, an idea often related to the work of the late economist Milton Friedman (see: AGENCY THEORY). Stakeholders, Freeman argues, expect to obtain benefits of corporate activities too (or at least not be harmed by them). However, the cutting theoretical edge of stakeholder theory is that priority of the interest of all stakeholders in the strategic decision-making process of corporations cannot always be taken for granted. In an ideal situation, the interests of different groups are balanced. In practice, we often see that only particular groups (for example, managers themselves) are privileged. One of the problems for stakeholder theory is therefore how it should bridge the gap between description ('what *is* the case?') and prescription ('what *ought* to be the case?'). Most of the models that were developed to bridge this gap have a distinctly instrumental and managerial quality about them. See also: NORMATIVITY.

Standards – Predefined rules and procedures for organizational behaviour with regard to social and/or environmental issues that are usually not required by law. Standards differ from CODES OF CONDUCT insofar as companies do not develop them 'internally'. Codes of conduct are developed by the very same company, which later on uses the code internally and/or imposes the code on its suppliers. In the corporate context, one can make a distinction between three types of standards: (1) *principles-based standards*, which outline broadly defined principles that are supposed to provide firms guidance while reflecting on corporate responsibility issues; (2) *certification standards*, which predefine compliance targets and assess a company's performance against these targets through audits; and (3) *reporting-based standards* that outline comparable performance indicators corporations can report on.

Structure–agency problem – In philosophy and social sciences, it is often asked whether individuals act out of their own free will and out of their own sense of AGENCY *or* whether they are determined by the institutions or structures in which they function. This classic APORIA is generally known as the structure–agency problem.

Sub-culture – This term is often used to designate a group of people with different characteristics as the dominant culture to which they nonetheless seem to belong. In organizational studies, the notion of 'sub-culture' has often been invoked in order to criticize corporate efforts to impose a dominant culture on all the members of the company. See also: CORPORATE CULTURE.

Sublime body – A concept used by Slavoj Zizek to refer not so much to the empirical body of the leader (or, in Zizek's case, the emperor), but to certain qualities of the leader that are being attributed to him or her by the followers: strength, CHARISMA, inspiration, perseverance, and so forth. As such, it is a concept that allows us to gain an understanding of the more radiating aspects of the leader–follower relationship. Zizek's concept also allows us to understand leadership in terms of a relation between follower and leader.

Subjectivation – A term used by Michel Foucault to describe the way in which the 'subject' is created. So, in a very straightforward sense, 'subjectivation' means nothing else than the 'making of a subject'. Foucault, however, proposes to replace the term 'subject' with 'subjectivation'. Roughly speaking, one might argue that he distinguishes between two kinds of subjectivation. In the first place, there are power processes in our society that make us think of ourselves as if we are subjects. Schools, tax offices, medical institutions, or business organizations all give us a sense of 'self' that has certain characteristics and responsibilities. For a long time in his career, Foucault seemed to have been only interested in subjectifying processes that turn people into governable subjects (see also: GOVERN-MENTALITY). In the second place, however, Foucault also alerted us, especially in his later work, to the role that people themselves play in these processes. In other words, they are not only passively involved in them, but also actively shape their own subjectivity. This is why Foucault became so interested in the concept of the 'self' or in what he refers to as the 'subject of freedom'. For him, the possibility of such a subject indicates nothing less than the possibility of ethics as such.

Sustainable development – The Bruntland Commission's influential definition of sustainable development is 'to meet the needs of the present without compromising the ability of future generations to meet their own needs'.

Target marketing – Corporations try to market their products and services. If they market it for specific groups (e.g. children, sportspeople, or musicians), we refer to this as target marketing.

Teleology – Within moral philosophy, teleology refers to an approach that privileges the importance of goals (*telos* = goal, or end) in determining what is morally appropriate. As such, it is often confused with the outcomes-based approach of UTILITARIANISM, but teleology has a different kind of goal in mind. Goals or end-states have to be understood from the perspective of Aristotle, who believed that normative guidelines lie in finding the right way to achieve one's purpose in life within a specific society. Each person's purpose is different because of the fact that we all occupy different roles in society. We can only reach our goal (*telos*) if we develop the appropriate VIRTUES.

Territorialization – A concept used by Deleuze and Guattari to describe how human beings organize their world into easily recognizable social patterns such as 'inside'/'outside', 'centre'/'periphery', or 'high'/'low'. However, and in line with much continental philosophy (see: DIFFÉRANCE and DECONSTRUCTION), this territory is not to be seen as a sedentary place with fixed borders. It is rather a mobile and shifting centre that always allows for '*escape lines*' or '*deterritorialization*'. There is always the possibility that things in the territory might shift and move to another place. In the discussion on GLOBALIZATION this is, for example, made clear when we think of the way that the meanings of words such as 'centre' and 'periphery' have profoundly changed.

Tort – A civil wrong or wrongful act from which convincing injury occurs to another person. Such wrongdoing can be accidental or intentional. Examples are fraud, assault, murder, battery, theft, and so on.

Transformational leadership – An approach to leadership that has been popular since the mid 1980s. This approach emphasizes that transformational leaders move beyond exchange relations with their subordinates (for example: 'I pay your salary and in exchange you do this and that task for me'). As such it implies a criticism of what is generally referred to as *transactional* leadership. Transformational leaders are said to create a common purpose for the organization through CHARISMA, inspiration, personal consideration, and intellectual stimulation.

Transparency – In laymen's language this term refers to the disclosure of all relevant facts and perspectives. It literally means to allow light to pass through objects, facts, events, or even people so that nothing remains hidden. Nowadays, transparency has become a kind of virtue for corporations and not-for-profit organizations as well. Critics, however, argue that the veneration of transparency seems to hinge on the idea that one can have immediate access to reality. This is misleading. Not only is there always the problem that power seems to determine what is relevant enough in order to be disclosed, but there is also the more general problem that access to reality always involves distortion. A financial manager, for example, has an entirely different perspective on the organization than a human resource manager or a professional. Under these circumstances, it is impossible to determine what is transparent or not.

Triple bottom-line – This is a term made famous by Elkington's book *Cannibals with Forks*. It refers to the fact that corporate success should not just be measured in terms of financial success, but that social and environmental performance should also be taken into consideration. This has led to triple bottom-line reporting, i.e. reporting on economic, social, and environmental performance.

Undecidability – This term is used by philosophers such as Jacques Derrida to indicate that there are sometimes situations in which it is impossible to make a decision. Somewhat paradoxically, however, Derrida adds that it is exactly this kind of situation that makes a decision a decision. See: APORIA.

Utilitarianism – Within moral theory, this approach has been described in terms of a cost–benefit analysis that is employed to judge whether something is morally acceptable or not. Within utilitarianism, it is argued that whatever maximizes pleasure for the majority involved, is the morally appropriate course of action. One of its first proponents, Jeremy Bentham; defended the 'hedonistic calculus'. In reaction to this, John Stuart Mill developed a more detailed account, which emphasized the importance of ensuring quality pleasures and positive long-term outcomes for all in society.

Value attunement – Business ethicist Diane Swanson has argued that only a certain kind of receptivity among management executives will make possible: (1) an alignment of organizational behaviour with social expectations of RESPONSIBILITY; and (2) an affirmative and proactive response to a variety of stakeholder concerns. Such receptivity is what Swanson describes as value attunement and she has developed a model that should help practitioners to develop it.

Value-based leadership – A leadership approach that emphasizes the importance of values, like INTEGRITY and FAIRNESS, of leaders. The best leaders are the leaders with the most desirable values. Of all the concepts related to LEADERSHIP, value-based leadership is probably the one that has attracted most attention among business ethicists.

Virtue – Virtues can be described as moral habits that are derived from acting on one's values over a long period of time. It therefore has to do with the development of a moral character. Aristotle's account of virtues remains influential, and has since been employed within COMMUNITARIANISM.

Vitalist empiricism – This expression is sometimes used to describe the work of Gilles Deleuze, who always considered himself to be a vitalist and an empiricist. The first problem is that Deleuze never referred to his own work as 'vitalist'. The second problem is that it is by no means clear what 'vitalism' exactly means. Yet, it is clear that Deleuze has a strong appreciation for 'life' as such. Like Nietzsche, one of his sources of inspiration, he believes that life is a force of itself that cannot only be explained by referring to physical elements such as 'atoms' or 'molecules'. Deleuze's famous remark, that only an organism but not life as such dies, is generally seen as a token of his alleged vitalism. Deleuze combines this with a strong empiricism, a term he *did* use to describe his own work. In philosophy, empiricism is the theory that all knowledge derives from sense experience. Deleuze, however, has never been interested in empiricism as a theory of knowledge (epistemology). He embraces empiricism because it does not explain the world in terms of entities that are 'above' this world (e.g. God, the good, soul). Deleuze's philosophy is, as he explained himself over and over again, profoundly 'immanent': it assumes that processes and forces in the world never belong to something that encapsulates them. For example, the processes and forces that make up a person's body never belong to this person's individuality or identity. They have a *life* of their own. Deleuze himself referred to this position as 'transcendental empiricism': we all undergo experiences that do not belong to our identity or individuality but rather transcend it.

Will-to-power – This is one of the most contested concepts in the history of philosophy. It is generally ascribed to Nietzsche who introduced it in *Thus Spoke Zarathustra*: 'Only where life is, there is also will: not will to life, but – so I teach you – will-to-power'. Even though there is a lot of debate about how the doctrine of the will-to-power should be interpreted, and also about the exact role it plays in Nietzsche's work, there is an agreement that it is linked to the idea that life is a process of *overcoming*. Whenever there is A, it will be overcome (absorbed, replaced, beaten, killed) by B, and B will be overcome by C, and so on. For Nietzsche, life is a constant flow. He decries notions such as 'substance' or 'soul' since they suggest a stability that is, in his view, merely a figment of our imagination. It is hard to underestimate the influence that these ideas exerted on many continental philosophers. See also: VITALIST EMPIRICISM.

Whistle-blowing – When a person considers a certain practice within the organization they are working for as harmful to the public weal and decides to report it either to someone else in the organization or to the public, this person will be referred to as a whistleblower. Business ethicists speak of *internal* whistle-blowing when the wrongful practice is reported through the appropriate channels within the organization. The internal whistle-blower uses a confidential hot-line or makes a report to an ethics officer or an ombudsperson. Whistle-blowing only becomes *external* when the wrongful practice is disclosed to somebody outside the organization (e.g. a journalist). It is especially the external variety of whistle-blowing that is considered to be morally problematic for it breaches the bond of loyalty in order to answer to a certain public concern. Moral judgements on whistle-blowing differ across countries and cultures. For example, in the US it is increasingly considered as a moral duty, but in Europe it is, differences between countries notwithstanding, considered to be reprehensible. Due to legislation and media attention, however, attitudes towards whistleblowers are constantly shifting.

World – This is a word that people often use in all of its ordinary senses (the planet, the people inhabiting this planet, the earth, the globe, and so on). However, it is also a philosophical concept used by many continental philosophers. To mention just one example, for Jean-Luc Nancy, the world is a 'touching of everything with everything'. This means that people now inhabit a 'world' where others increasingly affect our lives while we affect theirs.

Worldwide nature – This concept is used by Michel Serres in his book *The Natural Contract* to indicate that nature manifests itself more and more as a global phenomenon. For most people, Serres argues, nature is no longer the forest where children used to play or a river where men used to fish. It is a rather abstract entity that occasionally imposes itself upon us as a threat or a catastrophe. When people nowadays talk about nature, they talk about global warming, earthquakes, or tsunamis. The paradox Serres alerts us to is that the more we have distanced ourselves from the forest, the river, or the mountain, the more nature seems to have become a threat.

Name index

Note: Page numbers in *italics* indicate Glossary entries

Subject index

CPSIA information can be obtained
at www.ICGtesting.com
Printed in the USA
LVOW06s1519300716

498418LV00008B/150/P

9 780521 137560